Effective
Executive
Compensation

Effective Executive Compensation

CREATING A TOTAL REWARDS STRATEGY FOR EXECUTIVES

Michael Dennis Graham
Thomas A. Roth
Dawn Dugan

American Management Association
New York • Atlanta • Brussels • Chicago • Mexico City • San Francisco
Shanghai • Tokyo • Toronto • Washington, D.C.

This publication is designed to provide accurate and authoritative information in regard to the subject mater covered. It is sold with the understanding that the publisher is not engaged in rendering legal, accounting, or other professional service. If legal advice or other expert assistance is required, the services of a competent professional person should be sought.

Library of Congress Cataloging-in-Publication Data

Graham, Michael Dennis
    Effective executive compensation : creating a total rewards strategy for executives / Michael Dennis Graham, Thomas A Roth, and Dawn Dugan.
        p. cm.
    Includes bibliographical references and index.
    ISBN-13: 978-0-8144-1012-7
    ISBN-10: 0-8144-1012-X
    1. Executives—Salaries, etc.—United States. 2. Employee fringe benefits—United States. 3. Incentive awards—United States. 4. Compensation management—United States. I. Roth, Thomas A., II. Dugan, Dawn, III. Title.

    HD4965.5.U6G73 2008
    658.4'072--dc22
                                                                2007038372

To Elizabeth, Ellie, Scarlett, TBD, Rivendell, family, friends, clients, and associates. All of my "learnings" are still from you and I am, and will be, forever thankful.

MDG

To my wife Margaret, my love and my best friend, to my colleagues at Grahall, and to our clients.

TAR

To my husband Barry and to my sons Jack and Nate. You are my greatest rewards.

DD

Contents

Preface

The State of Executive Pay or Better Known as the Don Quixote Way

You can't escape the controversy that surrounds executive pay. These days, it's impossible to pick up a newspaper, fan through a business magazine, or catch a TV news program without being subjected to excessive hand-wringing over how much the top executives at America's largest corporations are being paid.

Much of what you read or see is hyperbole, exceptions to the norm being presented as the norm, guilt by inference, and maybe even a small amount of envy. And some of it is reality. We say this not as mere onlookers, but as people who have been practicing the art and science of executive compensation for more than 50 years combined.

For most of those years, we've remained publicly silent on the issue. But not any more. It's time to break the "code of silence." We hope that by doing so, they won't revoke our memberships in the Compensation Consultants Guild, better know by the Warren Buffet nickname of "Ratchet, Ratchet, and Bingo."

So why the change of heart? Well, it certainly isn't attributable to the compensation we'll receive for writing this book (which could be wiped out by your average dinner and a movie). Nor to any expectation of fame that will follow publication. We do not expect to suddenly be invited to important cocktail parties where our every thought, pronouncement, and expression will be hung on by important guests. Executive compensation consultants are usually relegated to the corner where the proctologists are gathered.

More likely, we're writing this book because we are fed up with telling clients and consultants one at a time how the process of executive compensation consulting *should* occur. It is far more efficient to write a book to the profession, and to the Boards and executives who hire those in the profession, explaining what we believe the vast majority of the compensation consultants have been missing the last 50 years. To the extent that others—the general public, academics, reporters, legislators—read this material in an effort to understand the issue, so be it.

The Problem

So what exactly is the problem? Simply put, most of America thinks that CEOs are overpaid. And it's not a case of sour grapes where the little guy who is barely scraping by is incensed by the millions being raked in by corporate titans. One poll in early 2006 pointed out that this belief crosses into far more segments of the American population than you'd think.

The headline from a *Bloomberg News* report says it all: "Affluent Investors Agree With Most Americans: CEOs Are Overpaid."[1]

The story explained that in a *Bloomberg/Los Angeles Times* poll taken in February and March 2006, 84 percent of respondents that identified themselves as earning over $100,000 annually said they believe CEOs are paid too much. This may be the one thing that both rich and poor in American can agree on. Even Warren Buffett, one of the richest men in America, has something to say about the state of executive pay in his letter to shareholders in Berkshire Hathaway Inc.'s 2005 Annual Report.

"Too often, executive compensation in the U.S. is ridiculously out of line with performance. The upshot is that a mediocre-or-worse CEO—aided by his handpicked VP of human relations and a consultant from the ever-accommodating firm of Ratchet, Ratchet, and Bingo—all too often receives gobs of money from an ill-designed compensation arrangement," he writes.

And the shrill noise continues today—as we write this preface, a presidential candidate is on the television making another harsh statement about CEO greed.

The rich may get richer in America, but clearly there is a limit to how rich the rich want the richest to become. How did we get to this point?

The Blame Game

The problem with executive pay is multi-layered and complex, and goes well beyond the sound bites and sensationalism of the media picking apart proxy statements for the most egregious examples of out-of-whack pay programs. But as Americans, we've been raised on a steady diet of short news bites that boil down even the most convoluted story into a quick, easily digestible nugget. All the better to leave room for the pseudo-news about Britney Spears' latest debacle, or stories about Dennis Kozlowski's fantastic parties on the shareholder dime. That is what keeps people reading and tuning in.

So rather than view current circumstances as a set of outcomes from a series of systematic interactions of complex forces inside the context of a historical framework, Americans want it simple. We want someone to be credited for the success of a particular endeavor, or blamed for the failure.

So let's take a look at the press coverage. When you pour through all the reports, you find that there are at least ten targets of blame for the shape of the U.S. executive compensation situation: the CEOs themselves, the economy, economists, the government and certain government agencies, the Boards of Directors, customers, institutional investors, lawyers (we couldn't leave out lawyers!), human resources people, and consultants (as consultants ourselves, we doubly couldn't leave out consultants!).

Greedy CEOs Are to Blame!

In some cases, it can be argued the CEOs cashing lavish pay-checks are themselves to blame for the state of executive pay. After all, these are the guys (and yes, they're mostly guys) who go after the exorbitant pay days.

Greed can cause CEOs to simply not pay attention to the curious things going on around them. We have all heard former Enron Chairman Kenneth Lay repeatedly defend himself by saying that he "wasn't aware of the details" of what was happening in his company. These executives keep their heads in the ground, and then profit from it.

The billion dollar stock option cache is not hyperbole. William McGuire, the CEO of UnitedHealth Group Inc., was granted stock options that were backdated that added up to $1.6 billion in unexercised options at the end of 2005. Yet McGuire somehow thought it was okay to point out that this money didn't come out of the premiums of health care recipients. The money came out of the pockets of shareholders instead! Regardless of the source, he also admitted that the sum is "a lot. You can't get away from that."[2]

This issue of backdating options is not limited to Minnesota-based health care CEOs. As of the end of 2007, the Securities and Exchange Commission had opened investigations on hundreds of companies because it looked as if they had backdated options of their executives. CEOs are resigning over the issue, and restatements of previous years' financial reports are becoming common. According to other reports based on statistical analysis, as many as 1,200 companies may have followed the modern version of the Aztec Two-Step, something we like to call the Backsteppin' Backdating Boogie!

So the media blame the CEOs and we can't argue with that, even though it's easy to assume that they are, to some degree, victims of media hype. These stories make for good copy and, like a car accident, it's hard for us to turn away from them.

The Economy Is to Blame!

In industries where business is booming—the way oil, housing, and defense are right now—economic windfalls are to blame for the largesse of the lucky executives in these fields. These CEOs take cover behind a screen of "it's not my fault." Their companies did fabulously and they profited, which is what "pay for performance" is all about, right? Well, not exactly.

Here's how *The New York Times* business reporter Gretchen Morgenson wrote about the issue: "Linking executive compensation to a company's results was supposed to align managements' interests with those of shareholders and to bring fairness to pay practices. But when a company does well mostly because of a rising commodity price rather than managerial genius, pay-for-performance becomes an unfunny joke."[3] The same article quotes Harvard law, economics, and finance professor Lucian Bebchuk as saying that the rising oil prices that have fueled the executives' windfalls "had to do with the Iraq War and the Chinese demand, but it certainly did not have to do with the managers' own performance."[4] If you are anything like us, you'll contemplate this particular contributor to the problem every time you empty your wallets to fill up your SUV.

In some ways, economic windfalls in booming industries are to blame for out-of-control pay days for executives. But there is something fundamentally wrong with the way the rising tide is lifting all boats, without factoring out elements of success that have nothing to do with the way executives are performing or the decisions they are making.

Economists Are to Blame!

Occasionally, economists will try to weigh in on the state of executive pay. But economists are notoriously bad at crafting the simple sound bite that Americans crave.

Until Steven Levitt, economist and coauthor of the wildly popular book *Freakonomics*, takes a crack at executive pay, we're left with this, a passage from a Massachusetts Institute of Technology Department of Economics working paper. The authors call this a "simple assignment framework." It's the *beginning* of their research on CEO pay hikes.

"There is a continuum of firms and potential managers. Firm $n \in [0;N]$ has size S (n) and manager $m \in [0;N]$ has talent T (m). As explained later, size can be interpreted as earnings or market capitalization. Low n denotes a larger firm and low m a more talented manager: S' $(n) < 0$, T' $(m) < 0$. In equilibrium, a manager of talent T receives a compensation w (T). There is a mass n of managers and firms in interval $[0; n]$."[5]

There's much more to this paper, but we couldn't find the right characters on the keyboard to reproduce it here. Since we're entirely in the dark on what this means, let's blame the economists. Whatever they say to defend themselves won't be understandable, anyway.

The Government and Certain Government Agencies Are to Blame!

When it comes to criticism of executive pay packages, stock options usually bear the brunt of the critique. For years, companies could give stock options freely because they weren't considered an expense for a company. The government gets the blame because lawmakers essentially took a ten-year hiatus on the issue and allowed stock options not to be expensed. The Securities and Exchange Commission, and those responsible for accounting standards, deserve the spotlight. Two of the most critical contributing (a.k.a. blame) factors for the executive pay mess are (a) the accounting system, which for years treated stock options as freebies; and (b) the proxy disclosure rules set by the exchanges which did not require complete disclosure of executive compensation.

In addition, the SEC has tread ever so lightly on the issue of proxy disclosure, and only in 2006 has begun to require substantive and thoughtful disclosure of executive compensation in each year's annual reporting by most major corporations. For years, the SEC has taken an approach very similar to the military's "don't ask, don't tell" policy. They've essentially been saying, "We're not going to ask you about the details of executive pay, and you don't have to tell us in your proxy statements."

The Board of Directors Is to Blame!

Certain company Boards have made the premise that they themselves are to blame very easy to support. After all, a company's Board of Directors has the power—and the responsibility—to review and approve the pay packages of company executives. In one case, what a Board did with that power and responsibility landed them in court. When Disney's Directors allowed Michael S. Ovitz to be paid $140 million in severance for little more than a year's work, the shareholders sued the Board. Certain Boards do appear to be asleep at the wheel, and they are not limited to one entertaining entertainment company. Boards need to wake up. People are paying attention, and more than your reputations are on the line.

Customers Are to Blame!

If you don't like what corporations are doing, should you continue to support them with your pocketbook? The simple answer is no, but the complexity of American consumerism muddies the waters a bit.

Still, some customers stand up and protest, and we support this kind of Don Quixote tilting at windmills effort. The customers of the power company Atavista Corp., for example, wrote letters to their legislators objecting to the fact that their power rates tripled as the company tried to keep up with enormous salaries.[6]

Yes, customers are to blame for not being more proactive, and we're surprised that there aren't more of them objecting to the extremes of executive compensation. Even though we are reluctant to join adventures which have any characteristics similar to Don Quixote's, we do know that customers have great influence when marshaled correctly.

Institutional Investors Are to Blame!

It's pretty clear that those with larger-than-normal ownership of company stock are to blame. On a smaller scale, institutional shareholders—the mutual and pension fund managers that add companies to the stock portfolio of the fund—are to blame for essentially sitting back and taking all the things that are going on within corporations without using the power they could be wielding. Institutional investors need to be working in the best interest of their shareholders. When they sit by silently, they're saying that big executive pay days are okay by them.

Lawyers Are to Blame!

You don't have to be the stereotypical, ambulance-chasing lawyer to be able to smell the money that is to be made in this effort to control executive compensation excess. Over the last 30 years, behind all of the most egregious instances in executive compensation excess, there stands a lawyer who has gotten "the best employment deal for his client" regardless of the other stakeholders concerned.

In a way, it's hard to fault lawyers. We actually envy them because they have the benefit of a single loyalty focus. They are the advocates of their client at the expense of everyone else in the system, with no need to provide an outcome that balances the needs of many. They sit firmly on one end of the teeter totter and as such, balance can't be defined by them. In fact, the lawyers are working hard to defy balance.

Human Resources People Are to Blame!

Is there an individual who works in a major corporation today who has *not* felt the pressure from his or her supervisor to alter the facts associated with a particular issue so that the executive would be presented in a better light?

Obviously, the human resources executive at the New York Stock Exchange has been in that situation. And she probably did not understand the gravity of her actions. How could she? All she did was click "hide column" on a spreadsheet that detailed former NYSE head Richard A. Grasso's compensation when presented to the Board. This is the executive vice president of Human Resources we're talking about. We really question what she was doing anywhere near a spreadsheet in the first place.

Are the human resources people to blame? Absolutely. When human resources professionals take the opportunity to obfuscate compensation information and not portray the true cost of a contract to the compensation committee, there is room to blame them for the state of executive pay.

The Consultants Are to Blame!

We've saved the best for last. Consultants. Everyone seems to feel that our profession should be singled out for a large portion of the blame associated with excessive executive compensation. Surprisingly, we agree.

Some consultants, especially those new to the field, are just inexperienced and easily swayed by the commentary of some of the most persuasive individuals on the planet—chief executive officers. But it's a different story when a consultant is so blind that they doesn't see an obvious conflict of interest. For a good example, consider the unusual case of a phone company whose directors couldn't see or hear. The crux of the issue is the payout of Ivan G. Seidenberg, Chief Executive of Verizon Communications, who got some $19.4 million in compensation in 2005—nearly 50 percent more than the previous year. Yet the company's stock dropped 26 percent that year. The package was devised with the help of an "outside consultant" who reports to the committee. The consulting firm's independence is highly questionable, since the same firm apparently had other work with Verizon to the tune of hundreds of millions of dollars.

We've been in those situations and we can tell you that even if the consultant doesn't think about how much a particular client may be worth to the firm overall, a colleague will remind them. A conflict of interest as large as the one in the Verizon case could only be missed by a deaf, dumb, and blind person. So of course executive compensation consultants are to blame.

The fact of the matter is that there's enough blame for this problem to go around and around and around.

On the Other Hand

If what we believe about executive pay is based on what we read in the papers, then there is a lot more reading to be done. That's because the excesses get covered, well, excessively, one might say. But there are also stories that refute the generalization that all executives are overpaid. We had to look harder for theses stories, but they're out there. Consider Richard Kinder, Chairman and CEO of Kinder Morgan, Inc., who has received only $1 in salary for the past six years.[7] And he's not alone. Chief executives of some of the largest and most successful corporations in America—Google, Capital One Financial, Apple Computer, and Pixar Studios—all receive $1 per year in salary.

There are a large number of instances where the poor performance of the organization has resulted in substantial reductions to the chief executive officer's pay. Of course, there are always reductions to the extent that a portion of the chief executive officer's pay is in the form of equity-related compensation. If the underlying price of the equity value is reduced substantially, the chief executive officer's total compensation program is also substantially reduced.

If we were to step away from the individual instances, both bad and good, that have been mentioned in the press and look at the aggregate picture, it is possible to see from 50,000 feet that executive pay has, in fact, correlated to and risen with the value of the U.S. stock market.

From 1973 until 2003, the salaries of chief executives rose from approximately $300,000 per year for the top individuals, to just over $1,200,000 per year. Total cash compensation, which includes bonuses paid, rose from around $350,000 to $3,250,000 per year. The stock market index rose from approximately $1,000 to $11,000. As you can see, the total direct compensation of CEOs—which includes base salary, short-term incentives and long-term incentives in the form of stock options, and other equity awards—rose to around $11 million per year which would indicate an extremely high correlation.

Admittedly, these are averages. But still, they would lead us to conclude that on average, the compensation paid to executives is directly proportional to the value they create in the stock market.

What Does It All Mean?

We have now taken a look at both ends of the spectrum and a small piece of the middle—everything from the egregious situations to instances that make us feel as if there is some hope for logic-based executive compensation, to a relatively simple conclusion that, on average, executive compensation has grown in proportion to the value created for shareholders in at least this sample of companies.

Nonetheless, we have a system that allows way too many egregious situations. Even worse, we have a system that is not effective, even if it doesn't result in eye-popping payouts. Too many times, results are based on serendipity at best because pay is so linked to stock or other equity-related reward vehicles.

The fact is, things have gone wrong with the state of executive compensation, and there's plenty of blame to go around for how we got into this mess. But there is a way to fix it.

This book encourages a methodology for executive compensation that relies on a more thoughtful and intense evaluation of the organization's condition to develop a better executive reward strategy. It's the framework that Boards of Directors and compensation committees should be reviewing, and that the executives themselves should be abiding by. It's a framework that leads to compensation strategies that reward organizational and individual's performance. Period.

We admit, this method requires doing your homework to set things up correctly. It's not a quick fix or designed to appeal to anyone looking for the lazy way out. But it will also keep you out of the headlines.

References

1. "Affluent Investors Agree With Most Americans: CEOs Are Overpaid," Bloomberg News, 21 March 2006.
2. "UnitedHealth CEO discusses stock cache," Associated Press, 30 April 2006.
3. "Rising Prices Lift All Bonuses," The New York Times, 5 February 2006.
4. Ibid.
5. "Why Has CEO Pay Increased So Much?," Massachusetts Institute of Technology Department of Economics, 8 May 2006.
6. "Utility's customers complain about executive compensation," Seattle Post-Intelligencer, 22 February 2006.
7. "Executive Compensation Linked to Good Corporate Governance," Oil and Gas Financial Journal, 4 April 2006.

Introduction

If you bought this book thinking you picked up the latest quick-fix, simple answer book on creating an executive reward strategy, well then, our apologies. There's a good reason we didn't call this book *Jump Start Your Executive Reward Strategy: 10 Easy Steps to Developing a Winning Strategy in 24 Hours or Less (While Also Slimming Your Waistline)*.

If you are looking for a book like that, there are plenty of pop management authors who sell their books for much less than this one. You can pay someone a lot less than us to give you the wrong answers. There is certainly no dearth of books out there that fall into the "how-to" genre when it comes to executive compensation. Books that show you "how to" manage, lead, or shortcut your way to success. Books that also, unfortunately, dramatically understate the complexity of managing today's large, diverse organizations in a world that is hyper-competitive and extremely dynamic.

Okay, enough about the other guys' books. What makes this book so great?

First of all, when we talk about an executive total reward strategy, what is the goal? It's quite simple, really: to reward both organizational and individual performance in such a way that a company is the absolute best it can be. While the traditional objective for the executive within a corporation is to increase shareholder wealth, most individuals would understand that the mutual benefits of all stakeholders, shareholders, employees, customers, and partners is also a major balancing endeavor of most organizations, and therefore a major consideration for the executive reward program.

3

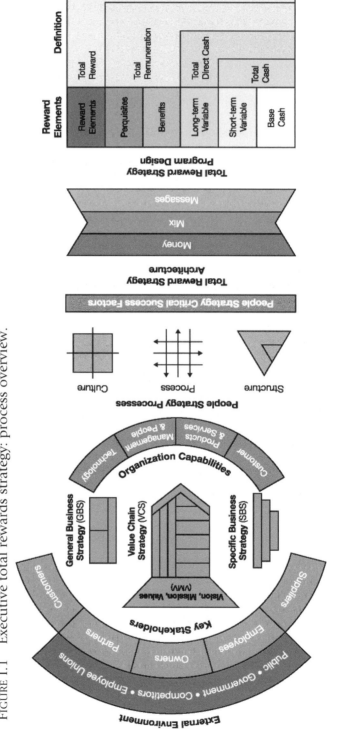

FIGURE I.1   Executive total rewards strategy: process overview.

Okay, now let's own up to the fact that there is evidence that things have gone terribly wrong with the state of executive compensation. These days, it's hard to pick up the *Wall Street Journal* without seeing something scandalous *a la* Enron or Dennis Kozlowski. It's hard to get through the news without shouting "Hey, honey, get a load of this!" as a result of some guy's blindingly shiny golden parachute or flagrant perk abuse.

It's no secret that the system has gone awry. And that's why we've decided to write this book. Between us, we've spent more than 50 years in the compensation industry looking for the "Holy Grail"—the unifying theory of all things related to management and reward theory. We've read, we've researched, and we've been in the trenches. We've worked with companies of all different sizes, in a wide variety of industries, with many different types of structures. We've worked with executives with incredible integrity, but have also experienced the opposite. We've seen effective internal human resources executives and boards who have put exceptional executive rewards strategies into place, and others that have not quite risen to the challenge.

The goal is pretty simple. So why is getting there so hard? The fact is, there is no simple answer when it comes to executive total rewards. There is no one-size-fits-all strategy. And that's what makes coming up with an effective reward strategy so challenging. Because every business is unique, a good executive rewards strategy is tailored with that particular company in mind. A strategy that works beautifully for one company may not cut it for another, even if the two companies make the same product and are similar in size!

In order to develop an effective executive total rewards strategy, you must understand the business, the entire range of reward components, and how to best motivate management to accomplish critical business strategies. And *that's* where this book is different from others you'll find on the market. This book shows the reader a method for developing an executive reward strategy that evaluates the organization's condition to develop the best strategy possible. And yes, the method leads to compensation strategies that meet the ultimate goal—to reward both organizational and individual performance. Which is what we're all looking for when all is said and done.

How This Book Is Organized

Remember a few paragraphs ago when we mentioned we've spent more than 50 years combined looking for the "Holy Grail?"—that ever-elusive unifying theory of all things related to management and reward theory?

Well, the following diagram summarizes what we've learned on our quest. Simply put, we've taken everything we've read, learned, and experienced throughout our careers, and this diagram is a conceptual outline of the process one should use when developing a successful executive total reward strategy. No, it doesn't tell you the answers. But it does outline the process required for success.

We think it's effective—okay, and a bit hard to admit at the same time—that we've managed to summarize conceptually all of the knowledge we've gained with respect to the process of developing executive rewards strategies in one diagram. Even if that diagram may appear somewhat complicated upon first view!

In fact, there is a very specific method to our madness. The diagram is laid out so that the steps to designing an executive total rewards strategy appear in order, from left to right. This book is organized in the same fashion as the process which we have created. You'll learn how each part of this diagram individually contributes to an overall executive total rewards strategy, as well as how the individual parts of the diagram relate to and work with one another.

In addition, we've outlined small case studies to illustrate some of the most important aspects. Even further, we've installed investor alerts for those of you looking for "buy" or "sell" signals in the "DNA" of the executive reward strategy. Lastly, we've put into the appendix an overall "macro" case study and a "micro" case study showcasing analytical techniques we use to develop our insights.

This book isn't meant to replace your deep subject matter expertise from people like us (we didn't wish to put ourselves out of business), but rather an attempt to reach a broader audience. If you wish, there is an appendix in the back of this book that lists our favorite resources, as well as sources for deeper technical material.

Basically, the first part of this book shows you what factors must be considered when designing an executive total rewards strategy—factors such as the effects of the business environment, key stakeholders, business strategy, organization capabilities, and people strategy. We'll show you why these concepts are meaningful when designing an executive rewards strategy, and help you understand them. The second half of the book shows you how to design an effective strategy based on the understanding of these concepts.

That being said, we know how tempting it is to jump ahead in order to "just get started." Don't. Spending the time to understand the prerequisite subjects like business environment, stakeholders, business strategies, people strategies, and their linkages to the executive reward strategy program is crucial to the success of your outcome. So be patient and take the time to read all the chapters. Hey, we didn't promise an easy, traditional, or even safe journey. Merely an effective one. Sometimes it's not about the destination, it's about the journey. So think about that when you get frustrated or impatient. If you follow the steps in this process, you are much more likely to have success. And you can take that to the bank—or the board, if you prefer.

Michael Dennis Graham

Tom Roth

Dawn Dugan

CHAPTER 1

Business Environmental Impacts

You may be wondering why we start out this book—and our total rewards strategy model—with business environmental impacts. After all, how much impact could the outside business environment, when all is said and done, really have on a company's total reward strategy?

The answer is that the external business environment has an enormous—that's right, enormous—influence over organizations in general, and specifically in the development of executive reward strategies. Think about it. Let's say a university catches wind that executive compensation is a growing topic of interest across the nation. So what do they do? Professors begin running research studies. They feed their statistics to the press, who write articles and run juicy news bits. Next thing you know you can't open a newspaper or turn on the television without being greeted by the countenance of the overpaid and underperforming executive *du jour*. The ruffled state of the public's feathers goads legislators into creating change. You can see how quickly, and easily, one voice can be turned into thousands. We award Gretchen Morgenson of the *New York Times* our annual award for press coverage impact. We don't always agree with her conclusions or points of view, but we can't debate her impact on the dialogue of the subject of executive pay.

So how does this affect executive reward strategies? Well, some cases are so egregious that laws are put into place to prevent history from repeating itself. In other cases, the publicity alone is enough to make companies reconsider how their executives are being paid. If you are Britney Spears, any publicity is good publicity. But if you are a top executive, not only do you have to wear underwear, it's also probably not a good idea to be rewarded, at the shareholders' expense, with silly amounts of money. Buca has Joseph Micatrotto, DHB Industries has David Brooks, and Tyco has Dennis Kozlowski. Believe us, they all wish they didn't. And you can bet these superstar CEOs' 15 minutes of fame have put other companies on high alert. They think twice before making rewards decisions that could land them in a negative spotlight.

It's an unfortunate sign of the times, but we've never opened the *Wall Street Journal* to a headline that says, "XYZ Company has a GREAT Executive Total Rewards Strategy!" Until good rewards strategies are rewarded by the media, you can bet companies are going to want to stay out of it.

By the way, we're not the first guys to write about environmental impact on business strategies. Henry Mintzberg, in his book titled *Power In and Around Organizations*,[1] provided the best academic handling of how environmental factors affect organization performance since Paul R. Lawrence and Jay W. Lorsch wrote *Organization and Environment: Managing Differentiation and Integration* in 1979.[2] While both books are academic in nature and not nearly as fun as this one, we do find them exciting because of their clarity. We've taken what we've learned from them and broken the environmental category into two coalitions: the general business power coalition, which we'll cover in this chapter; and the company specific power coalition, which we'll explain in the following chapter on key stakeholders.

The general business environmental coalition can be further broken into four categories: the public, government and government agencies, competitors, and employee associations and unions. Each of these groups has an amazing influence when it comes to the development of an organization's total reward strategy. Our goal in this chapter is to define each category in the external coalition, and show how they impact an organization and its executive total reward strategy.

From Football Fields to Foosball Tables

If these three groups—the public, government and government agencies, and employee associations and unions—have one thing in common, it's that they effectively define the playing field when it comes to executive total reward strategies. Much as you would define a football field, these groups define the playing field only by determining what is out of bounds.

For those non–jock readers who are scratching their heads at that analogy, here's another try. You've all heard someone say "I don't know art, but I know what I like." Well, these external groups may know absolutely nothing when it comes to executive reward strategy, but they certainly know when something isn't right.

And here's something we always find interesting. More often than not what these groups find wrong is generally wrong. The degree to which organizations can't seem to understand what is truly out of bounds is surprising to us. It's interesting that the people making the decisions are people considered to have a good working knowledge of total reward strategy. It is downright amusing to imagine the "aha" moment when General Electric's board of directors realized that Jack Welch's retirement perk package was a little, er, excessive. We think it probably went something like this (by the way, if this were a movie we would put Jack Black and Ben Stiller in these roles):

> *Board of Director 1 (reading the* Wall Street Journal*): "So all this brouhaha has really got me to thinking. Did you have any idea—I mean* any *idea—what we meant when we decided that Jack would `have access in retirement to all of those benefits that he had access to as the chief executive officer?'"*

Board of Director 2: "Nope."

Board of Director 1 (scratching his chin, thoughtfully): "Me neither. I'm talking no clue. Actually I still don't know. But do you think . . . I mean, is it possible . . . that we could have avoided this whole scandal if we had kinda, you know, hashed that out at some point?"

Board of Director 2 (slapping his forehead): "Darn it! I had that on the agenda but then we got into that debate about who was really the father of Anna Nicole's baby, and it to- tally slipped my mind. Well (chuckling), we won't make that mistake again!"

You think?

Don't get us wrong. Many organizations have pretty good to- tal rewards programs. Not great total rewards programs, mind you, but good enough to stay out of the headlines. But some really don't understand what is truly out of bounds. Let's go back to our football field analogy again. As more organiza- tions react to stories about what is truly out of bounds, the playing field will be substantially reduced. Instead of playing on a football field, we'll be playing on a foosball table! And that's a big mistake. If there is anything worse then getting called for a foul, it's not using the entire range available.

What do these business environmental groups define as "out of bounds" and why? That's what we want to hash out right here. Sometimes an organization is so intent on staying out of the headlines that it inappropriately shortens the playing field for their own executive rewards. Nobody wants to be the next Tyco or Enron. No way. But sometimes organizations that really go nuts trying to stay off the evening news don't opti- mize their executive reward resources. They are guided by what everyone else is doing, instead of developing a reward strat- egy that is designed to drive their business strategy.

As a matter of fact, executives often make three cardinal sins when developing executive reward strategies.

The Three Cardinal Sins

Sin #1: Mismanaging the "money;" the competitive market attachment

Let's face it. For the most part, executives are a pretty predictable bunch. They read the same newspapers, watch the same TV commentators, and pick up the same magazines in the airport. They are all too aware of what the limits are, and they don't want any press. So, while many execs can be ruthlessly surgical when it comes to allocating other resources under their command—things like marketing, research and development, operations, patents, and advertising, to throw out a few examples—they somehow lose their mettle when it comes to allocating the oftentimes more scarce resource of reward dollars. To make matters worse, they are too often swayed by the human resources folks who bandy about terms like "equity," "fairness," and "values." So what happens? They often end up with the "opt out strategy" or "default strategy" of positioning everyone at the 50th or 75th percentiles. The result? Most of the time, the market attachment place where companies choose to place their competitive market is so poorly chosen, it may be one of the biggest single sources of waste in the entire corporation.

Sin #2: Making the average company's mix of compensation components in the marketplace their own

To compound sin #1, companies often position the mix of reward components to reflect the mix most often found in the marketplace. What ends up happening? Well, maybe they'll have enough variable compensation, or maybe they won't. Maybe they'll have enough long-term incentives versus short-term incentives, or maybe they'll have too much. And perquisites? They'll just do what the other guy is doing. As a matter of fact, one of the most compelling reasons for a perquisite program is that "everyone else has them!" For those of you who thought his kind of reasoning was reserved for toddlers and teens, we've got news for you. It works for grown-ups in suits too.

Sin #3: Muddling the messages

The third mistake is in the development of the messages delivered by the reward program. We wish we had a dollar for every time a CEO or his human resources head called to ask for a survey on some obscure reward program component provision, just so they could know what other companies are doing. All this results in is averaging down to the mean. And that's not leadership.

So, let's get back to our football analogy for a second. If you don't understand the real size of the playing field, it will be like playing the entire football game inside your own "red zone." In other words, it's going to be pretty hard to score consistently. But if you understand how the general public, government and government agencies, and employee associations and unions define what is out of bounds when it comes to executive total rewards strategies, your organization can play within the bounds . . . but still use the whole playing field.

Some of the key business environmental influence groups are the public, government legislators, government regulatory bodies, judiciary groups, and, last but not least, employee associations and unions. Each of these listed groups' impact is discussed in the remainder of this chapter.

The Public

While the general public, at first glance, seems fairly detached from an organization, it's also somewhat influential. Let's consider, first of all, who comprises the general public—the media, newspaper editorialists, priests, teachers, friends, spouses, and children.

What kind of real impact do these groups have when it comes to how an organization rewards its executives? Well, we hate to ruin the executive image of cool confidence, but most executives we know would go to great lengths to preserve a positive public impression or image. Even the coolest of the cool get a little red in the face when they find their mugs front and center in *Fortune* magazine's annual article that lists those executives that produced the worst return for the most compensation. What do you say to your golfing buddies? Who needs it?

Well, nobody. And that's why there is an awful lot of time spent on making sure that executive rewards strategies are clean enough to stay out of the headlines. But remember what we said earlier, about not playing the whole field? The fact remains that most outcomes from executive reward strategies— let's say about 90 percent—are not going to attract negative attention.

Unfortunately, it's the ten percent or so of companies who do have reward strategies that warrant public outcry that land on the front pages of the newspaper or on the evening news. How come you don't find stories about the other 90 percent of the average, normal, organizations in the media? Well, because a journalist's job is to sell newspapers. What sells newspapers? Stories of excess!

But here's the clincher. Despite some titillating headlines, research shows that when all is said and done, these headlines don't make all that much of a difference in how corporations actually develop their reward programs. Research done by David Larcker, the James Irvin Miller Professor of Accounting at the Stanford Graduate School of Business, and his colleagues John E. Core and Wayne Guay of the Wharton School, tried to determine what might put constraints on excessive executive pay.[3] One of the things the research—which was called "The Power of the Pen and Executive Compensation"—looked at was the role of the press in catching and curtailing excessive levels of compensation.

The research looked at more than 15,000 press articles regarding CEO compensation from 1994 and 2002. The findings? While the press understood and reported on executive compensation with some degree of accuracy, it didn't completely "get it." In keeping with its reputation for sensationalism, the press tended to focus on large payouts, even when the pay was from multi-year compensation programs. When all was said and done, the research found that the press didn't have much at all to do with how an organization structured its total reward strategy.

So what do we take from this? Well, when the reporters only partially "get it," the public isn't going to "vote it." We'll bet there will be more legislation enacted regarding cell phone usage in cars than legislation driven by the "marching of the masses" on executive pay.

Have the efforts of the general public or press coverage ever resulted in a specific redesign of an executive rewards program? The answer is yes. However, in general, the answer is no. While there's nothing good about bad publicity, the sensationalism perpetrated by the media, as well as the fact that the public is presented only one side of the story, means that of all the outside business environmental influences, the public is the last group we should be concerned with when designing an executive reward strategy.

It's good to stay out of the headlines. But you don't want to get so hung up on avoiding bad publicity that you short-change your reward strategy. Listen to what the public says is out of bounds, but don't go overboard and use only half of your field.

Government Legislators

You Don't Need a Weatherman to Know Which Way the Wind Blows

What's the goal of a government legislator? To get votes! And what gets bucket loads of votes? When legislators promise to nip egregious business practices in the bud.

That's right. Believe it or not, legislators are highly influenced by public opinion. Are you a legislator that needs a vote? Well then, with any luck there will be a business scandal right around the corner. In our opinion, quite a few laws that have been passed—and Sarbanes-Oxley is a good example of this—have steamrolled through Congress on the back of some major business scandal. Just as the default of pension promises by Major Steel Co. provided us with the benefits of ERISA in 1974, the incredible bankruptcy of Enron, corruption of WorldCom, and debacle at Tyco have provided us with legislation giving us guidance on what most executives know they should be doing anyway.

So what's the issue? Well, when legislators attempt to buck the free market system and perform the art or ritual of social engineering using the tax code or other regulatory system, then the results aren't always what were intended.

Take Bill Clinton, who in 1991, right after launching his presidential campaign, had what he thought was damn near a revelation regarding the toning down of excessive executive paychecks.[4]

Clinton's idea? To use the tax code to curb soaring paychecks. At the time, companies were allowed to deduct all compensation to top execs. Clinton wanted to allow companies to write off amounts over $1 million only if executives reached certain performance goals. Despite compensation guru Graef Crystal's proclamation that the plan was "utterly stupid," Clinton went ahead with it anyway.

Did it work? Nope. Some 13 years later the only effect of the law is that $1 million is now too often considered the minimum base pay of any CEO. Wasn't the goal here to *curb* pay packages, not watch them explode? Irony, anyone?

Of course, some legislative efforts have resulted in significant changes. Take Sarbanes-Oxley, also known as SOX, which was designed to improve the quality of corporate governance in the wake of Enron, WorldCom, and a host of other scandals. According to research done by the Business Roundtable,[5] almost six out of ten companies (57 percent) report an increase in the pay-for-performance element of senior executive compensation in the last year, compared to 49 percent in 2005 and 40 percent in 2004. So this means that in one year another eight percent of companies got religion. Alright!

Sarbanes-Oxley doesn't come without its costs. Critics say that U.S. securities exchanges are losing market share to overseas rivals because companies can avoid SOX's burdens by doing their capital-raising beyond the statute's reach. But despite its costs, SOX puts a bit of fairness back into corporate capitalism, and shows that potential conflicts of interest between executives and shareholders can be managed. Best of all, Sarbanes-Oxley sends a loud and clear message that politicians aren't afraid to act if executive behavior becomes excessive.

Of course, direct legislation such as Sarbanes-Oxley is not the only area legislators impact, since, in conjunction with the IRS, they've changed significant portions of the tax code. We particularly applaud last year's effort, Section 409A, to clear up the approach to the practice of deferring compensation. This rule basically applies to any arrangement in which payment of compensation is deferred to another year, and again, is the result of business lobbying groups struggling to do the "right thing" by shareholders and the public. This little piece of legislation and the resulting regulations have resulted in a big level of change to deferred compensation programs as a result of 400 pages of regulations.

In 2005, the Democratic Leaders of the House led by Representative Barney Frank have recently introduced "The Protection Against Executive Compensation Abuse Act." The Act, which did not become law, would require companies to include an executive compensation plan on the ballot for shareholder approval. It would also require shareholder approval of golden parachutes, as well as a simple and clear disclosure of compensation arrangements on the company web site.

So when all is said and done, do legislators affect how companies structure their executive reward strategies? They sure do. Highly influenced by public opinion, legislators aren't afraid to send the message that executive hijinx won't be tolerated on their watch.

Government Regulatory Bodies

Rules, Rules, and More Rules

We continue to be genuinely impressed with those government agencies that attempt to regulate the complexity of business in today's world. The IRS and the SEC, along with the various accounting professional associations, have done a remarkable job given the complexity and the dynamic nature of business enterprise today. While each group has exhibited, in our opinion, a remarkable amount of consistency in its approach to the issue of executive rewards, the outcome of the various groups is, again in our opinion, the cause of a vast majority of the complexity associated with executive compensation today.

Let's cut to the chase. On July 6, 2006, the SEC unanimously approved its final disclosure rules. It only took a mere 436 pages of rules to instruct companies how to file their proxies. That's right, 436 pages. Of rules. So you can correctly file the executive pay portion a company's proxy statement. Which is a business's annual "state of the business statement" to stakeholders.

Once you've spent, oh, a week or so mulling through these rules (and we don't want to hear any whining) you'll be ready to disclose compensation info about your CEO, CFO, and three other highest-paid executives. In addition, information about the members of the board of directors will also have to be disclosed.

The disclosure rules also require companies to detail all pension payments and change in control provisions. And because of recent option backdating scandals, there are new disclosure rules regarding that as well. Rules, rules, and more rules. To be exact, 436 pages of them.

The rules don't place any limits on executive pay. Instead, the rules allow for more shareholder scrutiny in areas like pension plans and severance packages, and will most likely change the way boards design pay packages. Companies have to disclose perks if their total value is more than $10,000, and dividends on restricted stock grants will also be disclosed in companies' proxy statements.

Despite its complexities, the SEC has potentially done something wonderful for investors. We think that their efforts are finally going to bring some leverage to the issues of executive compensation disclosures. How that is going to impact the state of executive compensation is everyone's guess, but many of the worst-reported instances would have been disclosed, and in many of those cases probably rethought.

And Another Thing to Put on the To-Do List

For both private and public companies, January 1, 2007, ushered in more than just the new year.[6] It was also the deadline for compliance with FAS 123R, the Financial Accounting Standards Board Rule that mandates companies with calendar year ends to expense their stock options.

If you aren't familiar with this rule—if you live in a cave—123R says that companies have to show fair value of their stock option awards on their income statements. Before, companies generally didn't record compensation-related accounting charges when stock options were granted with exercise prices equal to the market value of the underlying stock.

FIGURE 1.1 Ultimately each organization/industry has a different level of governmental regulations, i.e., "guidance." From a survey of over 200 major corporations, it is easy to see that the range varies from regulation-free to heavily regulated.

Regulation Free
9%

Slightly Regulated
13%

Moderately Regulated
24%

Heavily Regulated
36%

Significantly Regulated
18%

So what happened? Well, take a trip down memory lane to the early 1990s, when internet start-ups and high-tech companies were giving away stock options to anyone who came to the door, just like candy on Halloween.

So what kind of impact has this rule had so far? Well, the complexities involved with complying with the standard—did we mention it's another tree killer and weighs in at more than 400 pages—have caused companies to simplify their stock option-grant policies. Of course Silicon Valley was in an uproar, saying that the rule takes away their ability to hire top-level executives. Well, maybe so. But we still think that the good far outweighs the bad. Still wondering whether government agencies can have a huge impact on total reward strategies?

Government Judiciary Groups

Is it possible to find senior executives today who are unaware of the efforts of the judiciary branch of the government and its impact on executive reward strategy? Doubtful. Almost all of the executives we work with have developed a new sense of awareness to the implications associated with their rewards.

Why? Because executives are being called on the carpet for their transgressions—and are expected to pay up, too. Consider Henry C. Yuen,[7] former executive of Gemstar-TV Guide International, who was ordered to pay $22.3 million by a federal judge for his role in a fraud that led the company to overstate its revenue. Or how about HealthSouth Corp.'s founder, Richard M. Scrushy, who was ordered by an Alabama judge to return around $36.4 million in bonuses paid to him as a result of a massive accounting fraud.[8] And of course let's not forget our friend Dick Grasso, who has been ordered to return $100 million of his $139 million total compensation he received for heading up the New York Stock Exchange. Hope he hasn't spent it already!

Yup. There's no doubt about it. Judiciary groups are just one more external group that has an impact on an organization's total reward strategy.

Employee Associations and Unions

Historically, employee unions have not played a significant role in the influence of executive reward programs. We're not aware, nor do we really understand, the reason why they have not been more active, given the high degree of influence that the rank-and-file employees could exert. And we do admit we are suspicious that the unions with the influence have executives running the unions that practice one of the golden rules, "Don't throw rocks if you live in glass houses."

We're not the only ones who smell hypocrisy. In April of 2006[9] the Center for Union Facts called union leaders out on their blatant hypocrisy. It seems like the new AFL-CIO's new "Executive Paywatch" report, which brings to light the compensation of corporate executives, somehow forgot to include the exorbitant pay of its own leaders. It was brought to light that the Plumbers paid former General President Martin Maddaloni $1.3 million in total compensation, while the presidents of unions for players in national sports associations made more than a million each. Oops!

Until recently, the cases where employee associations and unions have had some influence over the design of total reward strategies have been pretty isolated. Today, however, employee unions are becoming increasingly active in trying to influence not only board governance, but also executive reward program design. For example, a proposal submitted to 3M by the United Brotherhood of Carpenters Pension Fund requested that the company establish a pay-for-performance standard for senior executives.[10] While the AFSCME Employees Pension Plan submitted proposals to 26 different companies that outlined a program designed to hold corporate America accountable to shareholders.[11]

So what do we think about all this? We predict the past is a prelude to the future. In other words, unions will not significantly influence total reward strategies, except, perhaps, at the very boundaries of the issue. It's just not in their best interest, when you consider the other platforms they have on their plates and the amount of resources they have. When all is said and done, they may be better off deploying their resources in an effort to attain better governance by addressing board of director elections.

Competitors

Keep Your Eye on the Competition

What about competitors? Competitors are a huge outside environmental factor when it comes to poaching good executives. It's a dog-eat-dog world out there, and you can't expect the competition to "play nice." The competition will go for your best people, and they'll inflate the structure to boot. The most dangerous competition is those companies who are performing poorly and need your executives at just about any price. All of a sudden your vice presidents are someone else's president. The better your company performs, the more your executives become a target for head hunters. And this inflates the market for executives. In this type of environment, holding on to your executives can be downright tricky.

In the competitive business environment factor, the key aspects are to appreciate the economics of the industry in general, and where, specifically, your firm stands.

Also, competitors for customers and for executives may be different. There are no longer (if there ever were) limits by industry for executives to be recruited from company to company.

Some Final Thoughts

So now that you understand how each external environment group can influence not only your organization, but also your total reward strategies, let us ask you a question. How important are they to your overall reward strategy? If you've been paying attention, you know you need to understand how the external environment plays into a total reward strategy; in other words, how it defines what is "out of bounds" for businesses in general. But, that being said, we caution you to keep environmental elements in perspective. While this group of entities is influential in shaping the general dialogue of total reward strategy, with the exception of competitors for both customers and executive talent, it really has very little specific impact on the reward strategy of a specific organization. Don't do something just because the other guys are doing it. Don't let the headlines cajole you into placing limitations on your strategy. And remember, the best reward strategies are those in which you stay within bounds, but play your whole field.

References

1. Mintzberg, Henry. *Power In and Around Organizations*. Englewood, NJ: Prentice Hall Business Publishing, 1983.

2. Lawrence, Paul R. and Jay W. Lorsch. *Organization and Environment: Managing Differentiation and Integration*. Boston: Harvard Business School Press, 1986.

3. Larcker, David, John E. Core, and Wayne Guay. "The Power of the Pen and Executive Compensation." Stanford Graduate School of Business Working Paper, 2007.

4. Epstein, Keith and Eamon Javers. "How Bill Clinton Helped Boost CEO Pay." *Business Week*, 27 November 2006.

5. Business Roundtable. "Companies Report that Sarbanes-Oxley Implementation Costs Have Stabilized." Washington, D.C.: Business Roundtable Four Annual Survey of Corporate Governance Practices, 2006. Press Release.

6. Shaw, Helen. "Another To-Do Item: Expense Options-Small and private companies are struggling to comply with an upcoming deadline to expense stock options." *CFO.com*, 29 November 2006. Available online at http://www.cfo.com/article.cfm/8348861?f=search, accessed 21 September 2007.

7. "Henry Yuen's Civil Penalty is Among Largest Sought by SEC Against Individual." *Wall Street Journal*, 9 May 2006.

8. Dade, Corey. "Scrushy is Told to Repay Bonuses." *Wall Street Journal*, 5 January 2006.

9. Press Release, The Center for Union Facts, 6 April 2006.

10. MarketWatch. "3M Seeks Support Against Executive Compensation Proposal." *MarketWatch*, 2 May 2006.

11. "AFSCME Plan 2006 Shareholder Proposal: Board Accountability Needed to Rein in Excessive Executive Pay," *PR/Newswire*, 7 December 2006.

CHAPTER 2
Key Stakeholders

Now that you have an understanding of the external business environmental influences and their impact on total reward strategies, let's talk about the internal environmental influences or company specific power coalitions: key stakeholders. There are groups or individuals that care if a specific company is successful since, in many cases, their own success is affected.

If you don't think key stakeholders greatly influence total executive reward strategies, then the stories we're going to tell you in this chapter should make a believer out of you. Owners, board members, employees, partners, customers, and even suppliers have lots to say, especially in today's world where executive compensation is a hot topic. Of course, not all these groups wield the same amount of power. Nor do they necessarily impact certain aspects of the design. But all have *some* input—and impact—on executive total reward strategies.

With the issue of executive compensation heating up, all these stakeholder groups are being asked, and are asking themselves, tough questions. Are the high-level rewards provided to their high-level executives really performing their intended function, giving these powerful executives a more powerful stake in the company's future, and motivating them to ever-greater heights of inspired, money-making leadership? Or are the purposes of these grandiose packages going wildly astray, driving a stake into the company by unwontedly fueling unjustified and greedy personal profit-making? Is the current state of executive compensation an out-of-control, under-investigated, and deeply hidden form of board of director-sponsored cor-

FIGURE 2.1   In a survey of over 200 organizations, the variety of owner-ship strength shows a wide variety from widely held to tightly controlled.

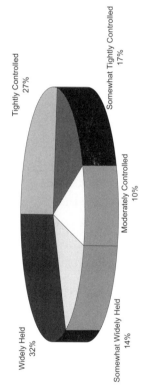

Tightly Controlled
27%

Somewhat Tightly Controlled
17%

Moderately Controlled
10%

Somewhat Widely Held
14%

Widely Held
32%

porate vandalism? Are these over-rewarded and unapprecia-tive CEOs and other top company officials sucking the value out of shareholders' present and potential earnings, creating a massive divide between the reality and appearance of com-pensation for the sake of profitability?

Tough questions, all of them. But they are being asked, and you can bet that key stakeholders want the answers.

As we take a look at key stakeholder groups and how they im-pact executive total rewards strategy, let's start with the cate-gory that packs the most punch—owners of company stock. These owners include general investors, investment houses, and fund managers.

General Investors

Chicken Man and the Fly-By Banner

A man in a chicken suit from the AFL-CIO standing outside of a hotel, a woman owning just $2000 of company stock spearheading a 2003 shareholder resolution to a major com-pany, an airplane towing a banner protesting a CEO's pension fund. What do these strange—okay, even bizarre—visions have in common? They are all visible signs of shareholder un-rest connected to executive compensation.

It's not like you have to search high and low to find an exam-ple of shareholder concern regarding executive compensation. Gone are the days of boring, ho-hum shareholder meetings. These days, shareholders are organizing themselves to makes sure their discontent regarding excessive pay packages is heard. Let's take Home Depot's CEO, Robert Nardelli, who was given a plush $3 million a year guaranteed bonus.

Despite the fact that Nardelli was no slouch—in fact Home Depot's revenues had grown 12 percent per year for the last 6 years and profitability had doubled to $5.8 billion—share-holders, having seen their stock go down by 13 percent since Nardelli took office, weren't exactly jumping for joy. It was the fact that the bonus was guaranteed, regardless of performance, that had their knickers in a knot. Ultimately Nardelli was terminated, but that's a story for another chapter.

Enter CtW Investment Group, an investment group associated with their union, and the California Public Employees' Retirement System, the largest pension group in the United States and a large shareholder.[1] CtW wanted an explanation from compensation chairman Bonnie Hill. The California group expressed their desire for a shareholder proposal requiring an advisory vote by stockholders in the area of executive compensation. The long and short of it? Two significant shareholder groups wanted more accountability from the Board.

So let's cut to the board meeting, which was held on May 27, 2006. The first clue that something was amiss was the Board didn't, er, show up. Nor did Home Depot personnel. Nardelli was there, flanked by big, gruff individuals wearing Home Depot t-shirts. Bouncers at a board meeting?

Nardelli oh-so-considerately placed two large digital timers in view and set up a few ground rules. The rules were basic. Each speaker could ask one question and had exactly 1 minute on the floor.

The meeting was contemptuous of shareholders, no doubt. But few shareholders were there. In fact, the meeting was poorly populated. Hardly a packed convention room filled with angry stakeholders. The aforementioned guy in the chicken suit was at the meeting, but one does wonder how angry you can really get when you are wearing a chicken suit. So what was the end result? Even though there were some shareholders at the meeting, they had very tiny tendrils with which to affect the compensation of their top executive, a matter which had already reached newsworthy proportions.

In a sense, the shareholders at Home Depot mirror the fate of the voters in a modern television-controlled republic. Their vote is largely controlled by special interest groups, which leverage their apathy with very little difficulty. Even so, given the existing rules and protocol for shareholder activity, it is doubtful that even a fully mobilized group of shareholders could exert enormous power over an insensitive, public company like Home Depot. In this case, the winners of this meeting were clearly the nonattendant Board and perhaps the bouncers, who certainly must have enjoyed telling the story of the chicken man over a pint or two later that night. What we find most interesting about this meeting, however, is that the façade of shareholder power was totally stripped away. Oh, and when all was said and done? Nardelli chose to resign and take his resignation pay of more than $200 million.

In the last 4 years, shareholders at Cendant, AT&T, Pfizer, and Merrill Lynch asked boards to take a closer look at how top execs are paid—and have been met with resistance from company officials. Why? Well, shareholders usually question executive pay when something catches their attention. Something like, poor performance. Shareholders don't like to see top executives getting fat bonuses when their stock has fallen for the last 6 years in a row. It makes them, well, bitter. And while company officials really don't enjoy shooting the breeze with shareholders in these circumstances, they are certainly not going to submit to shareholder demands and admit they were wrong. Not in a public forum. No way.

INVESTOR ALERT #1

ANNUAL SHAREHOLDERS' MEETING
RESEMBLES A ZOO

Just because the annual shareholders' meeting will be a place for some form of democratic commentary, it is not a reason for executives or the board of directors to show their disrespect for the shareholders, environmentalists, or other people with agendas. Everyone deserves to be treated with dignity and their difference of opinions should be listened to. The company's reputation is built on every interaction it has with its environment. Shareholders' meetings are a very specialized forum, and should be treated with the most thoughtful forms of Democratic etiquette. If the company's attitude at a shareholder's meeting is not respectful, investors should be very concerned.

Well, not usually anyway. Back in 2003, several small share-holders of Bristol Myers Squibb were incensed at the executive pay packages. According to a Jim Lehrer television report on June 10 of that year,[2] there were several shareholder resolutions from the grassroots. Ann Sink, who owned a small piece of Bristol Myers Squibb, drafted a resolution that called for es-tablishing a ratio between highest and lowest salary, freezing executive pay during lay-offs, and having shareholders vote on severance packages. That same year, Steve Schneider wanted executive bonuses linked to performance. He said, "They still contend there's this wonderful link between compensation and performance. And it escapes me. I see no such connection. None." The result of these two proposals may not have been earth-shattering, but it was eye-opening. Sink got 13 percent of the vote. Schneider got 12 percent. This was quite a high num-ber for new shareholder resolution, which needs only 3 percent of the vote to requalify for resubmission in the following year.

Investment Houses

Strategies of Resistance and the Wall Street Walk

We remember reading Peter Drucker's book, *The Unseen Revolution*. For those of you who haven't read it, Drucker pre-dicts that, as a result of the 1974 Employee Retirement Income Security Act (ERISA), which requires companies to fund pen-sion plan promised to employees, a communist-like revolu-tion would occur in which employees would end up owning those companies. According to Drucker, "The masses would own the means of production."

What he didn't foresee was the creation of the class of high priests associated with managing these funds, called by their more professional name, "investment advisors."

There is a growing sign of restlessness on the part of institu-tional investors and advocacy groups, who are bearing the torch for the sake of shareholders. Are they the sleeping tiger in this strange scenario?

A 2005 study of 55 institutional investors managing some $800 billion by Watson Wyatt Worldwide demonstrated a pronounced dislike of executive compensation packages. Ninety percent of those companies polled by the human capital consulting firm stated that American companies overpay their executives, and 85 percent stated that there was a negative impact on America's corporate image. Sixty-four percent complained of disclosure problems. A slight majority of those polled believed that there was a high level of stock ownership by executives. Watson Wyatt's research has indicated that stock ownership by executives seems to boost performance.[3]

As the concern regarding executive compensation grows among investment houses, we want to remind you that their concern hasn't been sparked by just a few small companies. The way companies like Merrill Lynch, Time Warner, Pfizer, Verizon, Merck, and Wal-Mart pay their top guns has made institutional investors sit up and say "hmmmmm." Just consider what Denise L. Nappier, State Treasurer of Connecticut and custodian of a whopping $23 billion in retirement plans and trust funds had to say: " . . . the most important issue that stands in the way of fully restoring investor trust— and eliminating the trust gap that was caused by the scandals of the Enron era—is the issue of executive compensation." This was a prelude to her efforts to try to block the re-election of compensation committee members at some of the top companies in America.[4] Her strategy? To withhold voting from these members and from board directors and executives.

When you are talking about investment houses and their impact on executive total rewards, you can't forget Pfizer and former CEO Hank McKinnell. Before he was ousted, McKinnell and his $83 million pension, added to his $65 million paycheck, didn't sit well with the Connecticut State Treasurer's office.[5] After all, their stock had lost 43 percent of its value since he had come on board. So why the largesse?

In fact, the State Treasurer's Office of Connecticut sponsored a resolution by the shareholders that stated, " . . . we believe that there is a disconnect between the company's perform-ance and CEO compensation in 2004—and that the Compensation Committee report does not give shareholders sufficient justification for the CEO's compensation given the underperformance of the company's return to shareholders."[6] So what did the Treasurer's Office want? They demanded that Pfizer's compensation committee report include disclosure in a tabular form of all relevant compensation, including dis-closure of any quantitative and qualitative performance met-rics used with regard to the five highest paid executives of the company.

While nobody in a chicken suit showed up at the April 27, 2006 meeting, there were some signs of discord. Union pro-testers chanted "Hank McKinnell, rich and rude, we don't like your attitude" outside the Lincoln, Nebraska, hotel site, while a plane flew overhead, jauntily pulling a banner that turgidly proclaimed, "Give it back, Hank!"

Did this, combined with the activities of two proxy advisory groups and the shareholder activist organization, really change anything? Nope. All of the company's directors were elected. Nonetheless, somewhat notable support, around slightly more than 21 percent for each, was withheld from two of the Board directors, including Director Dana G. Mead, who headed Pfizer's compensation committee, and was chairman of the MIT Corporation, and Director George A. Lorch, chairman emeritus of the floor and ceiling manufacturer, Armstrong Holdings. Was the tiger making noises in its sleep? Was it get-ting restless?

We think so. There's a certain posse of investor groups out there now commonly referred to as shareholder activists. Their *modus operandi*? To shake things up and initiate change by publicly challenging a company.

Just look at Nelson Peltz, a major investor in H.J. Heinz Company, and his investment vehicle, the Trian Group.[7] After the mother of all proxy fights, Peltz won some seats on the Heinz board in August of 2006, ensuring a future say in the company's direction. Like ImClone System's Carl Icahn and General Motors' Kirk Kerkorian, Peltz focuses on what he likes to call "operational activism," in which outraged investors focus on invigorating companies by finding efficiencies in their operations, and not just on their balance sheets.[8]

One possibly effective strategy by institutional investors, according to a study done by the Stanford Graduate School of Business, is the so-called "Wall Street Walk."[9] In this strategy, a pension or mutual fund investor can decide to divest itself of the company's assets. Nice idea, but in reality there are three major problems with this plan. Sure, the threat of a walk-out could produce change. Change, we might add, that comes with a much smaller price tag than shareholder initiatives and proxy battles. The problem? Once the investor leaves, the war is over. And this means no more controlling interest in the company until it re-invests.

Another problem? Once the investor leaves, it has lost its chance to profit from its involvement in the company. A quick, short-term pullout because of undesirable policies might not be in the long-term interests of the shareholders— to whom the pension fund or mutual fund owners are ultimately responsible to in the long run.

Finally, some of these institutional stakeholders feel they are making progress in communicating with the management, and the Wall Street Walk—or its implied threat—isn't really necessary.

On the other hand, in some cases, institutional investors can't participate in proxy combativeness. For them, as well as for those who have reached a much heightened level of concern for the company's future, the direct or implied Walk may be the only venue they have.

C*ase Study #1*

One of our clients, an oil company, had joined forces with three other major oil companies to create a new internet entity. The goal? To agree on an appropriate reward plan for the internet company's CEO. We started by interviewing the internet CEO, to understand the strength of his convictions and the source of his information on standard reward packages on internet startups. The big challenge was getting the four companies to agree. We divided, and somewhat conquered, the four key shareholders by discussing with each the importance of their investment in the internet company. We then proposed a total reward strategy that reflected something of what each key shareholder had offered as important in their individual interviews but obviously not all, and in some cases not much. With a few revisions, we were able to get an agreed approach to the proposed reward strategy for the CEO of the internet version.

Sometimes you have to determine whose side you really have to work for to get the client's goals accomplished. When there are four very different stakeholders on one side of the negotiations and one on the other, it's better to represent the one instead of the many.

Fund Managers

The SEC and the Sleeping Tiger

In June of 2006, the American Federation of State, County, and Municipal Employees (AFSCME), a large pension plan, sent a letter to our shareholder-friendly organization, Home Depot, asking them to explain their stock option procedures.

Huge surprise? Not really, considering that dirty stock option practices were selling newspapers and keeping millions of Americans glued to the nightly news to see who the latest executive bad boy was. It was this public awareness, as a matter of fact, that fueled the SEC's new compensation disclosure policies just a month later.

And why not? According to Marcy Gordon, an AP business reporter, stock options are turning into "corporate America's scandal of the year." More than 120 companies were investigated either by the SEC or by the Justice Department, with 18 CEOs forced out by the ill-conceived policy. It is estimated that back-dating of options may have wiped out as much as $5 billion in profitability, a matter not to be ignored by an intelligent shareholder.

Hedge fund, mutual fund, and pension fund holders are probably the newest kids on the block when it comes to grabbing the spotlight on issues involving executive compensation. Until recently, they've been habitually silent about key executive compensation proposals. But times have changed, and these groups are developing more traction in the area of executive compensation. They are already publicly concerned about this issue. So what's next? We foresee this group of owners, and their direct and indirect representatives, becoming a more substantial force in the world of executive rewards.

That being said, this type of activism is nothing new. As a matter of fact, Disney shareholders pioneered this type of activism way back in 1997, when they initiated a lawsuit against Walt Disney Co. over former President Michael Ovitz's $140 million severance pay. That's a hell of a parting gift, and shareholders found it none too entertaining.

The suit, it turns out, served a greater purpose than the retribution/recompense scenario the shareholder's were conducting. Shareholders of Disney found out, under the direction of a judge in the case, that they could, themselves, investigate reasons for the company's decision to fire Ovitz after only 14 months, as well as the reasons for the excessive severance.

All of this means that we've entered a new era in company acknowledgement of and divulgence of facts to shareholders.

While in the end the handling of company funds in regards to Ovitz was deemed as clean as Snow White, the case pioneered the way for shareholders of other companies to begin inquiring into their own companies' internal documents as a matter of scrutinizing fiduciary activity if mishandling is suspected.

All of this means that today, fund managers have immense power when it comes to calling companies out on the carpet. The pension fund of the American Federation of State, County and Municipal Employees (AFSME) submitted a proposal at five companies—Merrill Lynch & Co, U.S. Bancorp, Bank of America Corp., Home Depot Inc., and Countrywide Financial Corp—designed to allow shareholders to vote on the total compensation of the top five executives.[10] What did these companies have in common? All of them had excessive pay practices, but performed poorly. Red flag, anyone?

Other proposals have no interest in dictating pay practices, but just want to be in the know when it comes to executive pay. Connecticut's retirement-investment fund, for example, is asking for rules and regulations that would force companies to disclose all aspects of pay, including the current retirement benefits and targets for performance-based pay.[11] And the California Public Employees' Retirement System (CalPERS) targeted Brocade Communications, Cardinal Health, Clear Channel Communications, Mellon Financial, OfficeMax, and Sovereign Bancorp for poor financial and governance performance, urging them to make changes and improvements.

Putnam Funds, Glass Lewis & Company, and Institutional Shareholders Services withheld their support from directors who had approved excessive pay for executives at Pfizer.[12] But while these funds did, in our mind, the right thing, there were others whose lucrative relationships with Pfizer kept them rubber-stamping management's proposals and directors despite the fact that this might not be in the best interest of the share-holders they are supposed to be protecting.

So who supported Pfizer's board? Mutual funds operated by Barclays Global Investors, Dodge & Cox, and Northern Trust all said a-okay to the company's directors.[13] Now, will it surprise you when we tell you that all of these companies—that's right, every single one—receive revenue doing other work for Pfizer? Barclays earned $2.65 million as an investment manager in a Pfizer pension plan. Dodge & Cox earned $1.06 million in 2004 as an investment manager to Pfizer retirement plans. Northern Trust earned about $2 million from Pfizer in 2004 as trustee of its pension plan. But all of these mutual funds, wouldn't you know, said their votes had nothing to do with revenue generated by Pfizer or other relationships with Pfizer. We think it's reasonable to be suspicious.

What it all boils down to is that, when, it comes to fund managers and their effect on executive total reward strategy, there are good guys and there are bad guys. The good guys are trying to make a difference by publicly getting angry about excessive pay packages and demanding change. These are the guys that are looking out for their shareholders' interests first. The bad guys, on the other hand, passively allow companies they have financial relationships with to go about their business. And this is why owners aren't wealthy in corporate America, but managers are. In a nutshell, the bad guys, with their lack of care to corporate wrongdoing, allow continued wrongdoing. It is our hope that, as activists draw more attention to poor pay practices, fund managers will sit up, pay attention, and exert an impact that allows them to support their shareholders, not betray them.

Case Study #2

A new hedge fund client called with a crisis of significant magnitude. They had developed a large amount of client assets, and were starting to make real money as a result of the performance of the fund. Those investment people who were contributing more of the profits wanted more of the perform-ance bonus than was due them as a result of their equity shares, which had been awarded more on a historical basis. The CEO wanted us to referee the reallocation process.

We developed a formula that reallocated the bonus pool, and ultimately the equity, over a three-year period based upon the performance of each of the portfolio managers and equity holders. This was faster than some wanted, but slower than others wanted. The reallocation process would re-shuffle the bonus first, and the equity somewhat later in the process.

We believed that the formula was the best compromise we could come up with. With much rancorous debate, the group decided to agree not to agree. In a relatively short time the hedge fund bled assets and dissolved, leaving the partners with nothing of significance. Ultimately, instead of getting hundreds of millions of dollars in performance bonuses, the individuals received unemployment checks.

Sometimes you can lead a bunch of horses' asses to water but you can't make them drink.

Board Members

Maybe the Bucks Won't Stop Here Anymore

Are board members too much a part of the club? Probably. Despite government regulations, executive compensation has always been a tough animal to tame, and only time will tell whether or not the latest SEC rules will manage to curb exces-sive rewards. However, here's something we *do* know. According to a recent study done by researchers at Cornell University's Johnson School of Management and the World Bank, regulations governing the structure of corporate boards that were implemented in 2003 by the New York Stock Exchange and NASDAQ are stopping the bleeding when it comes to executive compensation.[14]

The regulations, suggested by former SEC chairman Harvey Pitt, are designed to reward "independent directors"—those with no personal or financial connection to the company—with greater influence on the board. So how has this shaken out? The majority of any listed company's board must now be independent, while compensation and nomination committees must be made up entirely of independent directors.

Is CEO pay still on the rise? Well yes, it is. And we don't pretend that there's not still a lot of work to do before this issue is under control. But the good news is that compensation fell by up to 25 percent at companies that restructured their boards. The main reason? Researchers who looked at 940 companies between 2000 and 2004 found that restructured boards with independent directors granted fewer stock options.[15] All in all, this concept isn't too hard to dissect. You have a board made up of independent directors, and you can bet they are going to do a better job of independently evaluating the executive pay situation. No need to worry about which side their bread is buttered, so to speak!

INVESTOR ALERT #2

STAKEHOLDER TRENDY

Whenever an organization is run with too much concern for certain groups of stakeholders at an unreasonable cost to other stakeholders, we call that organization "stakeholder trendy." We often see organizations doing window dressing when it comes to governance issues. If ownership guidelines become a topic of discussion among investors, and the company immediately installs a set of weak ownership guidelines in order to "check that box off," then the organization is being run on a stakeholder trendy basis.

For an example, an organization without retention problems that replaces stock options with restricted stocks that vest on a time basis is most likely being trendy, not thoughtful. Stock options are not the same as restricted stock. They should be used for very different purposes. They shouldn't be exchanged on some Black & Scholes ratio basis because they are simply more fashionable today.

So what happens when members of the board are tied personally or financially to a company? Well, we're all familiar with the backdating scandal that has put more than 200 companies in the media spotlight and sent top executives packing. But here's something you might not know. About 1,400 directors at 460 U.S. companies have benefited from backdating practices, according to a study done by Harvard Law School's Lucian Bebchuk, Cornell University's Yaniv Grinstein, and Insead's Urs Peyer.[16] And don't for a second think that these directors are unknowing bystanders who just happened to get "lucky" as a result of these grant manipulation practices. Since the study found that directors' backdated options were more likely to have occurred when executives also got a grant on the same date, it doesn't take a genius to figure out what's going on here.

Case Study #3

> *One of our private companies came to us with a request to review their total reward strategy. Performance for the organization had been slowly decreasing on a relative basis, and the individual who owned the majority of the company's stock was dissatisfied. After interviewing senior management it was decided to evaluate the range of general, value chain, and specific business strategies. Each of the organization's many businesses fell into each of the three major general business strategies. They had, in effect, a full house that was all the different colors of the rainbow at each of the business strategy levels.*
>
> *We then turned to the human resources department to determine what type of total executive reward strategy they had been applying. Based upon the HR department's analysis, as well as our interviews of key human resources department executives, we determined that the market attachment (money), the mix between the various reward*

> *components (mix), and the various performance and incentive plan messages (messages) were in fact uniform for the entire organization.*
>
> *When we asked the HR department for an explanation for the single uniform executive total reward strategy, we were told that the owner felt that it was important to be able to transfer people across organizational boundaries in order to be able to use the executives where they were needed. When we asked how many executives were actually transferred across organizational boundaries in the last three years, we found that less than 5 percent of the executives actually made transfers between organizational units.*
>
> *Sometimes a pronouncement by the key shareholders can remain with the organization long past the time when it should've been reviewed and challenged by staff.*

Take James Johnson, for instance. Johnson, perhaps best known as a former chairman for Fannie Mae, sits on the boards of six corporations and is on the compensation committees of five of them. Why is Johnson such as stand-out? You can bet that wherever he is, there will be a controversy regarding executive pay. What do five out of six of the companies at which Johnson sits on the board have in common? They've been singled out by two research groups for excessive executive pay practices and poor performance.[17]

Yes, boards have a large influence on executive total reward strategies, and everyone knows it. As more ties that bind result in shareholder suffering, activists are demanding more say regarding who sits on the board. Our friend Home Depot, for example, recently gave a nod to angry shareholders in the wake of the Nardelli scandal when it agreed to require a majority vote from shareholders for the election of board members. As more companies follow suit, we should start to see a new generation of boards who put a stop to excessive pay practices and put the needs of their shareholders first.

*C*ase Study #4

We were making a presentation to one of our favorite clients in the retail industry, when one of the key founders and present shareholders sat up and called us a poster child for the HR department—and the reason why he did not have an HR department at the company.

Some background. We were presenting our findings on a review of the executive reward strategy program at the client board meeting. What had brought the organization up to $3.5 billion in revenue was somehow not working as effectively as it once was. FAS 123A had required that the organization account for all of the stock options that it had previously not recorded as income statement items as an expense. Since the vast majority of its executive compensation was in the form of options, the organization faced a dilemma. Should they exchange the options for cash, putting the organization into a substantial cash drain? Or should they cut back on the formula that created the options allocation? We felt strongly that the formula that created the options allocation was off the chart with respect to the amount it provided the executives.

Looking at it from a macro economic point of view, the same formula could not work unless something major changed in the organization. We explained that in order to get a 90th percentile performance utilization, they only needed to pay 40 percent more in pay. They were presently paying almost 200 percent in additional compensation as result of the options formula.

Everyone except the key shareholder had reviewed the material and believed that we were making the right recommendation. Once the key shareholder stood up against the change in the formula, there was not a person in the boardroom who would lend their support to the recommendation. Ultimately the company floundered and the stock

> *became depressed. The next year it was purchased by a venture capital firm.*
>
> *Sometimes the founder and key shareholder shouldn't have any more than their nominal vote on the board of directors.*

Investment Advisory Firms

Heads or Tails? Does It Really Matter?

What did you do when you opened your mailbox last spring and removed—with two hands, mind you—the 132-page Exxon-Mobil proxy statements? Did you hunker down and read it, page by page, in an effort to determine how to vote?

Our guess is, probably not. As a matter of fact, there are very few investors who ever take the time to cast a proxy vote, let alone read a statement. Instead, most of us rely on our mutual funds, pension funds, hedge funds, and the like to make the right decisions.

And this is where investment advisory firms come in. Investment advisory firms tell institutional investors like mutual funds, hedge funds, and pension funds how to vote at company shareholder meetings. As a result, they have tremendous power when it comes to the state of executive pay.

How much power? Well, Institutional Shareholder Services of Rockville, Maryland, the largest advisory firm, claims to affect the decisions of professional investors controlling $25 trillion in assets. Just in case you're wondering how big that number actually is, it's half of the world's common stock. That's a lot of influence! Not to mention that not everyone gets a personal visit from former Hewlett-Packard CEO Carly Fiorina and her nemesis, Walter B. Hewlett, in the same week. When the two butted heads over Hewlett-Packard's potential acquisition of Compaq Computers, both made a personal appeal to ISS to vote in their favor.

ISS put the brakes on "money for nothing" in favor of "pay for performance" with its updates to U.S. and international proxy voting policies for 2007. The new policies, which will be applied after February 1, 2007, call for a majority vote standard for board elections, as well as a definition of "independent" directors. Key modifications to compensation policies include those dealing with backdated options, as well as shareholder proposals on disclosing measures for performance-based pay.

The growing influence on the proxy system of advisory firms has certainly gotten the attention of the NYSE, who recently asked the SEC to do a study on the role of these firms, citing a "potential for possible conflicts of interest." The problem? Since ISS both sets the governance standards and helps clients meet them, some wonder how pure their intentions really are.

Missouri's pension fund didn't like the fact that ISS sells its services to the very same corporations it criticizes, so they dropped them. Gary Findlay, the executive director of Missouri State Retirement System, said the ISS could not convince him that their interests were in line with those of shareholders.[18] But whether or not ISS operates under a conflict of interest, their message is a good one: pay for performance.

There are two other advisory committees that are embracing the new type of nose-to-the-grindstone, pay-for-performance executive. The Glass Lewis Co. of San Francisco and Proxy Governance in Vienna, Virginia, are two companies with one slight—or some might believe not-so-slight—difference from ISS. They do not advise on governance issues.

And they pack a lot of power, just the same. In January 2006, Glass Lewis Co. did a study in which they identified how pay related to performance in 2,375 companies.[19] All the companies were in either in the Standard and Poor's 500 stock index or in the Russell 3000 index. Their findings? Of the 25 worst companies, CEO pay averaged $16.7 million in 2005.

You would hope someone taking home that kind of bacon would make raising company stock his #1 priority. Guess again. Of the 25 worst companies, stocks fell an average of 14 percent. So how about the 25 best companies? Well, their executives were paid a measly $4.4 million on average in 2005, but the stocks in those companies rose an average of 44 percent. We guess the guys at these companies weren't too busy spending their money and had plenty of time to work.

So what's the point of this study? Jonathan Weil, a managing director at Glass Lewis, said the goal of this study was simple: to identify companies and directors that should be held accountable at next year's annual meeting.[20] Studies like this go a long way toward putting excessive executive pay in the limelight, and show investors how costly some pay practices can be. While certain companies and certain executives might gripe about advisory firms and whine about "conflict of interest," investors with the goal of someday retiring comfortably should be thankful that groups like this can shake things up and positively influence the state of executive pay.

Employees

Power to the People

It's no easy task to assess the percentage of employee stakeholder membership in U.S. companies. Still, the National Center for Employee Ownership (NCEO) took a stab at a statistical profile of employee ownership, and here's what they came up with: There's a clear $675 billion in fairly easy-to-define categories of employee ownership with ESOP plans (stock bonus plans and profit-sharing plans primarily invested in employer stock), comprising $600 billion of these assets, with the remaining $75 billion being held by 401k plans. There are also several hundred billion in broad-based stock option plans, not so easy to define in terms of potential stakeholder activism.

And what percentage of company stock is owned by employee ownership plans? Well, according to the NCEO 34 percent of public companies are owned in an area between 11 and 30 percent by employee ownership plans. So what are we getting at here? Somewhere in this picture is an enormous amount of power, ultimately defaulting to whoever represents these shareholders, votes their stock, or advises them.

Now here's the point. On the one hand, we can categorize mutual funds, pension fund holders, and proxy group advisors in the ownership category. But, in so far as many of these owners or representatives actually default to employee-owned stock, it is also very accurate to say that the owners are actually employees. Behind all this institutional energy are people who work for the companies they own. And if they want to enjoy their retirement, they had better start caring about the stock they own.

Some employees are clearly paying attention to the executive pay imbroglio, and it's making them sit up and take stock— no pun intended—of what's going on around them. In 2006, shareholders representing Verizon's unionized workers and retirees protested CEO Ivan Seidenberg's 12 percent pay raise.[21] They weren't too happy about the fact that their stock declined over a five-year period while Mr. Seidenberg took home more than $75 million in compensation.

It's interesting to note that of the 30 resolutions shareholders brought to Verizon's board, only one won the majority vote. But what's even more interesting is how little it matters. Even if resolutions are formally defeated, a bunch of angry employee shareholders sure can influence the board. Consider that Verizon directors have responded to griping by cutting perquisites and pay, tightening rules on director independence, and restricting severance packages. Talk about power of the people!

Speaking of people and power, have you seen the damage a bunch of irate retirees can do? Try standing between a retired

FIGURE 2.2   From our survey of over 200 organizations, it is clear that the level of specialization of key employees covers a substantial range from highly specialized to generally unspecialized.

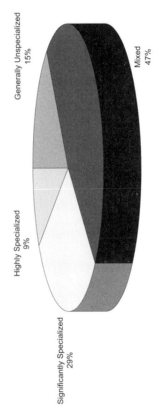

Significantly Specialized
29%

Highly Specialized
9%

Generally Unspecialized
15%

Mixed
47%

employee and his comfortable retirement and, well, don't say we didn't warn you. If there's ever a group that had the shareholders' backs, this is it.

Let's once again visit our beleaguered telecommunications company, Verizon. We know their employees are already giving them a run for their money, but which investor is giving our friend Verizon the toughest time when it comes to corporate pay? Give up? The company's Association of BellTel retirees.[22] When it comes to executive pay, this savvy group has been asking all the right questions and scoring some major wins for the shareholder team.

This group has 111,500 members, with a mere 214 shares, but that doesn't matter. They encouraged the board to revamp their golden parachute policy, and also convinced the board to seek approval for severance agreements exceeding 2.99 times base salary. They also challenged Verizon's supplemental retirement plan, resulting in top executives and managers getting the same smaller percentage contributions. So what's on the future agenda? Retirees jumped on the performance-based pay bandwagon and are urging the board to raise the bar when it comes to stock awards. And in November 2007, Verizon agreed to put the company's compensation plans to an annual vote by investors, beginning in 2009.

Verizon isn't the only company where retirees are taking a stand. Lucent Technology, General Electric, International Business Machines, Prudential Financial, and Qwest Communications are all being challenged by retirees looking out for the best interest of both the company and shareholders.

And what about the executives themselves? Well, no one wants to be a celebrity CEO these days, especially when being a celebrity CEO means scandalous paychecks and poor performance. All this bad press has some executives rejecting ridiculous pay practices. Former chief of Mercantile Bankshares Corp. Edward "Ned" Kelly, recognizing that people were "irritated" by big payouts, suggested to his board members that they drop provisions in his contract that would bring him a cool $9 million should the bank ever be sold.[23] And discount clothing and home goods retailer TJX cut the salaries of top executives 10 percent after Bernard Cammarata, who also took the cut, stepped in as president and CEO. The goal of the cut, according to Cammarata, was to save $18 million, and also align the goals of the company with those of its investors.[24] These decisions, which have the best interests of both the company and the shareholders in mind, illustrate the power of the people behind the organization.

Partners

Packing a Punch

When we use the word partners we're talking about law firms, bankers, accountants, unions, and . . . er . . . consultants.

You may have noticed our hesitancy to mention consultants in this group of key stakeholders. That's because compensation consultants have been getting a bad rap lately. And we don't like that.

Nevertheless, the story of Cablevision's shareholders suing consultant firm Lyons Benenson & Co. for knowingly participating in the illegal backdating of options does illustrate the direct role that consultant's play in executive pay strategies.[25] As compensation companies come under more attack, 13 large pension funds have banded together to urge the U.S.'s 25 top companies to carefully monitor their use of compensation consultants, saying that conflicts of interest could cause scandal. Their main worry? Consultants who advise on compensation, but who also work with management, could inflate executive pay. And that's just not good for the company, or for its shareholders.[26]

As we mentioned before, with all of the governance rules that must be followed, it's a great time to be a compensation consultant. But consultants have a duty—and responsibility—to remain objective when advising on the structuring of pay strategies. While gobs of money can turn one's head, it's important for a consultant to remember that the overall goal is to do what's best for the company and ultimately its shareholders—and not for a few individuals in management. Consultants who remember this wield the same power on executive pay that those who don't, but their power is positive. In our view, there are some good consultants, many average consultants, and also some bad consultants. Corporate compensation committees who keep an eye on their consultants to make sure they remain independent and are giving neutral advice will avoid scandal—and they won't have to sue anyone either.

INVESTOR ALERT #3

THE COMPENSATION CONSULTANT

Whenever a compensation consultant is either not listed by company name or you don't know the name of the firm when it's listed, that's a pretty sure bet that the consultant being used doesn't have sufficient experience to handle the assignment.

We're sure there are a lot of individuals who are in one-person firms working out of their basements who are doing a very good job of advising larger organizations how to structure their compensation plans. We just don't know of any.

If you see the name of a firm reported in the Compensation Discussion & Analysis section of the company proxy that you don't recognize, that should be a concern as an investor that the executives or board of directors don't have the kind of connections or resolve to hire someone who might have less need for revenues from the firm. Watch out!

Speaking of lawsuits, lawyers are another stakeholder group who can make a mark on the state of executive pay. Just take M & A lawyer Martin Lipton, who in November of 2006 passionately defended executive pay, saying that our friend Dick Grasso's exorbitant pay package was completely on the level.[27] Lipton argued that companies needed to pay a high price to retain top management. Lipton also defended curmudgeonly IAC/InterActiveCorp's Barry Diller, as well as UnitedHealth Group's Bill McGuire, saying that their creation of successful companies justified their ridiculous pay packages. Hmmmm, we wonder who was paying his salary.

Joseph Bachelder is another lawyer who has made the news for his ability to wrangle excessive pay out of companies for his clients.[28] Clients of his have included Lawrence Bossidy of Allied Signal Crop., George Fisher of Eastman Kodak Co., and Patricia Russo of Lucent Technologies. At $975 per hour, Bachelder might be one of the more expensive corporate attorneys around. But he gets results. Even as lavish CEO pay is being lambasted in the media, he and his clients are laughing all the way to the bank. Lawyers like Bachelder show why it's hard to curb executive pay. He'll haggle and rearrange contracts until he feels he has won the best deal for his client, often giving up common but relatively minor perquisites in favor of more important loot like restricted stock and wow-factor pensions. But why do compensation committees listen up? They're afraid that if they don't toe the line, they'll lose their shot at top executives.

Of course, while lawyers might make the job of reining in executive pay a little more difficult, no one can criticize them. They are working for their clients, make no apologies, and are up front about which side their bread is buttered on.

Customers

To Date, an Unknown Quantity

We're never completely sure of the impact customers have on the design of executive reward programs. The more customers are concentrated in number and have an influence on the supplier, the more they can exert influence. In this manner, their influence could be similar in power to that of the owners.

If, for example, an organization has a relatively small number of customers and those customers are critically important with respect to its long-term performance, it is less likely that the competitive levels will get substantially out of bounds. No one can easily face a major customer if their compensation levels are dramatically higher than is normal.

(text continues on page 60)

FIGURE 2.3   Customer influence is a function of how concentrated the organization's customers are. As you can see from the survey of over 200 organizations, the concentration varies from few customers to many customers.

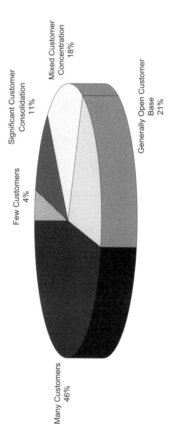

Significant Customer
Consolidation
11%

Mixed Customer
Concentration
18%

Few Customers
4%

Generally Open Customer
Base
21%

Many Customers
46%

FIGURE 2.4   As with other key stakeholders, the range of supplier concentration varies greatly as will their influence over the executive compensation framework.

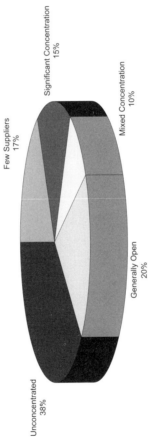

Few Suppliers
17%

Significant Concentration
15%

Mixed Concentration
10%

Generally Open
20%

Unconcentrated
38%

On the other hand, organizations that have very a large number of diverse customers, which exert very little influence, if any, on the supplier, are hardly a bother at all in regards to executive compensation. In fact, in regards to this issue, they may as well not exist. Because the small number of organizations that have customer groups that exert large influence is relatively minor this stakeholder group tends to influence executive reward strategy only by exception.

For boards who wish to exercise free form policies in regards to their customer base, they don't need to worry about this kind of scrutiny.

Are customers to be seen in the same light as the general shareholder? Nope. In fact, they are virtually powerless.

Suppliers

An Occasional Flex of the Biceps, Perhaps

Suppliers can exert influence over executive reward strategy design in many ways similar to the concept of customers. If the suppliers are few in number and important in respect to the organization's ability to deliver its services and products, suppliers will have an influence on executive reward strategy design. The opposite is also true to the extent that if the suppliers are very diverse and, with little overall influence, even the impact on executive reward strategy design is minimal if at all.

Where Do We Go from Here?

We wish we could wave a magic wand and make all the excesses and stupidity in executive compensation practices go away. But we're under no such illusions.

We can blame the system—with all its myriad weaknesses—but let's face it, if we are a democracy, and the voting machines still function on our behalf, we can fix it anytime.

Does the comment Plato said of governments and men, "The penalty good men pay for indifference to public affairs, is to be ruled by evil men," have any bearing on the relationship between a company and its shareholders? Perhaps the word "evil" is too strong. Shall we say "primarily self-interested?" Perhaps, understandably, these words are not as strong. But they are sad words, nevertheless.

As compensation consultants for so many years, we believe we are, and have been, quite often ruled this way—by both our government and our companies.

It would be hard to believe that the way the most visible members of a company are rewarded does not trickle down to the whole body. What $30,000 a year worker would not notice that his upper echelon is making a few million a year, just in their salaries? They may concur that the upper echelon needs large salaries—but to what point, to what end?

A company is much more than its board or CEO. It is, in fact, a giant engine of commerce, mostly composed of its workers and managers whose goal is to service a customer base. Engines like this compose the bulk of the world economy. If board members and executives have lost the sense of their primary mission—to serve a segment of the economy which not only contains their own customers, but their shareholders, workers, suppliers, and partners, and exist solely to serve themselves then they undoubtedly have lost their mission.

References

1. Grow, Brian. "Home Depot's CEO Cleans Up." *Business Week Online*, 23 May 2006. Available online at http://www.businessweek.com/investor/content/may2006/pi20060523_284791.htm, accessed 21 September 2007.
2. "Taking on the Company," *The Online News Hour With Jim Lehrer*. PBS, 10 June 2003.
3. "Institutional Investors Dissatisfied With U.S. Executive Pay System, Watson Wyatt Study Find." *Insurance Newscast*, 13 December 2005.

4. Morgenson, Gretchen. "The Shareholder Spring: Investor Discontent Fills Annual Meeting Agendas." *The New York Times*, 27 April 2006.

5. "Pfizer's Compensation Heads Under Fire, More Than 20 Percent of Shareholders Withhold Support for MIT Corporation Chair Mead." *New York Times*, 2 May 2006.

6. "Executive Compensaton 2006—Pfizer Inc." Interfaith Center for Corporate Responsibility, State of Connecticut Treasurer's Office, 2006.

7. "Investors Demands Rebuffed by Heinz." *Bloomberg News*, 25 May 2006.

8. Sorkin, Andrew Ross. "Enough Anger to Make Ketchup Boil." *New York Times*, 27 July 2006.

9. "Lifting the Lid: Threat of Selling Shares Can Force Change." *Long Island Press*, 9 June 2006.

10. Plitch, Phyllis and Kaja Whitehouse. "Executive Pay Faces New Tactics." *Wall Street Journal*, 27 February 2006.

11. Ibid.

12. Morgenson, Gretchen. "How to Find a Fund's True Colors." *New York Times*, 10 September 2006.

13. Ibid.

14. Holland, Laurence H.M. "Capping CEO Compensation." *Forbes.com*, 31 July 2006. Available online at http://www.forbes.com/leadership/2006/07/29/leadership-ceo-salaries-cx_lhmh_0731compensation.html, accessed 21 September 2007.

15. Ibid.

16. "Study Links Directors to Options Scandal." *Financial Times*, 18 December 2006.

17. Mctague, Jim. "Meet Mr. Generosity." *Barron's*, 21 August 2006.

18. Starkman, Dean. "A Proxy Advisor's Two Sides: Some Question Work of ISS for Companies It Scrutinizes." *Washington Post*, 23 January 2006.

19. "Shareholder Firm Says Lennar CEO Was Paid Too Much." *Reuters*, 15 October 2006.

20. "The Best and Worst of Executive Pay." *New York Times*, 12 September 2006.

21. Ibid.

22. Dvorak, Phred and Joann S. Lublin. "Verizon Tries to Mute Criticism of CEO Pay." *Wall Street Journal*, 3 May 2006.

23. Syre, Steven. "Retirees on the Watch." *Boston Globe*, 6 April 2006.

24. Smitherman, Laura. "Golden Parachutes `Tarnished'." *Baltimore Sun*, 15 April 2006.

25. "TJX To Pare Top Exec Pay 10%." *Boston Globe*, 9 March 2006.

26. Taub, Steven. "Cablevision Investors Sue Comp Advisor." *CFO.com*, 28 November 2006. Available online at http://www.cfo.com/article.cfm/8347091/c_8347143, accessed 21 September 2007.

27. Guerrera, Francesco. "Investors Warn on Use of Pay Consultants." *Financial Times*, 2 November 2006.

28. Anantharaman, Muralikumar. "Top M&A Lawyer Defends High Executive Pay." *Reuters*, 13 November 2006. Available online at http://www.reuters.com/article/InvestmentBanking06/idUSN1320265220061113, accessed 21 September 2007.

CHAPTER 3

Vision, Mission, and Values

We are firm believers that executive reward strategies—and the philosophies behind them—must reflect the organization's vision, mission, and values. A good mission, vision, and values statement provides a significant amount of directional guidance for decision makers within an organization—a guiding light, if you will, when the decisions get tough. And the decisions do get tough. We wonder if the scandals at Enron, Tyco, WorldCom, and UnitedHealth would have happened if there was a strong sense of mission and underlying values that governed the behavior of top executives. Considering all the—*ahem*—"gray areas" that top executives at these organizations encountered, shareholders at these organizations sure would have appreciated it if these guys had encountered a guideline or two that kept them on the straight and narrow. How many executive compensation scandals would have hit the news if executives held themselves accountable to their organizations' mission, vision, and values statements? Well, a good vision, mission, and value statement won't completely stop executive malfeasance. There are always going to be a few bad apples in the bushel. But we believe that for the most part good statements—those that executives buy into—promote good decisions.

Most executives know that when an organization has a stated mission, vision, and values, and operates from a position of adhering to these tenets, the long-term impact on the organization is powerful, significant, and compelling. Why? Because these things not only serve as a guide as they pertain to the organization's long-term goals and inspire executives to meet challenges, they also tell executives what practices are considered right, and what are considered wrong.

Of course, the vision, mission, and values must be articulated and understood to have any effect. Do most companies have vision and mission statements? They sure do. Many of these vision and mission statements make impressive reception area wall plaques and look great on needlepoint pillows—and unfortunately that's where their impact ends. In other words, in many cases employees have no clue what their organization's vision and mission statements are, let alone what the company's key values are. So what good are they? Aside from looking good in the company's annual report, that is.

Used correctly, vision and mission statements can pack quite a punch. What kind of power do vision and mission statements have when they are clearly communicated and understood? Well, consider Mahatma Gandhi, who had a simple, well-articulated vision of freeing India from British rule. His mission was to accomplish this without violence. While Gandhi came up with many different strategies along the way he remained true to both his vision and his mission, allowing them to guide his decisions. Was he successful? He certainly was. So what's the point? Powerful vision and mission statements are imperative for any company that hopes to succeed, and should guide the development of the executive reward strategy.

You've Got to Have Vision!

If you don't believe us, then we suggest you go out and buy a book called *Will and Vision: How Latecomers Grow to Dominate Markets* by Gerard J. Tellis, Peter N. Golder, and Clayton Christensen.[1] This book is basically devoted to debunking the myth that market pioneers have advantages over those companies who come on the scene a little later. It's a popular theory that's gained a lot of acceptance in the business world, but the authors' ten years of research studying 66 industries shows it just isn't true. So, according to the authors, what separates the men from the boys? Vision. Vision—and an indomitable will to realize that vision—is the real cause of enduring market leadership.

A vision statement defines where the organization wants to go in the future, without specifying the means that will be used to achieve those desired ends. It is the image that a business must have of its goals before it sets out to reach them. A powerful vision provides everyone in the organization with a shared mental framework that gives form to the often abstract future that lies before the organization.

A good vision statement is short, succinct, and inspiring. It paints a clear picture of a bright future, but can also be realistically achieved. A skillfully created vision statement not only describes what the organization wants to accomplish in the future; it also inspires executives to join the organization in meeting the challenges that lie ahead. A good vision statement inspires executives to make the right decisions, even if those decisions are personally painful.

A Man Should Have a Mission

Organizations that enjoy enduring success have a core purpose and core values that remain fixed, while their strategies and practices endlessly adapt to a changing world.

A mission statement defines the core purpose of an organization. In other words, why it exists. A mission statement examines the organization's reason for being, and reflects employees' motivations for engaging in the company's work. It should describe how an organization is serving the public interest—the true responsibility of any organization.

Unlike strategies and goals, which may be achieved over time, you never really fulfill your mission. It acts as a beacon for your work, constantly pursued but never quite reached. A mission is a compass by which an organization is guided.

So what makes a good mission statement? Well, first of all, it should be simple and clear. And while a mission statement itself shouldn't change, it should be designed to inspire change within the organization. Take these examples of great mission statements and you'll see what we mean:

United Way—To increase the capacity of people to care for one another.
3M—To solve problems innovatively.
Wal-Mart—To give ordinary folks the chance to buy the same things as rich people.
Merck—To preserve and improve life.
Walt Disney—To make people happy.
Mary Kay—To give unlimited opportunity to women.

Notice that all of these mission statements address how the organization will positively affect its customers as well as the world in general. Good mission statements, for example, don't say things like "To make our executives obscenely wealthy," "To make enough money to buy a company jet we can all use whenever we feel like it," or "To enable our executives to buy $5,000 shower curtains." Though you would never know it from the headlines.

INVESTOR ALERT #4

A BULL$%*T-SOUNDING VISION, MISSION, OR VALUES STATEMENT

We'll admit it's hard to keep our dander down when we hear a bull$%*t mission statement. Most investors, and most people for that matter, can smell cow manure from some distance. A good example of a mission statement gone bad is one which says, "We want to be a $1 billion company." To whom is this mission statement directed, anyway?

Is the statement communicating to the employees, since it seems to say a $1 billion company is better off than a $500 million company? Doubtful.

Is the statement communicating to shareholders, since it seems to say that they care more about big money than better returns on their equity? Doubtful.

Is the statement communicating to customers, since it seems to say that the company cares more about increasing total revenues than giving them the best value for the revenue dollars they spend?

If the vision, mission, or values statement comprises a lot of platitudes, it's a sure bet that the management team who wrote it is superficial and knows little about business strategy. Expect such a management team to operate poorly during the tough times.

It's a Matter of Principle

Now we come to values. Values are integral to an organization, as they are the timeless principles that guide that organization. They represent the deeply held beliefs within the organization, and are demonstrated through the day-to-day behaviors of its staff. To put it quite simply, values make an open proclamation about how an organization expects everyone to behave.

Is there a universal set of right or wrong values that exist? Absolutely not. In fact, each organization must discover the core values that comprise its essence and hold importance to those within it. Most organizations we work with have created a small number of core values that reflect the organization. While practices, processes, and strategies should change over time in answer to the many challenges that come, it should be expected that the core values remain the same. And what is the main job of the company's core values? They provide an enduring source of strength to executives focused on the company's vision. Face it, not all decisions in business are easy. Few answers are black-and-white. Strong company values can help an executive make the right decision for the company, even if it's not necessarily the right decision for him. Sure, it's oh-so-tempting to back date options, but if an organization's values include maintaining an excellent reputation, an executive invested in those values is going to think twice before doing something that has the potential to make his name, and that of his organization, front-page news.

Here's one way in which values differ from vision and mission. While a company can forego a vision or mission statement (though we wouldn't recommend it; the Maine

Mariner's have a saying, "For the person without a rudder, any wind is the right one"), every company has a set of values. And we mean every company, regardless of whether or not those values are officially stated.

So that means when it comes to values, the real issue is whether these values are conscious, shared, and lived, or remain unconscious and not discussed. Former good, latter bad. When values are not defined, the culture of the organization is subject to the vagaries of the personality of the leader.

INVESTOR ALERT #5

CELEBRITY CEO

Whenever a CEO becomes a celebrity for something other than good performance, it's probably time to reconsider your investment in the company. Unless the company is in the entertainment business, there is very little value to be attributed to the company for the support of high-profile CEOs. Often the case is that the executive is interested in promoting his or her career instead of the company's products and services.

Whenever a CEO suggests that his reputation and that of the company are inextricably linked, it's time to get out of the one-horse town quickly.

Walking the Talk

Which brings us to the importance of "walking the talk." It's not enough to have a conscientious mission statement, a quick and punchy vision statement, or a published set of ethical values if no one is paying attention. Leaders, and the executive rewards strategies they choose, must "walk the talk" when it comes to the values of an organization.

Okay, to illustrate how important it is to "walk the talk," here's a question for you.

Ready?

Whose corporate value statement was "communication, respect, and integrity?"

It's quick, punchy, and sends a good vibe, doesn't it? So who does it belong to? Think long and hard now . . .

Enron!

We know, it's hard to believe knowing what we know today. Did the executives at Enron "walk the talk?" Hardly. The Enron debacle is a great example of the company's value statement not being aligned with the company's vision, mission, or values. In fact, Enron's executive total reward strategy encouraged—even facilitated—the objective of making the numbers an overriding requirement to remain with the organization. And look where it got them!

Also, consider Pfizer's statements:

> *Vision and Mission: "Pfizer will strive to achieve and sustain its leading place as the world's premier research-based pharmaceutical company. The company's continuing success benefits patients, customers, shareholders, business partners, families, and the communities in which they operate all around the world. Pfizer's mission is to become the world's most valued company to all of these people."*

We know what you are thinking. Are we talking about the same Pfizer that paid ousted CEO Hank McKinnell $65 million in compensation and $83 million in retirement, even though during his tenure Pfizer shares lost 46% of their value? We're still trying to figure out how any of this is in the best interest of the shareholders, and where the values of integrity, leadership, performance—yada, yada, yada—come into play. Did McKinnell's pay package go hand-in-hand with shareholder and business partner success? Hardly. The only ones who are still remotely happy with Pfizer are the ones taking Viagra. The rest of them are pretty furious.

Most company statements that pertain to vision, mission, and values put the success of the company, and its shareholders, at the forefront. But executives who engage in shady activities like the backdating of options or flagrant perk abuse are messing with company values and sending a message to the rest of the company that they are not really accountable to the values they profess. Tyco, WorldCom, Parmalat, UnitedHealth—their statements didn't make a lick of difference because their leaders didn't live out those values and set the example for others. Leading by example—"walking the talk"—is the key.

So how does an organization ensure its executives lead by example? First of all, the power of vision, mission, and values shouldn't be belittled. And by this we mean it's not enough to come up with a nice-looking statement and consider the job done. Vision, mission, and values should be consistently reviewed and discussed so that they are not just relegated to a page in a manual, but reverberate throughout the organization's walls.

A total rewards strategy must be in line with the company's vision, mission, and values. In other words, the strategy must make it easy to do the right thing, and hard to do the wrong thing. The rewards philosophy should reflect vision, mission, and values, and should not send a conflicting message.

Case Study #5

One of the most unique and forward thinking organizations we've ever worked with developed its first people strategy in 1974. The strategy not only outlined how the organization would relate to its people, it also set expectations for those people in their relationship with the organization. The chief executive officer responsible for this strategy knew productivity was a function of the employee's desire to go the extra mile. He also believed in running a decentralized organization with the individual 50-plus company chief executive officers running their own shows. He felt strongly that these executives needed to understand their obligations and responsibilities, and also had to follow certain norms or behavior when it came to conducting business. The people strategy outlined safety, compensation wages, the importance of productivity, a nondiscriminatory culture, a meritocracy, and a mutual requirement for respect of the individual.

> *This people strategy guided the company's relationship with its employees for more than 20 years. The CEO who fathered the people strategy made it a personal campaign and ultimately walked the talk. Compare this to Enron's 100-page set of ethics and policies, and it's quite easy to see the difference. The chief executive officer knew that he was working in an organization decentralized across multicultural elements and many countries. He knew people would have to use their judgment to interpret the policies. He made to the policies clear and the penalty for not following them clearer. He simply said, "We operate to a higher requirement than `legal.' We demand a certain way of behaving altogether."*

Program design can become a real issue when problems crop up. Consider Robert J. O'Connell, Massachusetts Mutual Life Insurance Company's chief executive who was fired amid allegations of extramarital affairs with employees, illegal activity in trading accounts, and the misuse of the company aircraft. Despite all of this, a three-person arbitration panel found O'Connell was not dismissed for "cause" as he did not breach his fiduciary duties. The board argued that O'Connell was being fired "for cause," as he had made improper stock trades in a deferred compensation account using the prior day's closing price. This allowed O'Connell to benefit from gains in the stocks made from the news and information that occurred after regular trading hours.

So while the board considered this reason to terminate "for cause"—who wouldn't?—the arbitration panel disagreed. Why? Well, here's where that design flaw comes into play. The arbitration panel found that under the terms of the supplemental account, the company had the right to reject any trade or challenge whether the trades conformed to the provisions of the account. Were these terms contradictory to a company that espoused integrity and honor? You bet. In fact, these terms more or less gave O'Connell the green light to make improper stock trades. All in all, it was a pricey lesson that MassMutual learned. Organizations that want to ensure that executives lead by example when it comes to the company's vision, mission, and values statements should carefully examine their executive rewards program design to ensure that the statements and the compensation plan design are strongly linked. A total executive rewards plan should not give executives any tools that allow them to behave in a way that goes against company values.

Case Study #6

We met with the chief executive officer of one of our clients, which was one of the most successful grocery store chains in the United States. He had worked his way up through the organization, starting with the position of grocery bag filler. Because of this, he understood the importance of being extremely customer-focused. After significant discussion, he proposed a very unique approach to the executive compensation program.

He suggested that he and his top four executives each take home a $200,000 base salary. In addition, a 50% annual incentive and an amount of long-term incentive options would bring their total direct compensation up to the 50th percentile of the marketplace for organizations of their size and industry. Each of the executives would be appraised based on the overall organization's performance. It was truly a five-person team.

While the board had problems with the concept of their chief executive officer being paid the same salary as the other four executives, ultimately he and his logic carried the day.

Throughout the years we worked with the organization, they continue to have the highest profit of any of their competitors. They were known as the most innovative, and had the highest per customer revenues. They doubled every five years just like clockwork. We're sure that this was not due solely to the chief executive officer's unique decision on his executive reward strategy. That being said, his executive reward strategy was a reflection of his philosophy, his vision, and his values. The statement that he made was extraordinarily public and transparent. Because the organization's stock grew so well, we're sure the chief executive officer did better than his peers. After all, most of his rewards were in the form of stock instead of salary and short-term incentives.

Sometimes you have to go back to a time when the owners of today's public companies took only the amount that was a function of the organization's increase in value as compensation. Sometimes you have to express your value system publicly, and have no problem with using the proxy statement to do so. Walking the talk can provide a uniquely successful organization.

Putting It All Together

So now you've got the basic premise of this chapter: an organization is well served if its executive total rewards philosophy and strategy reflects the framework of the organization's vision, mission, and values. Seems simple enough, doesn't it? But if it were simple—if Enron, Tyco, Worldcom, UnitedHealth, and every other organization that has recently landed on the front pages because of corporate malfeasance had a vision, mission, and values structure that guided its decisions—the world would be a much nicer place, wouldn't it? Instead of headlines like "UnitedHealth's Options Scandal Shows Familiar Symptoms"[2] and "Burgeoning Stock Option Frauds Throw Corporate Ethics to Winds"[3] we would be opening the paper to headlines like "Popular Trend Shows Executives Walk the Talk; Shareholders Thrilled!" Are we going to see headlines like this one in our lifetime? Probably not. Why not? What's up?

Quite simply, while it's a great idea to link a company's vision, mission, and values statements to its executive total reward philosophy and strategy, it's a lot harder to do than you would think. Why? Because the quality of most organization's statements are generally so poor that they are uninspiring at best, and misleading at worst.

The majority of the vision, mission, and values statements that we read go something like this: "We will be the (best, pre-eminent, complete) provider of (goods, products, services) within our (country, industry, region) for our (size, clients, markets) etc . . . " You get the point. The combinations are un-limited, but the meaning and usefulness of these statements? Completely limited. We like to think in this case it's an in-stance of simple math: anything divided by zero is infinite.

In some cases, the founder is a truly inspired individual and is able to pass on that inspiration through a vision, mission, and values statement. Hewlett-Packard's founders David Hewlett and William Packard are good examples of leaders who lived their company's values, and inspired their execu-tives to live them as well. It wasn't until Carly Fiorina came on board and tampered with company culture that that their egalitarian message—and the company's values—somehow got muddled.

But let's get back to inspiring statements. Inspiring statements can impact the executive total reward strategy in several ways.

Sometimes, the vision, mission, and values statements address the environment and the organization's relationship to the environment. Remember, in our terms "environment" means the influential groups that do not have a stake in the particu-lar organization's success, but do exert influence on the indus-try in one way or another. Other statements speak to the or-ganization's significant or specific stakeholders.

In either case, vision, mission, and values statements are of-ten reliable sources for the limits of executive behavior. If these statements speak to key stakeholders, there will be implica-tions for executive compensation strategy.

- If there are influential customer groups that seek to limit the bottom line—the measures of success for the organization (profits made at their expense)—then the use of measures such as profitability as indicated on the income statement are going to be less likely, or, if used at all, very measured.
- If the statements address shareholder's wealth accumulation, the level of shares available to the executive rewards program, as well as the share dilution levels for equity compensation, will most likely be affected.
- When partners are important to an organization, they will often encourage a "be like me" type of influence in the executive total reward strategy.
- When employees are important to the organization as key stakeholders there will often be dialogue on the things that are most important to them—things like security, professional growth, or freedom. Some good examples of this are IBM's former no layoff policy, high tech companies that gave stock options to all employees to foster a "we are all in this together" environment, and one of the most interesting examples ever, when ice cream mogul Ben & Jerry's made the commitment that the CEO's compensation would be no higher than seven times that of it's lowest paid employees. Of course, as warm and fuzzy as this practice was in theory, it was scrapped when it was found that the company couldn't find the right kind of executive for seven times the salary of an ice cream scooper. This type of compensation practice is also not great for shareholders, but it is certainly more defensible than backdating options!

When we read vision, mission, and values statements we always try to determine their history, origin, and impact on key stakeholders—and therefore on the executive total reward strategy. In many cases the framework for key aspects of an executive total reward strategy may find its origins in the company's statements, or may even be a direct result of the company's statements. When these things are misunderstood—or don't align—things can go awry.

Certainly UnitedHealth's stock option program is going to be under pressure because it misunderstood that patients may also be shareholders. You know—the one where CEO William McGuire may have been granted stock options that were back dated to the most advantageous days and added up to $1.6 billion.

Anyway, in an Associated Press story about his compensation, McGuire was quoted as saying, "This isn't a giveaway of money that occurs out of the premiums of health care recipients. These are shareholder dollars." He also admitted the sum is "a lot. You can't get away from that."[4]

Well, we're certainly glad that the money doesn't come out of the premiums of health care recipients, and only comes out of shareholder pockets! One problem. There's a good bet that some of those same health care recipients are also shareholders. But apparently this didn't occur to McGuire. And the even bigger question is who says it's okay to be overpaid as long as it comes from shareholders? We doubt very much that UnitedHealth's vision, mission, and values statement condone this type of behavior. Most likely the statements aren't strong and inspiring enough, and haven't been integrated into the company's culture. Most likely they are buried in the back of UnitedHealth's annual report somewhere. In the end, it's a question of the CEO "walking the talk."

What's the moral of the story here, as well as of this chapter in general? Those involved in developing and designing an executive rewards strategy must be aware of—and respond to—the company's vision, mission, and values statements, in particular how those statements stand to impact compensation plan design. Those designing an organization's total reward strategy have an obligation and responsibility to ensure that the strategy complements—or at the very least is not obstructive to—the intent of the vision, mission, and values statements.

References

1. Christensen, Clayton, Peter N. Golder, and Gerard J. Tellis. *Will and Vision: How Latecomers Grow to Dominate Markets.* Los Angeles: Figueroa Press, 2006.
2. "United Options Scandal Shows Familiar Symptoms." *Washington Post*, 18 October 2006.
3. "Burgeoning Stock Option Frauds Throw Corporate Ethics to the Winds." *tradingmarkets.com*, 18 December 2006.
4. Freed, Joshua. "UnitedHealth CEO Discusses Stock Cache." *Associated Press*, 30 April 2006.

CHAPTER 4
Business Strategy

Understanding your business strategy, and aligning that business strategy with your executive total rewards program, is another key element when it comes to gaining competitive advantage for the organization and its shareholders. Allowing someone to design your total rewards strategy—whether we are talking about a consultant, human resources, or the board—who doesn't have a clear understanding of business strategy is, well, let's just say it's not a good idea. You better hope that everything is as everyone hoped it would be and nothing unusual happens, because there won't be a capacity to deal with anything other than normal situations.

We've done a great deal of work in the initial chapters trying to convince you that an organization's environment, key stakeholders, and vision, mission, and values statements create a unique situation for each organization—and therefore dictate a unique approach to executive total rewards strategy. Now that we find ourselves discussing business strategies, we want to make it clear that we are not going to give up that hypothesis. To drive the point home again, we want to make sure you understand that each company's unique business strategy should result in a unique total executive rewards strategy.

Is this always the case? Hardly. Even people who make their living designing executive reward strategies sometimes overlook the important linkage between business strategy and total executive rewards. Why? Because understanding an organization's business strategy takes time, and some compensation consultants have an unfortunate need to collect clients like baseball cards, which is great for the consultant, but pretty lousy for the clients who expect their reward strategies to play a part in their organization's success.

Mine Is Bigger Than Yours

To understand this mentality consider the following story. Michael was in an airport on the way to a client meeting when he happened to bump into another consultant he had worked with 10 years ago. They fell into the old, familiar routine of complaining about the life of a consultant (yep, occupational habit). Once they were done complaining, they engaged in another typical consultant behavior, which is comparing client loads. Just like other things we tend to compare (unless, of course, you are comparing cell phones), bigger is always better. So his former colleague told Michael that he has 60 clients and attends about 120 compensation committee meetings in a year.

Well, what can you say about that? Michael's 15 clients and 30 or so compensation meetings a year by comparison resulted in a, well, "girly man" moment.

But Michael was a firm believer that you can teach an old dog new tricks. And he wasn't about to let this guy get on his plane without learning his secret. When asked how he could possibly understand that many business and reward strategies the man gave Michael a befuddled, "what language are you speaking" kind of look, then stated that there was really no need to understand business strategy in order to determine pay levels. This guy's *modus operandi* was to let the market's "best practices" determine his recommendations to the compensation committee. You can bet at this point Michael breathed a sigh of relief and the "girly man" moment—thankfully—passed. Why? Because he knew—and by the end of this chapter we will have convinced you too—that if you design your rewards program to look like the average—or even the "best practices"—of the competition then, all things being equal, your company will be rewarded by approaching the mean, and your company will begin to look and operate like the crowd of lemmings headed for the cliff.

Looking in the Rearview Mirror Doesn't Work for Nascar Drivers, and It Won't Work for Your Organization Either

Sometimes executives focus on strategies they have used with success in the past and present, instead of focusing on strategies they'll need to keep them on top of the game in the future. While this is a comment on management in general, it is a notoriously prolific area for the misalignment of business strategy and executive reward strategy. A good portion of our new clients come to us with executive reward strategies that reflect their past successes or failures, instead of having executive reward strategies that focus on future challenges.

If we just had a dime for every organization we've seen develop a reward strategy looking in the rearview mirror, well— we'd have a lot of dimes. The results are, of course, the same as the proverbial driver who drives his car looking in the rearview mirror. Ultimately, the sweet sounds of success are replaced by the sickening sounds of a crash. Don't like blood and guts? Then we suggest learning to look toward the future and developing successful responses to what you see.

We often hear management complaining that shareholders are focused on the short term. The funny thing is, we often hear shareholders and investors complaining that management is focused on the short term. So what's the deal? Well, you could easily argue that this is a chicken-and-egg-type circumstance.

Why didn't IBM see the importance of the minicomputer, which resulted in competitors such as Digital Computer? Why didn't Ken Olsen understand the importance of the microcomputer? Why didn't manufacturers of personal computers see the importance of computer online purchasing and customization, which made Dell so successful? Why didn't any of the hardware makers see how important software was going to be for customers? Why didn't Microsoft see how big the Internet was going to become?

Why, indeed? Well, like many other people, we believe that a certain amount of success blinds an executive team to threats in the marketplace. A reward strategy focused on incremental improvements over prior years tends to develop and encourage a lack of market sensitivity on the part of the executive management team. In the end, what's the damage? A study done in March of 2004 showed that 40 percent of Standard & Poor's top 200 companies between the years 1990 and 2000 were different after the year 2000. That's a pretty high extinction rate, don't you think?

So what's the lesson here? First, business strategy is complex, but decoding an organization's strategy for purposes of designing an executive reward strategy is the responsibility of the management team, the board of directors, or the outside consultant. There *is* no "best practice" program that will fit the unique needs of any particular organization. If a consultant comes in and suggests executives be paid at the 75th percentile because that's what others in the market are doing, well, we think that's about as close to malpractice as you can get. And you know what? It happens all the time. It has become "common wisdom," and in most cases is pretty commonly wrong for the company.

Breaking the Code

We don't favor any one approach to decoding business strategy for the purpose of developing an executive reward strategy. And we don't advocate any one particular business strategy framework either. But we are big champions of an organized and disciplined process that allows an organization to develop and understand a business strategy or model that can gain competitive advantage for the organization and its shareholders. Much of the value of a strategy isn't found in absolute correctness, but in its message value to those who are allocating scarce resources among competing needs—the essence of leadership's execution of strategy.

Over the years we've developed a relatively straightforward approach to decoding business strategy for the purpose of developing a total executive reward strategy. In this approach, we look at strategy on three levels: general business strategy, value chain strategy, and specific business strategy. The key to designing an effective executive compensation program lies at each of these levels.

We'll explain these levels in detail in a second. In the meantime, we like to think about the levels of business strategy almost as if they were ways of looking at the business strategy at different altitudes. The general business strategy is like looking at the business strategy at 30,000 feet. The value chain strategy is like looking at the strategy from 10,000 feet. And the specific business strategy is akin to looking at the issues of strategy from 1,000 feet. We like the analogy of altitude because, similar to levels of altitude, there is a function specific to time span associated with each strategy level. And while executives also like to compare the creation of strategy to soaring with the eagles, we find that comparing the various levels and layers to an onion is closer to reality—in both sight and smell.

The General Business Strategy

The general business strategy is typically the longest form of directive, after vision, mission, and values, when it comes to developing an executive total rewards strategy.

We've mentioned before that we don't endorse any one predetermined framework for strategic analysis, so in the absence of one we're going to rely on Michael Porter's definition of general business strategy. For those of you who don't know

(text continues on page 92)

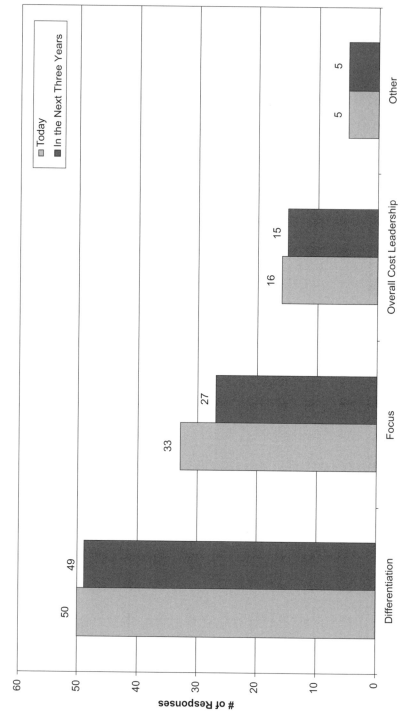

FIGURE 4.1 From a survey of organizations. The general business strategy that best described the organization's strategy.

Legend:
- Today
- In the Next Three Years

Differentiation: Today 50, In the Next Three Years 49
Focus: Today 33, In the Next Three Years 27
Overall Cost Leadership: Today 16, In the Next Three Years 15
Other: Today 5, In the Next Three Years 5

# of Responses

F$_{IGURE}$ 4.2   A general business strategy requires adding value to customers to build competitive advantage. It comes in different forms, as shown here. Adapted from Porter, Michael. *Competitive Advantage*. New York: Free Press, 1989, and Grant, Robert. *Contemporary Strategy Analysis*. Malden, MA: Blackwell Publishing, 1991.

Cost Advantage

Maximize every opportunity to increase efficiency.

Sources include:

•Economies of scale

•Economies of learning

•Production efficiencies

•Design

•Material costs

•Capacity utilization

Differentiation Advantage

Matching the customers' demand for differentiation with the firm's capacity to supply it requires an:

•Understanding of customer needs/preferences

•Commitment to customer

•Knowledge of organization capabilities

•Product/service differentiation

Focus - Deliver a Cost or Differentiation Advantage to a specific buyer.

who Michael Porter is, he's a Harvard Business School professor and guru when it comes to competition and strategy.

Porter categorizes general business strategy into three distinct and separate classifications. He states that general business strategy is either cost-based, differentiated, or focused.[1] Each of these three general business strategies have significant implications for the design of executive reward strategies, as each calls for different skills and requirements for success. When all is said and done, the general business strategy has a pretty big impact on organizational structure and culture, and ultimately the reward strategies. Let's further define the three categories of general business strategy, and you'll see what we mean.

The Cost-Based Strategy

What's the easiest thing about a cost-based strategy? Well, just about any executive can understand the benefit of having a cost advantage when it comes to selling their products or services in the marketplace. But despite the fact that a cost-based strategy is easy to understand conceptually, it's one of the most difficult strategies to implement operationally. Why? Well, the whole strategy falls apart in the hands of an unsophisticated management team who thinks a cost-based strategy means pinching pennies across the board—including when it comes to securing good executive talent.

If the general business strategy were the key to developing the executive reward strategy—by the way, it's not—then it's quite likely that a cost-based strategy would indicate a lower level of overall competitiveness, a higher reliance on both short-term and long-term variable compensation, and a modest amount of benefits and perquisites. This would, of course, be a direct reflection of the desire by the executive team or shareholders—or even a result of marketplace realities—that the associated costs of executive compensation had to be minimal, as well as directly related to the organization's performance.

If only life were this simple! In our opinion, any organization operating under a cost-based strategy better make sure that certain individuals are upper quartile performers. As a matter of fact, one of the keys to developing a good cost-based strategy is to look long and hard to determine where organizational capabilities such as cost control exist within the company, and to ensure that the very best executives who manage that capability or function are developed and retained within the organization. We also believe that a sustainable cost advantage general business strategy takes a little time to develop. What does that mean? It means that when you are reviewing the mix between short-term compensation and long-term compensation, lean toward long-term for the folks in the positions that control the organization's cost capabilities. It's interesting, but in the marketplace we often find the exact opposite.

In addition to the issue of determining where the capability of competing on a low-cost basis is located, our general belief and experience is that organizations that pursue a cost advantage strategy tend to be more centralized than those that pursue a differentiated or focused strategy. What's this mean? Well, when all is said and done, a relatively small number of individuals located at the strategic apex will make the critical decisions.

Further, a cost-based strategy can be implemented using the "second" component to costs, which is the number of individuals in the executive ranks. In fact, a 25th percentile market attachment can be accomplished by paying the 50th percentile pay strategy with just 20 percent fewer executives. In this case, the total cost of the executive group would be below market overall.

So where along the scale should these executives be paid? Well, think of it this way. When you fly on an airplane from one place to the other, you are usually one of many passengers. There are only two pilots. These pilots are making the critical decisions that keep the plane from unceremoniously plunging into the earth below. The thing is, you share the same fate as the two pilots, even though you aren't making the decisions. If you are anything like us, you hope that the two pilots in charge are the very best paid, and therefore the very best skilled, pilots there are. Similarly, a centralized organization might have only a few "pilots," but other employees, shareholders, partners, and suppliers will share their fate. No one wants their company to take the plunge either. So you want the best, and as we all know by now, you get what you pay for.

What about the rest of the organization? Let's get back to our friendly skies analogy. Aside from the pilots flying the plane— the people making the decisions that keep the organization aloft—few individuals need to be particularly well-paid. For organizations with a cost-based strategy we would recommend that only the strategic apex be paid in the upper quartile, based upon their long-term performance. We would also identify, vertically, those functions that contribute to the cost advantage and pay them in the upper quartile, all the while balancing the mix of rewards depending upon the level within the organization.

Need an example? Sure. Let's take Wal-Mart, where purchasing and logistics are very obviously the core organizational capabilities which allow the box store behemoth to pursue its cost advantage. We would place those in purchasing and logistics in the 90th percentile, and would recommend that senior executives in those functions be paid on a long-term basis, mid-level executives be paid on a mid-term basis, and low-level executives be paid on a short-term basis. Make sense? (We guess we'll sell at least a couple of these books, since we're sure now that everyone in the Wal-Mart purchasing and logistics department will buy one and give it to their corporate compensation department.)

All other job families would be paid at market, or even less than market assuming that this practice wouldn't decrease the organization's ability to execute its cost advantage. All other executives within the organization would probably be paid predominantly base salaries, and since their positions are not critical to the accomplishment of the competitive advantage, there would be little justification for any significant bonus program. The salary ranges for these individuals would be truncated, since any significant compensation paid above the market rate would be unjustified by a substantial return on the investment for the organization.

In order to run a cost-based strategy an organization might also remove a significant number of managerial layers that its competition might be willing to fund. Organizations that go this route should pay senior executives substantially above the market average to ensure that they are able to run the company on a centralized basis, without the benefit of multiple layers of expensive middle management.

Also, in terms of key messages, it might be very important to reward the key individuals on a "look forward" and "look around" basis. Individuals should be given incentive to both attain key future goals and remain in the upper relative cost performance categories.

The Differentiated Strategy

The second category of general business strategies we want to talk about is differentiated business strategies. Organizations with differentiated strategies focus on the ability to separate themselves and stand out from their competitors. The goal? To have a unique product, or be unique at something, that is valuable to potential buyers. Differentiation allows the firm to command a premium price, to sell more of its product at a given price, or to gain equivalent benefits such as a greater buyer loyalty during cyclical or seasonal downturns.

Apple Computers is a great example of an organization that uses a differentiated business strategy, proving that a personal computer isn't just a personal computer. Apple has successfully separated itself from other computer makers through ease of use as well as hip, eye-catching design. One of the areas in particular that Apple has been successful with is customer loyalty. Most Mac users have bought into the product to such a degree that using a lowly PC is just unthinkable. One of us is such a dyed-in-the-wool Mac user that when the first version of OS X crashed left, right, and center, we took it in stride. The Mac is still on the desk—and always will be.

So what are the implications for executive reward strategy when it comes to a differentiated strategy? Well, they are strikingly similar to those associated with the cost-based strategy we just talked about. The first step in determining how to compensate the executives is to figure out where within the firm the organizational capabilities to execute the strategy exist. At these tipping point positions it's important to understand the organizational processes required to develop and execute the differentiation strategy. To the extent that knowledge, decision-making, planning, communications, or managing change exist within a core group of positions ultimately responsible for the company's ability to differentiate itself, these positions need to be paid consistent with market and behavioral requirements for success in the long-term.

Rewarding these executives is more a function of determining how to measure their ability to provide customers with what they want and how they need it. To that end some of the performance-based rewards plans should be based on such things as market share, new customer accounts, retention of old customer accounts, and customer satisfaction.

A differentiated business strategy will also have some bearing on where you find executives. It just makes sense that a strategy focused on giving customers what they want and how they need it requires executives with significant marketplace insight. Since a broad understanding of the marketplace usually goes hand-in-hand with varied experience, it's quite likely that executives will need to be recruited from the outside. Executives recruited from the outside are usually considered mid-career hires. What does this mean? Well, mid-career hires carry a premium that must be met in order to acquire their services. As a general rule of thumb, this premium requires that they be compensated at the 75th percentile or higher, and that any benefits that they are losing from their former firm—such as unvested retirement or stock shares—be made up to them in the form of special allowances like hiring bonuses.

The Focus-Based Strategy

So now we come to the last category of general business strategies—the focus-based strategy. We saved this one for last, because in order to understand it you have to have a working knowledge of both cost-based and differentiation strategies. Why? Because focus-based strategies use either cost advantage or differentiation within a defined market segment.

In other words, a focus-based strategy focuses on a particular buyer group, segment of the product line, or geographic market. This particular choice of generic strategy is different because it requires the selection of a unique set of competitive scope within an industry. If a firm achieves sustainable cost leadership or differentiation in its segment, and the segment is structurally attractive, then the organization will most certainly be an industry leader. Talk about a one-two punch! Goldman Sachs is a great example.

Again, when following a focus-based strategy you use the same rule of thumb: figure out where within the firm the organizational capabilities to execute the strategy exist, and pay those executives at the 75th percentile or higher, while also using long-term incentives.

The Importance of Getting It

Every business has some sort of business strategy. The key is to understand how that strategy operates through to the ground level of tactical execution. If you want to really understand how important the linkage is between business strategy and reward strategy, look at any industry in which there is a major evolution. A change in the industry structure or a change in a critical element of competitive advantage can result in an important change in both short- and long-term incentive goals. If the goals don't change with the times, executives will find themselves being rewarded on a "look back" basis. Remember our analogy of the car crash a few pages back? Executives rewarded in a "look back" basis find themselves in an uncomfortable position. Basically, they are set up so that they are torn between doing what is best for the organization versus what is best for them.

Intel's gutsy move to respond to an evolving industry by changing things up is a powerful example of why executives should be encouraged to look forward, and not back. Their move also illustrates how pay strategies are inextricably tied to overall business strategy.[2] Back in January of 2006 Chief Marketing Officer Eric B. Kim and CEO Paul S. Otellini decided to dump old conventions—Intel Inside, the Pentium brand, even the company's logo—in an effort for Intel to keep up with changing times. Otellini also unveiled a new strategy. While the company had formerly buried the competition by narrowly focusing on the microprocessors that power personal computers, the new strategy called for Intel to play a key technological role in half a dozen fields, including health care, consumer electronics, and wireless technology.

Why did Intel switch things up? Quite frankly, they needed to. PC growth is slowing while other markets are growing. In order for Intel to remain viable, it had to be reinvented.

Did the company's total reward strategy change as a result? Of course. It had to. Otellini reorganized the company from top to bottom, creating specific business units for each product. High-level engineers no longer enjoyed celebrity status; instead the focus was on procuring software developers, sociologists, ethnographers, and doctors to help develop products. Major emphasis was placed on executives with marketing expertise. And for the first time in Intel's history, Otellini hired outsider Kim, whom he snagged from competitor Samsung, to report directly to the CEO.

What's the point of this story? It goes to show you that as Intel gears up to introduce a whole cache of new products—more products than it ever has in history—its leadership is shifting as well. Intel's actions are a good example of a "leap ahead" philosophy, rather than a "look back" philosophy.

The Value Chain Strategy

Now that you know how general business strategy is linked at the 30,000-foot level to executive total rewards, let's drop lower to the next altitude of 15,000 feet—the value chain strategy. Again, it's another concept provided by our friend Michael Porter.

Value chain strategy is a fairly simple concept. Basically, it suggests that there are various points along the value chain in an organization where extra resources can be applied in order to gain a competitive advantage in the marketplace.

Unfortunately, most companies we work with aren't in the position to throw unlimited resources to create a competitive advantage at all points along the value chain. If you can, all the more power to you! Most organizations, however, need to pick and choose where they are going to spend their critical, competitive advantage creating resources. Here are a few examples. Some companies stay in the game by having the very best purchasing and sourcing divisions, allowing them to either reduce costs or come up with a product that is more useful to their customers. Others—pharmaceutical companies are a good example here—spend their extra money in creating the research, development, engineering, or technology portions of their value chain in order to stay competitive.

A lot of organizations we work with still believe that it is efficiency of operations that ultimately win the day. We've seen some who believe that logistics and distribution are the critical components of the value chain. Still others believe that the customer portions of the chain are critical to success and spend lavishly on marketing, sales, and customer service.

(text continues on page 102)

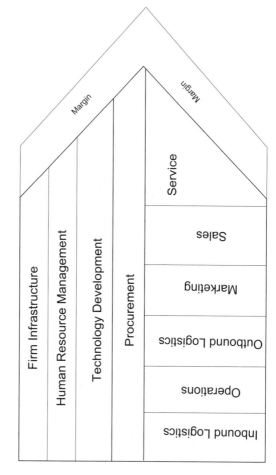

FIGURE 4.3 Porter's value chain.

FIGURE 4.4 From a survey of organizations asked the question: Where along the value chain would you characterize your organization's competitive advantage?

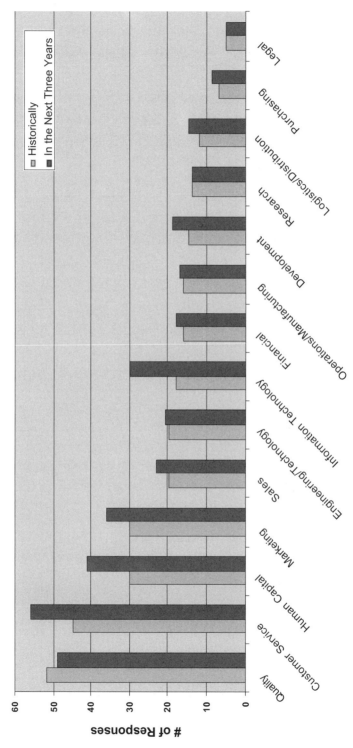

Some organizations even believe that certain staff functions—financial, legal, human capital, and information technology, for example—must be bolstered with extra money in order to create that competitive advantage.

The value chain strategy plays into the heart of executive reward strategy in very straightforward ways. Certain job families are clearly associated with creating and maintaining competitive advantage. As a result, the executives heading up those job families should have the opportunity to be highly compensated, and the performance factors inside their executive reward performance program should be specifically and directly related to their success in managing those key strategic functions.

Since all this is begging for an example, let's go back to our pharmaceutical company, where research is king when it comes to the organization's success. We would expect to see the vice president of research have the opportunity to be paid at the 90th percentile, with his short- and long-term incentive program directly tied to revenue associated with new products from research. Here's a simple rule: if you can identify a specific value chain area for the organization that is integral to its success, the executives responsible for that function should be well-paid if they produce results. The factors that drive their success—and let's not forget that of the company when all is said and done—should be uncovered and targeted by the total reward strategy.

As simple as the concept is, getting companies to put it into practice is one of the most frustrating aspects we face as compensation advisors. As a matter of fact, on the frustration scale it weighs in just above people not wanting to talk to us at parties.

Here's why. Most companies love to brag and boast about how aggressively they allocate and redeploy resources in the name of developing competitive advantage. But for some reason this aggressiveness always seems to come to an abrupt halt right outside the executive suite. Organizations don't like to differentiate between executives. Instead they apply an across-the-board percentile—the 75th percentile is always popular—and maintain that executive team cohesion is more important than calling attention to those executives who head up value chain functions that drive the success of the company. Short-term, mid-term, and long-term incentives, as well as benefits and perquisites, are also often designed in the same uniform manner.

Is there a price to pay for this one-size-fits-all, membership mentality? You bet. Because it positions all executives in a similar competitive percentile, the focus is on generic executive performance factors like earnings per share, operating profit, EBIT, etc. The sharp focus on what the organization needs to do to perform better than the competition in any particular market is lost. If the organization is lucky, the penalty will be mediocre performance. At worst it's dinosaur time—in other words, extinction.

What we've found over the many years we've been doing this is that the number of critical positions in any organization is relatively small. And yes, we know—that belief seems inconsistent with the premise held by our friends in the personnel department who maintain that all positions are critical and all people are corporate assets. Well, we don't mean to come across as unfeeling when we say "Bull!" But you don't have to take our word for it. In a study done for a very large insurance carrier, it was found that the 90th percentile performers produced close to 250 percent more than the average performer. And the best part is that the firm only had to pay these superstar performers 40 percent more than average performers. So why don't CEOs put together entire organizations made up of 90th percentile performers? According to the analysis, such a company would produce 250 percent more products or services for only 40 percent more money. It seems like a no-brainer! You don't need to be a math genius to figure out that company would certainly blow all of its competitors out of the water! Sure it would, but before you get too excited you do need to know that identifying 90th percentile performers is no easy task. So while it sounds great in theory, developing a strategy based on filling the ranks with high performers would, in reality, be prohibitively difficult. Some firms, like GE, practice a variation of this by regularly culling poor performers from their ranks.

Before we move on, we want to say that in our experience very few organizations actually understand or use value chain concepts, or the simple concept of allocating scarce resources among competing needs in general. Nor do they understand how to apply the principles to the design of a competitive executive reward program. One simple question can make a world of difference. Where along the value chain would you characterize your organization's competitive advantage?

Ask it. Then ask how surgical the competitive market attachment for those positions is, how their mix of reward components compares to both the market and other positions within the firm, and lastly, what messages are being delivered by the executive reward program.

Specific Business Strategies

The third layer of business strategy—imagine you are at now at an altitude of 7,000 feet—we believe should play into total executive reward strategy is what we call specific business strategies. These sit a layer below general business strategy and the value chain strategy. Specific business strategies might include growing through a merger, growing market share, optimizing margins, expanding operations geographically, expanding distribution, decreasing production capacity, growing from within, increasing cash flow, building better customer relationships, using joint ventures, managing costs for reengineering, or becoming more global. Each of these specific strategies results in the need for organizational capabilities that are unique to the specific time, maturity, or phase of business strategy execution.

Specific strategies can be thought of in a more operational short-term manner than the types of operational strategies employed to reinforce or execute value chain or general business strategies. These types of strategies usually run in the six-month to three-year timeframe. While they are different in time frame, it is not the time frame, per se, that makes these strategies a different animal than general or value chain strategies.

Rather, specific strategies have a transient, even temporary nature. We sometimes think that's because it's the management fad of the day. In our opinion—of course—management fads are a real problem. Why? Well, they prescribe simple, generic solutions to complex, individualized business situations. That being said, we do want to make it clear that there are a significant number of specific business strategies that are valid, and have been developed as a result of an appropriate amount of analysis at both the general business strategy level and the value chain business strategy level.

Specific business strategies such as growth through merger, grow market shares, retain market shares, increase profit regardless of market shares, optimize margins, expand operations geographically, expand sales force, decrease production capacity, etc. all have a very operational imperative in common. These are the types of strategies at which executives and designers should be targeting substantial short-term compensation. There is no need for the strategies and the resulting rewards to be annual. We are a major proponent of milestone incentives. Which means that these incentives are tied to the accomplishment of goals and are paid in cash when the goals are accomplished—regardless of the time of year.

Case Study #7

A client, which is a large systems house, had run into a significant slump in its new business efforts. Individual client relationship managers from the different sectors seemed to be only interested or able to sell products and services from their historic sector. The organization's fu-

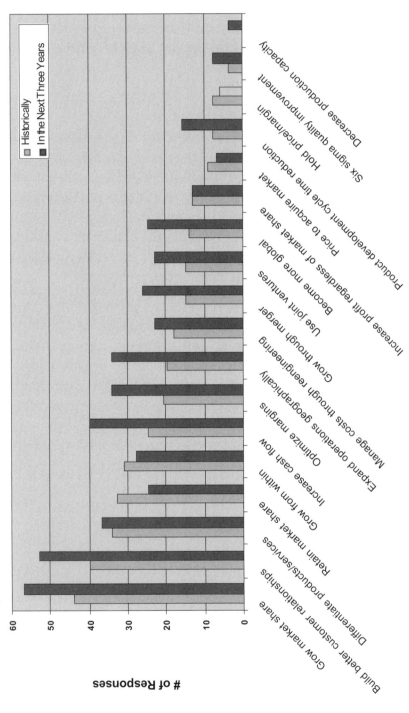

FIGURE 4.5 From a survey of organizations when asked the question: What best describes your organization's specific business strategy?

ture success was dependent upon a significant group of key executives, who were responsible for client relationship management to be able to sell all the organization's products and services. This would transform utilization from selling differentiated products to focusing on finding solutions to client problems, thereby opening the door for long-term client relationships.

The key was to design a measurement system that reflected the required performance of selling client-based solutions, rather than merely selling products. We recommended a scorecard methodology for the executive client relationship managers that included the following aspects: the relationship with the organization was measured by whom the executive client relationship manager worked with, how many services were sold to the particular client, and what the strategic level of the service was. In addition, we measured the size of the client in terms of the client's revenue.

Revenues dramatically increased from a core group of clients and, as is usually the case, profitability dramatically increased. Certain executives performed well on the new performance requirements, and other ones failed by just trying to sell more services, ultimately resulting in lower margins.

Sometimes when you lose money on each assignment, you can't make it up on volume. Executives are no different than other employees. Most of them (but not all of them) will study a performance measurement in order to maximize their own compensation. When the performance measurement is specific, you can expect the executive behavior to be specific too.

Hopefully by now we've convinced you of the strong link between business strategy and total executive rewards strategy. Remember, we don't advocate "best practices," unless a company comes to us and tells us their goal is to be average. Understanding your organization's business strategy—and aligning that strategy with your executive rewards program—is a necessary step for any organization that hopes to gain competitive advantage.

References

1. Porter, Michael. *Competitive Strategy: Techniques for Analyzing Industries and Competitors.* New York: Free Press, 1980.

2. Edwards, Cliff. "Inside Intel." *Business Week Online,* 9 January 2006. Available online at http://www.businessweek.com/magazine/content/06_02/b3966001.htm, accessed 21 September 2007.

CHAPTER 5

Organizational Capabilities and People Strategy

A lot of companies attempt to go directly from the business strategy to the total executive reward strategy. Even though we've given some examples of that type of linkage, we think that's a big mistake. Why? Because designers who do this are missing a huge—really huge—piece of the puzzle. What's the missing piece? Organizational capabilities and people strategy. Plain and simple, we don't believe you can design an effective total executive reward strategy without factoring in organizational capabilities and people strategy.

That being said, plenty of companies do. (Frankly, for that matter a significant number don't really factor in the business strategy either.) But designing a reward strategy without identifying, understanding, and determining the firm's organizational capabilities and people strategy is like driving a car with a faulty transmission. You can punch the accelerator as hard as you can, but the only place you'll go is nowhere—fast. You can have all the horsepower in the world, but if you can't put the car in gear it's not going to make much difference in the end. Should a successful company have its executive reward strategy rooted in strategic goals? Of course. But it should be rooted in organizational capabilities and its people strategy as well. The connection should be as clear and explicit as, "Because our business strategy is x, our key capabilities are y, and our people strategy is z, our rewards strategy is a function of x, y, and z."

Organizational Capabilities—That Certain "Something"

All this talk about organizational capabilities and we bet you want a clear definition of what they are. Well, within each company, there is an indefinable *something* that sets it apart in the competitive landscape. More than a single accomplishment, a visionary leader, or even a distinctive strategy, there is a set of business attributes that creates a unique identity in the minds of its employees and customers. That *something* is called organizational capability, and fostering it is every executive's most important job. As a matter of fact, Baruch Lev, a professor of accounting at New York University, says that intangible assets like a skilled workforce and know-how account for more than half of the market capitalization of America's public companies. Accenture, a management consultancy, says that intangible assets have risen from 20 percent of the value of companies in the S&P 500 in 1980 to around 70 percent today.[1]

McKinsey makes a similar point by dividing American companies into three categories: "transformational" (turning raw materials into finished products), "transactional" (scripted or automated interactions), and "tacit" (complex interactions using a high level of judgment). McKinsey says that in the last six years jobs that fall under the "tacit" category have grown two and a half times as fast as those that fall in the "transactional" category, and three times as fast as employment in general.[2] According to McKinsey, "tacit" jobs make up 40 percent of the American job market and account for 70 percent of all jobs created since 1998.

Organizational capabilities are unique to each organization. They are distinctive and difficult—if not impossible—for another company to replicate. They include the collective expertise, knowledge, values, and practices that create a competitive edge. Building organizational capability means learning to compete from the inside out—identifying strategic goals, developing internal processes and systems to support those goals, and directing the skills and efforts of employees toward a common objective. Organizational capability isn't actually about producing good ideas or results, but rather the path in between—how a company translates ideas into action.

To understand how important organizational capabilities are, we want you to take a few seconds to think about companies you really admire. Why do you admire them? Do you admire them because of their management techniques or because of their business strategies? Probably not. Chances are, you have no clue what their management techniques or strategies even are! Perhaps you admire Apple for its ability to bring innovative new products to the marketplace, or maybe Intel has your respect for its ability to respond to a changing marketplace. Maybe you picked JetBlue for its ability to bring great service at a low cost to its customers, or maybe Ben & Jerry's came to mind for its unparalleled ability to create and build brand awareness. Regardless of the companies you chose, we're pretty sure that their intangible assets—their organizational capabilities—are the reason they stand out to you. Although anything is possible, this exercise probably didn't result in you saying, "I dig General Electric because its management structure rocks!" The things that most often stand out for a successful company can't be touched or seen. But they make a huge difference when it comes to an organization's market value. In each of the above examples—Apple, Intel, JetBlue, and Ben & Jerry's—organizational capabilities provide a source of competitive advantage for each company.

Organizational capabilities comprise a company's skills, abilities, and expertise, and are a direct result of how an organization decides to invest in its human resources. And that's where the whole people strategy comes into play. Regardless of what a company's mission statement is, they aren't going to be able to fulfill that mission unless they have the people who have the skills and abilities to do so. A total executive reward strategy should be designed in order to ensure that the people with the right skills and abilities are attracted to—and retained by—the organization. So now it's becoming clear how organizational capabilities and a total executive reward strategy all tie together! So how do you do this? Again, it's simple in concept. If you want to attract and retain the right talent, you need to give the talent what it wants.

We have found it useful to identify a starting point or initial list of organizational capabilities in several key categories. Most organizations' critical capabilities are more specific than this generic list. These categories are customers, products and services, management and people, and technology. These key categories have several subcategories:

Customers
- Acquire new customers
- Build better customer relationships through high-quality service
- Match services to customer needs
- Identify and work with key customers to predict joint business opportunities
- Solve strategic problems for customers
- Solve more problems for existing customers

Products and Services
- Provide excellent, innovative customer service
- Strive to continuously improve products and services
- Create and build brand awareness
- Bring new products and services to market

Management and People
- Hire the best talent
- Strive to retain valuable, high-potential people
- Manage employee skills and knowledge
- Provide ongoing training and development programs
- Terminate non-performers effectively

Technology
- Apply the best technology to solve client problems
- Apply technology to reduce costs
- Continuously improve existing technology
- Acquire and implement new technology

Plumbing the Depths

Organizational capabilities aren't easy to measure. So sometimes it's harder for organizations to decide how best to invest in them. Managers often pay less attention to intangibles and instead focus their energies on tangible investments like equipment or software. Those who dig a little deeper, however, and place importance on organizational capabilities are amply rewarded. Remember, these intangible assets make a company what it is in the marketplace. Differences in intangible assets might explain why, for example, Nike's market valuation is significantly higher than that of Reebok's. Are Nike's sneakers of a better quality than Reebok's? Are their tennis skirts cuter? Debatable. But what's not debatable is Nike's far superior ability to create and build brand awareness. Whose technology is better? Who cares! When we buy Nike products over Reebok products we're not doing it because their sneakers offer more support or their tank tops breathe better. We're doing it because their ads are better. Nike and Reebok use similar material to make their products. Their executives most likely possess a comparable amount of knowledge and expertise when it comes to making the products. The companies may have similar goals and strategies. But where Nike really converts is in its organizational capability to market its product. Nike's branding makes them who they are—and gives them the competitive edge in the athletic equipment and apparel market. A company whose bread and butter comes from creating brand awareness would obviously want to create an executive total rewards strategy that would allow—and encourage—executives to build on these capabilities.

One of our major objectives with any client is to create a systematic connection between organizational capabilities and rewards. The company needs to identify, understand, and determine key compensable issues so that the appropriate portion of the total reward strategy architecture—money, mix, and messages—can be tied directly to each executive's contribution.

INVESTOR ALERT #6

ORGANIZATIONAL LAYERS

Whenever the CEO has few direct reports but is not near retirement age, you question if the CEO is not getting enough feedback from a diverse group of individuals with diverse opinions. It is not unusual for a CEO to create a horse race during the last few years of his tenure. This is typically done by developing several senior positions that have both line and staff organizational responsibilities across diverse business lines. In many cases the organizations also define ways to ensure that each prospective CEO candidate has an equal amount of challenge when it comes to their business portfolios. This is good organization structuring, and is a good organizational succession planning process as well.

If, on the other hand, the CEO is 10 years away from retirement, extra layers of management may be just a way of allowing the CEO to retire while on the job. The extra layer of management only creates an extra layer of politics. The extra layer of politics will have its casualties. Many of these casualties will be some of the best executives in the organization.

So if you see a lot of extra departmentalization occurring below the executive suite, you can expect the politics to increase and your investment performance to decrease with them.

Let's say that a company's organizational capabilities lie in acquiring new customers. The incentive elements arranged at each different level of the executive hierarchy should be oriented around ensuring that organizational capability is nurtured at a level sufficient to execute the various business strategies. Is it enough to put "acquire new customers" in the sales executive's goals and objectives statement and call it a day? Hardly. Creating an organizational capability to acquire new customers may involve issues with product quality, delivery logistics, and even pricing. The point here? Developing organizational capabilities is an effort to understand how the organization itself creates and executes key portions of its business strategy. The concept is sort of similar to that of value chain strategies, but on an intangible level. Is one of your organizational capabilities retaining and attracting talent? Then you need to staff the areas that pertain to this capability with the right people, and you need to reward them in a way that motivates them and retains them. A good example of this is Goldman Sachs, who in 1999, after an in-depth internal review, increased its emphasis on formal training and put together a program designed to reward senior execs who put effort into developing talent. It also reconfigured its internal organization to better appeal to talented young people.[3]

Here are some more examples. Is one of your organizational capabilities the ability to make important changes happen fast? Then ask yourself which areas of the company contribute to making this happen, and reward them in a way that ensures this capability endures and grows. Are you good at building trust and relationships with your customers? Managing costs? Providing excellent service? Introducing a steady stream of innovative products? Same deal. Find out who makes it happen and give them what they want to make sure it continues to happen.

If you really want to understand how organizational capabilities can be used to a company's advantage, take a look at Albany International.

Albany International is the world's largest producer of paper machine clothing, with manufacturing plants in 15 countries and nearly $1 billion in worldwide sales. Here is how the company describes itself:

> *"Albany International is recognized as the industry's technological leader. A strong investment in research and development has resulted in the successful introduction of breakthrough products that provide innovative solutions for our customers' challenges."*

This company has a strong commitment to a focused strategy: delivering technologically superior products. In fact, the company has become so proficient in developing advanced products that it has been suspected of holding back new products from market while its competitors catch up with the existing product line, thus ensuring a continual technological lead.

The company's strategy is clear, and so are its organizational capabilities. Albany International's competitive advantage comes from superior research, development, and engineering. You can bet its capital resources and executive reward strategies are aligned with these organizational capabilities. For instance, in many organizations, the chief technology officer is lower in the hierarchy than marketing, sales, finance, or other positions. But at Albany International? The technology managers reporting to the chief technologist are top performers recruited from the best colleges and universities. They are promoted from within based upon performance, given extensive resources for ongoing learning to ensure that they remain at the forefront of paper machine manufacturing technology, and are rewarded for their contributions. We bet the executive in charge of technology is one of the highest paid executives in the company after the CEO.

People Strategy—Leveraging Your Most Important Asset

So now we understand the importance of organizational capabilities and how they play into a company's competitive stance in the marketplace. To use our car analogy again, these organizational capabilities are the transmission for the business model engine, and are also critical to understand the organization's overall strategic intent. The business strategy—or the business model if you prefer—needs to be "translated" to get its people requirements in gear. How is this done? Through the organizational capabilities and a corresponding people strategy. Think of it this way. The organizational capabilities must be understood in order to know which portions of the organizations are critical to accomplish the organization's business strategies. The people strategy, on the other hand, will ultimately identify and put into motion the business strategy component with respect to its human capital element. In other words, no people, no strategy.

But before you slap your forehead and have a "Why didn't I think of that" moment, it's a little more complicated than that. It's not just enough to have people whose job descriptions say things like "Increase customer sales," "Build brand recognition," or "Develop innovative new products." That would make things a lot simpler, wouldn't it? Too bad. Instead, you have to have the right people in the right job, positioned in such a way that they are able to contribute in the way you want them too. They must be compensated in a way that is meaningful to them—that encourages them to perform and doesn't send them packing when other companies come calling.

Case Study #8

A hedge fund came to us with a unique problem. Its founder and chief investment officer wished to sell the organization to a large bank, but could only do so if he agreed to stay with the organization for five years following the acquisition. The individual did not wish to work for the large bank, but did wish to sell the organization. He asked us to solve this circular unsolvable problem of how to sell the organization, and yet not have to work for the buyer.

We developed the people strategy/reward strategy solution. The individual picked five additional investment strategies he wished the organization could pursue. We recruited the very best individuals in those new strategies from other well-established investment organizations. In the process of negotiating for the first individual's entry into the hedge fund, it became clear that what these individuals desperately wanted was some of the equity in the organization. We came up with a plan that allowed the individual to purchase equity in the organization. Over time, with each individual recruit, the organization became more and more successful. Instead of managing $2 billion in assets it began to acquire the opportunity to manage close to $10 *billion in assets. Ultimately, the individual who had planned to sell his position to a large bank ended up selling a minority interest to the five individuals who were recruited from other investment entities. Ten years later, he is still managing an organization that is worth five times what it was when he was planning on selling it to the bank.*

Before you say (as virtually all CEOs do at some point), "People are our most important asset," think about whether your organization actually manages its human resources—including executives as well as rank-and-file employees—as explicitly and thoroughly as other assets. It's all too frequent that the same guys who espouse the "People are our greatest asset" tenet pay attention to strategies such as marketing, research and development, operations, legal, sales, and customer service and hope the whole people strategy thing will take care of itself if they hire people with lots of talent. Big mistake!

We are often surprised by how little organizations know about handling talent once they have it on board. Enron, for example, certainly hired its share of talent. And look where it got them. Perhaps it was their across-the-board policy of rewarding talent over experience and performance that got them in trouble? What's our point? You can hire all the MBAs and Nobel Prize winners you can afford, but if you don't align your people strategy with your executive reward strategy, there isn't much point to it. Good management isn't all about hiring the best of the best and hoping for the best (unless you are running a large horse breeding conglomerate, in which case breeding the best to the best and hoping for the best is actually pretty good management indeed). Good management is hiring the best talent and then ensuring that your total executive reward strategy encourages them to best use their skills and experience in a coordinated way to ensure the organization's accomplishment of its business strategy and ultimate success in the marketplace.

One note on the limitations of this discussion: there are countless theories on how to develop a people strategy, and every executive could benefit from reviewing some of them. Don't believe there's any one single approach to understanding people strategy. There isn't! That being said, our goal isn't to tell you how to develop a solid people strategy, but rather how to connect your existing people strategy with an effective executive rewards strategy. Would our approach to the development of a people strategy be helpful to human resource executives? Of course we like to think so! Nevertheless, it's not the purpose of the concepts.

What Makes a Successful People Strategy?

A company's people strategy comprises its organizational structure, organizational process, and organizational culture. And this is where things get dicey. No two companies approach their people strategy in quite the same way. Again, this contributes to the fact that there's no such thing as a one-size-fits-all executive rewards strategy. Instead, a good executive rewards strategy is based on a company's own unique organizational structure, process, and culture.

Let's begin by defining people strategy in terms of structure, process, and culture. By the end you'll understand why these components are critical in determining an executive rewards strategy.

Organizational Structure

The Great Pyramid

The most effective way that we have found to understand organizational structure for the purposes of developing an executive total rewards strategy is to see or understand the organization as a series of departments both vertically and horizontally. In addition to the vertical and horizontal lines that designate the degree of compartmentalization in the organization, there are, conceptually, a number of staff organizations which support, inform, or advise the line organization structure.

So let's picture a pyramid. A series of overlaying vertical and horizontal grids will represent the organizational line departments. Now let's add a series of triangles to the grid, to represent various staff departments.

Okay. Now that we've got that down, let's think about the workflow of product moving through the organization from the left-hand side of the pyramid to the right-hand side. The left-hand portion of the triangle represents the company's inbound logistics such as purchasing, research, development, and engineering. The middle portion of the triangle represents the operations where the actual product is created and assembled. And the right-hand side of the triangle includes the company's outbound logistics, such as distribution, sales and marketing, and customer service.

So why do you have visions of pyramids dancing in your head? Because it's important to understand the organizational structure in order to appreciate how the executive total reward strategy will be cascaded down through the organization.

A company's executive total rewards strategy will include performance management criteria. It is critical, when designing the strategy, to choose factors that address shareholder concerns but, at the same time, are also effective when used to cascade objectives and tactical plans down throughout an entire organization.

As a matter of fact, organizational structure is such a critical element to understand when designing an executive incentive and executive rewards program, that there is rarely an assignment begun without complete review of the executive organizational chart. And this is appropriate. A good, hard look at the executive organizational chart will tell you two things: (a) who is eligible for various incentive plans; and (b) how the position levels compare with various survey sources' descriptions of executive position responsibilities.

Unfortunately, while these two uses of an organization chart are valid, they are, in our minds, only partial conditions. And here's where we differ from most other executive compensation consultants.

When we look at a company's organizational structure, we're looking to understand its present and future "intent."

INVESTOR ALERT #7

LONG-SERVING CEO'S

Whenever you have a long-serving CEO whose initial 5- or 10-year time in the position was deemed brilliant, but whose performance has trailed off substantially in the last few years, it's a pretty good bet that the CEO has overstayed his welcome.

There was a great article in a major magazine which fundamentally headlined the issue. What happens to all those risk-taking, hard-charging CEOs once they have been CEOs for 10 years? The answer? Quite simply, they get soft and risk-averse because they are much more concerned about their retirement years than they are about their working years.

Don't invest in a person who's got their eyes on something other than what they're doing today.

The Game of Telephone

All of this is just begging for an example, isn't it? Well, we'll start by asking you to take a trip down memory lane and think about a childhood game most kids play at one time or another called "telephone." You remember the game—one child begins by whispering a sentence into another child's ear. That child passes it down, and so on and so on. What was the objective of this game? To see how garbled the message was once it reached the final recipient.

Well, much like the game of "telephone," hierarchical organizations that have lots of horizontal layers make the cascading down of specific objectives more difficult. Picture your pyramid again. By the time the message reaches the person furthest away from the top, the message may have little in common with the original. Unfortunately, the results are not nearly as amusing as they are when playing "telephone."

This information is critical for the designer, as it would tell him he needs to create an incentive plan that rewards effective communication of goals and objectives. One product we like to use for this type of organization is called a scorecard, which starts at the top and is linked as it cascades down. A scorecard allows you to look either up or down and see how communication of goals and objectives are connected.

When an organization has lots of demarcations in a vertical direction, it usually means that value is added by a large number of specialized functions. How does a company like this reach its fullest potential? Well, the more transfer of knowledge between the separate departments and job functions, the better. And how would the designer use this information? It would tell him that he needs to design an executive rewards strategy that increases the interdependency among departments, to help them operate as a single entity. The incentive plans should emphasize the larger organizational entities goals to encourage cooperation that might not naturally occur.

Different Strokes for Different Folks

By now you probably understand that organizational structures are as unique as the companies themselves. As a matter of fact, two organizations of approximately the same size, with the same number of employees, who produce the same product, can have drastically different "line" organization structures. One company could be extremely hierarchical, but could have relatively few vertical demarcations. The other could have fewer hierarchical layers but more vertical demarcation. Or virtually any combination thereof.

If you put the concept of hierarchical and vertical demarcations as an organizational structure principal in a box matrix, you'll

FIGURE 5.1 Four general types of organizations.

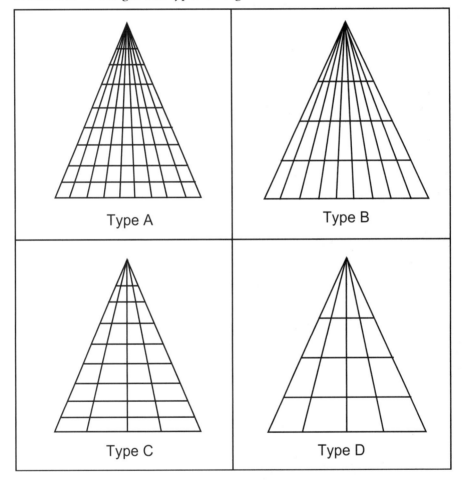

see there are four general types of organizational structures. Each of these four general types of organizations has very different operating characteristics and, for that matter, has very different reactions to executive compensation strategies. So what's the key here? The total rewards package must be designed in a way that complements the organizational structure. At the risk of over-simplifying things ourselves, we've broken out four types of organizational structure to represent extremes.

Type A. Organizations which have very high horizontal and vertical hierarchies.

Often described as highly departmentalized, these organizations are typical of businesses that have existed in a relatively stable environment, and have delivered a relatively complex product or service.

Type B. Organizations which have a high vertical hierarchy and a low horizontal hierarchy.

These types of organizations usually develop relatively singular, simple, or uniform products, but have either existed for a long time and have developed a significant hierarchy, or have existed within a stable industry but have built up a hierarchy because competition requires a significant degree of control by the managerial layers of the organization.

Type C. Organizations that have a low vertical hierarchy but a high horizontal hierarchy.

These organizations typically deliver relatively complex hand-offs from one organizational job family to another without a large number of managerial layers.

Type D. Organizations that have a low level of vertical hierarchy and a low level of horizontal hierarchy.

These organizations are extremely flexible regarding both managerial issues as well as product, development, design, and delivery issues.

What makes things even more interesting is that there are, of course, a number of combinations of organizational types within a single organizational entity. For example, sometimes the left-hand side of the pyramid, or the inbound logistics side, will have a low vertical hierarchy, while the middle of the pyramid will have a moderate hierarchy and the right side of the pyramid will have a relatively high hierarchy. So what's the solution? In this particular example the designer of an executive reward program would have to consider that cascading down objectives inside the purchasing, research, and development areas of the organization would be simple and effective, while cascading down objectives within the sales, marketing, and customer service areas would prove a greater challenge.

Why Staff Functions Are Like Airplane Flaps

Now that you've grasped the meaning of the vertical and horizontal layers within an organization, consider this: while they are important to understand, they do not operate outside the context of the staff functions associated with various parts of the organization.

In fact, staff functions are like airplane flaps that direct the flow of wind over various plane surfaces. Just like these flaps create a directional dynamic for the plane to respond to, staff functions create a directional dynamic for the organization to respond to.

That being said, there are three issues to consider with staff groups. The first issue is the size of the staff group, the second issue is the location of the staff group, and the third issue is authority.

Let's tackle location first. We can begin by picturing the polar axes—North, South, East, and West. Where is the staff group located? If it is located near the strategic apex, or North on our axis, the staff group will have significant directional force on the organization. If the staff group is located in East,

FIGURE 5.2   Staff group location.

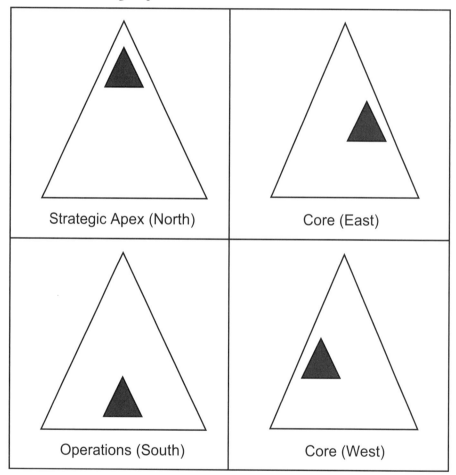

| Strategic Apex (North) | Core (East) |
| Operations (South) | Core (West) |

they will have influence over the right-hand side of the organizational structure, where sales, marketing, and customer service reside. If the staff group is located in the West, it will have influence over the inbound logistical area where purchasing, research, and development live. You get the picture.

Once you know where the staff group is located, you need to consider its size. Quite simply put, the larger the staff group, the more influential it is in affecting the company's direction.

The third aspect when it comes to staff groups is the authority they are given by the key executives. The authority can best be defined in four different categories:

Primary: This is when the authority for decision making is absolute. In other words, the staff group is the decision making entity. This is rarely the case, thank God.

Shared: This is when staff groups and line managers share the responsibility for a decision.

Advisory: This is when the staff group advises the line group, but has no authority to enforce its will on the line group.

Informational: This is when the staff group provides information but does not advise the line groups.

By now you should have a pretty good idea of how to determine a company's organizational structure. And while you know the number of combinations and permutations are only equal to the amount of unique companies out there, that shouldn't scare you anymore. Analyzing organizational structure is the first step to determining a company's people strategy. Sure, a company's business strategy is critical to its success. But who executes the business strategy? People. And it is the people behind the business strategy that the executive rewards strategy should be designed to motivate.

Now let's spend some time learning about how organizational processes are integral to the design of an executive total rewards strategy.

(text continues on page 132)

FIGURE 5.3   Size of staff groups.

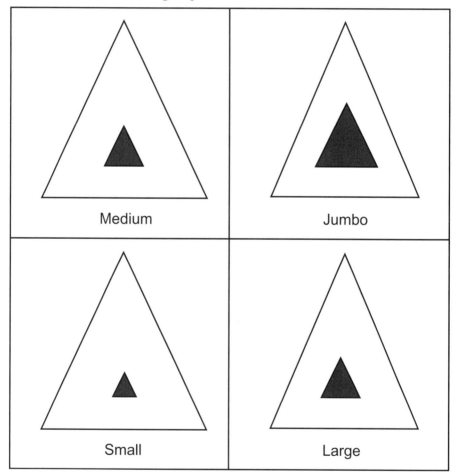

FIGURE 5.4   Management processes fit into five categories.

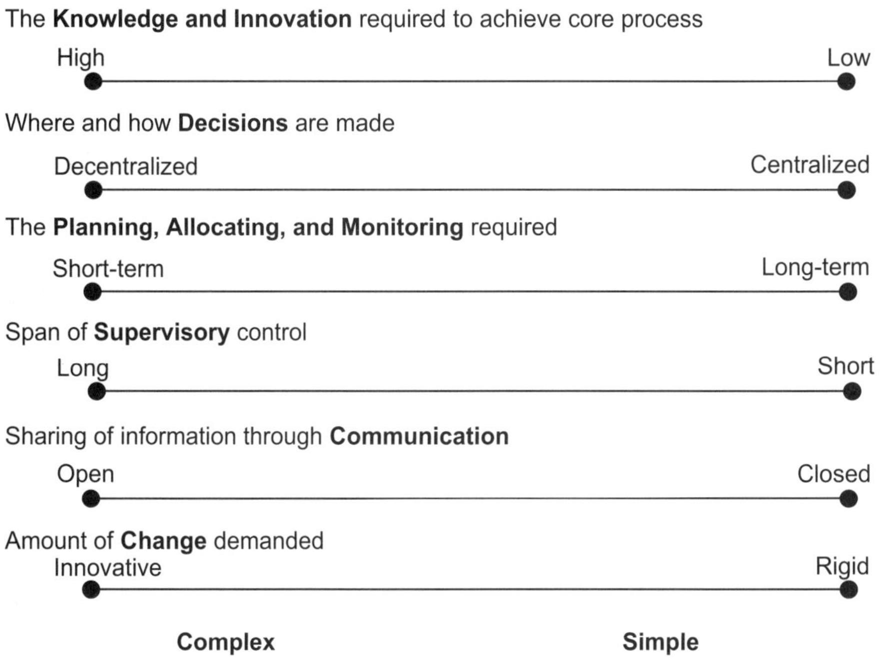

The **Knowledge and Innovation** required to achieve core process

High   Low

Where and how **Decisions** are made

Decentralized   Centralized

The **Planning, Allocating, and Monitoring** required

Short-term   Long-term

Span of **Supervisory** control

Long   Short

Sharing of information through **Communication**

Open   Closed

Amount of **Change** demanded

Innovative   Rigid

Complex   **Simple**

Organizational Processes

Measuring Up

Organizational structure defines how a company is organized so that people get things done. Organizational processes, on the other hand, define how an organization measures and communicates success. To further simplify organizational processes, think of them as managerial accounting.

But organizational processes have something in common with organizational structures, and that is that they must be understood in order for an effective total rewards strategy to be developed.

While there are many processes that are specific to an organization based upon its unique products and services, there are also a number of organizational processes that are more generic. We'd like to focus on six generic processes and show you how, by fully understanding them, you can develop an appropriate total rewards strategy. The six processes are organizational knowledge management; decision making; planning, allocating, and monitoring; supervision; contacts and communication; and management of change.

Organizational Knowledge Management

How much knowledge exists within an organization, and where does it reside within various individuals, databases, and other storage structures? In order to design a good total rewards strategy, you'll need to understand how that knowledge is spread day-to-day, month-to-month, quarter-to-quarter, and year-to-year. You'll need to know how the organizational knowledge compares to that of the company's competitors. When all is said and done, a thorough study of organizational knowledge management should give you a good idea of the depth and breadth of knowledge needed to successfully produce the organization's products and services.

Decision Making

Who makes the decisions, and where within the organization is the effect of those decisions felt? This process should bring to light the information needed by and given to the decision makers, as well as the time frame in which decisions should be made. The degree of guidance should be understood, as well as the impact of poor decisions and how long it takes the company to feel the effect of them. Without a full understanding of how an organization makes its decisions, it's tough to design an appropriate executive total rewards strategy.

Contacts and Communications

This organizational process will help the designer understand how the company communicates within its own organizational structure, as well as how it communicates with stakeholders and the environment in general outside of the company.

The contacts and communications process is one of the golden keys to total rewards strategy, particularly the extent and speed of the communications exchange. Why? Well, let's picture our pyramid again. When the communication flows quickly and effortlessly from top to bottom and from side to side between departments, the organization requires less formal planning. Now let's think about an organization in which info *doesn't* flow vertically or horizontally. This will have severe ramifications on the types of synergy needed in most successful businesses today.

Supervision

There's been much to-do surrounding the issue of supervision, and understanding how supervision is exercised within an organization is certainly important to designing a total rewards strategy.

Some companies keep their executives under very close supervision, while others allow some or all executives the freedom to do their jobs without direct supervision. If there is significant departmentalization—if a supervisor is intimately knowledgeable with an individual's efforts and performance— then it's perfectly appropriate for the executive to use his discretion concerning rewards. If, on the other hand, the executive does not have first-hand knowledge regarding the efforts and performance of the individuals reporting to him, the reward program must have more effective indexes to measure performance so compensation is fairly allocated among the individuals.

Management of Change

As few aspects of organizational life remain stagnant for long periods of time, the management of change process is particularly important in designing an effective total rewards strategy.

When looking at any organization from a management of change point of view, you should ask yourself how important the company feels it is to gather information that identifies the need for change, either internally or externally. Who is responsible for identifying the need for change, and once it is identified, who manages it?

In some organizations managing change is very widespread, while in others managing change is confined to a specialized group. Why is the management of change process so important to identify? Because when all is said and done much of a company's success, and the executive compensation that goes hand-in-hand with that success, is based on identifying and responding correctly to threats and opportunities in the marketplace.

INVESTOR ALERT #8

ORGANIZATION STRUCTURE EVIDENCE OF SUCCESSION PLANNING

An experienced organizational observer should be able to see evidence of succession planning within an organization's structure. If the organization is too flat, too hierarchical, or too departmentalized, there's very little evidence that the organization understands that one portion of its organizational design is to fulfill the responsibility and role to develop leaders.

In order to be a great investor you have to be an organizational archaeologist. Once you sift through the sands of the structure you'll see how the organization creates leadership, or in some instances doesn't create leadership.

Planning, Allocating, and Monitoring

Most modern-day organizations with a reasonable level of sophistication spend a great deal of time planning, allocating, and monitoring the effectiveness of their resources. As a matter of fact, much of the last few decades have been spent developing more effective and more sophisticated planning, allocating, and monitoring methods among our client base.

At the same time, much of the world has become less predictable and more interrelated. So what are we getting at here? Well, in our opinion the increase in sophistication of most of the organizations we work with has not matched the increase in variability and environmental change on a one-to-one basis. Okay, this might be a gross generality, but still, we think it's better for most organizations to develop organizational capabilities and people strategies that allow them not only to cope with, but to take advantage of, the increased inability to project the future on all strategy levels. And here's another opinion: the integration of and reliance on plans has been a mistake in the design of executive total rewards systems.

Losing a Few Pennies

The recent and abrupt termination of J.C. Penney's Chief Operating Officer, Catherine West, after only five months on the job, highlights the hazards of hiring an executive who doesn't understand the company's operational processes. West was hired to oversee store operations, property development, and logistics, with special emphasis on the store's expansion plan. It was an operational role with lots of detail and substance.

Before joining J.C. Penney, West was the former president of Capital One Financial Group. This alone, because of her lack of retail experience, made her an unconventional choice for the job. As a matter of fact, the retail environment is so unique that few industry outsiders who have joined retailers in senior roles succeed.

When J.C. Penney ousted West they paid her a severance package worth close to $10 million. Costly mistake—and let's not even talk about the organizational opportunity lost—wouldn't you agree? This story is a cautionary tale for anyone wondering how a lack of understanding of organizational processes can negatively affect a company and its executives.

Now let's have a little fun and move on to organizational culture. We say this tongue-in-cheek, as understanding organizational culture and how to apply it to a total executive rewards strategy is often the designer's biggest challenge.

Organizational Culture

We've already mentioned that of the three components that comprise people strategy, organizational culture is the most difficult to understand. So it just figures that it's clearly the most powerful component, as well as the most important to master, for the chief executive and his team of top management executives. Everyone seems to associate success and failure with the ability of the executive team to, among other things, manage, respond to, and create an organizational culture oriented around the success of the business.

For all its importance, only one company that we're aware ever put an effort into defining organizational culture and incorporating the measure of organizational culture into their performance goals for top management. For the rest of us, it seems the definition of culture and the difficulty in operationalizing it continues to be a subject of major debate.

Despite the fact that it's missing a formal definition, organizational culture is often seen as the glue that holds an organization together. Organizational culture is responsible for the answers to questions like "What is it like to work the company?"; "How do executives feel about their relationship with their employer?"; "Does the executive feel valued?"; and "Does the executive feel that he is recognized for the job he does and how it contributes to the overall success of the organization?" If you want to think about corporate culture in another way, think of it as a company's "personality," or "feel."

Case Study #9

The only time we've seen an attempt at capturing organizational culture as a performance factor was with a well-known telecommunications company. When we did a review of the incentive program performance factors for this company, one of the performance factors was the result of an employee attitude survey. If the results of an employee attitude survey were above a certain level with respect to the average positive response, then the executives received a portion of their bonus plan payout. While the concept was fairly innovative at the time, the execution was, in our opinion, flawed. Employee attitudes, like customer attitudes, are a function of their overall environment. It was assumed that happy employees made for more productive employees and for better overall performance by the organization. It could also have been assumed that the com-

pany's employees were an important stakeholder group, since they probably also used this company's services.

So where's the flaw? An employee attitude survey is not a measure of the organization's actual culture type. It's a measure of employee attitudes—nothing more and nothing less. You have to ask yourself what the folks at this organization were thinking when they measured executive performance via scores of employees on the employee attitude survey. Our only guess is that if you can't control the business environment, and you don't have a great business strategy, and you are not willing to evaluate your value chain in light of the new competitive non-regulated environment, then maybe the best you can do is keep your employees happy as you go out of business.

INVESTOR ALERT #9

ORGANIZATIONAL CULTURE MYSTIQUE

Whenever an organization and its culture are spoken about in mystical terms, it is quite likely that organization has a case of "look backitis." Quite often this disease is deadly. An organization that continues to comment about what it was, rather than what it is or should be, is most likely ill-equipped to face future challenges.

We believe organizational culture should be spoken about in business terms. Yes, there is room for "organization speak" on vision, mission, or values. But it is important that an organization be able to manage the people strategy it has chosen. That means it has to be operable. If you hear someone say that the organization's culture is that everyone likes each other, or it's a fun place to work, the best thing you can do is ignore the commentary and try to understand what the real culture is.

If the real culture is a reflection of a business necessity such as "we will go to any length to meet customer needs" the organization possesses a culture that is based on a business imperative and is probably being managed as a business-based factor.

Culture is the most important of the three people strategy factors. If culture is described in non-business terms, and if the culture is not defined as part of the organization's people strategy repertoire, you can bet the people strategy engine is not running on all three cylinders.

Culture Clash

To appreciate just how important it is to understand organizational culture, consider the story of Hewlett-Packard and former Chief Executive Carly Fiorina.

Founders William Hewlett and David Packard were the anti-executives, inviting people to share ideas, encouraging an open-door policy, and referring to their executive style as "management by wandering around."[4]

Fiorina, by contrast, was a very different type of manager intent on reinventing the company. Fiorina didn't eat in the company cafeteria as her predecessors did, nor was she easily accessible. She bucked tradition from the start by negotiating a huge compensation package, and finagled perquisites that divided her from other employees. The egalitarian feel of the company faded, as did the family-like atmosphere.

Fiorina took 83 different business divisions, each with their own management structure, and whittled them down to half a dozen. She overhauled the worker evaluation system. She set into motion a $200 million campaign in which she changed the logo of the company, dropping the founders' last names, and put herself front-and-center as the driving force behind Hewlett-Packard's innovation and change.

In 2001 Fiorina found herself the subject of vehement criticism when she announced her decision to buy Compaq Computer. A public and nasty battle with Walter B. Hewlett, the company's largest individual shareholder and the son of the founder, ensued. To top it off the merger meant a planned layoff of 15,000 people.

Hewlett-Packard used to be known as a place you could work your whole life. But now it had the feel of just another big business.

INVESTOR ALERT #10

BIG COMPANY HIRES CEO FROM OUTSIDE

When a big company that should be creating layers of leadership underneath the CEO hires its next CEO from outside, not only has the board of directors failed, the former CEO has failed as well. Why? Because one of his primary responsibilities is the continuity of the organization through the sustainability of leadership.

There's little or no excuse in a large, talented organization when a CEO can't be found from within. Although there are some very rare (and highly publicized) exceptions, most CEOs hired from outside preside over an organization that performs worse than their competitors.

If people are their most important asset, as most companies claim, then we wonder about any company that doesn't build replacement parts for it's most important asset, the CEO.

And that wasn't just a perception either. Hewlett-Packard had been listed in *Fortune* magazine's list of top 100 places to work. But not after Fiorina took the helm. And the icing on the cake? An early-morning mid-August phone call in which it was announced that the company would miss its revenue projections in the last two quarters of the year. Fiorina had failed to produce the kind of profits she had promised.

Case Study #10

When the CEO of an optical company hired an individual from outside the organization to take over his job, the person he hired brought with him a culture of "making the numbers." This culture soon pervaded the entire organization. At the same time, higher levels of performance were being demanded from outside investors and the community. These two forces—the pressure to make the numbers and the pressure to have the numbers be even higher—ultimately resulted in gamesmanship within the divisions. What kind of gamesmanship? Here's an example. In order to make the numbers salesman would tell a distributor to accept more product than they expected to sell, just return the unsold at the end of the fiscal year, at no cost. The company booked the entire amount as current year sales.

The culture so pervaded the entire organization that it became a slave to the predictions of each year's budgeting sessions. The pressure to produce ever-higher levels of performance collided directly with the culture to hit those levels of performance, regardless of the cost. It is a poor practice, not to mention illegal, to produce income statements and balance sheets that result from the phantom sale of product.

Sometimes understanding the reality of one's performance characteristics will allow the divisions within the organization the liberty to be truthful. American industry as a whole has an obsession with making quarterly numbers. This is because if they do not make their quarterly numbers, their stock is penalized substantially by individuals investing for the short-term. The fact is that very few environments are as predictable as we would like them to be. It's best to be more realistic in determining the kinds of variances that are appropriate in today's complex and competitive environment. Designing incentive plans so that they require making the numbers is a short road to hell, and this organization ultimately found that out. The accounting irregularities were found on audit, the chief executive officer lost his job, and the organization lost its way.

It probably won't surprise you to know that Fiorina didn't make it at Hewlett-Packard. When she messed with Hewlett-Packards revered and sacrosanct culture, the people behind the business were no longer "feeling it." There's no doubt Fiorina was a talented, smart woman, and Hewlett-Packard probably was in need of some change. And we don't want to suggest that not understanding the company culture was the sole reason for the downfall. There's never any one reason, and we're sure that other issues factored into the equation. But did this culture clash have something to do with HP's downward spiral? You bet. Had Fiorina understood the company's culture, Hewlett-Packard's story, as well as hers, would probably be quite different today.

C*ase Study #11*

We were once called in to the office of the chief executive officer of the consulting firm we were working with and asked if we would accept an assignment with two of the firm's major clients. They wanted to develop an entirely new product that would be competitive with one of the major industry's dominant market competitors.

Shortly after we arrived at the meeting, one of the organizations showed up with five layers of executives who were prepared to talk about, and then recommend to another layer of management, the executive total reward strategy for the combined organization's new separate joint venture. The five executives of ever-increasing titles all wore blue suits and white shirts. Somewhat late for the meeting, the potential joint partner's executive came in by himself wearing blue jeans, a polo shirt, and cowboy boots. He said he was there to make the decision, not recommend it to higher powers.

As the morning wore on it was clear that it would be impossible to develop a single unified executive reward strategy for the new venture. The "suits versus the boots" is what the meeting became known as inside our organization. The suits wanted high base salaries, low short-term incentives and nonexistent or low long-term incentives of restricted stock, and a healthy supplemental executive retirement plan. The boots wanted low base salaries, high short-term incentive plans, bundles of stock options, and no retirement plan.

> *In addition, one of the executives wanted to be able to re-turn to the mother company if the venture somehow went wrong. We dubbed that the, "If the game gets a little rough take a ball and go home" strategy.*
>
> *We recommended the Cortez strategy. Cortez lined his men up on the beach upon arriving in the New World and burned the boats in the bay. The message was clear: prevail in the New World or be buried there, and never go home.*
>
> *While the boot man cheered, the suit men voted with their feet and left the meeting. Ultimately, the suits prevailed and each individual sent to the new venture was to keep his or her own company's executive reward program, with a transfer back if things did not work out for them.*
>
> *The new venture was a disaster, and produced nothing but discourse between the individuals located within the com-pany. The discourse even overflowed to the two parent organ-izations. After a number of years it was quietly closed down.*
>
> *Sometimes you can tell the difference in cultures as soon as the individuals walk in the room. And sometimes it's important to have the right people in the room when mak-ing decisions on executive total reward strategy. The boot man was a line man and the suit men were staff men. He was ready to make decisions and they were ready to make recommendations. It was a mismatch from the get go.*

Four Basic Cultural Types

When it comes to cultural concepts, a book we've found re-ally helpful (and one we steered you to in the last chapter as well) has been *People, Performance, and Pay* by Flannery, Hofrichter, and Platten.[2] They outline four general cultural types: process, functional, network, and time-based. Each type of culture would call for a different type of total rewards strategy.

• *Functional Culture*.

When you take an airplane flight from the United States to Aruba, the baggage claim person checks your baggage, the pilot flies the plane, and the flight attendant makes sure you are flush with gin and peanuts. And you can pretty much count on the fact that this is how it's going to be, flight after flight. Well, an airline is a good example of a functional culture, in which everyone has a specific function. Other examples might include a doctor's office, where the receptionist checks you in and the doctor does the diagnosing, or the Army, where the Sergeant makes orders and the enlisted men follow them.

Functional cultures tend to focus on stability, reliability, and consistency. They are highly organized, and clear lines of authority and accountability are maintained. Functional cultures are often hierarchical, with those at the top giving orders to those who follow them.

• *Process Culture*.

Process cultures are prevalent in companies that rely upon processes to meet customer satisfaction and improve quality. Process cultures usually focus on teamwork, and each participant is equally skilled in their job. Good examples include chemical or pharmaceutical manufacturers. Process cultures are intent upon understanding the customer's point of view, and strive to gain the confidence of the customer. The most important result in a process culture is a consistent product or service, so clear, well-documented work processes are established.

• *Time-Based Culture*.

Time-based cultures are focused on getting their product or service into the marketplace in a timely manner. Instead of a management hierarchy, project work groups that cross functional boundaries are used. Time-based cultures are usually developing new products and services, so there's a high sense of urgency in the company, and it's focused on capitalizing on windows of opportunity. Time-based cultures

FIGURE 5.5   Organization culture. From Flannery, Thomas P., David A. Hofrichter, and Paul Platten. *People, Performance, and Pay.* New York: Free Press, 1995.

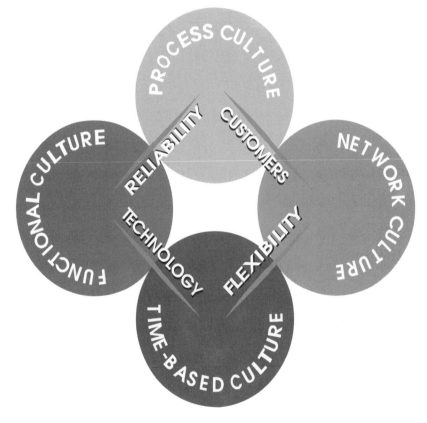

adapt quickly to changes in the business environment, and are flexible when it comes to their approach. These companies often accept a certain level of error so they can be first on the marketplace.

In today's high-tech world, we're certainly not at a loss for examples of time-based cultures. Internet companies, computer companies, and cell phone companies are all good examples of companies that strive for speed to market.

* *Network Culture.*

A network culture strives to bring together certain people and alliances with specific skill sets and competencies in order to complete a project. A film company is a good example of a situation in which the traditional management hierarchy is replaced with people who coordinate and direct the network's efforts. A network culture is involved in developing new products and services, and in establishing new ventures or new lines of business. Strategic alliances with other organizations are a big part of the network culture.

As you see, there are many ways to define and think about a company's culture. But when all is said and done, defining it is not nearly as important as understanding it. We can't stress enough how important understanding a company's culture is to developing a total rewards strategy. The organization's culture can affect any or all of the reward architecture elements— money, mix, and messages.

Putting It All Together

Now that you understand operational structures, processes, and culture—what we like to call the people strategy of an organization—we would like to explain how this dimension relates to the executive reward architectural element.

To make this clear, we would like to give the example of two organizations that produce similar products in the consulting industry. The first company, which we'll call "Tickled Pink,"

(TP) has eight layers of management. The second company, which we'll call The Wild Wild West Company, otherwise known as "Why in the World are We Working?" (WWW), has three layers of management. Now let's talk about the structure, processes, and culture of each company. In the end you'll understand that even though the organizations produce similar products in the same industry, they require drastically different rewards strategies in order to be the best they can be.

Ponying Up for Cowgirls and Cowboys

WWW is an entrepreneurial organization whose success is heavily dependent upon the quality of the more than 70 office managers around the world. The office managers have very little staff support from either "corporate WWW" or within each of the offices themselves. In fact, they have little direction other than producing a good return for the shareholders over a long period of time.

The organizational structure is incredibly simple. The 70 office managers report to the CEO of the organization. Up to 10 practice leaders report directly to the office manager. All other employees report directly to the practice leaders.

What about WWW's organizational processes? The knowledge in the organization exists within the consultants, and is not consolidated particularly well into any central depository. The organization doesn't plan, monitor, or allocate particularly well on a long-term basis, but is highly effective in deploying consultants on a tactical basis. Consultants are usually highly "billable."

WWW's culture fits into the "network" category, as it is very person-to-person dependent and not institutionalized. While there are a number of national practice leaders, everyone knows that as long as you and your team are highly billable you can easily ignore any "dictum" without concern for any penalty.

The WWW organization is a loose confederation of "cowboys" and "cowgirls" doing their own thing and responding to client needs based upon their own understanding of those needs. Each office manager and practice leader is a king or queen in their own fiefdom.

So what kind of executive rewards strategy works for these "cowboys" and "cowgirls?" Because the consultants are independent and survive on their own merits, combined with the fact that there are no major "corporate staff groups" with any significant authority, the executive reward strategy that is successful at the organization is an extremely large range of "money" for any one position, strictly based upon that person's ability to generate revenue and profits. This means that people in two similar positions can be paid quite differently. The reward program is highly decentralized, and therefore the messages are highly discretionary and discriminatory. Some offices run an executive reward strategy that is very practice-based, while others reward the practice leaders on a very office-based measure of performance.

So why is this type of rewards strategy successful? Because ultimately it rewards practice leaders and office managers for success in the marketplace as they define the market. Sure, the organization is hodgepodge and messy. But so what? Democracy always is.

Keeping the Boat Afloat

Let's compare WWW to TP. TP is constantly reorganizing the practices, regions, and staff group so that each manager of managers can wear his own "party hat." Staff groups dictate the type of clients that are delivered to, as well as the services and fees that are delivered. Consultants are deployed often by the national or global practice leaders. Leads are delivered by the practice leaders, and the business results are also quite good.

The executive reward strategy at TP is completely opposite of that at WWW. The "money" for a position is within tight bands, with practice leaders, for example, making similar amounts.

At TP everyone is in the same boat, and it is important for them, as a team, to keep the boat afloat. There are no heroes, and the message is "We are all in this together." So practice leaders all receive similar bonuses, regardless of performance. The higher performing practices subsidize the startup or poorer performing practices by both sharing resources and sharing bonus pool dollars. While there is a significant annual bonus, the larger component of the reward structure is the longer term reward elements such as partner stock and the generous retirement plan.

The Moral

The moral of this story—in fact, the moral of this entire chapter—is that two successful organizations with different organizational capabilities, people strategies, structures, processes, and cultures should have different executive rewards strategies. What would happen if, just for fun, we switched the reward strategies up? You can bet it would result in chaos, confusion, and ultimately the demise of the organizations.

References

1. "Tossing Out the Chief Executive." *New York Times*, 14 February 2006.
2. Flannery, Tom, Dave Hofrichter, and Paul Platten. *People, Performance, and Pay*. New York: The Free Press, 1996.
3. *FT.com*, 19 May 2006.
4. "The Battle for Brainpower." *The Economist*, 5 October 2006. Available online at http://www.economist.com/surveys/displaystory.cfm?story_id=7961894, accessed 23 September 2007.

CHAPTER 6

Total Reward Strategy

So now we've come to a pivotal chapter. Let's take a couple of seconds to check in with the chart at the beginning of this book to get a sense of where we are. If you've come away with anything from the first five chapters let's hope it goes something like this: there is no one-size-fits-all answer when it comes to a total executive reward strategy.

When we think about the last few chapters and all the information and analysis we've encouraged in order to develop the context for creating an executive total reward strategy, it becomes important to clearly outline the various levels of reward strategy.

First, we think of "strategy" as having layers. The overall 30,000-foot level of thinking is what we mean by "strategy." Generally, this involves statements that in some way link the key environmental, stakeholder, business, and people strategy findings and their implications for the key concepts of attract, motivate, and retain. This chapter addresses both the general linkage between these business issues and reward strategy, and gives examples of analytical tools we developed to measure, understand, and interpret these executive reward strategies.

Chapter 7, Total Reward Architecture, moves these general linkages from the 30,000-foot altitude down to 15,000 feet. In Chapter 7 we describe the process as one of building the architecture of the executive total reward program. This architecture generally plays out in three key axes: "money," "mix," and "messages." In other words, how much in total (money), what the balance of the various components should be (mix), and what points are delivered to the executive through the executive reward strategy architecture (messages).

FIGURE 6.1

Reward Component	Type of Company			
	Start-Up	Growth	Mature	Declining
Base Salary	Below	At	Above	Above
Short Term Incentives	Below	At	Above	At
Long-Term Incentives	Above	Above	At	Below
Benefits	Below	At	At	Above
Perquisites	Below	Below	At	Above

Chapter 8, Executive Total Reward Strategy Components, brings the design process down to the separate design aspects of each reward component.

Hopefully, this layered approach will assist you in an orderly development of the executive total reward strategy. It has certainly assisted us.

When we talk to our clients, about 90 percent of them say that the mission of their executive total reward strategy is to attract, motivate, and retain. Great idea, but the words alone won't get you too far. An organization's reward strategy must be specific about who it wants to attract, as well as how it will motivate and retain. Details! It's certainly not enough to base your compensation strategy on what the guy in the next building is paying his similarly positioned executive, and adhering to so-called "best-industry practices" in the best-case scenario can leave you with a total reward strategy that doesn't make the most of motivating executives. And what's the worst-case scenario? This type of thinking can land you in weird places, like the front page of the newspaper or the nightly news. And you don't have to take your eye off the ball for all that long to land yourself in a nice pile of trouble. Just ask the folks at the New York Stock Exchange after Dick Grass' pay package was disclosed. And while being mentioned in a negative light in the press is problematic, it is far more damaging to the competitive effectiveness of the company if the executive reward strategy isn't customized to the organization's specific situation.

What's it take to get your total reward strategy right? Well, if you've been paying attention you know that outside business environmental factors, as well as issues surrounding key stakeholders, must be taken into consideration. An effective total executive reward strategy can't be crafted without a workable knowledge and understanding of the company's vision, mission, and values. Nor can a company's business strategy, organizational capabilities, or people strategy be ignored. And it's not enough to take one—or even a few—of these things into consideration. The most effective total reward strategy considers *all* of the above factors.

The Way Some Other Guys Look at Executive Compensation

Are we the first guys to write a book on executive compensation? Hardly. There are lots and lots of books out there on how to structure your total executive rewards strategy. But we approach things a little differently. Here's how. Go to your local library or bookstore—or even raid the shelves in your human resource department—and you'll see that when it comes to how to structure total executive total rewards strategy most of the experts are all singing the same tune. We're not going to name names here. Some of these authors might be your friends. Okay, some of these authors might be *our* friends. The point is they kill a lot of trees getting the same concept across. What's the concept? Here it is:

"If you are *a*, then your total reward strategy should be *b*."

While this is refreshingly simple it's . . . well . . . *too* refreshingly simple. It's like deciding to build a Victorian because you love *Great Expectations*. In other words, there are few more things you should probably consider, don't you think?

We don't mind saying here that most of the reward strategy "solutions" that portray themselves as "strategic" are really fairly pedestrian. Take a look through any of these books and you'll get more or less the same information. The general consensus is that there are four kinds of companies:

- Start-up companies
- Growth companies
- Mature companies
- Declining companies

Historically, there's been a simple answer when it comes to the total executive reward strategy for each kind of company.

Start-up companies, which are notoriously low on cash, are told to structure their reward strategies with a low base pay and no short-term incentives, but lots of long-term incentives like stock options.

Growth companies are told to structure their reward strategies with small base salaries and some short-term incentives, while their long-term incentives should be more moderate than those of start-up companies.

Mature companies are told to structure their reward strategies with a high base salary and balance between short-term and long-term incentives.

And finally, *Declining* companies are told to structure their reward strategies with low base salaries and short-term incentives, and are encouraged to reduce long-term incentives even further.

Sounds fairly cut-and-dried, doesn't it? So what's the problem? The problem is that not all start-up companies are the same. Not all growth companies are the same. Not all mature companies are the same and not all declining companies are the same. It's likely that two start-up companies, for example—let's say they are even the same size and produce a similar product—have somewhat different business environmental factors and dramatically different key stakeholder issues that should affect how they structure their total executive rewards strategies. The vision, mission, and values of one growth company could be drastically different from that of another growth company. Shouldn't their executive reward strategies reflect the difference? Two mature companies could have business strategies and people strategies that are completely dissimilar. So it stands to reason that their total executive rewards strategy would be structured differently as well, right? And two declining companies could have two very different organizational structures in place. Wouldn't their executive reward strategies contrast as well?

If we've done a good job with this book so far you shouldn't hesitate very long before you answer yes, yes, and yes! Taking environmental and key stakeholder issues—vision, mission, and values—and people strategy and business strategy into consideration when planning your total executive reward strategy is the way to go. "If you are *a*, then your total reward structure should be *b*" isn't a great strategy. Sure, it's quick, easy, and doesn't take a whole lot of time or thought—that's the way it usually goes with the easy way out.

In Search of the Magic Number

Let's think about this for a second. When you take a trip down memory lane and think of all the executives that have attained—ahem—*celebrity status*, why do you think their stories cause such an incendiary reaction? If you think it's because they are taking home too much money, think again.

A study by Bain and Co., in which they interviewed more than 40 institutional investors in both the U.S. and the U.K., made it clear that it's not *how much* we pay our executives, but rather how much bang we're getting for our buck.[1] Consider that of the investors interviewed, just about 100 percent opposed option repricing, 82 percent wanted to nix excessive severance packages, and 70 percent were against awarding bonuses tied to acquisitions. The clincher? Sixty-three percent said senior managers deserved a larger share of the value they created for shareholders—as long as executives also shared in the downside.

So does this mean we link compensation to shareholder returns and call it a day? Nice try, but you're going to have to work a little harder than that. Simply linking compensation to shareholder returns means management can focus on the wrong priorities but still benefit from a rising market. On the other hand, they could be focused on all the right things, but forces outside their control could conspire against them. So what's the answer? Well, think about what would happen if the compensation system was structured so that management and shareholders were aligned. Executives would be motivated to beat internal goals, as well as others in the stock market. Good news for everyone, right?

*C*ase Study #12

A new chief executive officer had arrived at a utility company with a whole new business strategy. The organization was planning to get out of the energy generation business and into the energy transmission business. As the energy business was deregulating, the CEO believed the best return for the shareholders would be in the energy transmission business. The energy transmission businesses had a much higher business risk, and were fully deregulated.

We put together a conclave process for his top 11 executives. They were to go through 2 days of intensive efforts to redesign the executive total reward strategy to reflect the new and much more competitive business environment associated with the energy transmission business. Eleven executives put in long hours, and openly debated all of the three major strategic axes.

In order to be competitive they attached themselves to the marketplace at the 50th percentile of commercial competitive businesses, not utilities. In addition, they proposed to have substantially more variable compensation than was typical of the utility industry and their history. Finally, they developed a "look forward" scorecard system. And while the reward strategy was a dramatic departure from the present program, all 11 people agreed it would be in the best interests of the company shareholders, and probably themselves, to transition over to the new program as fast as possible.

Not only has the company prospered over the last ten years, it has acquired several other energy organizations. Its stock has risen consistently faster than its competitors

> *in the overall stock market in general. Sometimes change requires the executive team to make a common commitment to sacrifice and a common commitment to a higher goal in order to sustain the kind of change in opportunity required to fulfill a business opportunity.*

This point can be underscored by research Bain did on sustained-growth companies.[2] Of the couple thousand companies Bain included in their study, they found that only 1 in 10 enjoyed sustained, profitable growth (defined as revenue and net income growth greater than 5.5 percent and positive return on capital) over a 10-year period. What separated the wheat from the chaff? The study found that the senior managers at top-performing companies made strategic, well thought-out decisions designed to clearly define their businesses and achieve market leadership. Performance at these companies was measured based on these decisions as well as how they were executed. Was executive compensation an important lever? You bet. There was a strong and defined link between pay and performance.

If we haven't yet convinced you of the link between pay and performance, consider the fact that a study of CEO pay done by Watson Wyatt in 2005 showed a very strong pay for performance link.[3] Companies that gave above-median increases in base salary and annual incentives to their CEOs generated significantly higher performance for their shareholders—a one-year median total shareholder return (TSR) of 19.4 percent, compared to a 8.6 percent median TSR among those companies that gave below-median total cash compensation (TCC) increases to their CEO. So what are we getting at here? Well, the study shows that companies whose executives have real share ownership tend to outperform those that do not. Does this show a strong link between executive pay and financial performance? You bet. And here's more evidence. Another survey of 500 companies showed that companies actively using pay-for-performance programs showed twice the shareholder returns as those who were not actively using these programs.[4] In *The Growth of Executive Pay*, Harvard University's Lucian Bebchuk and Cornell University's Yaniv Grinstein examined the relationship between growth in executive pay and firms' performance between 1993 and 2003.[5] Their conclusion? The growth in compensation can't really be explained by growth in performance. Therefore, compensation has not been designed in the most cost-effective way to provide a given level of incentives. In 2005 Bebchuk teamed up with Jesse Fried, also of Harvard University, and found evidence that not only does most executive compensation fail to produce incentives to enhance shareholder value, but much compensation is paid in ways that provide perverse incentives.[6] Plans that give executives broad freedom to unload options, for example, allow executives to benefit from increases in short-term stock prices that come at the expense of long-term value.

Sports Stars and CEOs: Is It a Game Either Way?

As the public decries the rising paychecks of superstar CEOs, defenders say that hikes in executive pay are no different from the pay increases associated with football players, baseball stars, and those who make their living playing basketball.

But isn't it? The rationale in the above statement is that today's pay practices are a product of market forces; in other words, rising executive pay is a product of efficient markets and reflects the productivity of senior executives.

But before you buy this rationale hook, line, and sinker, think it over a bit. Harvard B-School professors Lucian Bebchuk and Rakesh Khurana say the above belief is a myth that nicely benefits CEOs.[7] How so? Well, let's talk about the professional athlete first. The team executive negotiating with the athlete is looking out for the club's interest, while the athlete's agent is looking out for the player. Makes sense so far, right?

So now let's put this in the context of a business executive. The person negotiating the salary with the executive is looking out for the company and its shareholders, right? Not necessarily, say Bebchuk and Khurana. There are a lot of other factors—some social and some psychological—that come into play. Board members often share personal relationships with executives, whether they have worked together at another company, get together once a week for a game of tennis, or are linked socially through shared status, organizational affiliations, or social standing. Does this make things complex? No doubt.

In the end, what do ball parks and businesses have in common when it comes to executive compensation? Well, there are two views. Defenders like Xavier Gabaix of MIT and Augustin Landier of NYU believe executive pay, like pay for professional athletes, follows a free market system.[8] Our friends at Harvard, Bebchuk and Khurana (as well as lots of other folks out there), think the market is rigged and that directors must be given strong incentives to focus on shareholder interests. What do we think? Aside from the fact that there might be a Harvard/MIT rivalry going on here? We think both sides have a point. Sure, the way things are currently set up, directors are not guided solely by the interests of the shareholders. That being said, we really do believe that most compensation programs are good attempts at pay for performance.

It's interesting to note that while Bebchuk and Khurana have lots to say about how lack of board accountability to shareholders results in compensation snafus, they have yet to come up with a solution that most companies and investors are willing to embrace. It bears repeating that much of the public teeth-gnashing that goes hand-in-hand with today's inflated pay packages has less to do with the actual amounts being awarded and more to do with the lack of a relationship between compensation awards and actual corporate performance. If more companies linked pay to performance and developed unique compensation strategies that answered questions like "What kind of results is this strategy likely to produce?" and "Will the results of this strategy help the business meet its needs and goals?" we bet we'd see a lot less hand-wringing and a lot more support. After all, every time David Ortiz hits one out of Fenway, the fans hardly stand up and shout about his $52 million paycheck. As long as the ball keeps sailing over the Green Monster, everyone at Fenway is happy.

Tools of the Trade

When all is said and done, the design team must identify and understand the organization's environment, key stakeholders, and business and people strategies in order to put an effective executive total reward strategy into place. While all of these things are important to the organization's success, some are more important than others. It is the duty of the design team to figure out where along the value chain each of these things lie, and to structure the total rewards program so that it is properly aligned with each business dimension.

Brilliance helps. But if you are not brilliant, we have some tools that will help you analyze, conceptualize, and measure certain areas of your business. These tools are designed to help you create an executive total reward strategy that is completely aligned with your business goals.

Putting Your Tally Sheets on Steroids

We know where executive pay trends have been. Where are they going? It's becoming increasingly clear—witness the Disney and NYSE debacles—that boards themselves are in need of better information on pay.

Why does it appear that many organizations are playing out of bounds? When Richard Grasso's stint as celebrity CEO *du jour* had the nation wringing its collective hands over his $139 million pay package, directors at the NYSE claimed that they didn't realize the full extent of Grasso's pay package. To the average person reading the newspaper or tuning in to the nightly news, this lack of board understanding seems ridiculous. Is it possible for someone to take home close to $140 million without the people in charge knowing exactly what's going on? If you work in the compensation industry you know something the general public doesn't: it can be difficult to keep your eye on the ball. Is it possible for an organization not to understand the full range of an executive's pay plan? It sure is. The NYSE wasn't the first group of directors to lose sight of what they were paying their top executives, and they likely won't be the last.

Why? Well, the way in which firms traditionally view executive compensation annually, through the use of competitive analysis, doesn't provide a complete picture of compensation. Instead, it provides a "static" point-in-time snapshot of the amount of compensation delivered at target. The result is that boards are not focused on what an executive could earn above and below target, assuming various levels of company financial and stock performance achievement.

Don't get us wrong—we're not completely dissing competitive analysis and are the first to say that it serves an important purpose. But what does the above tell us? It tells us that firms and boards should no longer be solely focused on the finding from the same annual competitive analysis, as this only provides a partial view into the world of executive compensation. In addition, pay should no longer be set exclusively on "what is competitive in the marketplace."

The implementation of SFAS 123R and the new SEC disclosure rules, as well as stock option backdating scandals and a renewed focus on actual pay earnings and pay-for-performance alignment, means that we are in a new era when it comes to the state of executive pay. The only way to ensure the "appropriateness" of executive pay is for firms and boards to begin thinking about an executive's total compensation opportunity. In other words, what an executive could earn based on company and stock price performance under all possible scenarios.

Great idea! So how do you do it? We've come up with something called the grahall Economic Impact Analysis (gEIA), a new process that reviews an executive's total potential compensation and its relationship to all relevant performance factors.

What Exactly Is the gEIA?

Okay, we're all familiar with tally sheets. Tally sheets give you one number, the total compensation at target. The problem? The chances of actually being at target are fairly low. In fact, in most cases the target is exceeded. The gEIA *does not* result in one number. Instead, it takes into consideration both stock performance and company performance, and creates an entire set of scenarios that show the least an executive can make, the most an executive can make, and everything in between. Just think of a gEIA as a tally sheet on steroids. Tally sheets, with their one number, are unlikely to stop a "Holy Cow" moment. But a juiced-up gEIA very well might. Once the board or compensation committee is aware of exactly how much an executive can make there are no surprises, and boards can decide whether this figure is appropriate well before shareholders—and the public—decide it isn't.

So how does a gEIA work? Well, a gEIA provides a comprehensive analysis of potential executive payouts between the 10th and 90th percentile performance over time, incorporating historical performance as a predictor of future performance (or other appropriate predictions). The result is Figure 6.2, a grahall Economic Impact Analysis, which shows the total direct compensation value for all possible future company and stock performance scenarios.

Among the benefits of this broader and longer-term look at pay and performance is an understanding of plan leverage: in other words, the degree to which possible payouts are affected by incremental changes in stock prices or company performance. When all the potential scenarios are laid out, organizations can then ask themselves if the resulting numbers make

(text continues on page 172)

FIGURE 6.2   grahall Economic Impact Analysis (gEIA).

Stock Performance / Percentiles	Company Performance 10%	20%	30%	40%	50%	60%	70%	80%	90%
10%	$493,664	$567,975	$652,471	$760,990	$865,393	$964,990	$1,149,064	$1,498,452	$1,837,808
20%	$1,064,680	$1,138,991	$1,228,534	$1,347,296	$1,461,759	$1,570,631	$1,765,012	$2,126,827	$2,482,499
30%	$1,476,422	$1,550,733	$1,643,916	$1,770,065	$1,891,781	$2,007,340	$2,209,153	$2,579,930	$2,947,367
40%	$1,828,241	$1,902,552	$1,998,845	$2,131,305	$2,259,218	$2,380,492	$2,588,656	$2,967,090	$3,344,579
50%	$2,157,077	$2,231,388	$2,330,588	$2,468,947	$2,602,654	$2,729,269	$2,943,368	$3,328,958	$3,715,844
60%	$2,485,914	$2,560,225	$2,662,331	$2,806,589	$2,946,089	$3,078,045	$3,298,080	$3,690,827	$4,087,109
70%	$2,837,733	$2,912,044	$3,017,260	$3,167,829	$3,313,527	$3,451,198	$3,677,582	$4,077,987	$4,484,321
80%	$3,249,475	$3,323,786	$3,432,642	$3,590,597	$3,743,548	$3,887,907	$4,121,724	$4,531,090	$4,949,189
90%	$3,820,491	$3,894,802	$4,008,705	$4,176,903	$4,339,914	$4,493,548	$4,737,672	$5,159,465	$5,593,880

FIGURE 6.3 Key discussion points for a compensation committee to review. Compensation here reflects one year's award. TDC is total direct compensation, calculated as base salary and short- and long-term incentives.

1.) Is this to much compensation for a CEO performing between the 10th - 20th percentile for company and stock price performance?

2.) Is this an appropriate amount of compensation for a CEO performing at the 50th percentile for company and stock price performance?

3.) Is this an appropriate amount of compensation for a CEO performing between the 80th - 90th percentile for company and stock price performance?

4.) Is an incremental change in potential TDC of 9.7% (btw the 30th and 70th percentile for company performance only) enough incentive to drive executive behaviors on company performance?

5.) Is enough of the TDC package driven by company performance?

6.) Is an incremental change in potential TDC of 67% (btw the 30th and 70th percentile for stock price performance only) an appropriate amount of incentive to drive executive behaviors?

7.) Is an appropriate amount of the TDC package driven by stock price performance?

8.) Is the mix between company and stock price performance appropriate?

9.) Does this compensation program have a true pay-for-performance orientation?

10.) What behaviors does this type of compensation program drive?

Percentiles	10%	20%	30%	40%	50%	60%	70%	80%	90%
10%	$4,084,03x	$4,375,758	$4,586,170	$4,765,959	$4,934,003	$5,18x,070	$5,455,754	$5,771,371	$6,208,959
20%	$6,611,214	$6,902,939	$7,11x,550	$7,29x,15x	$7,4x1,1x4	$7,x1x,25x	$7,x6x,x9x	$8,298,551	$8,736,139
30%	$8,433,488	$8,725,21x	$8,9xx,625	$9,115,414	$9,283,459	$9,535,525	$9,805,209	$10,120,826	$10,558,414
40%	$9,990,555	$10,282,280	$10,492,692	$10,67x,x81	$10,840,525	$11,092,592	$11,362,275	$11,677,893	$12,115,480
50%	$11,445,908	$11,737,63x	$11,948,045	$12,127,834	$12,29x,x78	$12,547,945	$12,817,628	$13,133,246	$13,570,833
60%	$12,901,261	$13,19x,xxx	$13,403,397	$13,583,186	$13,751,231	$14,00x,x97	$14,272,981	$14,588,598	$15,026,186
70%	$14,458,327	$14,750,0xx	$14,960,464	$15,140,253	$15,308,297	$15,560,364	$15,830,xxx	$16,145,665	$16,583,253
80%	$16,280,xx2	$16,572,327	$16,782,739	$16,962,528	$17,130,572	$17,382,639	$17,652,323	$17,967,940	$18,405,528
90%	$1x,807,783	$19,099,508	$19,309,919	$19,489,708	$19,657,753	$19,909,819	$20,179,503	$20,495,120	$20,932,708

Company Performance

Stock Performance

FIGURE 6.4 gEIA graphic shows how base salary is constant regardless of company or stock performance.

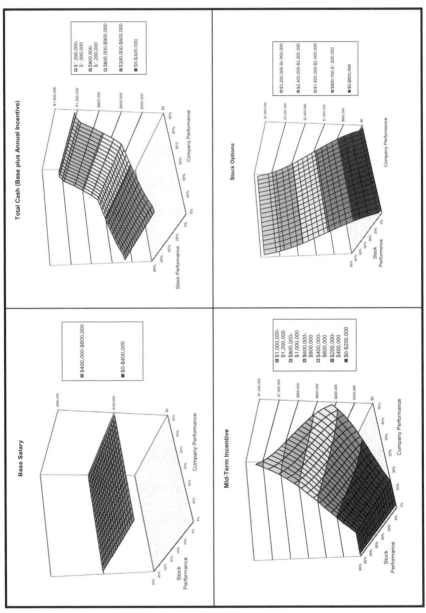

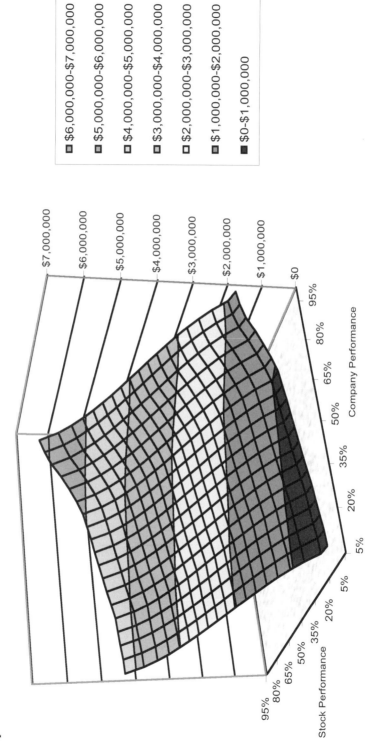

FIGURE 6.5 Total potential compensation: this shows how total cash (base salary plus annual incentives) varies only with the performance of the company on such factors as EPS, or revenues, which might be in the annual incentive plan.

FIGURE 6.6 Stock options: this shows how stock options vary across a range of probabilities from the 10th to the 90th percentile of probable stock performance. The values here range from $0 to $6,000,000 annually.

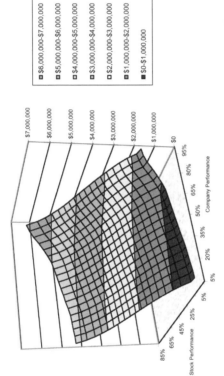

Percentiles	10%	20%	30%	40%	50%	60%	70%	80%	90%
10%	$459,411	$528,058	$608,470	$713,499	$814,640	$910,975	$1,085,831	$1,414,389	$1,735,496
20%	$1,030,427	$1,099,074	$1,184,533	$1,299,806	$1,411,006	$1,516,616	$1,701,778	$2,042,764	$2,380,187
30%	$1,442,169	$1,510,816	$1,599,915	$1,722,574	$1,841,028	$1,953,326	$2,145,920	$2,495,867	$2,845,055
40%	$1,793,988	$1,862,635	$1,954,844	$2,083,814	$2,208,466	$2,326,478	$2,525,422	$2,883,027	$3,242,267
50%	$2,122,825	$2,191,472	$2,286,587	$2,421,456	$2,551,901	$2,675,254	$2,880,134	$3,244,896	$3,613,532
60%	$2,451,661	$2,520,308	$2,618,330	$2,759,098	$2,895,336	$3,024,031	$3,234,846	$3,606,765	$3,984,796
70%	$2,803,480	$2,872,127	$2,973,259	$3,120,338	$3,262,774	$3,397,183	$3,614,349	$3,993,924	$4,382,009
80%	$3,215,223	$3,283,870	$3,388,641	$3,543,106	$3,692,796	$3,833,893	$4,058,491	$4,447,027	$4,846,876
90%	$3,786,238	$3,854,885	$3,964,704	$4,129,413	$4,289,162	$4,439,534	$4,674,438	$5,075,402	$5,491,567

Company Performance

Stock Performance

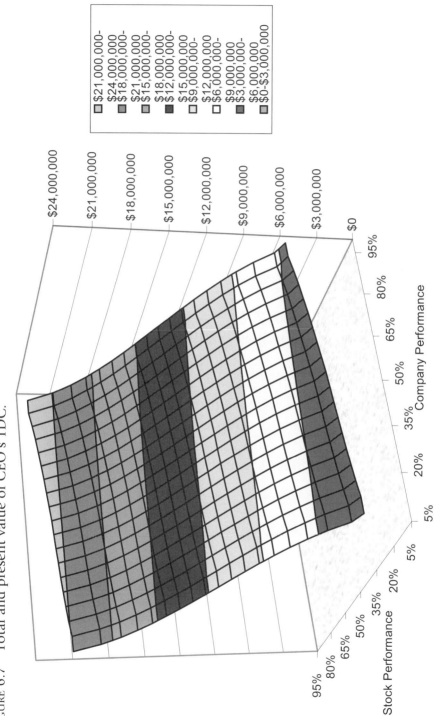

FIGURE 6.7 Total and present value of CEO's TDC.

Legend:
- $21,000,000-$24,000,000
- $18,000,000-$21,000,000
- $15,000,000-$18,000,000
- $12,000,000-$15,000,000
- $9,000,000-$12,000,000
- $6,000,000-$9,000,000
- $3,000,000-$6,000,000
- $0-$3,000,000

sense and are "within bounds." An organization, for example, that finds compensation at target perfectly appropriate might realize—after looking at a complete gEIA—that the compensation amount that corresponds to a CEO performing between the 20th and 40th percentile for company and stock price performance is not high enough to retain that executive. Or worse, they might find that the compensation amount that corresponds to a CEO performing between the 80th and 90th percentile for company and stock price is so high that it's bound to give their CEO some unwelcome celebrity status. Either way, a gEIA allows an organization to gauge and understand where they stand, across an entire range of likely outcomes. In addition to providing a comprehensive view of an executive's compensation in each and every scenario, a gEIA also allows an organization to delve deeply into the design of a certain plan and identify pitfalls. By arming companies with a frame of reference to examine the underlying drivers of pay, a gEIA helps facilitate discussions regarding plan design to help address:

- The degree to which possible payouts are affected by incremental changes in stock price or company performance.
- Whether there is sufficient performance orientation in the executive compensation program.
- Whether the design of incentive programs support the business strategy.
- Whether the compensation program provides the appropriate mix of compensation elements.
- Whether time-based LTI awards are appropriate.
- Whether the compensation program has a true pay-for-performance orientation.
- What type of behaviors the compensation program drives.

So, we bet you are dying to know what the method is behind this gEIA madness. In a nutshell, gEIA reviews current base salary, potential short-term incentive payout based on simulated financial results, potential long-term incentive award values based on simulated financial and/or stock price performance over the term of the award, as well as benefits and perquisites. The following pages show an example of how executive compensation components vary with company performance factors such as EPS and company stock performance.

So what's the outcome? The end result is that the numbers on the gEIA will help determine if incentive programs, as designed, help support the business strategy and its corresponding time horizon for the firm. By identifying potential flaws in the overall program design, this kind of analysis can result in changes such as amounts paid to executives, mix of instruments in the program, performance metrics and goal setting, payout opportunities, and even in the entire compensation strategy and philosophy. Organizations will also be able to assess the relationship between total potential payouts to executives and compare that value to the incremental market-value delivered to shareholders. Finally, the analysis will provide boards with the tools to fully evaluate executive pay, and make those "Holy Cow" moments a thing of the past.

How Much Wealth Is Too Much?

Another area that is being rethought in light of recent scandals is wealth accumulation. How many organizations would change their compensation plans if they knew how much wealth a particular executive were to accumulate over the course of his career?

The answer is, probably quite a few. While boards and organizations spend a lot of time determining how an executive is to be paid year-to-year, they often overlook how much wealth an executive accumulates.

Why is this an important figure? Boards that are aware of total wealth accumulation can decide whether the figure is appropriate, and adjust their plans accordingly. Once they have the figure in front of them, they can ask questions such as "How much wealth is too much?" and "What is the saturation point?" By this we mean the point at which additional compensation will most likely not have a direct correlation on how hard an executive works. For example, would the guy who is slated to accumulate $200 million in wealth over the course of his career be motivated by an additional $50 million in accumulated wealth, or would he have reached his saturation point at $200 million? Would that extra $50 million make him think twice before hitting the snooze button that one extra time? When all is said and done, would the additional $50 million benefit the company and shareholders because of the executive's increased performance? In other words, is this money well spent? We're not here to give you the answers, because the answers will vary from organization to organization, from executive to executive, from board to board. But we are telling you that in the best interest of the company and the shareholders, the questions should be asked.

Being aware of how much wealth an executive stands to earn throughout the course of his career can also prevent bloopers and "holy cow" moments regarding underperforming executives who are ousted. Understanding how wealth is accumulated—how base pay, bonuses, long-term incentives, deferred compensation, and retirement factor into lifetime earnings—allows organizations a snapshot of how much of that total figure is performance-based, and how much is non–performance-based. For example, will an executive earn significantly less wealth over the course of his career if he underperforms, or is that figure static regardless of performance? We can bet that Pfizer and Home Depot wish they had taken a few seconds to mull this one over! Understanding wealth accumulation should challenge boards to rework compensation plans until they are satisfied.

So, how can boards determine how much wealth an executive will accumulate over the course of their career? They can do so through a grahall Wealth Accumulation Analysis (gWAA) that takes into consideration base pay, bonus, long-term incentives, deferred compensation, and retirement. The end result? One figure that represents an executive's total accumulation over a period of time. The analysis is broken down so the board can see just how each of the above factors contributes to the executive's overall wealth each year. As we mentioned before, this is important because it allows the board to determine how much of the executive's lifetime compensation is performance-based, and how much is not. Once complete, the board will be able to determine whether the figure is too much or too little, as well as whether the plan appropriately attracts, retains, and motivates.

So how would you go about this analysis? First, the analysis is based on certain assumptions. The assumptions change based on the executive, the company, and the features of the compensation plan, but may include:

- Annual base salary increase estimates
- Annual bonus payout estimates
- Annual stock price growth assumptions
- Assumed age of retirement

What's the end result? An analysis that graphically represents total cumulative earnings potential for an executive year after year based on the assumptions. The graph will show how base salary, bonus, long-term incentives, deferred compensation, and retirement add up each year, as well as over the course of the executive's career.

The board will also be able to determine from the graph how much retirement the executive will earn and whether it's appropriate. A wealth accumulation analysis may show, for example, that $60 million of $200 million total accumulated wealth comes from the executive's retirement fund. Since retirement funds are not performance based, these numbers may spark dialogue among the board and foster discussion on whether the mix is appropriate.

(text continues on page 178)

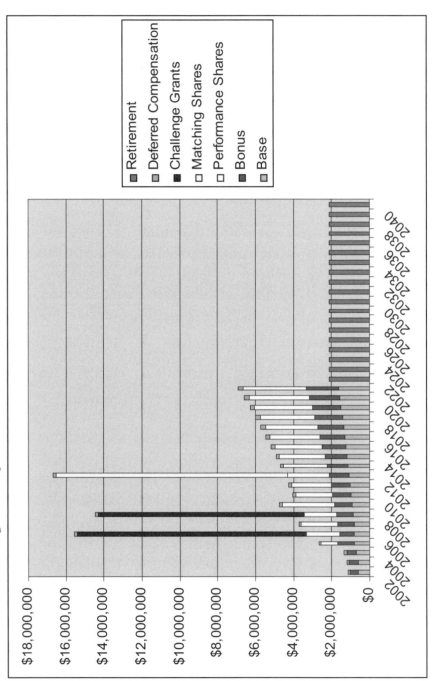

FIGURE 6.8 Annual total compensation for an example executive starting with the date of hire and progressing until projected death, based on target assumption.

FIGURE 6.9 Cumulative earning potential for an example executive based on target assumptions.

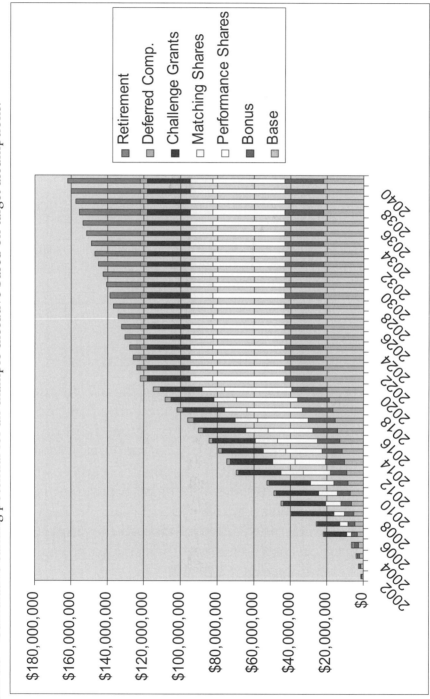

Retirement
Deferred Comp.
Challenge Grants
Matching Shares
Performance Shares
Bonus
Base

INVESTOR ALERT #11

NO DOWNSIDE PAIN ON THE TOTAL REWARD PROGRAM

Everyone normally focuses on the upside and the maximum amount that can be paid if performance is above target. Few focus on the downside pain, if the executive team doesn't accomplish the target. More often than we would like to see, we find that the executive team doesn't feel much financial pain on the downside below target performance. This is more than just having high base salaries and low thresholds on the incentive programs. It may be the constant overlapping vesting of the restricted stock "retention" program, or other similar programs.

If there is no pain, then we're reminded of the frog that, sitting in a pan of water brought slowly to a boil, won't jump out but will end up dying. Something similar happens to management if they don't feel any real downside pain. The cost of reassessing the situation is more than going home each night with a slightly reduced reward.

If there is a lack of performance make sure there is a stimulant in the total reward architecture that "gets `em off their ass" and doing some fundamental soul searching before it's too late for the money you have invested.

These Boots Were Made for Walking

What happens when executives leave a company? Besides finding new challenges ahead, they leave earned but unvested compensation behind in the form of "earned but unvested" compensation. The grahall Walk Away Analysis (gWAA) is an analysis that determines how much this loss can be. In Figure 6.10, an example executive compensation program is examined to determine the executive's loss at the walk-away point. Many executives do not really understand the complex vesting restrictions on each element of their reward programs. For that matter, many boards don't either.

What Have You Done for Me Lately?

A final analysis in the grahall Executive Reward Strategy toolkit is the grahall Incremental Pay for Performance Analysis (gIP4PA). Ever board of directors and, for that matter, every

(text continues on page 186)

FIGURE 6.10   Example assumptions for calculation of gWWA.

Variables

- base salary is assumed to grow at 5% annually. Bonus is calculated at 100% of base salary.

- Performance shares are until year 2009 are based on the number of shares granted times the end-of-year stock price. Thereafter performance shares are calculated at 200% of base salary. Stock price is assumed to grow at 10% annually.

- Matching shares vest in year 2012. The value reflects number of matched shares (20,000) times the end-of-year stock price.

- Challenge grants of 35,000 RSU's and 26,000 RSU's are assumed to vest in year 2006 and 2008 respectively.

- Retirement is calculated by taking the average of last three years' base and bonus times 66.67%.

Loss at Walk Away

- Calculated by taking the summation of each component (expect base salary and bonus) for all the years minus the value in year that he walks away.

- For example in 2007 Loss at Walk Away is $98.6M. This is equal to adding the value of (Performance Shares in all the years from 2007 – 2040 and then subtracting 1.9M(year 2007)) + (Matching shares from 2007 – 2004 and then subtracting 0.00M (year 2007)) and so forth.

- However for retirement component in loss at walk away we have actually calculated the loss of value based on number of years of service. For example, if the CEO left in year 2007 he would not get anything in retirement since he would have less than 5 years of service. However if he left in 2008 he would have 5 years of service, so his retirement would equal pro rata portion of what his retirement would be if he were there for 15 years or more.

- We have made the assumption in this scenario that he would vest in the challenge grants in year 2006 and 2008.

- If Executive A were to walk away in year 2007 he would lose all of his retirement money, since he would not have completed 5-years of service with the company. He would also lose the second challenge grant and matching shares since they vest in 2008 and 2012, respectively. Thus he would lose approximately $98.6M.

- However after year 2008 he would only lose a portion of his retirement money since he now has completed 5-years of service and is eligible to receive a pro-rata portion of the retirement.

FIGURE 6.11 Calculation of loss at walk away.

	Base	Bonus	Performance Shares	Matching Shares	Challenge Grants	Deferred Comp.	Retirement	Loss at Walkaway
2002	$600,000	$450,000	$0	$0	$0	$97,200	$0	0
2003	$624,000	$468,000	$0	$0	$0	$108,864	$0	0
2004	$700,000	$518,007	$0	$0	$0	$122,109	$0	0
2005	$800,000	$900,000	$855,000	$0	$0	$139,369	$0	0
2006	$800,000	$800,000	$1,725,000	$0	$12,075,000	$140,749	$0	0
2007	$840,000	$840,000	$1,897,500	$0	$0	$147,340	$0	$98,618,696
2008	$882,000	$882,000	$1,669,800	$0	$10,853,700	$154,671	$0	$79,085,957
2009	$926,100	$926,100	$2,755,170	$0	$0	$162,402	$0	$74,820,844
2010	$972,405	$972,405	$1,944,810	$0	$0	$170,522	$0	$70,959,219
2011	$1,021,025	$1,021,025	$2,042,051	$0	$0	$179,048	$0	$66,829,969
2012	$1,072,077	$1,072,077	$2,144,153	$12,223,771	$0	$188,000	$0	$50,192,215
2013	$1,125,680	$1,125,680	$2,251,361	$0	$0	$197,400	$0	$45,475,350
2014	$1,181,964	$1,181,964	$2,363,929	$0	$0	$207,270	$0	$40,436,349
2015	$1,241,063	$1,241,063	$2,482,125	$0	$0	$217,634	$0	$35,054,791
2016	$1,303,116	$1,303,116	$2,606,231	$0	$0	$228,515	$0	$29,309,017
2017	$1,368,271	$1,368,271	$2,736,543	$0	$0	$239,941	$0	$23,176,060
2018	$1,436,685	$1,436,685	$2,873,370	$0	$0	$251,938	$0	$16,631,566
2019	$1,508,519	$1,508,519	$3,017,039	$0	$0	$264,535	$0	$6,494,176
2020	$1,583,945	$1,583,945	$3,167,891	$0	$0	$277,762	$0	$3,326,285
2021	$1,663,143	$1,663,143	$3,326,285	$0	$0	$291,650	$0	$0
2022	$0	$0	$0	$0	$0	$0	$2,113,709	$0
2023	$0	$0	$0	$0	$0	$0	$2,113,709	$0
2024	$0	$0	$0	$0	$0	$0	$2,113,709	$0
2025	$0	$0	$0	$0	$0	$0	$2,113,709	$0
2026	$0	$0	$0	$0	$0	$0	$2,113,709	$0
2027	$0	$0	$0	$0	$0	$0	$2,113,709	$0
2028	$0	$0	$0	$0	$0	$0	$2,113,709	$0
2029	$0	$0	$0	$0	$0	$0	$2,113,709	$0
2030	$0	$0	$0	$0	$0	$0	$2,113,709	$0
2031	$0	$0	$0	$0	$0	$0	$2,113,709	$0
2032	$0	$0	$0	$0	$0	$0	$2,113,709	$0
2033	$0	$0	$0	$0	$0	$0	$2,113,709	$0
2034	$0	$0	$0	$0	$0	$0	$2,113,709	$0
2035	$0	$0	$0	$0	$0	$0	$2,113,709	$0
2036	$0	$0	$0	$0	$0	$0	$2,113,709	$0
2037	$0	$0	$0	$0	$0	$0	$2,113,709	$0
2038	$0	$0	$0	$0	$0	$0	$2,113,709	$0
2039	$0	$0	$0	$0	$0	$0	$2,113,709	$0
2040	$0	$0	$0	$0	$0	$0	$2,113,709	$0

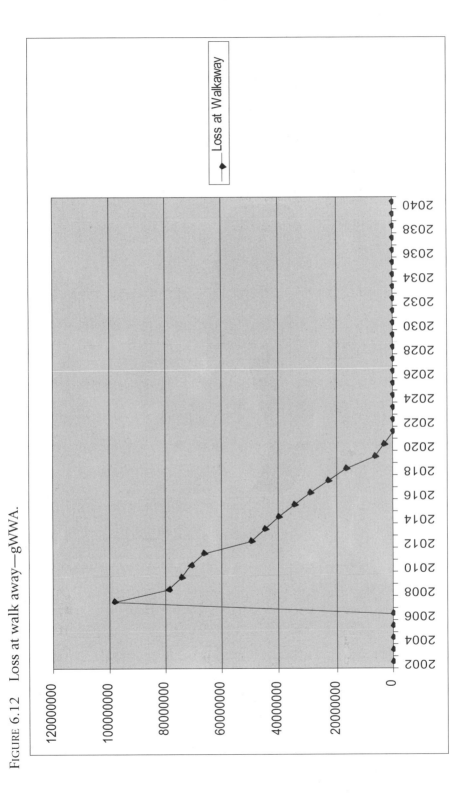

FIGURE 6.12   Loss at walk away—gWWA.

FIGURE 6.13 grahall Incremental Pay for Performance Alignments Analysis (gIP4PAA).

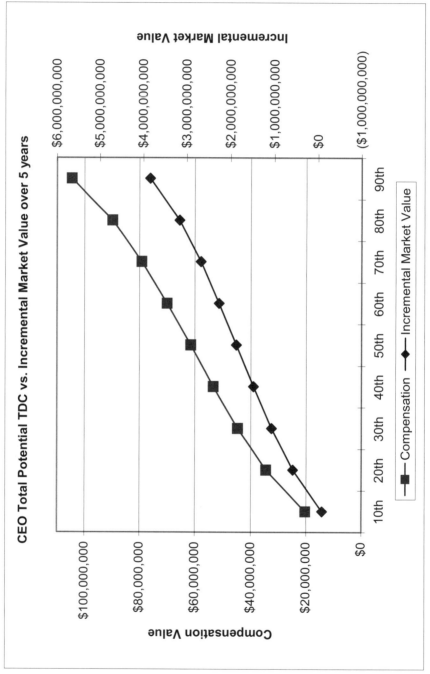

CEO Total Potential TDC vs. Incremental Market Value over 5 years

FIGURE 6.14 CEO total potential TDC comparison using the grahall Incremental Pay for Performance Alignment Analysis (gIP4PAA).

— This set of gIP4PA shows a comparison of three firm's CEO total potential total direct compensation (TDC)

— Comparator Firm A, X and Y background:

- Firm A is in the biotechnology industry with revenues of $2.2Billion.

- Firm X is in the property/casualty insurance industry with revenues of $2.1Billion.

- Firm Y is in the entertainment retail industry with revenues of $3.0Billion.

— The following pages compare:

- Compensation programs of the three firms.

- The value of CEO total potential TDC by performance percentile.

- The incremental percentage change in CEO total potential TDC as compared to the incremental value delivered to shareholders.

FIGURE 6.15   CEO total potential TDC comparison program comparison in standard "English" term sheet form.

Compensation	Firm A	Firm X	Firm Y
Base Salary	✓	✓	✓
Target Annual Incentive	• Target: 100% of salary • Maximum: 250% of salary • Metrics: Sales, Operating Income, EPS, ROA	• Target: 50% of salary • Maximum: 75% of salary • Metrics: annual EPS, subject to 1 year growth in book value per share hurdle	• Target: 150% of base and deferred compensation. • Metrics: Operating income.
Annual Time Vested Long-Term Incentives	• Stock Options • Restricted Stock	• N/A	• Stock Options • Restricted Stock
Annual Performance Vested Long-Term Incentives		• Target: 150% of salary • Payout: 0%–150% of Target • Performance Period: 4 years • Metrics: 4-year growth in book value per share	
Challenge Share		• Award of number of performance based restricted stock • Vested based on Company's compound growth in stockholder's equity per share • Threshold: vesting starts upon achievement of Company 60th percentile historical performance	
Matching Share		• The Company awards 2 restricted share units up to a maximum for each share CEO purchases.	
Transition Grant		• Grant based on $ value • Performance period: 3 years • Vesting of award from 0% to 100% of the grant based on 3 year growth in EPS	
Compensation Program Observations	• More traditional in nature. • Driven primarily by stock performance. • Minimal company performance focus.	• Driven both by company and stock price performance. • Larger upside award opportunities.	• More traditional in nature. • Driven primarily by stock performance. • Minimal company performance focus.

FIGURE 6.16 CEO potential total direct compensation comparison in grahall Incremental Pay for Performance Alignment Analysis (gIP4PAA) form. These charts show the relationship between the incremental market value of the three firms and the corresponding amount of compensation delivered to the CEOs over five years. We can see Firm X requires a greater shareholder incremental wealth be created for less total CEO rewards. Compensation is flat until the incremental shareholder wealth is above the 50th percentile.

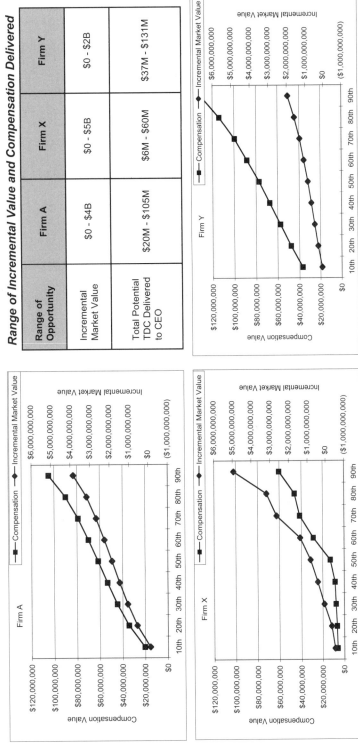

Range of Incremental Value and Compensation Delivered

Range of Opportunity	Firm A	Firm X	Firm Y
Incremental Market Value	$0 - $4B	$0 - $5B	$0 - $2B
Total Potential TDC Delivered to CEO	$20M - $105M	$6M - $60M	$37M - $131M

shareholder should have a sense of how much incremental value needs to be created by the executive for the executive to receive in compensation in return.

In Figure 6.13, the chart outlines the potential value of the CEO's total direct compensation (TDC) and how it varies with incremental wealth creation for shareholders. The exhibit shows the compensation over a five-year period as stock price performance increase from the 10th percentile to the 90th percentile. Firm A, the example firm, will pay the CEO between $20 million to $105 million for the five-year period. In turn, Firm A's market value will have increased up to $4 billion in incremental market value to shareholders. All those associated can now see the "exchange" rate.

Which Executive Total Reward Strategy Would Your Prefer if You Are a Shareholder?

In the end, it is all about getting what you pay for. As an illustration, the pay programs for CEOs have been analyzed for three different companies using the various analyses outlined earlier in this chapter. Figure 6.14, a standard term sheet; Figure 6.15, a grahall Economic Impact Anaylsis; and Figure 6.16, a gIP4PA, all serve to illustrate the three companies' executive pay programs.

A Few More Thoughts at 30,000 Feet

In the end, it's all about "how," and not "how much." Aligning the reward strategy to an organization's challenges is far more important than the value of the reward itself. As a matter of fact, the more the reward programs are customized to the organizational unit, job family, or individual, the greater the influence in driving results.

Now that we've got a broad overview of total reward strategy, let's take a closer look. When we are talking about total rewards strategy, this is where we get into more detail by looking at money, mix, and messages.

References

1. Gadiesh, Orit and Marcia Blenko. "Creating The Right Numbers For Executive Pay." *Forbes.com*, 18 January 2006. Available online at http://www.forbes.com/columnists/2006/01/17/sec-executive-comp-bain-cx_og_0118bain.html, accessed 24 September 2007.

2. Ibid.

3. *CEO Compensation Practices in the S&P/TSX Composite Index.* Watson Wyatt, 2005.

4. "Business: Pay Purview." *The Economist*, 27 August 1998.

5. Bebchuk, Lucian Arye and Yaniv Grinstein. "The Growth of Executive Pay." *Oxford Review of Economic Policy*, Vol. 21, pp. 283–303, 2005. Available online at http://ssrn.com/abstract=648682, accessed 24 September 2007.

6. Bebchuk, Lucian and Jesse Fried. *Pay Without Performance: The Unfulfilled Promise of Executive Compensation.* Cambridge: Harvard University Press, 2005.

7. Bebchuk, Lucian and Rakesh Khurana. *The Compensation Game.* Harvard Business School, 30 August 2006.

8. "Are They Worthy?" *Financial Times*, 29 October 2006.

CHAPTER 7
Total Reward Architecture

Why We Talk About "Architecture"

When we talk about building executive total reward strategies, why do we use the word "architecture?" Because if you compare building your strategy to building a house, things suddenly seem a lot clearer!

If you were thinking about building a house, what would be your first step? Deciding what kind of house would fit your needs, right? For example, an English Tudor is going to fit a very different set of needs then, say, something *a la* Frank Lloyd Wright. A one-story ranch may be more convenient for those who—for whatever reason—appreciate one-level living. On the other hand, a sprawling, multi-level Colonial might meet your very specific aesthetic needs. When you build a house, you prioritize what's important to you based on the occupants of the house. You decide whether, for example, convenience or aesthetics will drive your construction decisions. Same thing with building a total executive reward strategy. You take a good, long look at the company—it's environmental factors, key stakeholder issues, vision, mission, and values, business, and people strategies—and decide what kind of total reward architecture will best fit the company. But instead of deciding whether to go rustic Cape Cod or reproduction Victorian, you are thinking about things like whether it better suits your company to pay for organizational or individual performance, short- or long-term performance, etc. However, the concept is the same.

If you've ever built a house, you know there are a lot of steps to complete before you can throw a respectable housewarming party. If you could just decide what type of house you wanted and call it a day, building a house probably wouldn't be an oft-cited reason for divorce. The fact is, once you've decided what kind of house you are going to build, you've got a lot of details to deal with. How big will the house be? Will the house be one story, or two? How many bedrooms? How many bathrooms? Will the garage be attached or separate? And just when you think you've got all that out of the way even more details come down the pike. Copper roof or asphalt? Aluminum siding or cedar shingles? Granite countertops or soapstone? Cherry cabinets or birch? Should that extra room on the first floor be a library for her or a card room/bar for him and his buddies (if they decide to go the latter route, we hope one of the buddies is a marriage counselor)? And how will you set up the electrical, plumbing, and heating systems?

Just as you build a house in steps, you should look at constructing a total reward architecture in steps as well. The first step is to determine the needs of your company and decide what kind of strategy you are going to put in place. Just as you would first decide what kind of house you are going to build, when building your total reward strategy the first thing you should do is determine what the goals of your strategy are. Again, look carefully at the factors previously discussed in this book—business environmental factors, key stakeholder issues, vision, mission, and values, business, and people strategies—and decide what kind of reward structure would best help your company reach its goals.

Coming In for the Close-Up

As we hone in a little closer on total reward architecture—we're hovering around 15,000 or so feet here—the way in which executives are linked to business outcomes should become more apparent. You've got a lot of information, from how outside business environmental factors affect your total reward strategy to how organizational structure, processes, and culture affects your plan. The key now is to take your information and leverage it in a way that motivates your executives. It all comes down to the age-old question, "What's in it for me?" In order to best answer that question you've got to have knowledge of the business, and you've got to use that knowledge to motivate executives through rewards. The goal here is to align the successes of the company to the successes of your executives. We don't care how much fun someone's job is, if they aren't being compensated in a way that is meaningful to them, they aren't going to show up. Or in some cases they are going to show up—if they have the corner office at Victoria's Secret, say—and that's about it. But is that going to go very far in helping you meet your desired outcomes? Doubtful.

So back to the question, "What's in it for me?" How best to answer it? Like we said before, the first step is to leverage everything you've learned about your company in a way that links executive success to overall company success. The next step— and this is critical—is to demonstrate to executives how that connection is made. How do you do this?

If only we could write a paragraph or two here under the subhead "You Have Found the Holy Grail" and call it a day. No such luck. There is no one path; there's no silver bullet. As you've learned in previous chapters there are just way too many permutations and combinations for there to be a one-size-fits-all answer.

But the good news—and yes, there is good news—is that you've done enough homework up to now to know that while there's no chartered bus to take you to your destination, there is certainly a navigable road map if you are willing to take the time and effort to drive yourself. What's the most effective kind of executive rewards strategy? One that allocates rewards in a way that directs the business to meet its goals and objectives. When developing your plan there are three factors that will make up the reward plan's total value. Used correctly together, these three strategic axes provide all the leverage you need while communicating to executives how their success is linked to the success of the company. So what are these three strategic axes? We like to call them the three Ms—money, mix, and messages.

Let's quickly define money, mix, and messages.

Money. What's money? Just what it sounds like. It is, when all is said and done, what the executive is compensated. It's the element that is considered to be the rewards in the marketplace where you compete for talent and the competitive levels that you establish for yourself in those marketplaces. We like to refer to money as the competitive market attachment. Money is the level of rewards, and is how total rewards are defined in terms of total cost to the company (internal) and relative competitive level (external) of the total of all of the rewards components paid to the executive.

Mix. This strategic axis answers the question of how the total executive reward strategy is balanced between various reward components, such as base salary, short-term incentives, long-term incentives, benefits, and perquisites. For example, is the overall program more fixed, or variable? Mix is how an executive total reward architecture is designed to distribute the reward elements most successfully.

Messages. Messages answer the final question of "why." Messages tell executives what the desired business outcomes are, and align the plan with people's efforts. You can look at messages as the philosophy behind your total reward program. Messages should make it clear to everyone what the reward plan is designed to accomplish.

*C*ase Study #13

An organization about to become an IPO came to us with a difficult situation. The two founding members of the organization were the two key sales individuals for the

(text continues on page 199)

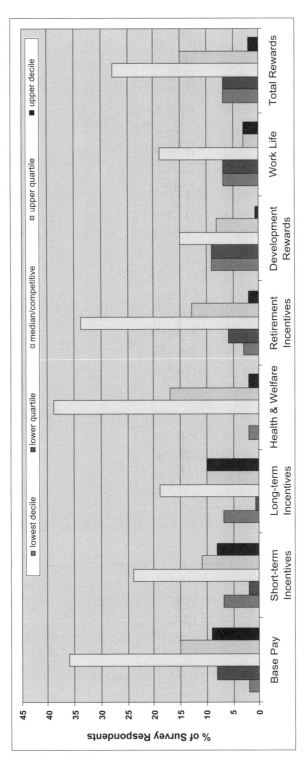

FIGURE 7.1 "Money" or competitive market attachment. The position in the market to which companies actually anchor various components.

FIGURE 7.2 "Mix" or the balance between the different reward components shown at various company and stock performance levels.

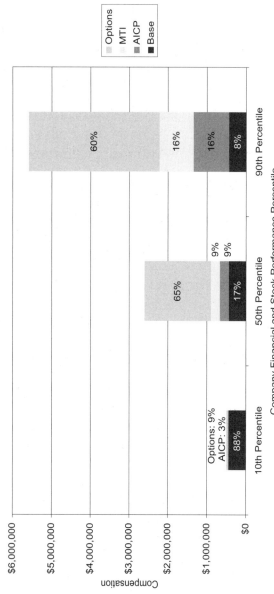

FIGURE 7.3   A. Example messages for executive reward strategy.

Pay for Which Organizational Unit? Individual Team Group/Unit Organizations	Pay for What Duration of Time Frames? Short-term Middle-term Long-term Life-term
Pay for What Type of Performance? Incremental performance Restructuring	Pay for Which Performance Levels? Absolute performance Relative performance
Pay for Ways to Measure Performance? Contribution/Effort Results Competency/Knowledge/Skills Behaviors	Pay for Which Business Stage? Start-up Emerging Growth Mature Decline
Pay for Which Types of Time Frames for Performance? Projects Milestones Termstones	Pay for What Performance? Look forward/Plan Look back/History Look around/Competition

Figure 7.3   B. Messages.

Performance Measures: Examples by Type

Measure Type	Examples	Pros	Challenges
Capability Measures	Employee satisfaction/turnover Response time/time to market Staffing/employee profile	Generally more directly controllable than other financial or shareholder measures Recognizes difficulty of financial, shareholder value goal setting Recognizes very long term objectives	Human capital value chain relationships to financial and shareholder value measures is poorly understood Requires strong ability to identify the key objectives
Operational Measures	Budget vs. actual Process quality Reliability/rework Accuracy/error rates Process improvements New product introduction	Generally more directly controllable than other financial or shareholder measures Recognizes difficulty of financial, shareholder value goal setting	A limited number of objectives may not adequately recognize business complexity Requires strong ability to identify the key objectives
Financial Performance Measures	Income statement Revenue, revenue growth Gross margin, gross margin growth Operating income, growth ROI, ROI growth EBIT, EBIT growth EBITDA, EBITDA growth Balance sheet Debt management Asset management Blend Earnings per Share Return on Invested Capital (ROIC) Economic Value Added Return on Assets Cash flow, cash flow improvement	Familiarity Simple approach — measures outcomes, not process Blends begin to reflect investor expectations	Generally modest relationship to long term shareholder value growth Line of sight is weak for most employees Understanding of measures is weak for many employees
Shareholder Value Measures	Actual Share price appreciation Change in market capitalization/MVA Total shareholder return Pseudo/Indicators (positive correlation to SV) Economic Value Added ROIC Return on Capital Employed ROA	Clear or clearer link to shareholder value May be effective for short to mid term Pseudo/indicators Best reflection of competitive nature of business, inherent risk and uncertainty	May not adequately recognize true long term objectives Pseudo/indicators may be difficult to understand; may require new measurement tools, processes Line of sight is very weak May be difficult to measure at local levels

> *acquisition. The founding individuals wanted to be called "Co-CEOs." They also generated the majority of the revenues for the organization. The dilemma: we couldn't pay two CEOs for one job.*
>
> *The solution was to cut the baby in half. We gave each CEO approximately half of the salary and incentive they would have received as sole chief executive officer. We also provided them with a unique producer bonus. The producer bonus provided them with a similar amount of compensation based upon their sales efforts.*
>
> *Sometimes the Solomon solution is the right solution. There's nothing wrong with designing half-assed programs if you've got a half-assed situation.*

When you put money, mix, and messages together, you have what we have been calling "total reward architecture." Let's go back to our house building analogy for one second. Once you've decided what type of house you are going to build, the next step is to determine its layout and features based on your family's needs. In comparison, money, mix, and messages are the layout and features of your total reward strategy based on your company's needs. Just like no two families are exactly alike, nor are any two businesses. The total reward architecture—the money, mix, and messages—will be unique to each company. You've probably figured out by now that we don't always stay within the lines, and for that reason you'll never find us suggesting the "standard" division of 30 percent salary, 30 percent short-term incentive, and 30 percent long-term incentive.

Money, Mix, Messages and the External Environment and Key Stakeholders

When it comes to the influence of key stakeholders and the external environment on total rewards, company ownership, the regulatory environment, and competitive posture are three of the biggest factors. Let's take ownership as an example. A company's owners have a big influence on how rewards are allocated. When it comes to mix, the fewer the owners the higher the variable and the more they focus the reward program message on financial returns. Companies with many owners have a more moderate variable, and the reward strategy tends to send a message that the organization is striving to serve its many stakeholders.

Case Study #14

One of our hedge fund clients asked us to develop a total reward strategy. At the time the CEO of the organization owned 85 percent of the company, with a prior investor owning the other 15 percent. All of the traders received annual bonuses in the form of cash plus a small deferral. The CEO wanted the individuals to have more incentive over the long term, as well as a stake or an amount of equity in the firm to ensure the long-term viability of the organization.

We designed a modest deferral of current bonus for the purchase of equity within the organization, after an initial small investment in the form of equity was given to some of the key trading people. To this day we feel the amount of equity given to the individuals was far overshadowed by the amount of value that would accrue to the individual trader on an annual basis. Ultimately, before we even finished the design or implemented the plan, the hedge fund blew up as result of one of the traders making short-term bets. We'll never know whether or not the change from a 100 percent short-term basis incentive program to a more balanced short- and long-term rewards program would have encouraged the individual to reconsider his extreme bets.

Sometimes you have to realize that when the rewards are extremely high and the risks are also very high, rebalancing the program is an imperative that needs to be done much faster and much larger.

Whether or not a company is heavily regulated will also determine reward design. When it comes to money, the degree of government regulation impacts the free market for organizations and employees. When it comes to mix, the degree of government regulation impacts whether the product is system controlled versus employee controlled. And when it come to messages, the degree of government regulation increases and decreases the risk orientation and time frame.

Case Study #15

A university came to our organization with serious concerns about retaining their two key investment professionals. Other universities had lost their key investment individuals to the hedge fund industry.

The investment professionals were paid a reasonable salary, with a short-term incentive plan typical of endowment incentive plans. The upside based upon superior performance was modest. The downside based upon extremely poor performance was not very penalizing. The individuals had performed between the 80th and 90th percentiles of all endowments in the United States.

We decided to fashion the reward strategy upon the direct competitors in the hedge fund industry. The professionals would receive substantial upside compensation when performance was superior, but would suffer hedge-like consequences should they perform badly.

Sometimes when designing a total reward strategy you can't look at the way direct competitors pay their people if the direct competitors are losing their people to other types of organizations. You're better off looking at the way the organizations recruiting your people are paying their individuals.

Finally, where a company stands in relation to its competitors will also be reflected in its reward strategy, since this factors in to the ability to attract, retain, and motivate executives. How an organization's products and services are viewed by consumers, how that position in the marketplace affects executive perception, and what the organization is best known for should also be reflected in the messages sent by the total reward strategy.

INVESTOR ALERT #12

INAPPROPRIATE COMPETITOR BENCHMARKING

As the saying goes, we wish we had $1 for every time a CEO gave us a list of their competitor companies, only to find said "competitor companies" were much larger when it came to size and performance. We would be rich indeed.

This is probably just a case of someone comparing themselves to someone they aspire to. And that's fine. We like CEOs who shoot for the stars. We usually deliver a cream-of-the-crop group of competitive companies to those individuals—but only after providing them a group of companies that are comparable to themselves in size, industry, and performance.

Money, Mix, Messages, and Vision, Mission, and Values

Lots of organizations think they have vision, mission, and values. The question is whether or not vision, mission, and values are understood and put into practice. If they are, they can—and should—be used as leverage in your executive total reward strategy. How much should you link these things to compensation? That's easy. The extent to which they are used in your organization should determine the extent to which they are linked to compensation.

When it comes to money, a good tactic is to pay for what the company values. For example, if your organization depends upon customer service for success, make sure you pay for it. As far as the mix goes, it should speak directly to how far into the future your vision extends. For example, if your vision statement focuses on three to five years from now, rewards should be structured for the long term. Finally, when it comes to messages, use vision, mission, and values to determine whether what you are paying for will drive executive behavior to reach the organization's goals.

Money, Mix, Messages, and Business Strategy

The first step in linking executive rewards to your organization is to completely understand the organization's general business strategy (GBS). You want everyone to know how you compete; for example, if you compete on research and development, you need to make sure your reward plan is structured so that executives don't forget that, and when all is said and done you reward for research and development. That's how you'll get your message across.

Both money and mix will vary greatly depending upon the GBS. For example, an organization with a GBS focused on low cost might have a lower fixed, higher variable mix of components that focuses on the long term, while an organization that focuses on differentiating its product in the marketplace might have a mix that balances short- and long-term rewards. The message conveyed in the reward strategy in the former company might be to focus on points in the process where costs can be impacted, while the message conveyed in the reward strategy in the latter organization might be to focus on standing out from the competition by being different.

Value chain strategy (VCS) can be used to deliver a message of how and where executives add value to an organization's products or services. When it comes to money and mix, focus on the critical links in the value chain and reward the right people and actions. Rewards should make it clear how each link in the chain adds value, and the mix should reflect the emphasis.

When it comes to specific business strategies (SBS) they vary so much that it's hard to get into particular strategies. However, we can offer one piece of tried-and-true advice: be consistent! Just make sure that the money, mix, and messages give your

(text continues on page 206)

FIGURE 7.4

General Business Strategy

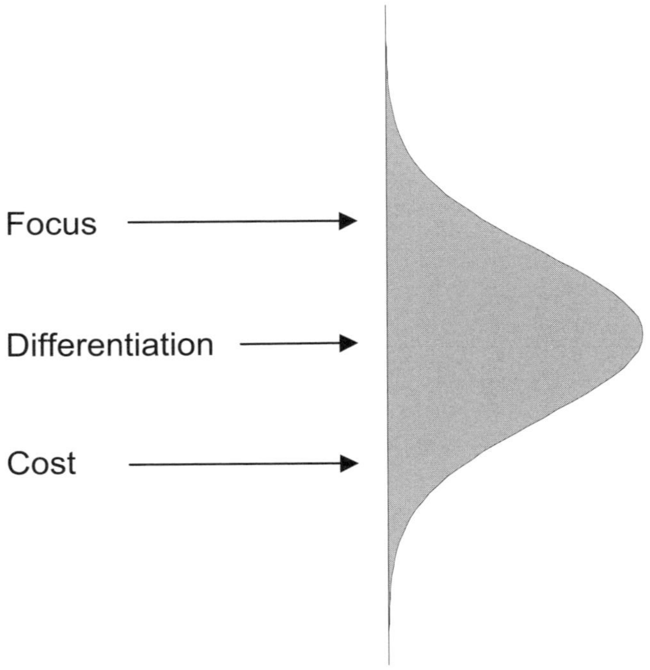

- **For any given position, there is a range of market pay levels**

- **The General Business Strategy helps to shape an organization's overall target pay position (across all positions)**

- **Typically:**

  - An organization that competes on a Focus basis will pay, on average, _above_ the 50th percentile

  - An organization that competes on a Differentiation basis will pay, on average, _near_ the 50th percentile

  - An organization that competes on a Cost basis will pay, on average, _below_ the 50th percentile

- **An organization's General Business Strategy is typically consistent year to year and changes over a 5 to 10 year time horizon**

Focus

Differentiation

Cost

FIGURE 7.5   Value chain strategy.

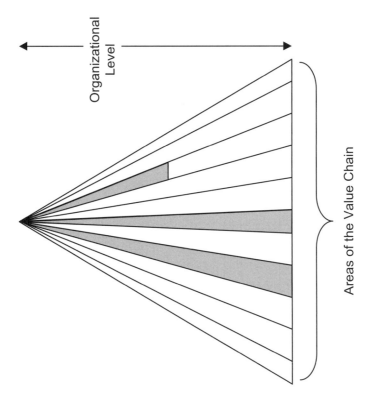

Organizational Level

Areas of the Value Chain

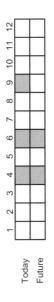

1 2 3 4 5 6 7 8 9 10 11 12

Today

Future

■ **The Value Chain Strategy helps to shape the target competitive position *for functional areas within the organization***

■ **Areas of competitive advantage would typically be targeted higher versus the external market (in comparison to other functions within the organization)**

■ **Where the competitive advantage is in the future, an organization may target particular organizational levels (where responsibility for implementing change may reside)** executives a clear indication of the direction in which you want them to go, as well as what you want them to accomplish. Specific business strategies fall into the categories of growth, value chain optimization, and maintenance/reduction. If those are understood and properly communicated, a properly designed reward program can heavily influence their success.

*C*ase Study #16

We were called in by a large instruction organization to assist them in integrating their five most recent acquisitions into a single consulting organization. None of the acquisitions had been integrated into a single reward strategy, nor had they been integrated into the organization overall.

To make matters even worse, each of the individual acquisitions had been given a different buyout formula. Since each organization negotiated a different buyout formula and a different set of buyout performance factors, the entire organization was headed in five different directions with no interest in working with each other to create the synergistic effect proposed as a rationale for the actual acquisitions. Not only was the result a clash of objectives and egos, but ultimately none of the key executives within the organization had any real desire to work with the parent organization if it meant a decrease in their buyout incentive payments.

In this case we recommended developing an overall total reward strategy for the five organizations, starting with the broad-based employee work force and using the five key acquired executives as designers of a single integrated reward strategy for their new entity. All five executives worked as a team to develop the new unified reward strategy for the overall organization, which gave them a good working knowledge of the organization's overall business strategy.

Sometimes it's not the results but the process. In order to create the required trust and credibility of the process, it

FIGURE 7.6 Specific business strategy.

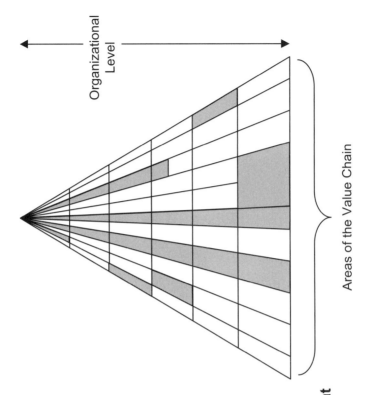

Organizational Level

Areas of the Value Chain

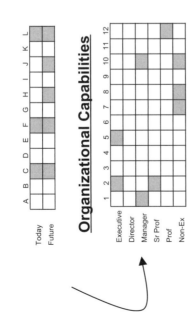

	A	B	C	D	E	F	G	H	I	J	K	L
Today												
Future												

Organizational Capabilities

	1	2	3	4	5	6	7	8	9	10	11	12
Executive												
Director												
Manager												
Sr Prof												
Prof												
Non-Ex												

The Specific Business Strategies (SBS) and the Organizational Capabilities (OC) help identify areas of the organization to target differentially versus the external market

The end result is an organizational "map" that identifies the market attachment strategy

> *was necessary to co-opt the executives into running through the process once for their employees, and a second time for themselves. The first time allowed them to develop a common goal, while the second time allowed them to make the compromises necessary because they understood and trusted the process.*

Money, Mix, Messages, and Organizational Capabilities

The money dimension should feel lots of influence from organizational capabilities. If you've determined where along the value chain success lies, you can focus rewards on where the leverage from those capabilities is the most significant. Mix can be used to organize rewards, and put the emphasis in the results and actions—as well as those behind them.

Money, Mix, Messages, and People Strategy

When it comes to structure, rewards should be aligned with how people move within the company, as well as whether the organization is focused on being functional, geographic, product/service-oriented, or process-oriented. The layers of management will drive the mix, while the characteristics of the structure—the number of layers and the predominant themes—will influence messages.

As far as culture is concerned, the three Ms (money, mix, and message) do much toward defining an organization's personality. Money and messages are used to attract and retain the people who define the company's culture, while mix and messages motivate those same people to keep behaving in a way that continues to define it.

It's Getting Hot in Here

How much do the external business environment and key stakeholder issues affect plan design? Dramatically. Just consider the heat that shareholders, boards, and even the general public are putting on companies to cut down on exorbitant pay and keep ethics in check. How do you think shareholders of Marvell Technology group reacted when Sehat Sutardja saw his paycheck explode 14,000 percent in one year as a result of cashed-in stock options? You could practically hear their blood boiling. But what is worth mentioning is that while most companies who earn so-called "celebrity status" have been involved in activities like backdating scandals, most of the companies that haven't been in the limelight have tried to improve their total rewards strategies. One of the major impetuses for change came from shareholders who were concerned that executives were getting giddily rich off of stock option plans. The logic behind this plan wasn't so bad. The idea was that executives who were sold future stocks at a current price would do everything to ensure that stock prices rose as much as possible.

Nice idea, but while CEOs were encouraged to ensure that stock prices rose as much as possible, this was only until the future date at which the shares were valued. From that point forward the executive had little—if no—incentive to see share prices continue to rise. There were other flaws too: high share prices as a result of "hype" meant the company's effectiveness and profitability were ultimately damaged, not to mention that the set-up made "backdating" not only possible, but very tempting. Options at Tyco and Enron, for example, certainly didn't prevent and may have even encouraged the widespread accounting frauds at either company.

So what's the result? As executive after executive enjoyed—we use the term loosely, of course—his 15 minutes of fame, the external environment and key shareholders did their best to ensure that the ethics-free period was over. They had lots to say, and the government was listening. According to the 10th Annual Corporate Board Effectiveness Study, 40 percent of directors thought that pay for CEOs was "too high in most cases," and 81 percent favored increasing the link between CEO pay and performance.[1] Sarbanes-Oxley and the new SEC regulations are designed to keep companies from straying out-side of bounds when it comes to executive pay. We won't know for a while whether these sweeping pay disclosure rules will manage to contain the executive pay beast. But our guess is that outside influences will most certainly play a part in rein-ing in ridiculously large paychecks.

As a matter of fact, companies are already bidding *adieu* to the "pay for a pulse" mentality. A good example is Smithfield Foods, which modified CEO Joseph W. Luter's pay plan so that he received a bonus only if the company surpassed $100 million in earnings.[2] Other companies are following suit by responding to investor outrage by spending time on more cre-ative compensation strategies. Some recent trends? Bonuses based on how a company compares to its competitors, elim-ination of guaranteed minimum pay, and severance accords that prevent big payouts despite poor performance.

Shareholders are driving the "new normal" in executive com-pensation. They are influencing the size and features of total rewards strategies, with an emphasis on looking at all elements of compensation. Thanks to shareholders, companies are say-ing goodbye to the almost exclusive use of stock options and are instead changing the long-term mix to a blend of options, restricted stock, and performance shares.

INVESTOR ALERT #13

75TH PERCENTILE PAY FOR 50TH PERCENTILE PERFORMANCE

Whenever the executive compensation program is targeted at the 75th percentile for the purpose of retaining the 50th percentile performing management, there is a pretty important disconnect.

Call us simple, but to pay above-average compensation for average performance just doesn't seem correct or fair to shareholders or management.

If we were investors and saw an organization that stated it wanted to pay the 75th percentile for target performance, unless we could truly determine performance was at the 75th percentile, we would target some other organization—one with a more reasonable pay and performance relationship—for our investment.

Peer Pressure

In many cases, boards and committees throw in the towel and decide to do what other successful companies are doing, in the hopes that they'll get the same results.

Flawed logic, at best. Your company can be in the same industry, with the same amount of employees, but unless your environmental and key stakeholder issues—vision, mission, and values, business and people strategies, and organizational structures—are identical, you are going to require a unique total reward architecture with a unique set of money, mix, and messages. Are you going to get the same results just by copying the other guy? Not likely. What helps a company with one strategy, culture, and environment might really hurt another. What makes your company successful may be very different from what similar companies are doing. Companies who are practicing this type of lackadaisical benchmarking need to slow down and ask themselves one simple, basic question: Will this total reward architecture that we are considering motivate our executives and enhance company performance?

Another problem that causes a poorly structured total reward architecture is when boards and committees follow ideologies that, while deeply believed in, are relatively unexamined. The use of stock options as a compensation strategy is a great example. Everyone jumped on the stock option bandwagon, thinking they were a great way for cash-strapped companies to ensure executives worked their tails off making sure stocks performed. In reality, the excessive use of stock options led to an ethical nightmare in which executives were motivated to take a short-term, selfish view. A few senior executives lied about their companies' performance, "hyped" their stock, cut nefarious deals—and were rewarded for it—even as companies went bankrupt and shareholders were left with nothing. And yet more and more companies continued to jump off this bridge just because others were doing it. The companies with the best total reward architectures don't allow ideologies to get in the way of examining all the data necessary to determine the right money, mix, and messages. The companies with the best total reward architectures don't follow another company's lead without demanding proof that the plan will work in their favor.

The Stories of Miller and Diller and a Few Others

Let's go back to that question we asked a while ago that all committees and boards ask themselves. The question is, "How much is enough?"

Again, there's no right answer. Even at the top, there are different views when it comes to the paychecks of CEOs. If you don't believe us, consider Biomet Inc.'s Dane A. Miller and IAC/Interactive's Barry Diller for a study in two contrasting opinions.

Let's talk about Miller first. When money was tight in Biomet's early days, Miller cut his salary by 25 percent and took home $12,000.[3] No, we didn't leave off a zero or two. Granted, this was all 28 years ago, but still. And Miller continued his approach throughout his tenure as CEO. In 2005, he took home $575,800.

According to a University of Notre Dame Study that tallied the top five executives at 460 companies from 1992 to 1997, a narrow pay gap at the top reduces management turnover. Executives were much more likely to leave companies with big gaps in pay distribution, regardless of the actual figure.[4] Biomet's philosophy emphasizes group decision making and compensation is based on how much authority a person has. And its low pay pyramid is in perfect alignment with that philosophy. Biomet preaches moderation, and Miller, who has never taken stock awards, and has no pension, employment contract, or golden parachute, set the example by walking the talk. So is it *really* about how much? Nope. It's about structuring money, mix, and messages in a way that encourages executives to operate in a fashion that leads to the success of the company. Biomet's compensation strategy works because it has been the basis for the company's management style since the beginning.

Now let's take an example for the other end of the spectrum. Who won the award for the biggest paycheck in 2005? The golden pig statue went to Barry Diller, CEO of IAC/Interactive. Two different companies estimated his total compensation— Corporate Library said his paycheck logged in at a hefty $295 million (if we did our math right that's about $14,000 an hour; we hate to state the obvious, but that's a lot of money)—while Glass Lewis & Company figured he was paid $85 million.[5] Both services used different methods to calculate the final damage, but both agreed Diller was the highest paid executive.

What else did both companies agree on? Both companies agreed that the company's performance—down 7.7 percent in 2005—didn't merit such obscene pay. Most of his compensation—less his relatively normal $726,115 base salary in fact— was made up mostly of stock options. Sure, stock options are often given to CEOs as motivation to improve performance, but when you've accumulated the amount of wealth that Diller has, do you really think the extra stock options are going to keep him in the office past 5? Not likely. Had the board or compensation committee really thought about it, there was probably a much better way to allocate money, mix, and messages that would have ensured a better return for the company.

For now, shareholders continue to contend with the daunting task of linking pay to performance. The 1980s brought us the idea that tying cash bonuses to rising sales or earnings would boost performance. And what was the result? Executives made decisions based on short-term results that often yielded long-term catastrophes. In the 1990s stock options were the hopeful "quick-fix" *du jour*, and we all know what happened as a result. Were executive's fortunes tied to those of shareholders? Hardly. The CEOs got richer, while the shareholders were often left holding useless pieces of paper. So what's the moral of this story? There is no "quick fix."

However, there are some new trends looming on the horizon. Companies are rethinking the different components that make up pay packages. Safety nets like golden parachutes and hefty "see ya" severances are no longer standard. Companies are trying to motivate executives by linking components like bonuses and the vesting of restricted shares to performance.

Slowly but surely, companies are responding to shareholders' call for total reward packages that reward executives who think long term. Many companies are structuring their pay packages so that executives and directors hold about five times their pay in stock, making it harder for them to cash in on any short-term boon. What message is this sending? It's sending the message that executives will not benefit from a short-term gain that isn't sustainable. Some companies are moving away from grants of restricted shares that vest after three to five years. Instead, companies are giving shares that vest only if the company hits certain measures that correlate to its success. What does this mean? It means that executives who aren't helping the company reach its goals may not enjoy the same kind of happy and carefree retirement of yesterday's executives.

Mix Masters

Do big-time executives care more about getting rich than increasing shareholder value? Well, CEOs are human, just like you and me. To be quite honest, some of the stock option offerings that executives were offered in the 1990s and the early part of the 2000s were begging to be abused. In these cases, the mix wasn't mastered.

The problem is that many total reward architectures reward short-term thinking—and that's just plain corrosive to organizations. Two groups—the Business Roundtable's Institute for

Corporate Ethics and the CFA Institute's Centre for Financial Market Integrity—have put together a report that illustrates the effect of short-term thinking.[6] In a nutshell, the report shows that companies focused on short-term earnings put long-term value creation by the wayside. Are there any solutions? The report has those too. It suggests eliminating earnings guidance and instead structuring pay plans to reward long-term strategic and value-creation goals instead of short-term stock market goals.[7]

If we haven't convinced you yet that a total reward architecture that rewards short-term thinking isn't good for anyone, consider this. In a 2005 study conducted by three economists for the National Bureau of Economic Research, 400 executives were asked questions about the importance of quarterly earnings.[8] They found out—and this shocked us—that just about 80 percent would decrease discretionary spending in major areas like advertising, maintenance, and research and development if that's what it took to make the quarterly numbers. Obviously, the typical reward architecture encourages executives to make decisions that are not good for the overall success of the organization.

Are we saying that boards and committees should check in with their executives every five years of so to see how they are doing? Of course not. Structuring your reward architecture so that it focuses on long-term value has its own problems, as we've all learned by now. So we aren't suggesting that you ignore short-term performance. No way. Rather, we're calling for a nice balance. Paying executives for achieving critical long-term strategic goals, while also including something in the mix that ensures short-term goals aren't forgotten, is something to consider.

The "Why" Dimension

The "messages" component of total reward architecture should answer the question "why?" The message component tells executives, through the reward system, what is expected of them. A well-articulated message allows executives to focus on business goals—it is where total reward strategies and the efforts of executives are aligned.

Here's another way to think of the messages component. It is the philosophy behind the reward plan. It is, in effect, the reason *behind* a reward strategy. In a nutshell, it tells you what the plan is designed to accomplish.

What message do you want to send? It's not enough to say, in general, the goal of your total reward strategy is to "promote company success" or something equally as vague. Instead, based on the factors discussed in this book—environmental and key stakeholder issues; vision, mission, and values; business and people strategies; and organizational structure—you'll decide what kind of messages best suit your organization. There are all different types of messages.

So what's the best message? The one that best suits your company. For example, a high-tech company that is introducing a new product and wants to be sure to get that product first to market might pay for short-term performance, while a pharmaceutical company that emphasizes research and development might pay for long-term performance. A company with a hierarchical organizational structure might send the message of pay for individual performance, while a company's whose success relies heavily on the sharing of information might send the message of pay for group or corporate performance.

But while there may be no best message, there are certainly ones that are more popular. Shareholder angst has more companies touting the pay for performance message, and indeed, companies from Coca-Cola to Google are making it known that they won't be paying money for nothing.

Other companies haven't quite clued in. Take Hewlett-Packard, which paid ousted CEO Carly Fiorina about $180 million during her five years at the company and a $21.6 million severance package despite a decidedly lackluster performance. Fiorina may not have done HP any good, but she'll still be livin' large much to shareholder chagrin. You would think the board and the compensation committee had learned from their mistakes, but no. New CEO Mark Hurd enjoyed the same kind of front-loaded non–performance-related package, complete with a $2 million signing bonus, $8.7 million in stock, and $5 million in price protection payments.[9]

But happy executives don't mean happy investors. A study done by the Corporate Library showed that front-loaded compensation plans hurt widespread efforts to link pay to performance, and certainly at no benefit to the offending companies. According to the study, over a five-year period 11 companies listed as the worst offenders paid their CEOs a total of $865 million—but also experienced a $640 billion decline in shareholder value.[10] If this isn't a good example of how people who should know better don't understand how incentive pay should work, then nothing is.

A study by Glass Lewis, in which they analyzed 2,375 companies, shows how the message component of the total reward architecture can make a big difference.[11] Glass Lewis graded the companies based on shareholder wealth and business performance: changes in stock price, per-share earnings and book value over the two prior years, and total return, return on equity, and return on assets for the previous years.

What did Glass Lewis uncover? Check this out. Of the 25 worst companies whose message seemed to be payment for a pulse, chief executive pay averaged $16.7 million in 2005, while the stocks fell an average 14 percent and their overall net income dropped an average of 25 percent.[12] On the other end were 25 companies that paid more modestly but had happy investors. CEOs at these companies earned an average of $4.4 million, but their companies' net income grew by 44 percent and their shareholders enjoyed one-year stock gains that averaged just about 40 percent.[13] So there you have it. The right message will tell executives what is expected of them, and the compensation plan will be structured so that when they heed the message, they will be rewarded. It's as simple as that.

Now that we've explained how money, mix, and messages make up a total reward architecture, our next line of business is to discuss the components of a total reward strategy. We are going to show you how the mix of these components—base salary, short-term incentives, mid-term incentives, long-term incentives, wealth creation incentives, benefits, perquisites, and development rewards—can be leveraged to motivate executives to make decisions that bode well for the company and its investors. Again, there's no magic formula. The money, mix, and messages are unique—and put an organization's executives in action.

References

1. Taub, Stephen. "CEO Pay is Too High, Directors Say." CFO.com, 12 October 2006. Available online at http://www.cfo.com/ article.cfm/8027003/c_8027107, accessed 24 September 2007.
2. Lublin, Joann S. "Goodbye to Pay for No Performance." Wall Street Journal, 11 April 2005. Available online at http://online.wsj.com/article/SB111265005063397590. html?mod=2_1147_1, accessed 24 September 2007.
3. "The Journal Report: CEO Compensation Survey." Wall Street Journal, 2005.
4. Ibid.
5. Fabrikant, Geraldine. "Diller Takes Prize for Highest Paid." New York Times, 26 October 2006. Available online at http://www. nytimes.com/2006/10/26/business/26diller.html, accessed 24 September 2007.
6. Nocers, Joe. "A Defense of Short-Termism." New York Times, 29 July 2006. Available online at http://select.nytimes.com/ 2006/07/29/business/29nocera.html?_r=1&n=Top/News/ Business/Columns/Joe%20Nocera&or ef=slogin, accessed 24 September 2007.
7. Ibid.
8. Ibid.

9. Kristof, Kathy M. "Upfront CEO Pay Growing, Study Says." *Los Angeles Times*, 1 April 2006.

10. Ibid.

11. "The Best and Worst in Executive Pay." *New York Times*, 17 September 2006.

12. Ibid.

13. Ibid.

CHAPTER 8

Executive Total Reward Strategy Components

Now that we've looked at total executive rewards strategy from afar, let's swoop on in for a close-up view of the components that comprise a plan. We've found, over the years, that in certain circles much of the executive compensation debate has centered on how much *money* should be paid to executives. And no doubt, money is important. No matter how fascinating and fulfilling your job, the fact is you aren't going to show up every day and make things happen if the money isn't there. Just consider professional athletes. A typical day's work includes shooting some hoops, hanging out with beautiful women, having people buy you drinks, and taking home lots of free swag at the end of the day (okay, okay, maybe we're exaggerating just a bit). But if you have to show up every day it's still considered W-O-R-K—and the brouhaha surrounding professional athletes' paychecks proves it.

That being said, while money is an important component of the executive total reward strategy, it really missed the point when it comes to building an effective executive total reward strategy.

So what is the point . . . if it's not money, that is? How much of the total reward strategy is delivered in the various reward components is just as important as how much money the executive is bringing home—and in some cases it's even more important. The extent to which the total is made up of more variable components than fixed components—and that the variable portion of the reward program is more short-term instead of long-term—is pretty critical in the design process, and will send very different messages to the executives.

FIGURE 8.1 Executive total rewards strategy components. Adapted from Manas, Todd. "Combining Reward Elements for the Right Team Chemistry." *Workspan*, Nov/Dec 2000.

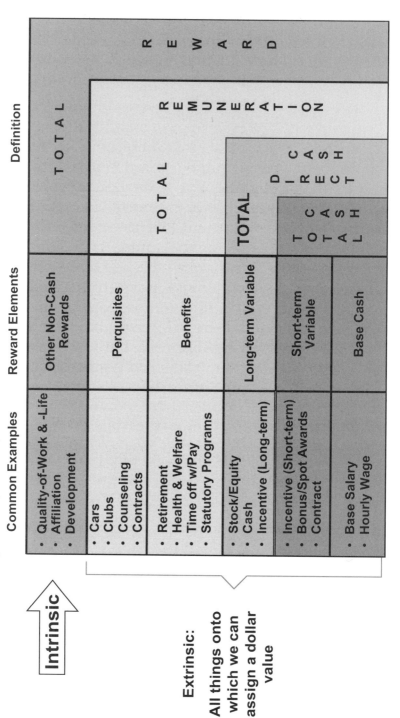

The major components of an executive total reward strategy and their subcomponents are numerous enough to be able to encode vast amounts of information to the executive in the form of key messages. We believe that the *real* power in developing an executive total reward strategy lies within these key messages. And how do you get these key messages across? By plugging them into the various reward strategy components in a way that ensures these messages are sent directly to the executive's motivational system. In other words, the various reward components carry the key message. Again, it bears repeating that there is no quick-fix, easy answer to total executive rewards. What motivates executives at one company may not impress executives at another organization. You'll have to take your business environmental impacts and key stakeholder issues—vision, mission, and values and business and people strategies—into account when figuring out the right mix.

The remaining chapters in this book are more or less devoted to diving deep into each of these components and showing you how they impact your executive total reward strategy. For now, let's define and quickly review each of the components.

A Buck or a Million? Demystifying Base Salary

It's no secret that there has been a big, bright spotlight shining on executive pay since the Enron and Tyco scandals. And it's fair to say that disgustingly large paychecks have fallen so out of favor with shareholders and the general public that CEOs themselves are reining in their own salaries. Just consider Viacom's Sumner Redstone, who cut his base salary from $1.75 million to $1 million and made his bonus performance related in order to garner shareholder acceptance and tie his performance with that of the company.[1]

Of course, Redstone wasn't the only executive to find his name in newsprint because of interesting base salary practices. News Corporation's Rupert Murdoch found his name in print when it was determined that he won the award for the executive with the highest base salary in 2006—$8.1 million.[2] Incidentally, when you do the math this translates into an extra $70,000 per week for Mr. Murdoch compared to his salary in 2005. That's one heck of a raise!

Yahoo CEO Terry Semel got just as much time in the press but for other reasons. Semel took a $599,000 pay cut—his base salary went from $600,000 in 2005 to $1 in 2006.[3] Google's CEO Eric Schmidt also takes home a buck a year. But don't feel *too* sorry for Semel. Sure, his base salary may weigh in significantly lighter than those of his peers. But he'll make up for it in the millions of stock options he negotiated in the hopes of adding to his already hefty $429 million stock option windfall. We would take Semel's buck a year any day, and so would you—if, in addition, we received his total reward package!

The dollar a year guys aside, there's nothing base about base salary any more. Base salaries for most executives run in the $500,000–$1,000,000 per year range. And the only reason they top off at $1 million is that any salary that exceeds $1 million is considered to be non–performance based and is not deductible under sections 162m of the Internal Revenue Code.

It's interesting to note that many of the organizations that we work with have given up on the message-carrying capacity of the base salary portion of the total reward plan. And we think this is a serious mistake. Why? Well, the vast majority of CEOs running large organizations have, throughout the time they have built their careers, been on the receiving end of annual performance reviews. These reviews often drive their annual merit increase. When an individual becomes a senior executive the worst message you can send them is that annual performance reviews are no longer important or valid. Because this just makes your executive feel like he's "above the law."

The annual performance review provides an invaluable opportunity for an organization to enhance an executive's understanding of the organization's fundamental value system. An annual performance review is where behavioral traits like integrity, teamwork, management of subordinates, and playing well with others are emphasized and reinforced. What happens if you send the message that base salary and annual performance appraisals aren't important? The executive will likely deliver that same message to their subordinates. And when that happens the company is at risk of being associated with failure of integrity—and earning some celebrity status for all the wrong reasons.

Getting Creative: Short-Term Incentives

Short-term incentives—incentives that speak for any period less than or equal to one year of performance—can be tremendously powerful when it comes to motivating executives, especially in cases where base salary has lost its meaning and long-term incentives seem just too, well, *long*. Both executives and designers love working with short-term incentives because you can get pretty creative with their structure. They can be a function of individual performance, business unit performance, or organizational performance. Another much-appreciated benefit? There aren't a whole lot of federal rules and regs to follow when it comes to short-term incentives.

Of course, with freedom comes misuse. And ignorance too. Yes, short-term incentives can be powerful, but creating a total reward strategy that obsessively focuses on quarterly returns, for example, creates greedy executives who are looking out for themselves today and not for the company tomorrow.

But if short-term incentives are properly used they can pack quite a punch. Consider Goldman Sachs, which paid out $16.5 billion to their employees in 2006. That's crazy, right? Not really, considering that when you average things out, each employee brought in $550,000 in pre-tax profit after paying themselves and their expenses. Angry shareholders? Doubtful. One of the keys to Goldman Sachs's success is their bonus structure, which works so well because it mimics free-market capitalism. Great employees are paid enough so that they don't jump ship at the first good offer to come down the pike, while freeloaders take home next to nothing. Goldman Sachs's strategy is structured so that compensation is cut in bad years—ensuring that profit margins aren't hurt and layoffs aren't necessary.

Goldman Sachs obviously has it all figured out. But what are some common mistakes that organizations make when using short-term incentives in their total executive reward strategies? Well, in many cases the time frames used in short-term incentives are at odds with the organizational or business strategy requirements. For example, if a turnaround situation existed where the executive should be making progress on a three-month or six-month basis, it makes no sense to apply a one-year timeframe for the annual incentive. As a matter of fact, in our experience there are many instances in which a shorter timeframe will deliver a much more appropriate message to the executive and his team.

Five Years Isn't Such a Long Time: Mid-Term and Special Incentives

What do you want your organization to accomplish in the next three to five years? Whatever your goals, mid-term incentives are designed to get you there. It's interesting to note that many in the compensation community file these under the definition of long-term incentives. Wrong! If you are hoping your organization will have some longevity, then five years isn't really all that long, is it?

In our opinion, mid-term incentives are absolutely integral for any company that needs to focus on increasing organization effectiveness or business plan execution over a three- to five-year period. It always surprises us to see how much more effective an organization can become when a new competitor enters its environment and it becomes increasingly sensitive to the operating effectiveness of its own organization. Well, mid-term incentives are positioned to increase operating effectiveness. The fact is that senior executives often take their eye off the ball when it comes to this mid-term business period. Quarterly performance? They're on it. Long-term performance? Good to go. Mid-term performance? It often falls by the wayside as executives become increasingly focused on—and sometimes obsessed with—short-term and long-term performance.

Unfortunately, this type of thinking causes organizations to become inefficient—and eventually non–competitive—in a dizzyingly short period of time. When an organization becomes ineffective in its intermediate time period it is no longer able to effect significant strategic changes in direction. And so the long-term strategic plan is doomed as well.

While mid-term incentives are critically important for any organization that suffers from a lack of ability to execute on a strategic plan, special incentives are a great addition to any total executive reward strategy when non-recurring opportunities are present or non–recurring problems need to be dealt with. Project-based incentives, challenge grants, milestone incentives, success fee incentives, development or royalty incentives, and turnaround incentives can all be leveraged and used to meet non–ongoing business goals.

What's All the Fuss About? Long-Term Incentives

Long-term incentives fall within the 5- to 10-year range, and when it comes to reward strategy components, should be considered the main horse an organization rides in the quest to communicate its business strategy to senior executives. By way of size, long-term incentives are the most important portion of an executive compensation program.

They are also the most likely incentives to draw key stakeholder and shareholder attention. Just consider that most of the corporate scandals you read about while eating your Wheaties involve—you guessed it—abused long-term incentives. The stock option scandal trend, for example, is a good example of long-term incentives gone badly. As the general public has waged war on stock-options and outlandish pay packages, long-term incentives are the area becoming most scrutinized—and governed—when it comes to total reward strategy components. The SEC's new disclosure rules, as well as the general desire to stay out of the spotlight, has organizations thinking about how their long-term incentives are structured, whether they serve investors and stakeholders, and whether there's room for abuse. Of course pay packages are still outlandish, it's just now they are outlandish in a different way. Executives may not be getting rich through backdated stock options, but believe us, they are figuring out other ways to get rich!

All that being said, long-term incentives—when used thoughtfully—are the foundation of any total executive reward program. It's safe to say that any major strategic imperative—whether it's a continuation of the present business strategy or model, a significant change in strategic initiatives, or a change in any component of the value chain strategy within the industry—should always be the subject of debate and discussion with regard to the most appropriate long-term incentives. But wait a second! While it's possible in most industries to predict competitive and environmental changes over a period of three years—making mid-term incentives more goal-oriented in nature—that's not the case when one evaluates periods of time associated with incentives associated with a 5- to 10-year timeframe.

Imagine attempting to predict what an organization's operating characteristics would be like 10 years from the present time. Are you Miss Cleo or a member of the psychic friends network? Only the most insightful—or psychic—individuals could be expected to make predictions—and to understand the implications for their own organization—over such a long period of time. And this is where a real conflict of circumstances occurs. When we talk about incentive programs we often use terms like look forward, look backward, and look around. Well, we just said it would be difficult or nearly impossible to develop goals and objectives that would be worthy of incentivizing an executive management team over a period of 10 years on the look forward basis. We're also not quite sure that incentives would be appropriate in a look back or look around basis either.

Why? Well, a look back basis of developing incentive goals merely encourages an incremental improvement over some period in a prior year. At first sight this might seem like a good plan. After all, every period will represent an improvement. But as comforting as this idea is, try comparing it to driving a car while keeping your eyes glued to the rear view mirror. Not too smart, right? Similarly, a look back strategy can mean extreme danger to the organization ahead.

We do believe that there is some value that can be directly attributed to the look around approach for developing long-term incentive plans for executives. And the economic theory is really quite simple. The organization is managing an asset for the shareholder. So it needs to provide—over a long period of time—the return that is consistent with the other opportunities shareholders have for deploying their wealth, commensurate with the risk that is consistent with the organization's mission and business strategy. Many organizations we've worked with have created innovative look around long-term incentive programs for executives, and on the whole we're in favor of them. Certainly, over a 5- to 10-year period executives should be required to provide a return equal to or greater than their risk category. And if they don't? If their long-term rewards incentives are structured appropriately they will be penalized. And in our opinion, any executive who isn't meeting this goal should be asked to hit the road.

FIGURE 8.2 Portfolio approach.

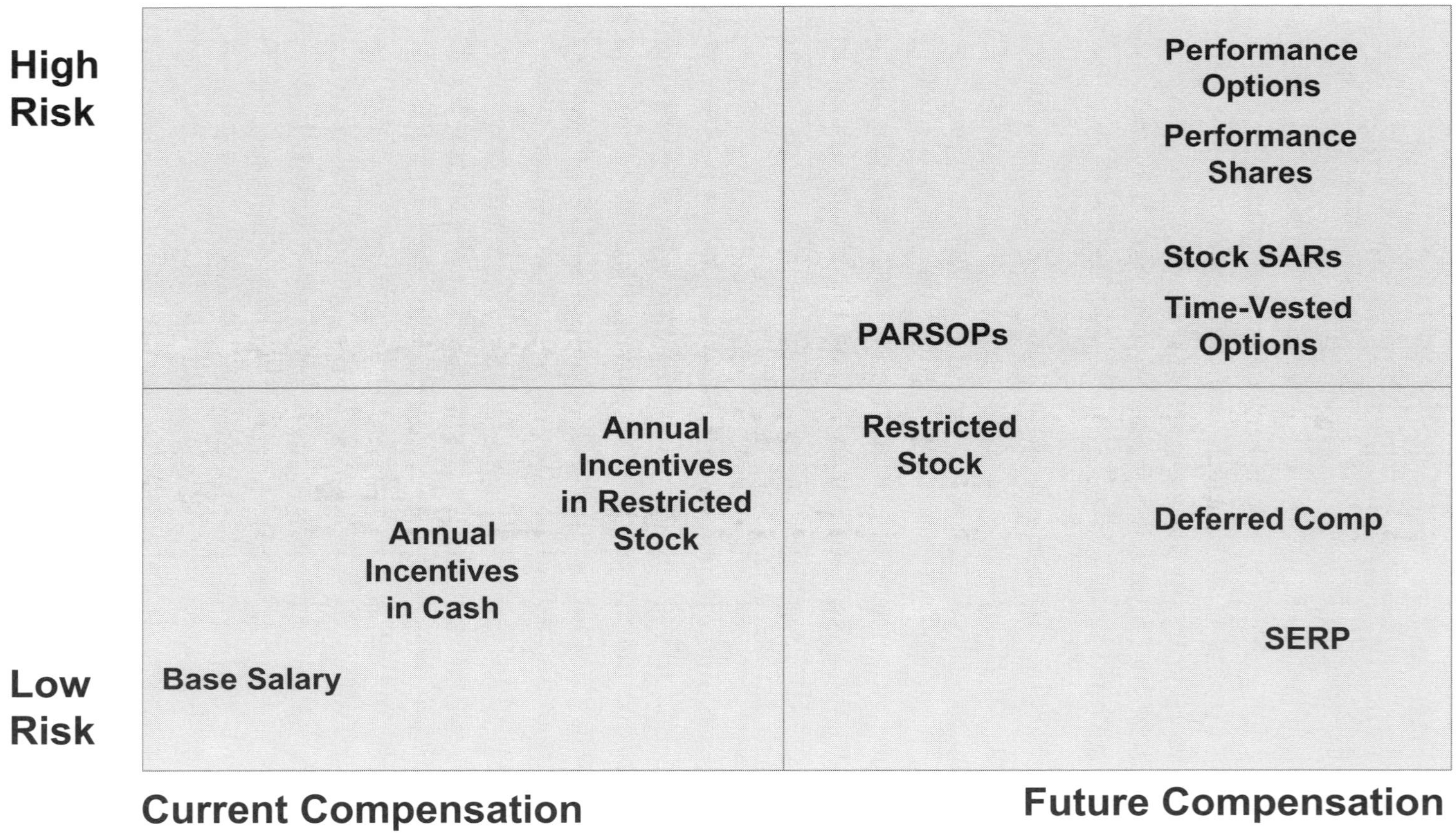

High Risk

Performance Options
Performance Shares

Stock SARs
Time-Vested Options

Deferred Comp

SERP

PARSOPs

Restricted Stock

Annual Incentives in Restricted Stock

Annual Incentives in Cash

Base Salary

Low Risk

Current Compensation

Future Compensation

How Much Is Too Much? Wealth Accumulation Incentives

The reward component we call wealth accumulation is a fairly new one for both executives and designers, and it's an important one. Used correctly, these plans are highly motivating and retentive. Used incorrectly, and we all start asking ourselves, "How much is too much?"

It's our belief that far too much of an executive's wealth accumulation in the form of Supplemental Executive Retirement Plans—fondly known as SERPs—is not performance-based. In our opinion, that's outrageous. Often an executive will work for a company for a period of, let's say, 10 years, and will walk away with a SERP that is roughly equivalent to 60 percent of their annual total cash compensation. In most cases, these SERPs are paid for a minimum of 10 years. Simple math here folks? This means the executive's cash compensation has been doubled for the 10-year period he worked for the company. Many people feel the abuse of long-term equity plans was the outrage of the 1990s. But we believe the real outrage has been the level of executive retirement plans provided by many of the large organizations.

So what's the answer? We've come up with something called a grahall Performance-Based Wealth Accumulation and Retention Program—or gPB-WARP. This plan consists of a relative measure of performance sustained on a long-term basis, which creates a deferral in the form of a defined contribution amount for the executive. This plan calls for long-term career vesting, with severe penalties for voluntary termination. We believe—strongly—that executives should accumulate wealth in direct proportion to the above-average wealth created for the shareholders by their efforts. What's the end result? Well, a CEO who wants to enjoy his golden years is going to realize that his success is directly tied to the success of his company. A good gPB-WARP is very motivating, and encourages good executives to stick around too.

These new gPB-WARPs are the kind of programs that should be developed for a significant number of the executives at the strategic apex of an organization. Performance should always be defined as above the norm of any peer group of similar organizations or similar investments available to shareholders. In addition, the wealth accumulated for the executive should be directly proportional, in percentile, to the wealth accumulated for shareholders. The vested portion of the executive's retirement plan should be consistent with his career contribution. In other words, no quick hits! We've seen our share of short-term miracles created, only to completely implode shortly after the miracle maker leaves his position with the company.

You heard it here first: gPB-WARPs represent the most significant breakthrough in recent times with regard to the opportunity to rationalize and rethink the concept of total executive reward strategies.

Gilding the Lily: Executive Benefits

First of all, let's define executive benefits. We want to make sure you understand that when we are talking about executive benefits we are not talking about perquisites—country club memberships, use of the company jet, redecorating the South of France villa, and other fun things. When we talk about executive benefits we are talking about those benefits provided to *all* employees that are, through congress's ill-conceived and poorly executed social engineering, capped in some statutory way. Executive benefits are those plans that restore the benefit above the "qualified" limits. We break this category into subcategories of income protection, income replacement, savings and retirement income, and holidays and vacation. While the executive benefits component is not generally performance-based, it is an important way to attract and retain top-notch executives.

Let's talk about income protection plans first. An income protection plan might be, for example, a life insurance plan.

While rank-and-file employees might be entitled to a certain amount, a life insurance plan turns into an executive benefit when executives are provided a higher amount. Here's an amusing (to some) story that shows how this works. You may remember reading about Kerry B. Skeen, CEO of bankrupt Independence Air. In March of 2005, a few months before the company filed for bankruptcy, Skeen renegotiated his pay package. He took a 15 percent pay cut, and asked for control over his life insurance policy, in which his deferred compensation had been invested. In effect he swapped an unsecured claim with one he owned outright—and saved himself more than $3 million. Pretty tricky, eh?[4]

When it comes to providing executives with supplemental medical or dental plans above and beyond those of the rank-and-file employee, you would have a hard time convincing us that this makes sense. We know companies do it all the time, but (a) anyone who is bringing in $500,000 or more per year can afford to get his teeth cleaned; and (b) shareholders and investors, many of whom *don't* take home an executive's salary, are in effect paying for some rich guy's teeth cleaning. Talk about gilding the lily!

How about income replacement? Income replacement plans comprise the categories of short-term disability, long-term disability, or worker's compensation disability. In this case, we do think the executive should receive more protection than rank-and-file employees. We're always shocked when we find out that a senior executive at a large organization is covered by their company's disability program at the same level as other employees. Most plans allow for 60 percent replacement capped at a certain amount, often $3,000. Since executives are paid significantly more, we think it's totally appropriate to develop an income replacement plan that allows them 60 percent of total cash compensation—at the very least 60 percent of base salary.

The savings and retirement component of executive benefits is where things can get a little juicy. Most executives are limited to saving just $20,000 per year under their organization's 401k plan. In addition to this limit on the organization's savings plan, the executives are limited by the amount of income they can receive from their organization's qualified retirement plan. These socially acceptable limits were set by a Congress eager to reduce discrimination and to provide only certain benefits for qualified plans. So is there some logic to developing supplemental executive retirement plans? Sure. But we find very little logic for developing supplemental savings or retirement plans that are dramatically in excess of those plans developed for all employees.

Consider organizations where a recent trend is to curtail or freeze their pension plans. Boeing, Xerox, Electronic Data Systems, Verizon, Unisys, Sears Holdings, and General Motors are all doing it.[5] For their rank-and-file employees that is. Their executives are still sitting pretty. Let's pick on General Motors for a second. General Motors used the excuse of "legacy costs" to explain recent slumps—and did away with pensions for 42,000 workers.[6] Executive pensions are safe. But here's the interesting fact. The account that holds pension plans for workers has an excess of $9 million, while the account that holds pension plans for executives has a liability of $1.4 million.[7] So what's this tell you?

When Judge Ramos colorfully ordered NYSE's Dick Grasso to return as much as $100 million in retirement money, that was his message that it is *not okay* for boards and investors to indiscriminately pour money into CEOs pockets in the form of supplemental retirement plans. His message got so much press that many organizations are taking a closer look at their pension practices. Pension plans that award executives obscene amounts of money but don't take care of the rank-and-file workers send the wrong message to executives, send the wrong message to employees, and are clearly wrong for shareholders.

Before we move on, let's touch on holiday and vacations. What we have to say may surprise you here, so pay attention.

We believe that executives deserve more vacation days than regular employees. Executives make sacrifices by spending time away from their families on weekends and evenings—so a little extra vacation time is a small price to pay.

The Icing on the Cake: Perquisites

With the new SEC disclosure rules stating that all perquisites in excess of $10,000 must be disclosed, our guess is that organizations are going to think a little harder before giving the stamp of approval on golf-club memberships, million-dollar parties, and booking the company jet for your German Shepherd.

Oh, you wouldn't believe what we've seen over the years when it comes to executive perquisite programs! The CEO of one of our clients, the credible, high-integrity Allegheny Corporation, once said, "If an executive wants a car, I hope we're paying him enough so that he will be able to afford to buy one." If other organizations took a similar approach to executive perquisites the abuses that are peppered all over the newspaper and television would diminish dramatically. Of course, we would all be a little less entertained, but we're willing to find other ways to amuse ourselves in the name of supporting hardworking shareholders and investors.

It's unfortunate that what we hear about are often the extreme examples of perk abuse, because executive perquisites are valuable when they are structured in a way that is designed to help the executive achieve better business results that make sense for all stakeholders. Unfortunately, many perk programs are status based and come to represent a category of rewards that tells the executive he is "special" and "different" from rank-and-file employees. Since we have yet to see any performance criteria associated with the development of an executive perquisites program, perquisites are clearly not a function of the executive's, or the company's, performance.

So how to handle perks? Well, we realize our recommendation may sound radical. We suggest you review and cancel a significant portion of your executive perquisite program. Ask yourself, "Is this perquisite helping the executive do better business, or is it just making him feel better in general?" If the perk is not helping the executive reach company goals, then it's quite simply not good business sense to keep it.

Executive Development—A Real Return on Investment

One of the most common mistakes is to forego a focus on executive development rewards. Many companies assume either (a) an executive has "arrived" and therefore doesn't need additional training or development; or (b) that they will manage the process on their own. In our opinion neither is true, and both are truly costly to an organization. Executive training, development, and mentoring are effective for many reasons, one of which is that it breaks the "cocoon of isolation" that builds up over time as an executive advances up the ladder of corporate success.

In addition to training, development, and mentoring, career pathing and succession planning are enormously valuable exercises for both the executive and the company. We'll spend some time in one of the upcoming chapters in an attempt to convince you folks that, dollar for dollar, these are well-spent investments.

We'll Leave You with Some Final Thoughts . . .

You now have a pretty good overview of the components that make up a total executive reward strategy. The next chapters will deal with each component in greater detail. Each of the components has many subcomponents in their design. The number of permutations and combinations that can be made from the components can at first seem a little mind-boggling! That being said, it is possible to send appropriate messages to an executive regarding performance, obligations, and business imperatives—and a good total executive rewards program is the conduit that gets that message across. It's up to the corporate executives, the board of directors, and the reward consultants to develop programs that are a reflection of the organization's current circumstances and future business requirements—and to be brave enough to cancel or redesign portions of the strategy that no longer cut it.

References

1. Fabrikant, Geraldine. "Redstone Takes a Cut in His Salary." *New York Times*, 26 September 2006.
2. McGeehan, Patrick. "His Salary Last Year? They're Still Counting!" *New York Times*, 13 August 2006.
3. "Yahoo CEO Negotiating Salary Cut for Options." *San Jose Mercury News*, 5 June 2006.
4. "Flyi's Skeen May Have Averted Pay Loss—CEO's Renegotiated Contract Makes $3.4 Million Harder for Creditors to Reach." *Washington Post*, 5 January 2006.
5. "Hidden Burden." *Wall Street Journal*, 26 June 2006.
6. Ibid.
7. Ibid.

CHAPTER 9

Base Salary

So where's all the information when it comes to base salary? It seems like you can pick up any book on executive rewards, and the subject of base salary is either conspicuously missing or given a scant paragraph or two. As a matter of fact, base salary is usually glossed over so that sexier components like long-term investments, perquisites, and retirement plans get more ink.

The fact is that most authors haven't paid all that much attention to the subject of executive base salary programs. And the reason is pretty simple. It's because they think *organizations and their executives* don't pay all that much attention to base salary. And for most organizations—as well as for their CEOs and other top executives—there may be quite a bit of truth to this. But there doesn't have to be and, in our opinion, there shouldn't be.

The typical CEO today makes between $500,000 and $1 million a year in base salary pay. That's not exactly chump change. Sure, it represents only a portion of the executive's total rewards plan. But think of it this way. For the sake of argument, let's say an executive with a total compensation of $6 million has a base salary of $1 million. Well, simple math tells us that this executive's base salary makes up one-sixth of his total compensation. How much are *you* currently earning this year? Now subtract one-sixth of that amount, and tell us how you feel. Unless you are disgustingly wealthy, the thought of subtracting one-sixth of your total compensation makes you feel uncomfortable. That's exactly what we're going after. It's not that we get satisfaction from making our readers uncomfortable—we just want you to understand that base salary is not as insignificant as it is sometimes portrayed.

Okay, we know what you are thinking. You are thinking that in previous chapters, in this very book, you read about executives with, like, $80 million compensation packages, of which a mere million was base salary. And sure, if you are lucky enough to be enjoying this type of windfall we can understand how losing a million or two wouldn't be any big deal. But you need to keep in mind that executives earning this type of money are examples of people earning *excessive* compensation—and are not the norm. We know that can be hard to swallow, considering the press is glutted with stories of over-paid executives. And yes, it's hard to tune into CNN for your daily Anderson Cooper fix without being rudely interrupted by outrage over one excessively paid CEO or another. But you should know by now that these are the stories that sell papers and news spots. And quite honestly, when it comes right down to it that's a bigger priority for a journalist than, say, reporting the news. We just don't live in a world where we'll ever hear these words out of Larry King's mouth: "Next up we'll meet John Smith, who will share his experiences about being a fairly compensated executive." That'll never happen.

So all that being said, in order to discuss base salary with some degree of accuracy in this chapter, we are going to focus on fairly paid CEOs and executives, with a sprinkling of renegades thrown in here and there when we need to make a point.

Garbled Messages

Here's the main problem—and yes, it's a big problem—when it comes to how most organizations pay their chief executives: their systems are not pay-for-performance oriented.

It's that simple. In most total reward strategies, a CEO's base salary is not structured to reflect how well they perform in their various responsibilities. As a matter of fact, when it comes to base salary most companies take the easy way out.

FIGURE 9.1   Salaries—no leverage; no news.

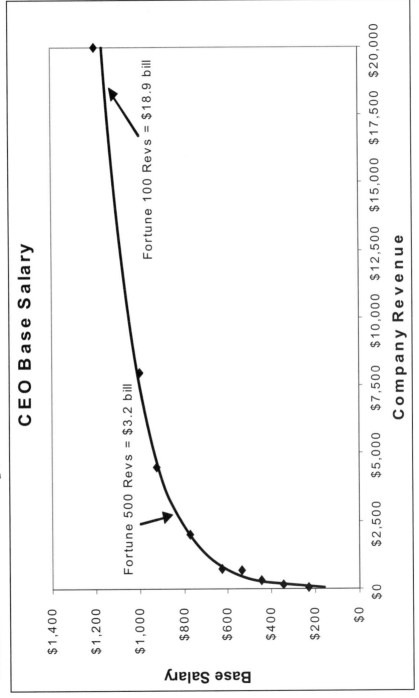

CEO Base Salary

Fortune 100 Revs = $18.9 bill

Fortune 500 Revs = $3.2 bill

Company Revenue

Base Salary

They look at the average market "going rate" for a CEO, then pay their executives at or just above the 75th percentile and call it good. This practice is generally agreed-upon and practiced industry wide—and it's extremely inadequate.

Why is this system inadequate? Well, it doesn't exactly motivate people to strive for excellence in the workplace. They *know* they are going to get paid their base salary, regardless of whether or not they perform well. And as we said before, base salary these days isn't exactly, well, *base*. We're talking upward of half a million of guaranteed pay for most executives. It's actually a pretty good gig when you think about it. Most executives can rest easy knowing that they aren't exactly going to starve—even if when all is said and done they just don't have the chops.

No wonder most people are under the impression that base salary is of little or no concern for these executives. Because executives know they are guaranteed a set amount, they have no need to be all that concerned with this aspect of their compensation plan. The entire system is built around blending in with the average market, rather than driving its company to success.

We find this lack of insight when it comes to base salary and its importance to the total executive reward strategy—in a word—appalling.

It's possible that base salary is paid so little attention because it is perceived that, compared to other components within the total reward strategy, it has a limited "message carrying capacity." Wrong! In our opinion, this way of thinking shows a real lack of sophistication for both the client and the consultant.

Every reward component has the ability to carry a message—and that goes for base salary too. If you don't see it that way—if you decide that base salaries are unimportant—then you are overlooking another opportunity to send your message.

So here's the deal. General Motors Corp., suffering from poor company and stock performance, cut CEO Rick Wagoner's base salary in 2005 from an excessive $2.2 million to $1 million.[1] This is more than a 50 percent cut! But here's where the message of such a cut becomes loud and clear. Wagoner's base salary cut was just about equal to the cut that GM shareholders took in their dividend level. So what's the message GM was trying to get across? If you don't perform, then you don't get paid. It's as simple—and as effective—as that.

Clearly, other stakeholders have figured out the importance of executive salaries. Too bad management still doesn't get it! But they will. And some are already. Take Imperial Sugar Company, for example. One of its major shareholders, New York's Schultze Asset Management, didn't like the way things were going. After all, Imperial Sugar reported a net loss of $19.3 million for its fiscal year ending September 30 2005, including a $13.9 million loss from discontinued operations. Not exactly a good showing, eh? So Schultze called on the company to freeze the compensation of CEO Robert Peiser and four other executives.[2] Their reason for the freeze? To more closely align executive compensation with the company's overall performance. When did the shareholder suggest the company lift the freeze? When Imperial Sugar Company's financial performance had consistently improved over multiple reporting periods. This is obviously a shareholder who understands that ignoring the component of base salary means a missed opportunity to send a strong message.

Imperial isn't the only organization whose stakeholders are starting to take a stand against inappropriate base salary compensation. Others are slowly but surely coming on board. Viacom, the giant media company that owns MTV and Paramount Pictures, had its chairman and controlling shareholder, Sumner M. Redstone, announce in the fall of 2006 that he would be restructuring his pay to more clearly align it with shareholder interest, and to base it on the company's financial performance.[3] The move came as Viacom has come under increasing pressure to reduce executive compensation—and restore investor confidence—in the face of poor stock performance. Viacom, which was ranked as one of the worst companies when it comes to overcompensation in a 2005 study done by Glass, Lewis & Company, lowered Sumner's base salary from $1.75 million to $1 million, eliminated deferred compensation, and linked his bonus to certain performance targets. Over time, we hope that more organizations will slowly get with the picture and make positive—and meaningful—changes to their base salary program. We don't exaggerate when we say the success of their individual companies depends upon it.

If You Can't Figure Out What You Paid Your CEO . . . It's Probably Too Much

Executive compensation should never be something that's hard for an organization to be accountable for, as in the case of the News Corporation's Chairman and CEO Rupert Murdoch. Remember Rupert Murdoch from the last chapter? If you don't recall, he's the guy that won the golden pig for the highest base salary in 2006—$8.1 million, to be exact. What we didn't tell you—and we're not kidding—was that Mr. Murdoch's total compensation was so complex that the company wouldn't divulge it.[4] Not because they didn't want to—although it was a little embarrassing—but because they actually weren't able to. It took, oh, about a month or so and a small city's worth of number crunchers to figure out where Mr. Murdoch finally weighed in on the pay scale.

Okay, no compensation plan should be quite *that* complex. But now that we've had our fun with News Corporation, let's shift the blame a little bit. To give credit where credit is due, some of these inflated, out-of-control, complex pay plans are simply a story of good intentions gone badly. Which brings us to Congress, the other bad guy in this story—a bad guy, incidentally, that the press just loves to ignore. When Congress gets into the process of legislating the free market system, things can quickly go from good to bad.

And Now, a Lovely Exhibit From the Museum of Good Intentions Gone Horribly Wrong

Executive greed is an easier story to sell, we suppose. But the same members of Congress who most deplore big CEO pay-days—yep, the very same members—are the same ones who created the incentive for companies to overuse options as compensation.

The story goes something like this. In 1993, amid more public hand-wringing and teeth gnashing due to—what?—envy?—over CEO pay, Congress capped the tax deductibility of base salaries at $1 million.

Good move right? Not really. Guess what happened? CEO salaries suddenly started weighing in at just about $1 million. Imagine that. You probably aren't surprised to hear that, and no one at the time was surprised either. But because companies still need to hire and retain the best, they have found other innovative, unique, and tricky ways to ensure their executives are adequately compensated. What are we talking about here? You know it! Stock options!

What happens when you shower executives with stock options? We're all too familiar. Stock options give executives a pretty good reason to capitalize all company profits back into the stock price. And so they contribute to their own pay, rather than paying out dividends to shareholders. Stock options tempt people to make the wrong decisions. So while Congress was trying to do the right thing when it capped base salaries, it ended up creating a much bigger problem. Sure, obscenely large base salaries are annoying to the general public, rarely serve the best interests of shareholders, and are in most cases a poor way to compensate executives. But they haven't ruined lives and companies like many of the stock options scandals did.

What would happen if we went back to the olden days—you know, those days in which Congress did the M.Y.O.B. thing and organizations were free to make their own decisions regarding base salary? For one thing, you can bet companies wouldn't rely on options to motivate executives. And the practice of backdating would become a thing of the past. We don't doubt that Congress laid down this law with good intentions. But they made a mistake, and now is as good a time as any to make good on it.

Size Matters

While we would love nothing more than to debunk the size matters myth in these pages (no doubt you would be getting your money's worth then), we can't. The fact is, when it comes to base salary, size really *does* matter.

Executive salaries are, in fact, generally a function of the size and complexity of the organization. For many years, executives have increased their compensation levels in lockstep with the size of the organization that they have managed. That's somewhat logical, and while in our opinion base salary levels should be more a function of the market value of the organization—rather than the revenue value of the organization—historically, executive salaries have been a function of revenues in general industry, assets in the financial services industry, or number of beds in the hospital industry and so forth. And so on and so on. You get the picture. Size matters, but there are different ways of measuring it.

The competitive level for executive salaries is generally thought to be a function of job-to-job comparisons within the marketplace, in addition to comparisons within the organization. The vast majority of companies assume—incorrectly—that the market for executive salaries within their organization is a singular group of competitive peer companies. This just isn't true.

But if you've made this mistake, don't feel too bad. This is the fundamental and foundational mistake that most executive reward strategy designers make. The mistake lies in the fact that every executive position within an organization may have a substantially different competitive market group of peer companies. So the initial decision—who or what organizations the comparison group will contain for each executive position—is made incorrectly. The CEO position, for example, can come from nearly anywhere. Need an example? Here's one: the new CEO of Ford comes from the airline industry. The "line" senior executives have a higher chance of being industry-specific, while the staff senior positions can come from a pretty wide range of industries. Research and development executive positions are more industry-specific than finance positions, for example. It's true that most organizations want people with experience in their industry and in companies of similar size. But it's also true that executives strive to attain positions in increasingly complex organizations. Sure, it's a disconnect. But that's business for you, right?

We're All in This Together . . . But Should We Be?

There's a second competitive issue, and that's the level of competitiveness within the marketplace.

Most of our clients, when we meet initially, insist that the competitive strategy for base salary be consistently applied throughout the executive ranks. Here's an example. Let's say an organization has chosen to place the competitive salaries at the 75th percentile. In a situation where base salary is consistently applied throughout the ranks, *all* executive positions will subsequently be slotted at the 75th percentile.

INVESTOR ALERT #14
HIGH EXECUTIVE SALARIES

When executives or CEOs have salaries that are high relative to their direct competitor's salaries, an investor should be a little bit concerned about the executive's view of their ability to perform. In most cases, a higher than normal base salary is a clear indication of an executive seeking more security in their overall reward program because they don't trust the organization's capacity to compete.

The exception to this is within the last few years of an executive's career, when salaries are sometimes increased artificially in order to give an executive a slightly larger retirement income.

If the executives have high salaries, you can bet that the managers and other significant portions of the workforce will have disproportionately high salaries too. Sometimes this can be sustained for long periods of time if the company has a substantial competitive advantage. However, generally speaking salaries that are substantially above the market going rate should be an indication for the investor to get going.

Remember the phrase, "High salaries, low expectations!"

What could the thought process possibly be for such a gross waste of organizational resources? "We are a team!" is the cry, which usually comes from the head of human resources. But while "go team, go" is a nice idea in theory, and certainly evokes warm and fuzzy feelings, it's an impractical compensation strategy.

Back in Chapter Three we discussed business strategies. We know it was a while ago, but take a trip down Memory Lane to the value chain strategy we discussed in that chapter. Remember value chain strategy? It's a way of thinking about strategy that says, in a nutshell, that executives who hold positions in areas that are critically important to the success of the organization should be compensated accordingly.

How will you know who those executives are? You'll have all the information you need from the analyses of the business strategy and organizational capabilities. Those analyses will provide information on your people strategy, which will indicate which jobs were critically important to an organization, as well as which jobs are less important. In other words, if it's determined that customer service makes your organization what it is, the executive that heads up the customer service area should be compensated more on a relative to market basis than, say, the executive that heads up the organization's information technology department.

Once you've defined the critically important jobs, they should be positioned in the upper percentiles of the most stringently applied competitive market. Those jobs that are progressively less important should be paid at levels that are competitive with a more general market—in most cases no higher than the 50th percentile, and in some cases substantially lower in base salary.

And we'll even go one step further. It may be appropriate—and a good strategy—for certain job families which are not critical to the delivery of the organization's products or services to be priced at the general industry markets, at the 25th percentile of base salary with a range maximum of no more than the 50th percentile. Remember—in the administration of executive salaries there is a significant range around the midpoint of the salary structure for each position. Which means that executives who perform well can be priced at a premium even if their midpoint salary rate is targeted at the 25th percentile of general industry.

This surgical strategy application to executive salaries is the first indicator that an organization truly understands the value of each position's capacity—and the executives in those positions—to contribute to the organization. It's also a major indicator that the executive team is surgical in all its allocation of assets processes. This type of strategy creates and maintains an organization's competitive advantage. Executive salaries are at the top of a hierarchy that cascades down throughout the whole company—and send the message that some job families are more important than others to the long-term success of the organization. So the "go team go" approach is all very well-intentioned, but can be filed under the category of "good intentions gone bad." We don't exaggerate when we say that billions of dollars are wasted annually by companies who apply an "even spread of the peanut butter" approach to their compensation strategy, instead of a more strategic approach.

INVESTOR ALERT #15

HIGH CEO SALARY

If a CEO's base salary is above average for his peer group, above $1 million, or both, then we would be very concerned as an investor. We see no good logic to have the CEO's salary above the 50th percentile for the competitor group. There is even less logic to have the CEO's salary above $1 million, which is the deductible salary cap for non–performance-based compensation.

There's a certain discipline about keeping your expenses in line with your fixed compensation. If a CEO can't live reasonably on his fixed compensation, or if he is so unsure of his variable compensation he needs to have an unusually high base salary, you might prefer to invest in someone with a little more budget discipline and a lot more confidence in his—and his company's—future.

Speaking of Competitive Advantage: What the Oakland A's Could Teach Corporate America

If baseball teams can understand how base salary and value chain strategy are linked, why is it sometimes so hard for corporate America?

We're talking about the Oakland A's. What happened was this. In 2005 the Oakland A's and executive on-field manager Ken Macha had a bit of a disagreement when it came to Macha's salary. The A's offered just under a million. Macha wanted $1.4 million.[5]

No doubt Macha was a great performer. He had turned the ball club around and they wanted to keep him. But in order to stay in the game they also had to put their modest budget where it counted most—on securing new ballplayers. So the A's wished Macha good luck and they parted ways.

How often do a company and its CEO part ways over pay? Not often. As much as the A's loved Macha they knew they could find someone else to do the job. If the ball club gave in and paid Macha the additional $400,000, that was $400,000 less they would be able to spend on a player.

In the end Macha capitulated and signed the deal. After all, he had a pretty good gig when all was said and done. The team ended up winning its division. No doubt the team's hard-headed approach regarding base salary had something to do with that. Don't you think corporate America could learn a little something from this story?

I Don't Care What You Call Me—Just Show Me the Money

Job titles are an aspect of base salary administration that you can't ignore. The fact that our feelings about job titles are somewhat out of the norm shouldn't surprise you if you've been with us the whole ride. Our philosophy when it comes to job titles can be boiled down to this: the fewer the better.

Okay, to illustrate our point here's a story. A new commander of the Marine training camp on Lejeune Island in South Carolina was dismayed to walk into one of the lowest morale situations he had seen his entire career. The junior officers were in the habit—because that's what their past commander did—of carrying a "swagger stick" (that's a riding crop to you and me) as a sign of authority. So the new commander sent out his first official communication: "If you need a swagger stick, carry one." The next day, not a single swagger stick could be found on the island! The moral of the story? Titles are like swagger sticks; they aren't necessary to gain authority.

When clients come to us for advice on titles, we tell them to put their efforts into something else. Titles are like the "third rail" of organizations. If you attempt to rehabilitate them you'll more often than not end up "electrocuted." And the organization will continue to roll on down the tracks—and over your once-promising career—without a moment's notice or remorse. That being said, in some organizations job titles are awarded in lieu of compensation. We've all seen it. And what do we have to say about this? Anyone willing to accept a title over base salary probably deserves the deal. On the other hand, any company that places more importance on titles than base salary deserves the type of executives who find this practice acceptable.

Did You Hear Something? Why Merit Increases Turn Down the Base Pay Volume

Salary structures are the main component of compensation administration that links the results of benchmarking and pricing to the pay delivery system. A salary structure basically guides the organization's base salary system, and has unique characteristics when it comes to salary range width and pay progression. The pay delivery system is an infrastructure for defining and valuing pay movement, performance level, promotional or normal increase pay actions, and a linkage to the assessment/employee development system.

Here's the problem: if the incorrect use of executive salary competitive analysis weren't enough, most organizations compound the problem by misusing the annual or biannual increment approach. The general state of affairs is that most executives receive an increase on an annual basis. That increase reflects the average increase in the marketplace, plus or minus a relatively small amount. Well, jeez! Is it any wonder that executives spend little time thinking about their base salary? Why should they, when little differentiation exists between extremely high performers and the average performer within the organization?

Let's say the average merit pay increase is 5 percent in the industry. If the executive performs extremely well and is with an organization that has an aggressive merit program, he might receive as much as a 10 percent increase.

So here's the problem. While the increase may seem like a high figure to you and me, the fact is the difference between the increase for the average performer and the exceptional performer is relatively small. The exceptional performer will quickly learn to pay more attention to the messages sent through the other reward components, like short- and long-term incentive plans, and will ignore any messages sent through the base salary.

By the way, this will have a nice—or rather not-so-nice—little trickle down effect throughout the rest of the organization with exactly the same result. A salary administration program that uses "merit" increases like this castrates (ouch!) the expenditures on salaries with respect to motivation, and sets a poor foundation for the other portions of the reward program.

Revenge of the Promotion Seekers

When merit increases are ineffective, executives quickly learn that one way to make more money is to seek a promotion. Promotional increases are typically rewarded at the time the executive goes from one position to a position of greater importance.

Makes sense in theory, but in practice appropriate promotional increases are few and far between. They are either too small or too large, and both come with their own set of issues.

Too small and the executive lands in a lower part of the new salary range than is appropriate—becomes fresh meat for hungry head hunters. Too large and it's disproportional to the merit increase, which sends the message that the executive's main focus should not be on the job at-hand, but on frequent promotion. Another issue with excessive promotional increases is that it makes it difficult for the executive to leave—even when it's time. Why? Because comparable jobs at comparable companies pay less. So who *wouldn't* want to hang on as long as possible?

One client we worked with actually studied the difference between the salary levels of a number of executives over their careers. What did they find? They found that the biggest difference in salary levels was due to the frequency of promotions, and not to the level of performance within a certain position. Will executives at such a company be concerned with performing well on a particular assignment? Not particularly, especially if the difference in salary increase between high performers and low performers is infinitesimal. But you can bet they'll be focusing much of their energy on getting their next promotion. And that's the equivalent of managing upward, when if fact, they should be managing downward (those people whom they are responsible for).

What's Fair Is Fair: Equity Increases

When it all comes down to it, sometimes it seems like people don't put a whole lot of thought into base salaries. How else to explain why the compensation of executives being promoted is viewed substantially—sometimes solely—in light of their own historical situation?

Here's a better idea. Organizations would fare much better if they reviewed, on an annual basis, the compensation of all executives who resided in horizontal bands of similar responsibility. If an individual executive's base salary is too low or too high given his contribution, responsibility, and potential compared to other executives at his same band, his salary should be adjusted by whatever amount was required both upward and downward. It is, in fact, internal inequity that is responsible for a substantial percentage of executive turnover we see at organizations today.

Another type of equity increase is the market equity increase. What are these? Well, they are a function of a mismatch between the executive's annual salary, which results from the more traditional portions of the base salary administration program, and the actual market that exists for the executive's talents at any one point in time. Like any supply and demand situation, certain job families, industries, or situations may require that a larger portion of the organizations in a particular market segment may need more executives than the qualified executives that exist. What's this mean? Simply a supply and demand problem. Unless you are in the mood to deal with a deficit in a critical job category, you are going to have to throw down some extra money. We recommend the use of market equity increases as a process for eliminating the gaps in retaining critical employees. And again, it isn't written in stone (like the Ten Commandments) that an executive's base salary can never go down. Just think about it!

So What if It's Not Sexy

Let's face it. When it comes to determining an executive's salary, performance focus is very rarely the focus of most management teams we work with. And okay, we agree, the development of performance factors for say, short-term and long-term incentive plans are much more sexy and interesting. But so what?

Here's the deal. The better organizations actively develop performance management programs associated with the distribution of base salary increases. This is an area of rich and untapped messages that can be sent to executives. In fact, it is through the base pay program that executives should learn to deliver performance within the greater context of the organization's value system. Why miss out on such a great opportunity?

Some organizations stress the word "competency" in base salary administration. Others emphasize the words "individual performance." And still others put the focus on various combinations of performance factors. It is clear to us that the base salary administration program should be the location for those threshold operating norms that an executive needs to exhibit consistently in order to remain an executive at the organization. The base salary administration program should emphasize factors such as teamwork, integrity, stewardship, and other critical behavioral norms. And performance should be a factor in determining the executive's pay after these special conditions are met.

Why Base Salary Died on the Vine

The average CEO base salary ranges from $500,000 to $1 million. That's a lot of money, right? It's really a shame that most of the companies we work with aren't spending the kind of time or effort they should in order to benefit from the big base salaries they are paying their executives. Why aren't they getting more bang for their buck?

In our opinion, one of the reasons for this is that base salary administration was handed over to our friends in the human resource department. Remember those nice folks who espouse that nice sentiment, "equity within the organization?" Once they got base salary administration in their hands they built a bureaucracy around it. It could have become a significantly motivational portion of the executive reward program—it really could have! Instead, it more or less died on the vine with respect to its role within the overall executive reward strategy.

No worries though. In most organizations there is significant opportunity to revitalize the delivery of executive base salary dollars. The formula is pretty simple. Set the appropriate competitive level against a well-chosen marketplace, then deliver pay increments on a frequent enough basis to be meaningful, and in a dramatically differentiating amount to be motivational. We advocate increases that go from minus 10 percent to 30 percent per year. That's right—that's a 60 percent differential, which is a full four times more than the differentials of the vast majority of our clients, which usually weigh in between 0 percent and 10 percent. Let the headhunters pull the lowest performing executives—so what?—while the highest performing executives are secured with high-percentage increases and high-percentile base pay programs.

Sounds radical? That's not surprising, considering the level to which base salaries have sunk. Sometimes we feel like breaking out the paddles and shocking base salary administration back to life. The bad news is that base salary programs are, for the most part, in a sorry state. The good news? It won't take much to turn them around. If you are wondering if it's worth the time and effort, consider this: the base salary program is, in effect, the foundation for an organization's overall reward strategy. So if you want average executives, pay them average base salaries based on the market's best practices. And don't be surprised when your organization is, well, *average*. If, on the other hand, you want outstanding executives—executives who perform—well then, pay them in a way that motivates them to perform. Start with base salary. It's that simple.

References

1. "GM's Wagoner Pulls in Bulging Salary Gut a Notch." *Bloomberg News*, 8 February 2006.

2. "Major Imperial Shareholder Calls For Freeze of Top Executives' Salaries." *FortBendNow*, 24 March 2006.

3. Fabrikant, Geraldine. "Redstone Takes A Cut in His Salary." *New York Times*, 6 September 2006. Available online at http://www. nytimes.com/2006/09/26/business/media/26viacom.html?_r=1& oref=slogin, accessed 25 September 2007.

4. McGeehan, Patrick. "His Salary Last Year? They're Still Counting." *New York Times*, 13 August 2006. Available online at http:// query.nytimes.com/gst/fullpage.html?res=9902E1DA163EF930A2 575BC0A9609C8B63, accessed 25 September 2007.

5. Leonhardt, David. "Why C.E.O's Aren't Sitting in the Dugout." *New York Times*, 4 October 2006. Available online at http://www. nytimes.com/2006/10/04/business/04leonhardt.html, accessed 25 September 2007.

CHAPTER 10

Short-Term Incentives

Short-term incentives are incentives that last no longer than a year and are typically paid in cash. Are they important? Absolutely! Short-term incentives can have a tremendous impact on a total executive reward strategy—that is, if they are designed correctly by someone who truly understands their function in the overall plan. Correctly used short-term incentives can create focus on short-term priorities, align rewards with business and individual performance, provide a competitive or differentiated pay package, align people costs with business results, and increase employee commitment. Those are no small tasks!

Companies—and executives—*loooooove* to use short-term incentives. What makes the use of short-term incentives so, well, *enticing*? In the last chapter we talked about the unfortunate fact that base salary has more or less lost its "oomph" as a motivator. And long-term incentives tend to take too long to provide that important, now-oriented turbo boost that most executives are looking for. Not to mention the fact that long-term incentives are often perceived as being fueled by events beyond executive control. So what component do boards and committees turn to? You got it.

As a matter of fact, a recent survey done by Towers and Perrin showed that short-term incentives are a vital—and important—component of overall pay packages. The study, which included 268 companies in the United States and Canada, showed that most companies advocated customized and thoughtful plans designed to link short-term incentives, variable incentives, and the performance of both individuals and the organization as a whole.[1]

The Slate and the Scalpel

Perhaps one of the most appealing aspects of short-term incentives is the variety of ways in which you can use them. They can be a function of the individual's performance, the team's performance, the business unit's performance, or an organization's overall performance. Because of our unimpeded ability to readily design and implement short-term incentive programs, they are, in fact, a favorite of most executives we work with. Short-term incentives allow the executive twin opportunities: they create a potentially clean slate to reward an executive, and a sharp scalpel to hone in on performance and reward surgically. You also don't need to be Einstein to implement them. There are no particular tax or accounting ramifications that need to be considered, there are no eligibility or maximum amount issues that are potentially bothersome, and as long as the factors meet the regulations of section 162m of the Internal Revenue Code, then the amounts associated with short-term incentives are fully deductible. The slate is almost immediately clean with no ugly complexities. And if the design is right, there is some traceable reward to be created for performance. A nice little scalpel.

We can divide short-term incentives into three major components:

1. Discretionary

Discretionary bonuses are unexpected rewards for past behavior. And here's how we feel about them. These rewards have little or no motivational impetus for the beneficiary and are somewhat arbitrarily conceived by the benefactor. We don't mean to imply that they have no place at all in potential bonus scenarios, because they do. It's just that they can't really be designed.

2. Pool

A pool percentage is premeditated and involves some type of percentage compensation based on the performance of a certain project. The benefit of this is that it is self-funding—much like a salesman's commission. Goal isn't met? Well then, the executive's bonus isn't as large as it could be. The disadvantage is that it does not target a successful individual, but disperses the percentage in a somewhat random way. In fact, the executive could be busting his hump and reasons beyond his control—an inherited unmotivated team, a stock market slump—could prevent the organization from meeting a goal. As you can well imagine, this dilutes its motivational power.

3. Target

Target incentives are very specifically measured, often using key performance indicators to indicate the challenges to be met. They require an understanding of the objectives of the company and the capacities and their potential to motivate specific individuals. This incentive could be combined with pool or discretionary incentives.

INVESTOR ALERT #16

THIS YEAR'S THRESHOLD FOR PAYMENT
IS BELOW LAST YEAR'S ACTUAL

If the short-term incentive plan, or any incentive plan for that matter, has a threshold that is well below the prior year's actual performance, then it's time to be concerned as an investor.

Two things could be happening if you see this particular occurrence. The management team could be attempting to set a low threshold for participation in the incentive plan payout. Or, the management team could not understand the mechanics of the plan, and may not have actually thought through the outcome. If either of these is the case, then it's time to think about where your investment money should go in the future.

For the designer, target incentives separate the wheat from the chaff, so to speak. In other words, the designer better have a lot of skill if he's hoping to pull off target incentives. One must really know the client company and its executives rather intimately to make these work effectively.

With this tremendous amount of freedom to design comes an immense opportunity for misuse. If the short-term incentive program is discretionary—and most are not—there isn't much for the designer to worry about. But if the program is non–discretionary, some key decisions must be made. The executives and designers of the short-term plan must take incredible care regarding those decisions because they could have an extraordinary impact on the company.

Okay, here's an example for you. Let's say a pharmaceutical company wants to make an investment and it's see-sawing between two decisions. It could acquire an interesting little company with a few top-caliber but underdeveloped products. Wouldn't that make an impressive splash in the business press! Or it could invest in a killer, long-term anti-cancer drug that has made an adroit performance in preliminary trials and could make them billions. An executive with stock performance on the brain just might make the decision to buy the little company. In the short term this might drive the organization's stock up a bit . . . just in time for his own bonus. But would this be a good long-term solution for the company? You've read enough of this book to now know the answer. So you tell us.

In fact, 2006 might be called the Year of the Bonus, if you wish to look at the November 2006 Executive Compensation Index, released by CareerJournal.com and the Economic Research Institute.[2] In a random sampling of 45 public companies, whose management featured some of American's super compensated executives, we find a dizzying, dazzling annual cash bonus increase of 48.2 percent with an increase of 31.21 percent more in total cash compensation. Even with a slight decrease in base pay, these lovely little bonuses accounted for an average total cash compensation of $4,795,096—31.21 percent more than 2005. The list of 45 companies was pulled from a total of 6,500 companies that reported on compensation to the SEC.

What does it all boil down to? The average annual cash bonus for the study's targeted executives in 2005 was a bouncy little $3,521,615. Last year was less—only $2,375,615.

Shareholder concern was evident when five Boston Scientific executives received special bonuses of at least $1.98 million as a result of the company acquiring Guidant.[3] The move raised the question of whether rewarding executives for acquisitions was premature and irresponsible—especially considering that mergers and acquisitions have a less than stellar record when it comes to increasing shareholder value. We usually prefer to recommend special incentives to ensure that the planned benefits (which were used by the board of directors to approve the merger) of the merger are attained by the management team.

Frustration with wrongly based short-term goals has surfaced in a very large but somewhat controversial outcry about quarterly guidance which certain groups, like the Business Roundtable Institute for Corporate Ethics and the CFA Centre for Financial Market Integrity, have found somewhat troubling. In their report, they called for more attention to be paid to long-term strategic objectives of companies, as well as better disclosure of the 'asset managers' incentive metrics, fee structures, and personal ownership of funds they manage."[2] By forcing the asset managers to disclose their stake in the assets, the public could better gauge their decision-making motivations. Until recently, even institutional investors were remarkably unconcerned when it came to how these very large bonus rabbits were pulled out of a seemingly infinitely generous top hat.

Commissioner Christopher Cox of the SEC, having reviewed the proposal, commented favorably, noting if frequent guidance tended to obscure and manipulate the overall earnings picture to shareholders, it might be a good idea to let the practice fade away into the sunset.[2]

The debate about quarterly earnings guidance indirectly re-flects on the problems related to using short-term incentives based on stock performance. Short term incentives based on stock can lead to bad decision-making, as can management's short-term obsessions with stock prices.

Placing the benefit square on the performance, earning-wise, of company stock, can have an enormous downside. Bonuses developed in this way can encourage self-oriented executives to make decisions that would have immediate impact on stock prices but might have detrimental long-term effects. Even ex-ecutives who aren't particularly self-oriented quickly learn to be so when placed in a position where it's downright difficult to do the right thing, considering that it sometimes comes at personal expense. After all, these guys are human, just like the rest of us!

A few examples of bonuses taken in 2005 show some of the problems with current practices regarding annual bonuses. A study of 179 companies done by Pearl Meyer & Partners showed that bonuses taken in 2005 exceeded those taken in 2004 by 38 percent.[4] That's no small number!

Here are a few executives who took home sweet bonuses—much to shareholder chagrin. Michael D. Eisner of Disney, who faced the ire of his shareholders and decided to leave his illustrious position a year earlier, took with him a nice fat bonus of $7.5 million because of his performance in 2004.[5] Raymond V. Gilmartin of Merck, whose product Vioxx was forced to vacate pharmaceutical shelves in that terrible year, still collected a $1.38 million bonus from the year before.[6] Hewlett Packard's Carleton S. Fiorina got $1.57 million even though she had to resign because of the board's assessment of the shareholders.[7] So as you can see, being focused on the short-term can cost an organization—and its shareholders—a nice chunk of change. Each of the above situations falls into a category we fondly call "money for nothing."

Sometimes "money for nothing" can extend across entire industries. Here's an example. A survey done by the Corporate Library studied 20 companies in the oil industry and found that even poor performance netted big rewards.[8] When all was said and done, the study showed that short-term bonuses were too high—way too high—in an industry that needed to rely on long-term focus in order to stay alive.

But don't get too depressed. There's some hope out there too.

Meet Robert I. Toll, CEO and one of the founders of the housing company, Toll Brothers. Toll was headed for a mega-bonus of $50 million as company performance found itself holding hands with a delightfully robust housing mega-boom (4). Yes, his company's shares were responding wonderfully and no one could fault his leadership.

But Toll had a problem with this amount of money. He found it, well, a tad *embarrassing*. With full approval of the board and compensation committee (what, like they were going to say *no?*) he gave $20 million back to the company. And probably slept better at night knowing he did the right thing for the organization as well as for its shareholders. Of course, if you were given a check for $30 million you would probably sleep pretty well too.

Another smaller giveback, but nonetheless perhaps as spiritually significant, was that of Revlon CEO Jack L. Stahl. Stahl, who made $1.3 million in salary in 2006, returned his bonus of $373,190 to reward employees' contributions for 2005.[9]

Despite some of these caveats, the right kind of short-term incentive can be just the ticket when it comes to effectively motivating management. The trick is to link the component to a factor of acceptable profitability that will not sabotage, but will actually add to, long-term goals. The incentive should be linked to the real-world performance of the executive achieving the goal.

The Tender Trap

A management team developing compensation plans on an executive level can fall into some very deep pits if they take their counsel from Human Resources.

Fine. We agree this isn't a nice thing to say. But it's true. HR people are too often in an environment that, in certain ways, downsizes their competitive instincts. And for the most part, they live and work in an environment quite different than that of upper level management. While HR people can help the machine function smoothly by assisting in the hiring process of day-to-day employees, they don't necessarily understand the psychology of the drivers of the business. We don't mean to say that egalitarian ideas of running a business have no validity, because they do. But accepting them across the board can mean falling into a tender trap from which a business may never recover.

Of course, you would also think that you wouldn't give short-term incentives to people in an organization whose behavior has virtually nothing to do with its success. But too often that's what HR will do if you let them. HR's enthusiasm to share information about the typical procedure for endowing certain levels of employees with short-term incentives can lead to the creation of disastrous policies. But we aren't interested in being typical here. We're interested in profitability.

Human resources departments may worry too much about employee equity in a situation that demands result-oriented impact. Eligibility should primarily be a function of impact—and nothing more. There are all kinds of other ways to raise the level of the water in a company, but the purpose of these short-term incentives is to extract powerful, profit-making focus from the *real* players.

Here's a cute analogy. If you are using a racing fuel in a high performance vehicle, you don't have to spread it around to all the cars in the parking lot. It has a purpose—to help win the race. Those who do not affect the outcomes should not be incorporated in the short-term incentive rewards program. If the people who design the plan can't determine the impact of specific individuals on the performance of the organization, well then, they shouldn't be designing the incentive plan. In fact, quite possibly, they shouldn't be running the organization at all.

We believe that, over the years, the level of short-term incentives has too often been extended way too far down in organizations. In our review of many, many companies, we've seen far too many examples of these programs reaching down to staff groups and additional line groups—groups that should never be on short-term incentive programs. Has this overextension of short-term incentives cost shareholders dramatically throughout the years? Of course it has.

If you haven't guessed already, we're opposed to the all too typical human resource view about the importance of internal equity, and that all individuals within a certain salary grade or at a certain salary level should be paid short-term incentives. This is, simply put, a misunderstanding of the function of these incentives and belies a huge waste of corporate resources. It is best to develop an insight into the organization and its critical value chain components, its general business strategy, and its specific business strategies to determine what job functions and level of executives should have significant portions of their annual compensation vary in the form of short-term incentives.

How to Avoid the Short Road to Mediocrity

We normally react very badly when either an executive or a human resources individual suggests that certain specific performance factors such as earnings per share (or some other "typical" or "best" practice) be the paradigm for compensation. Their justification is typically that this is the strategy used by 50 percent of their competitors as determined by a specific survey.

As you may have determined by now, we think that design-ing executive compensation packages by relying on surveys of "common practices" is a relatively short road to hell. At the very best, it is a short road to mediocrity. Short-term incen-tive factors are nothing to fool with. Those incorporated into the rewards design should be meant to fuel critically impor-tant company goals. They must also be in line with the gen-eral value chain and the strategic business strategies demanded to fulfill those goals.

Only the individuals who are in charge and capable of driv-ing those types of strategic goals should have their incentive paid on an annual basis.

No One Wants to Be a Pillar of Salt: The Importance of the Viewing Period

As with all types of incentive plans, there are three major ap-proaches to developing the type of targeting systems used in short-term incentive plans. They are:

1. Historical—sometimes called a "look back approach."
2. Business plan—sometimes called a "look forward approach."
3. Peer comparison—sometimes called a "look around approach."

All three approaches have some validity, and can sometimes be used in combination very effectively. If used properly, they will help push forward appropriate goals and payouts that are consistent with creating shareholder value. And that's what short-term incentives are all about!

So how do you choose which approach to go with? Much of that depends upon your organization's situation.

For example, if the organization is in a turbulent period, then it will be difficult to set specific look forward, or business plan, types of goals. The choice in turbulence is generally peer com-parison or look around goals.

That being said, if an organization is performing substantially better than its competitors, look around goals don't make much sense. Why should a successful organization, outpacing its competitors, want to set up goals similar to those of competitors with poorer performance? This same company probably doesn't need to look back either. Its past, after all, was simply a prelude to its current success. A successful company needs to look forward and set newer—even higher—goals. If the company is unique or new to its industry or has recently adopted a new business model, it might be advised to take a look at its recent achievements to set these new standards. A slight look backward might not hurt, in this case.

Those examples aside, in most cases we advocate look forward goals. Look around goals are sometimes appropriate. In general, we're very much against look back goals. A management that looks back at the success of its environment, business practices, and people strategies should hope—and pray—that nothing happens to change that projection of performance. Looking back doesn't work very well, but it is a common practice sometimes bordering on the criminally negligent. So don't say we didn't warn you. Unless your idea of a good time is being turned into a pillar of salt.

Performance Versus Payout: A Major Design Focus

We're often asked to review short-term incentive plans that have failed to work effectively. And time after time we find one major problem—the relationship between the various performance factors and the variability of the actual incentive itself has been out of sync.

We're not sure why this is so consistent a problem, but we have our suspicions. We think management often creates and accepts plans from which they will receive consistent payouts from the plan, without significant regard to the performance of the organization.

On paper, this doesn't sound so great. And yes, it's absolutely self-serving. That being said, we don't think the motive is all that terrible. Try thinking of it as a natural outcome of good management individuals attempting to eliminate risk in their business dealings. In this case, of course, that includes the payment of short-term incentives. We've too often noticed that they start the incentive at levels of performance they can very easily reach. Their target payout is normally positioned to a level that is 75 percent guaranteed. The maximum is set at a level which ensures they will reach it more often than not. This may serve their interest—and they may be nice people who haven't backdated any stock options lately—but creating ineffective short-term incentives that have no teeth doesn't really help anyone, particularly since the practice cascades down through the entire organization like cow manure through a "gravity barn."

INVESTOR ALERT #17

SHORT-TERM INCENTIVES PLAN PAYS TOO MUCH WHEN TARGET ISN'T ACCOMPLISHED

How much of the short-term incentive plan should be paid for performance that is less than satisfactory?

In most industries, threshold performance is somewhere near 90 percent of the target performance. A fairly significant drop-off from expectations should result in a fairly significant drop-off in the short-term incentive. Some management teams suggest that for 90 percent performance they should receive a 90 percent payout. While there is a certain odd logic to the suggestion, we might suggest that a 90 percent performance should receive a 50 percent payout of the short-term incentive plan. And if performance is below 90 percent of target, the payout should be zilch.

Make Sure the Trophy Can Fit on Your Shelf

Certain information is most certainly useful in determining the level of target awards for short-term incentives. But be careful using it.

When developing target amounts, time can be your best friend. Think carefully and deeply about each target and its purpose. Not every executive needs to participate in every type of plan. If an executive's major focus is on producing annual results, we see very little need for the executive to participate in plans that are mid-term, long-term, or that focus on wealth creation. On the other hand, if an executive is primarily responsible for long-term research or infrastructure development, then forget, or significantly limit, the short-term plans.

All decisions regarding the final target amount of the annual or short-term incentive plan need to be made in conjunction with the balance of the various reward components. The mix must be right, as well as the individual components.

We think it's good to have thresholds in short-term annual incentive programs. These ensure that the amount paid to the executive in base salary requires a threshold amount of performance prior to having the variable component payout.

However, we *don't* apply that same logic when it comes to developing maximums in a short-term incentive plan. Why should there be maximums? If the shareholders are continuing to make money, then the executive should continue to make money. That's the whole point of a performance-based incentive, right?

We understand some of our associates' concerns about the windfall incentives paid to executives when circumstances beyond their control deliver their performance for them. NYSE's Dick Grasso, after all, hasn't been the only executive in the news for raking in cuckoo bucks. There are certainly a fair share of examples out there of executives that have earned dizzyingly large bonuses due to circumstances beyond their control. But is this a problem with the idea of continuing rewards for continuing performance—or is it a problem with design of the short-term performance? Hmmmmm. Let's think about that.

We believe this is usually a result of the compensation designer's choice of performance factors, as well as the range within which the performance factors operate. In many cases—and this is the excuse the NYSE used when asked how they could have approved Grasso's enormous $139.5 million pay package—boards and committees know what an executive can earn at target, but don't focus on what an executive can earn below or above target. Boards and committees would do well to understand what an executive could potentially make under all possible scenarios. In the chapter on Total Rewards Architecture we discussed in some detail a tool called the grahall Economic Impact Analysis (gEIA), a new process that reviews an executive's total potential compensation and its relationship to all relevant performance factors. We suggest you take a few seconds to go back and review it. This is a great tool to use when plotting out short-term incentives as well.

It's interesting, but it seems to us that the same people who decry executives taking home healthy performance-related bonuses don't seem to have a problem when the executive is underpaid as result of an unforeseen circumstance, even if it is an industry-wide phenomenon. As long as the plan is designed responsibly and it's understood from the start how much the executive can make in all situations, we say let the chips fall where they may.

Cowboys Versus the Communists

Over the years, we have used the "OUTE" analysis to successfully determine the appropriate balance between organizational, business unit, team, and individual executive goals for each executive position. The analysis works within all incentive programs, whether short-term, mid-term, or long-term. There are two key determinants of the balance between the different organizational entities to receive targets within a short-term incentive plan. One is how the work is accomplished. The second is how the competitive advantage in the value chain and specific business strategies are executed.

We fondly call this analysis the "Cowboys versus Communists" proposition. To the extent that the contribution to shareholder wealth is created mainly through individual performance, the rewards should tilt toward the cowboy orientation. To the extent that wealth needs to be created for the shareholders as a result of significant team, business unit, or organizational performance, then the rewards should be tilted toward the organizational units involved.

It is our experience that tilting the rewards one way or the other is a critical decision in the design of various incentive plans. Like the phrase "buyers are liars" associated with the real estate industry, we want to warn most designers that individuals will consistently tell you that it is all about team or organizational performance. While that may be a gallant-sounding proposition, we really don't believe it has nearly as much truth as executives would like us to believe.

Yes, we realize that in the United States we have a "cult of the individual" and we tend to put individual performers on a pedestal. And, yes, perhaps popular historians and screenwriters have marvelously cultivated this tendency. And, yes, we Americans do love our Rockys and our Babe Ruths.

At the same time, the CEO catchphrase "If it is to be, it is up to me" also expresses a profound truth about our "cult of the individual." In our culture, individuals do make things happen—sometimes very big things.

And, realizing that, we always try to capture a certain degree of reality when determining what is the appropriate balance between organizational goals and individual goals. The individual and the team will always have a profound interaction in our culture.

Go Short Term, but You May Have to Kill the Clock

Most organizations pay short-term incentive plans out annually, and we think that in most cases that makes the most sense. But are there times when short-term incentives shouldn't be paid out annually? Of course.

If an organization is facing bankruptcy, coming out of a turn-around situation, or facing significant but dangerous competitive pressures on a narrow timetable, then it should consider how frequently it pays out its short-term incentives.

Our advocacy of this position should come as no surprise. Short-term incentives are like high-performance fuel. And sometimes, the annual payoff could completely annihilate its effectiveness.

We have used historically based plans as short as quarterly with senior executives. Sometimes these plans may look back at the last six months and pay on a quarterly basis, or they may look back at the prior twelve months and pay out on an every six-month basis. In either case, payouts are often more frequent than annual.

Milestone Incentives: When You Know How Much, but Not When

We are very much in favor of milestone incentives, and have used them in the past with a great deal of success. Milestone incentives are, in fact, incentives that are associated with the accomplishment of the objective. While it's relatively easy to determine if an objective was reached, a timetable associated with an objective may be altogether arbitrary. Associating a particular objective with a 12-month calendar year can dilute the power of the incentive, especially under the adverse conditions we have described.

In a milestone incentive, the goal and its preferred time period of accomplishment is determined. To the extent that the management achieves the objective earlier, its payout is increased. To the extent that it is achieved after the time, its payout is decreased in some proportional way.

We believe the milestone incentives are a much underused advantage. Why? They effectively break the mold of the annual drumbeat to which most American businesses operate. In a sense, the annual incentive is saying that management wants everyone's heart to beat at the same rate, a desire that is somewhat of an affront to the nature to the reality. Especially to the reality of the fleet of foot.

We all know great athletes' heartbeats tend to beat faster when, as Sherlock Holmes was fond of saying, the "game is afoot." For this reason, it still surprises us when management defaults to the annual plan incentive without so much as evaluating its appropriateness.

Short-term incentives are just tools. Don't overuse them and don't underuse them. You don't use a screwdriver when you should be using a hammer. And you shouldn't try to pretend a screwdriver is the only tool you need when making a cabinet.

And here's something else. Don't overstate the importance of short-term incentives.

There are many times when it is perfectly appropriate to discuss short-term incentive plans. But should the conversation go on forever? Please, no.

We've seen enormous amounts of time misspent on how to fund these incentives when, in effect, millions of dollars go unfunded in the form of long-term incentives associated with stock options. As usual, management wastes a tremendous amount time worrying about the insignificant while the significant runs out the door. If you haven't guessed by now, we're not great believers in spending a lot of time determining how to fund short-term incentive plans. That's because if they are designed correctly, they shouldn't need "funding mechanisms."

No Matter How Smart You Are, You Still Need to Read the Menu

Most management teams don't spend enough time communicating the goals of their short-term plans to incentive plan participants. And it's hard to figure out why. Do they believe their executives are so smart that they should catch on automatically? As flattering as that may be, it's a little like going to a restaurant with one of your more intelligent friends and foregoing the menu because you think they're so smart they don't need to read it. Even the simplest of menus needs to be read—at least once.

The simplicity of an incentive should not eliminate the need to communicate to executives. Management needs to be sure that executives understand how the short-term incentive plan operates by itself and, more particularly, how the short-term incentive plan operates within the framework of the overall reward program. Because incentives don't work unless they are understood.

We encourage the strenuous review of all variable compensation paid annually or more frequently. As someone once said in an old Western movie, "There's gold in them there hills!" We just believe it needs to be gold for both the executives *and* the shareholders.

References

1. Towers and Perrin Study, 2006.
2. Taub, Stephen. "Trade Groups: Dump Quarterly Guidance." *CFO.com*, 25 July 2006. Available online at http://www.cfo. com/article.cfm/7216954/c_7216090, accessed 27 September 2007.
3. Bowe, Chris. "Boston Five Share Takeover Bonuses." *Ft.com*, 14 May 2006. Available online at http://search.ft.com/ftArticle? queryText=Boston+Five+Share+Takeover+Bonuses&y=0&aje= false&x=0&id=060513000687&ct=0, accessed 27 September 2007.
4. Dash, Eric. "A Bad Year for the Chief (But Not the Bonus)." *New York Times*, 3 April 2005.
5. Ibid.
6. Ibid.
7. Ibid.

8. "Petroleum Industry Compensation Too Focused on Short-Term Results." *Market Wire,* 22 September 2006. Available online at http://findarticles.com/p/articles/mi_pwwi/is_200609/ai_n16741 899, accessed 27 September 2007.

9. Olson, Elizabeth. "Bucking a Trend on CEO Pay." *New York Times,* 7 May 2006.

CHAPTER 11
Mid-Term Incentives

Why do compensation consultants and designers love mid-term incentives so much? (That is, those who even know the category exists—which we estimate to be about 10 percent of the population!)

Have you ever been to a party and had a hard time picking out the compensation consultant? Probably not. He's the guy who is either standing alone or in a small group of other compensation consultants. Face it, we aren't exactly seen as the life of the party.

What a lot of people don't know is that compensation consultants have their wild side too. We get bored by base salary. Long-term incentives don't always float our boat. So when things get a little dull, where do we turn? To mid-term incentives.

That's right. While the rest of you liven things up by having a few drinks and taking in a Fergie concert, we compensation consultants are letting our hair down and getting creative with mid-term incentives.

Mid-term incentives are liberating for the same reason that they solve problems that other reward components can't—they have no general pattern that we can think of, except that they are best used on an *ad hoc* basis. Sometimes they focus on all employees, sometimes they focus on one key individual, and still other times they focus on a group of individuals. They target a period that can range from one to five years—a period of time critical to most companies' success. But aside from that they can target just about any issue a company needs to focus on—whether that issue is bringing new products to market or navigating bankruptcy, effectively completing an acquisition, or successfully handling a one-time project. Most mid-term incentives are typically not recurring, and eligibility for them is on a case-by-case basis. By their very nature, mid-term incentives give the total rewards strategy designer a little freedom to solve important—often unique—issues necessary for the success of the organization.

Three Years Isn't Such a Long Time

Okay, so now that we've convinced you how great they are, let's talk about mid-term incentives in a little more detail. Mid-term incentives are another form of variable compensation— and they sandwich quite nicely between short-term incentives and long-term incentives. You may have guessed, just from their name, how mid-term incentives differ from the short-term incentives we just talked about. Well, the most obvious difference is that the length of the performance period is longer—typically anywhere from one to five years. To a lesser degree the length of the distribution period, or vesting terms, also falls within this range.

So what do mid-term incentives do that short-term incentives and long-term incentives don't?

First, a Bit of Historic Background from Our Perspective.

Mid-term incentives came onto the scene in the 1970s and were given nifty names like "Special Awards Bonus Programs." Essentially, these types of programs were designed for individuals—and teams—who accomplished specific goals of a particularly important nature. Goals that carried with them significant financial consequences. As a general rule, the approach to the amounts of the bonus was "look back" in nature and, while significant to the individuals, they were insignificant to the organization as a whole.

Since their modest beginnings, what are now known as mid-term incentives—or sometimes special incentives—have become an important component of the overall executive total reward strategy. Not only have these types of incentives become more widely used across the board, they are more significant in their size and application. Like we mentioned before, mid-term incentives can be used to address a variety of business challenges—challenges like bankruptcies, mergers, or other specific business missions that are generally non-recurring or that need to be addressed within a certain time frame. Used correctly, mid-term incentives are extremely motivating—and effective.

INVESTOR ALERT #18

ACCOUNTING ADJUSTMENTS REQUIRED TO CALCULATE THE PERFORMANCE UNDER THE INCENTIVE PLANS

If company disclosure information indicates significant adjustments in the reported financials in an effort to be fair to executives, we would expect that the executives don't feel strongly about being in the same boat as the shareholders. Either that, or there is something wrong with the accounting system. Neither instance bodes well for the investor.

In many cases these adjustments are relatively trivial, which makes one wonder why they even bother. Well, the reason these trivial adjustments are normally made is to soften up the board of directors, so when a large adjustment needs to be proposed it has become a way of doing business.

Don't invest in companies that consider this "the way" of doing business.

We Hate to State the Obvious . . . but We're Going to Anyway

Mid-term incentives are designed to reward executives for the execution aspects of the strategic plan. That may seem like a rather obvious statement, but peel back a few layers and you'll see that it's not. Here's why. We can sum it up by saying "short-term fever." That's right. The most challenging responsibility of organizations and their executive teams is to exe-

cute the strategic plan when every investor and his grand-
mother are focused more on short-term and quarterly results.
Things don't seem so easy anymore, do they?

We could philosophize about the lack of execution capability
within most companies, but we could also blame the Harvards
of this world that have lots of courses on strategy, but not on
execution.

Many of the organizations we work with are great—really
great—at developing a strategic plan. They are also great at developing monthly, quarterly, and annual plans and budgets.
Where they fail miserably is going smoothly from point A to
point B. In other words, they nail the operating plan requirements, but somewhere on the way to strategic plan execution things go awry and never get accomplished, resulting in
the ever-too-frequent "hockey stick" strategic plan.

What's up with this? We're convinced that this monster is actually two-headed. First of all, we believe there are problems
in the planning. There's no doubt it's difficult to break down
those steps necessary to execute a good 5- to 10-year strategic
plan into shorter time periods. And let's face it. Most organizations focus on short-term incentives. The various equity
incentive programs are seen as more random and less of a sure
thing because of the ties to the overall stock market. There's
also the possibility that the executive will no longer be in the
same position when the long-term program pays out.

*C*ase Study #17

*One of our clients is a producer of laboratory-engineered
animals for use in research studies. The performance of
the organization had been reasonably good for a significant period of time. However, the organization had never
performed extraordinarily well.*

*Long-term plans were always well-designed and well-
received by the board of directors. These long-term plans*

provided substantial growth targets in both revenues and return on investments to shareholders. Year after year the short-term goals were accomplished, but after some review it was clear that the organization would never reach the more challenging long-term growth targets.

There was a gap. While the executives could put together very good long-term plans, they always felt that the challenges of accomplishing their short-term plans were so overwhelming that they were never able to focus on accomplishing key steps toward long-term sustainable high-end performance. The stock performed badly. While it never decreased in price very much, it also never increased in price very much.

The long-term incentives for typical stock option grants were supplemented with restricted stock grants. So while the executives did receive the benefits of the restricted stock grant's time-based vesting, there was never much appreciation in the form of stock option grant value.

The CEO and the board of directors became uncomfortable enough to ask us to create a mid-term incentive plan which balanced the short-term and long-term incentive plans. With the implementation of the mid-term incentive plan, executives began to focus on turning long-term strategy into three-year objectives. Since installing the mid-term incentive plan the organization's execution of the long-term incentive goals has substantially increased in quality and magnitude.

Sometimes you get what you pay for. These executives were paid extremely well for short-term annual performance, which they were quite effective at predicting and accomplishing. But if you want your long-term strategy executed, sometimes you have to pay for the steps it takes to get there.

In the end, figuring out how to relate rewards to organizational and executive performance over an extended period of time is a big old challenge. So don't be thinking that we executive compensation consultants have it easy all the time, even if as a whole we seem like a relaxed and jolly group. The truth is, we've had more than a few challenging moments figuring out how to break down the key drivers of the long-term strategic plan into operational factors. And once we've gotten over that hurdle we face yet another: determining how those drivers will be incorporated into an incentive program that is both the right amount of money, and encourages the right behavior. It's a tough task, no doubt. But done correctly, mid-term incentives provide exceptional value to both the organization and its shareholders. So is it worth spending a little extra time on this component? You bet it is.

Why Mid-Term Incentives Are Like Navy Seals or Green Berets

Mid-term incentives can save the day in ways that other variable reward strategy components can't. What do we mean by this? Well, say your organization has a fire to put out right away—let's say the company is planning an acquisition or merger and one of the main goals is to ensure that the company stays afloat (many don't—as many as 70 percent, believe it or not) during the transition. How do you ensure that your executives feel the heat and rise to the occasion? Well, we all know that short-term incentives probably aren't the ticket, as in these types of situations they often encourage the CEO to save his own skin before that of the company. And long-term incentives are more or less meaningless in this situation.

Enter mid-term incentives.

Many times boards, compensation committees, or CEOs will use this category of incentives like the military uses special forces like the Navy Seals. In other words, when a specific mission needs to be executed, mid-term and special incentives are an effective use of compensation resources. Used in this way, special incentives are a function of a special mission or the establishment of a new set of values for the organization. When

an organization needs to find a new approach that is so basic it affects or changes the fundamental vision, mission, or
values, we believe that instead of asking the imbedded reward
system to do the heavy lifting, it's much more effective to create a mid-term or special incentive program to create a sense
of urgency and uniqueness.

*C*ase Study #18

One of our technology clients called us with an issue. The
board of directors had determined that it was time for the
chief executive officer to step down as a result of accusa-
tions that he had acted improperly with regard to certain
female staff members. He resigned and the company was
left without a formal successor. After deliberations the
board decided to allow the office of the CEO to be created
using three key executives while the board searched for a
replacement.

We were asked to develop a retention and mid-term bonus
of appropriate levels in order to retain the three executives,
who had been told that they were not candidates for the
job.

It was a difficult situation. The three executives had not
been chosen to run the company, they were not going to be
allowed to choose their boss, and they were, in fact, candidates for termination by the new chief executive officer
upon arrival.

The board, however, felt strongly that to lose these three
individuals at the same time they had just experienced
their chief executive officer's resignation could potentially
be seriously damaging to the organization.

We developed retention-based restricted stock grants with
ratable vesting, which accelerated upon the hiring of the
new CEO. In addition, we granted each of the executives
an incentive severance program. The incentive severance

program prescribes a period of time for which the company will pay an incentive, and it is substantially longer than similar severance payments. In this case the severance payments were to be made for over three years once severance occurred. The difference between incentive severance payments and regular severance payments are that the company does not pay the full amount of severance once the executive gets a new position. Once the executive gets a new position, the remaining amount of severance is divided into one half, which goes to the executive in the form of a bonus. On the other hand, if the executive needs the full three years of severance it is available.

This combination of restricted stock grants for performance up until the new chief executive officer was hired, and the large amount of incentive severance upon possible termination, was sufficient to keep all three executives with the organization through the transition period. Ultimately two of the three executives remained with the company, even after the new CEO was hired. The company's position has rebounded and is performing better than it has in the past.

Sometimes the right combination of incentives, when targeted at a specific need, is quite simply all that needs to be done. In this case, restricted stock grants allowed for substantial wealth to be accumulated. The incentive severance told the executives that, should they be severed after the new chief executive officer arrived, they would receive three years of payment if needed. In fact, the ultimate payments, when looked at as a percentage of the total program's proposal, were less than 10 percent. Since it was paid only to one executive and in his case paid only for a short period of time, what looked like a significant exposure became a non–event for the organization.

Let's take the example of an organization undergoing a turnaround. What's the first thing we usually do? We eliminate incentives for the majority of employees, including the executive ranks. When people ask why we're doing this—and be-lieve us, they do—we say, quite simply, "We don't want peo-ple running harder in the wrong direction!"

After we've suspended—temporarily, we should add—the standard short- and long-term incentives, we locate the key organizational capabilities for the turnaround within the or-ganization. The special incentives are targeted *specifically* at these executives. How's that for mid-term incentives coming to the rescue? "Believe it or not," as Ripley would have said, we get better results by spending less. It's just more surgical and focused.

C*ase Study #19*

A large German chemical company came to us with an op-portunity to work with their new research facility located in the Carolinas. This facility was staffed by Ph.D. bio-physicists and researchers who were going to work on breakthrough plant designs.

One of the common difficulties with researchers and engi-neers is that there is a desire to have the effort 100 per-cent perfect before it is released into the marketplace. But 100 percent perfect is the enemy of revenue dollar cre-ation. So a developmental reward was designed. This re-ward started as a relatively small percentage of the prod-uct's revenue stream, and decreased exponentially over time until it ceased to exist after 10 years. This type of mid-term reward structure promoted developing and get-ting products to market, which, in turn, created a revenue stream needed to fund, build, and introduce more new products.

Sometimes you just have to measure what you can and reward for it. The development rewards concept sent the right message to the researchers, and allowed the organization to produce a lot of results earlier.

It's All About Execution

Mid-term incentives are often targeted at the gaps in the organizational competencies, which prevent a critical portion or aspect of the business strategy from being accomplished. Organization capability gaps can crop up just about anywhere, and they don't follow any particular rules. Sometimes they are about management; other times they are about technology. Whatever they are about, in almost all cases these gaps make it near impossible for the business strategy to be accomplished.

Mid-term incentives can be used to shore up the gaps and ensure that the things get done. Sure, sometimes an organization needs an executive to step up to the plate and work outside of his job description to accomplish a particular goal. A nice little mid-term incentive ensures that an executive working outside of his comfort level is a little more, well, *comfortable*.

There is some debate about how long mid-term incentives should be, as well as how they should be paid. Again, the beauty of mid-term incentives is that they are often used in special circumstances. So if you want to make them a little special as well, we see no problem with that. A company whose goal is to increase sales geographically, for example, is going to structure its mid-term incentives quite differently than a company whose goal is to seamlessly and successfully integrate a merger. While the former company could use an ongoing mid-term incentive until the goal is accomplished, it would be appropriate for the latter company to award a one-time incentive upon successful completion of the merger or even better, upon the generation of those all-so-elusive "synergistic" values that seem to disappear once the merger ink has dried.

While the category of executive rewards that we call mid-term incentives reflects all incentives that fall into the two- or three-year category, lots of people would argue that today's stock option plans and restricted stock plans—which vest over three, four, or five years—are examples of mid-term plans. And we agree. In our opinion there's absolutely nothing long about three-year or four-year incentive plans. They are certainly the plans that speak loudest when it comes to execution, which is why we are such big fans of them. Are there goals that can be met on a quarterly or annual basis? Of course. But for most large organizations, execution of major goals—those that have a long-term positive effect on both the organization and the shareholders—usually comes in three- to five-year periods. Today's organizations are much more complex than they used to be. So if we add a year or two to mid-term incentives, it's just because we're the kind of people who like to keep up with the times.

Choosing Wisely

One of the beautiful things about mid-term incentives is that, if used correctly, they can really complement a company's people strategy. How so? Mid-term incentives can be—make that *should be*—targeted at specific organizational strategies or capability gaps within the organizational structure, process, or culture. Remember when we discussed value chain management back in Chapter 4? When it's determined what portions of the organization are necessary to drive the organization to meet a specific goal or mission, mid-term incentives should be targeted at those particular portions of the organization.

As a matter of fact, we'll go so far as to say that the use of mid-term incentive plans should be limited to those executives who can truly have an impact or make a contribution over a three- to five-year period of time. For executives who fall into this category, a significant portion of the reward program should be targeted at mid-term incentives. Maybe even the largest portion!

In addition to specific departments or groups within an organization, mid-term incentives can also be targeted at specific organizational processes—processes like decision making or planning, allocating, and monitoring. Some major clients have even used mid-term incentives to improve their communications process! Mid-term incentives are not only powerful, they're incredibly versatile. And they can be used creatively to address just about any organizational issue.

Mid-term incentives come in all shapes and sizes—something that adds to their versatility and makes them a good choice in a wide variety of situations. These plans go by various names like project-based incentives, challenge grants, milestone incentives, and success fees. We've used them all at one time or another with great success. But how do you know which incentive to use and when to use them? Don't worry, we're going to help you out.

Make an Impact . . . or Come Home on Your Shield—Project Incentives

Project-based incentives, just like they sound, are specific to unique and identifiable projects, so they should be designed to motivate key groups of individuals. Project-based incentives are very versatile, and we've designed them for just about every job family within a value chain structure. Project-based incentives are also very unique because they can include not only the executive that's in charge of the project, but the entire team that can potentially influence the project's outcome. It's fairly typical in the design of project-based incentives for individuals making as little as $50,000 per year to participate in a single project-based incentive. Why are those being targeted by project-based incentives similar to the Green Beret? Well, project-based incentives are designed to ensure that a critical initiative is accomplished by a unique group with many different talents. While their number may be small when compared to that of the entire organization, their impact is disproportionately great. But what happens if our corporate Green Berets aren't successful? Not to be grim, but just like the real Green Beret's they should be prepared to come home on their shields. Hey, we never said corporate America was fun *all* the time.

INVESTOR ALERT #19

ALWAYS PAYING AN INCENTIVE

The future is not easy to predict, and setting goals can be difficult. If the executives are always in the money with respect to their short-term, mid-term, or long-term incentive plans, then their plan is just too darn good or the requirements to receive that incentive plan payout are just too darn low.

When all is said and done, it is just not possible to always predict all the various risks associated with performing as a modern major corporation in today's competitive environment. The executive ought to be out of the money at least one year per decade, and if they are in the same industries as many of our clients, then they ought to be out of the money at least two times per decade. Only because a company can't perform as expected year after year.

Most of the time it's not so much a question of performance, but rather one of becoming addicted or entitled to the variable component part of the executive reward program. Goals already set to low thresholds are set even lower—and the executive always receives his payout.

You can bet if the executives are always in the money, the shareholders are out of money at some part of the day.

Rising to the Challenge—Challenge Incentives

Challenge grants are a favorite mid-term incentive for us—as well as our design teams. As a matter of fact, we've used so many challenge grants throughout the past 25 years that it's hard to categorize them all. Challenge grants can be targeted toward all employees, toward an individual, or toward a specific group like management.

In order to understand how challenge grants can work, let's take the example of one of our clients that we'll call "French Corporation." French Corporation is a small start-up corporation in the biopharmaceutical area—one we feel has a bright future ahead of it. Why do we think French is so great? It has developed a number of drugs that are just beginning to be marketable. Of course, it's competing against Pfizer and Merck and other big-name pharmaceutical companies with deep pockets. Which means its bright future will only occur if it ruthlessly drives revenues in order to bring its products to market before its larger competitors. So what's the organization's objective here? Simple. To generate revenues to reinvest in the business and create additional drugs. In this particular challenge grant, all employees were eligible to receive the challenge award if—and when—the stock price reached a certain level. The goals are ambitious—really ambitious—and the organization is asking executives to work beyond the call of duty. So what keeps employees galvanized and focused on the task at hand? When the firm's performance is outstanding, the executives' rewards will also be outstanding. What's not to love about a challenge grant? It's great for the company, great for the executive, and great for the shareholder.

C*ase Study #20*

A French pharmaceutical organization came to us with a unique problem. They were a relatively new organization, only had a few drugs in the marketplace, and needed to focus the entire workforce on ramping up revenues while at the same time driving up share price. The solution? We developed a challenge grant award for all employees. The challenge grant was linked to selling $1 billion of revenues in any 12-month period at any share price that was double the current price. If this challenge grant was accomplished within three years, the individuals would receive a number of shares linked to their relative position within the firm. The feedback from the various stakeholders was excellent. The board of directors believed it was a good investment on the part of a firm, the executives felt that this would focus serialization effectively on driving revenues, and employees felt a significant sense of sharing and ownership in the company.

> *So what was the outcome? While the organization did accomplish its goal of driving revenues to $1 billion, it did not accomplish the goal of doubling the share price. It is our understanding that they have replaced this past challenge grant with a new challenge grant with even loftier goals. We only hope the amount they provided in the form of shares is sufficient to at least recoup some of the initial challenge grant's promise.*

Challenge grants can also be specific to an individual. Take "John Corp.," a $4 billion company that wanted to replace its retiring CEO with someone they were confident could continue the company's phenomenal performance. After narrowing their search down to 20 top-shelf executives, they finally found their man. Their pick was the chief financial officer of the "Big Insurance Group," an organization many times the size of "John." So how to woo away this talented individual? Enter the versatile challenge grant! John Corp. decided, based upon its situation and the individual's desire for substantial income related to key decisions, to design a challenge grant solely for that individual. This particular challenge grant involves the compounded increase in book value for the organization over a five-year period, paid at the individual's retirement. If the individual increases book value at a compounded rate of 10 percent or greater, he'll receive the challenge grant. Has this substantial challenge grant been effective? What do you think? In fact, the shares have gone up 250 percent in the last four years.

*C*ase Study #21

> *A client asked us to develop a reward program that would attract its next CEO. After significant discussion, we put together a package. The package, including direct compensation as well as several challenge grants and matching shares, would be worth, over a 10-year period, approxi-*

> *mately $10 million less than the candidate was presently making as the CFO of a larger company. We also knew this candidate was one of three individuals who were likely to be promoted to become the CFO of his present organization. While our client had no interest in trying to match the larger company's total reward program, they felt strongly that the candidate was a perfect fit.*
>
> *So what was the solution? We recommended two challenge grants. One challenge grant would occur when the individual was initially hired as executive vice president, and the second grant would occur if and when the individual was promoted to CEO. In addition to the challenge grants, we recommended a matching grant concept, where the individual would buy one share and get two shares free over an extended vesting period.*
>
> *Sometimes it's not the amount of the award that is critical to design, but the mix and messages of the key components of the overall total reward strategy. These challenge grants ultimately turned out to be effective at recruiting the individual, motivating him to restructure and maintain our client's phenomenal stock price growth, and are presently effective at retaining the individual since the vesting is over an extended period of time.*

"Sam's Corporation" is a client of ours that has grown from $400 million in revenues to close to $2,500,000,000 in just a couple of years, mostly due to acquisitions. Before going on its acquisition binge, the board was concerned—justifiably—that the acquisition was integrated so that the organization operated as a single high-performing entity. After all, it's a well-known fact that 70 percent of acquisitions don't achieve their objectives, nor do they increase shareholder value as a rule. So how to make sure that "Sam's" was part of the other 30 percent? A challenge grant—one that was fairly substantial in size—was designed specifically to accomplish the synergy associated with the acquisition. Only the very top executives were eligible for the award, and the goals were specifically those that the CFO presented to the board of directors to justify the acquisition.

Okay, we better stop now. We could go on and on giving you good examples of challenge grants we've used in the past, but we think we've made our point. Which is that when it comes to challenge grants, eligibility can be different, the objective can be quite specific to the circumstances associated with the organization and its five-year goals, and the amounts can be dramatically different. The only rule with challenge grants? Make sure they are significant in proportion to the overall total executive reward strategy. Other than that, be creative and go nuts.

Ah, Serendipity . . . or Not—Success Incentive

Sometimes when a particular goal is accomplished it is critically important to the success of an organization, and therefore to its shareholders. But what happens when circumstances beyond the executive's control have the possibility of playing a large part in when that goal will be accomplished? Milestone incentives are a unique category of mid-term incentives designed to address this very problem. Rather than artificially tying a goal accomplishment to a standard period of measurement—like a single year or three years—the goal is determined and a reasonable date for its accomplishment is set. To the extent that the goal is accomplished sooner or later than the set date, the executive receives more or less in proportion to the benefits that accrue to the organization's earlier or later accomplishment of the goal. Which means no more relying upon serendipity to determine when the executive will reach the goal!

George Washington Should Have Gotten One, and Ben Franklin, Too

If you ask an executive to tackle a goal outside of his normal responsibilities, a success fee initiative is a good way to get him out of bed in the morning. Success fee initiatives are a special category of milestone incentives in which a block of incentive is put aside and paid only when the objective is completed. It doesn't matter if it takes one year or five—the incentive is paid *only* when the assignment is completed.

We would have given George Washington a success fee at the end of the War of Independence from Britain (had his expenses not been in excess of $400,000, but we'll have some fun with Mr. Washington later in Chapter 16, which is on perquisites). And we certainly would have approved a success fee for Benjamin Franklin as he was clearly instrumental—not to mention efficient—in getting France to enter the war on the side of the United States. In fact, we've recommended approval for many success fees over the years when executives have truly accomplished something far and away above the line of duty. As a rule, success fee incentives should be relatively small and of recognitional nature in size.

There is a downside to success fee incentives, which is that the concept has been abused. Yep, if a reward component can be abused, you can bet someone will find a way to do it. They are typically abused when an executive is awarded a hefty success fee for something that is, by rights, part of his job description. We've seen the bar set pretty low. We've seen success fees paid in all kinds of situations, including when an executive makes an acquisition. Really now, isn't evaluating and making acquisitions part of a senior executive's responsibilities?

Getting Rewarded for Bringing It— Development/Royalty Incentives

Sometimes an individual or a group of individuals will have a unique impact on an organization's revenue due to things they create. For example, a pharmaceutical company's success is dependent upon creating new drugs, while a technology company's success may be dependent upon innovative new software. No products, no company! Someone is responsible for an integral set of decisions like choosing which drug to pursue or which software to create. How to ensure that the best products get out of research and into the market? Development or royalty incentives specifically reward those who "bring it" by paying incentives based on revenue from a particular creation. Many large organizations have stand-alone research and development entities, where it makes sense for not only the executive—but also the researcher—to be eligible for developmental or royalty incentives. Basically, those who are critically involved share a small amount of the revenues that result from their creations. The incentive is generally a decreasing proportion of revenues paid over a 5- to 10-year period.

Getting Back on the Horse—Turnaround Incentives

There are all kinds of reasons why a company goes into a state of decline. The reasons can be internal, like an unproductive workforce, poor decisions, or rising costs. They can be external, like new competitors, a changing market, or a declining market. Or they can be a combination of both. What's a company's first priority when it finds itself in a decline? To get back to an earlier—and better—stage. A turnaround is designed to reposition the company. What happens if the turnaround isn't successful? A sale, or maybe even a bankruptcy. And that's why a nice, hard-hitting turnaround incentive can mean the difference between getting back on the horse and biting the dust. Turnaround incentives may be targeted at successfully cutting expenses, or they may focus on repositioning the company to better meet the needs of the marketplace. In a situation like this where time is of the essence and creativity may be one of the keys to keeping things afloat, mid-term incentives are a good choice.

After Verizon's stock took a pounding in 2005, the company decided to try something new. Instead of focusing on long-term rewards, it decided to tie the compensation of CEO Ivan

Seidenberg to certain strategic objectives.[1] So goodbye to $7.6 million restricted stock grant, hello to more than $22 million in stock if the company's stock price and dividend return is among the top 20 percent of Standard & Poor's 500-stock index and its competitors in the telecommunications industry.

Here's the catch. Verizon was facing some stiff competition. And it wasn't rising to the challenge. The answer? To complete a fiber-optic project that would put them at the head of the class. Other targets included expansion of its wireless unit, integrating its merger with MCI, and making legislative objectives happen.

So what happened? We're still waiting to hear. What we do know is that these incentives are producing a much smoother rollout of the fiber-optic, especially when compared to companies who don't have such plans, like AT&T. But what would you do if offered Mr. Seidenberg's deal? We would personally roll out the fiber optic—and we bet you would too.

Back from the Brink

When a company enters bankruptcy it has one goal in mind— to keep creditors at bay while attempting to return the organization to a profitable state. That's no small task, and one that generally asks the executive to go above and beyond the call of duty.

If an organization can't bring itself back from the brink, it will go out of business. So it just makes sense that top executives would receive some fairly substantial mid-term incentives to ensure this doesn't happen.

Take Dana Corp. as an example. Dana Corp., which filed Chapter 11, promised CEO Mike Burns $6.75 million in cash and stock if the newly reorganized company met specific financial goals in a two-year period.[2] What was the deal if Burns didn't have the chops? He'd take home his base pay, but nothing else. With this type of incentive program the CEO has everything to gain and lose—with little or no risk on the part of the organization. What happens if Burns fails? He's out some money—and a job. In this type of situation, there's no better example of an executive's success being tied to the organization's success. And that's what mid-term incentives—and total executive rewards strategies in general—should be all about.

As you can probably now appreciate, we are big fans of mid-term incentives. They are often "tipping point" incentives in that a little money, mixed well, can carry a lot of messages and provide a huge "return on incentives" for shareholders.

References

1. "Verizon Ties CEO Pay to Project Success Instead of Company Stock Performance." *Wall Street Journal*, 18 October 2006.
2. "New Plan Ties Exec Payout to Set of Goals-CEO Could Receive Up to $6.75." *Toledo Blade*, 8 October 2006.

CHAPTER 12
Long-Term Incentives

One of the major differences between short-term incentives, mid-term incentives, and the subject of this chapter, long-term incentives, is the length of the performance period and, to a lesser degree, the length of the distribution period or vesting terms. When the length of the performance and distribution/ vesting period are added together, the typical long-term incentive program normally covers a 5- to 10-year period. Compare that to short-term incentives, which usually cover up to a year, and mid-term incentives, which usually cover a three- to five-year period.

This is a significant distinction. Why?

Because the organization's—and executive team's—most challenging responsibility is to position the organization for long-term success. Determining how to relate rewards to organizational and executive performance over an extended period of time is no easy task. When it comes to conducting business, there's a significant cyclical nature. This cyclical nature is a function of the world, United States, industry, and the individual company's natural—but unfortunately not fully predictable—business cycles.

It's too bad, really, that long-term incentives have gotten such a bad rap. Much of the song and dance regarding executive malfeasance has centered on stock options, a long-term incentive vehicle which has proven to be oh-so-easy to abuse. Apparently some executives thought their enormous compensation packages weren't enormous enough. A little backdating fixed the problem—but eventually ended up landing those same executives in somewhat of a fix.

Shareholders got angry—really angry—and who can blame them? Now the SEC, FASB, and IRS have so many rules and regulations regarding long-term incentives that you have to be a veritable math whiz to use them.

Why Use Them?

Used correctly, long-term incentives are a very powerful component of the total executive reward strategy designed to accomplish at least some of the following objectives.

- Align executive interest with that of key shareholders. When an executive's long-term incentive compensation is based on company performance over a long term, there is no doubt that the executive's personal interest will mirror that of key shareholders.
- Attract and retain executives. Since, in most organizations, long-term rewards represent the largest portion of the executive's total compensation, they are critical to attract and retain executives. Because most long-term incentive programs vest over an extended period of time, they are more successful in retaining executives than other portions of the compensation plan that are paid in cash.
- Promote long-term thinking. Long-term plans can promote long-term thinking, and are important to balance with monthly salaries, short-term incentives, and mid-term incentives.
- Share the success of the organization with the executive. Right from the pages of all employee gain sharing plans, the long-term incentive plan allows a unique approach to sharing the success of the organization. Especially when long-term incentives are paid in equity, with the executive's gain in direct proportion to the shareholders' gain.
- Long-term incentive plans can be used as a platform for wealth accumulation programs.

Everything You Wanted to Know but Were Afraid to Ask About Long-Term Incentives

The subject of long-term incentives has always been more confusing than the subject of their cousins, short-term incentives and mid-term incentives. But the recent scandals surrounding stock options, and the resulting new accounting methods, have sparked even more debate on the best long-term incentive methods to use. And this makes the whole subject even more unwieldy.

There are basically three types of long-term incentive vehicles: (a) appreciation-based awards, such as stock options and stock appreciation rights; (b) full-value awards, such as restricted stock with time vesting, and performance shares; and (c) cash-based plans.

Appreciation-Based Awards

Let's talk about appreciation-based awards first. Two types of stock options are incentive stock options (ISO) and nonqualified stock options (NSO). An ISO is valuable to the executive when the stock price increases over the exercise price of the option. When the executive exercises the stock, he is paid the total exercise price and receives the shares of stock. The executive gets an amount equal to the difference between the exercise price and the fair market value of the stock on the date of exercise. No income is recognized at the time of exercise, as the taxable event is triggered upon the sale of the underlying stock. If the executive holds the stock for more than two years from the date of grant of the options and one year from the date of exercise, then the whole gain on the sale of the stock is seen as a long-term capital gain. If the stock is sold before the holding period is up, the ISO is turned into a nonqualified stock option (NSO). The difference is taxed as ordinary income, with any appreciation after the above full market value (FMV) on the date of exercise treated as capital gains. According to FAS 123, the Black-Scholes value of the options shows up as compensation expense in the income statement, and is spread over the vesting period or performance period.

INVESTOR ALERT #20

ANNUAL BURN RATE

If the annual burn rate or the number of shares used for employee and executive equity programs is high compared to other organizations, there's a good chance the company has lost its sense of balance.

There are only two ways to have a high annual burn rate. One is to give too many shares to executives. The other is to give too many shares to everyone. Neither are good signs for the investor.

Which brings us to NSOs. An NSO benefits the executive when the stock price increases over the exercise price. At the date of grant, the exercise price may be more than the fair market value (FMV). When the executive exercises the stock, he pays the employer the total exercise price and receives the stock shares. The executive benefits in an amount that is equal to the difference between the exercise price and the FMV of the stock on the date it was exercised. That difference is taxed as ordinary income. Any appreciation of the shares after that is taxed as capital gain. Just like incentive stock options, the Black-Scholes value of the options shows up as compensation expense in the income statement, and is spread over the vesting period or the performance period.

A Shareholder-Friendly Alternative

We defined SARs a bit earlier. Now we want to tell you why shareholders love 'em.

Stock appreciation rights, while they give the same benefits to recipients, are seen as a more shareholder-friendly version of options. Basically, SARs are similar to stock options—their value is tied to company stock price. So what's the difference? Options require executives to pay cash when exercising them. With SARs, the executive may choose cash or stock equal to the price increase in company stock based on when the SARs were issued.

Shareholders like SARs because they often create less dilution than options, and they are also exempt from deferred compensation taxes when settled in stock. Executives also don't need to put up their own cash to purchase them. Good news for many executives now that loans are no longer allowed!

Are SARs perfect? Nope. As long as company shares appreciate, SARs have a guaranteed value.

Stock appreciation rights, otherwise known as SARs, are basically the same vehicle as stock options. The only difference is that the instrument doesn't allow the executive the right to a particular share of stock. Instead, this long-term incentive program allows the executive the value of appreciation, and no exercise price is paid. When exercised, the value of the appreciation is paid in cash or stock.

When paid in cash, the difference between the FMV upon grant and stock price is paid to the executive, and is recognized as ordinary income. Under FAS 123, cash-settled SARs fall under the "variable" accounting category, which means that they are measured from period-to-period using the Black-Scholes valuation model. If there is an increase in the Black-Scholes value, that increase is expensed over the remaining vesting period.

When paid in stock, the difference between the FMV upon grant and stock price is paid in stock to the executive. The transfer is recognized as ordinary income, and under FAS 123 receives the same accounting treatment as an ISO or NSO.

Full Value Long-Term Incentives

Now that you have a good handle on appreciation-based awards, let's move on to full value incentives. Restricted stock, restricted stock units (RSU), and performance shares are the three different types of full value long-term incentives.

When it comes to restricted stock, a grant of actual stock is made to the executive, subject to vesting. Once vested, the FMV of the stock is taxable, just like ordinary income. No additional transfers or payments are made upon vesting, as the shares have already been transferred to the employee on the date of grant. Appreciation that occurs between vesting and the sale of stock is considered capital gains. Under FAS 123, restricted stock is expensed over the vesting or performance period.

INVESTOR ALERT #21

WHEN THE CEO HAS LOTS OF STOCK OPTIONS AND NO OWNERSHIP

Research indicates that when CEOs have large amounts of stock options but hold no company stock in the form of restricted stock, or have purchased stock in the open market, then the company's stock will be highly volatile and will perform worse than the average organizations in the industry. Options are an invitation to roll the dice. If risky strategies such as an acquisition or merger work out, the stock will appreciate substantially. If the risky adventure does not work out, the stock will not appreciate. Who loses? Not the executive, since they never really owned anything.

We'd be reluctant to throw our own money into a craps game where the individual could win money but the only money he could lose was ours.

A restricted stock unit (RSU) is similar to restricted stock. The main difference? No actual stock is transferred to the executive at the date of grant. Instead, an RSU is actually a right to receive a share of stock at the time of vesting. The value of an RSU is equal to the FMV of one share of stock. As far as taxes are concerned, RSUs are taxed like ordinary income, based on the FMV of the transferred shares. RSUs are accounted for under FAS 123 in the same manner as restricted stock.

Performance shares promise a certain number of shares of actual stock if an executive achieves a goal or milestone. The

FMV of these shares is taxed as ordinary income. FAS 123 accounting is similar to restricted stock and restricted stock units.

Cash-Based Awards

Just like they sound, cash-based long-term incentives take the form of cash awards based on the achievement of long-term goals. As far as taxes are concerned, cash-based awards are treated as ordinary income, and are treated as compensation expense under FAS 123.

What's Not to Love?

During the dot com boom of the 1990s, stock options were the long-term investment plan of choice. Not only did they enjoy certain tax and accounting benefits, but companies didn't have to report them as expenses, which meant that they didn't affect a company's bottom line. Stock options were a great way for cash-strapped technology start-ups to attract the talent they needed, and because of their vesting periods ensured that good talent stuck around for the long haul. Furthermore, stock options were seen as a great way to align executive success to that of the company and shareholders. It just made sense that CEOs with stock options would do their damndest to make sure that company stock price was always on the upswing. Best of all, stock options were, well, *invisible*. Companies could hand them out by the truckload—and many did—and still tell their investors that they cost nothing. What's not to love?

Another interesting fact is that the federal government has played a significant role in enhancing the emphasis on long-term incentives. When Congress imposed their tax penalties on all base salaries above $1 million, performance-based pay became the latest fashion. When equity compensation in the form of stock and stock options was determined to be performance-based, the natural shift from fixed compensations (base salaries and entitlement-based retirement plans) to variable compensation was an unintended consequence that was put into motion.

INVESTOR ALERT #22

HIGH DILUTION LEVELS

High levels of dilution as result of executive and employee use of equity in various compensation programs should be a concern to investors. Equity can be an important source of motivation for key executives. If there is a substantial amount of shareholder equity that is being used for either motivating a few executives a great deal, or attempting to motivate a large workforce a small amount, it's our feeling that executives are probably not allocating other scarce resources efficiently either.

If you can't allocate someone else's—the shareholders'—money effectively, you probably cannot allocate the company's money effectively. If the executive isn't allocating the company's resources effectively then the company will be a loser sooner or later—usually sooner.

We wouldn't let an executive who couldn't allocate his money very effectively allocate ours.

So popular were options in 2002 that a study done by the National Center for Employee Ownership (NCEO) showed that about 10 million United States employees were getting stock options.[1]

So what went wrong with stock options? Why is the number of people in the U.S. today who are receiving stock options 7 million and shrinking?[2]

Here's the problem. Stock options are perhaps not as motivating as they were once thought to be. Or, should we say, the way they were being used doesn't always motivate executives to make good decisions with long-term success in mind. Part of this, at least, can be blamed on the fact that options make it too easy to sacrifice long-term success for short-term gain. In other words, the motivation of stock options as a long-term incentive vehicle is contraindicated: they motivate the executive to focus on pumping up the stock price on a quarter-to-quarter basis, without focusing on sustained performance over the long haul. And that's most certainly not what stock options are meant to do. Meanwhile, back at the shareholder ranch, greater share issuance is diluting the value of existing shares.

Where Oh Where Did the Options Go?

Here's another statistic. Stock options granted to employees hit $137 million in 2001. In 2005, according to a study done by Watson Wyatt Worldwide that looked at 793 companies in Standard & Poor's Composite 1500, stock options granted fell to $40 million.[3]

While just about all public companies issued options a mere five years ago, now only about two-thirds do, and they are pickier about whom they give them to. In addition to the fact that stock options are easily abused, there are two other reasons why companies are shying away from options. The first is that since the tech bubble burst companies have needed to look for other ways to attract and retain top executives. The second is FAS 123R, is a regulation that requires the expensing of options—and, for all intents and purposes, removes their cost advantages of options versus other forms of long-term incentive compensation. In many companies, stock options are being replaced with restricted stock as well as performance-based stock plans in the hopes that organizations will get a bit more for their money.

Those companies who are still using options aren't being so cavalier with them. As a matter of fact, they are being much more thoughtful when it comes to long-term incentives in general. Take Agilent Technologies, a measurements products company that did a study that showed half of their share price movement was driven by economic and industry factors, while the other half was driven by company performance. So Agilent changed its long-term incentive program to reflect their findings. Instead of being made up entirely of options, the company split their long-term incentive plan evenly between options and performance shares. Makes sense when you think about it, doesn't it?

Some investors are refusing to play with companies that grant options. After all, what better way to avoid the potential problems of options than to avoid companies that grant options? We all know how much Warren Buffet, CEO of Berkshire Hathaway, hates options. Other companies, like the investment-advisory firm Bastiat Capital, also avoid companies that grant options because they want to avoid the stuff that goes with it—difficult accounting, dilution, and of course backdating.[4] Instead, Bastiat chooses to focus on companies like CompuCredit, who not only have stopped issuing options, but provide a thoughtful and detailed explanation of their compensation philosophy in general.

Parlez-Vous CEO?

With stock options, of course, came a whole new fun language. While we all agree that the main reason for granting options was to get managers and shareholders on the same page, I doubt even industry gurus suspected that stock options would have such a huge impact on our vocabulary.

For example, we bandy about the word "backdating" like we've been using it for centuries. As a matter of fact, you would have to live in a cave not to know what it means. Okay, for those of you who do live in a cave, backdating is the practice—widespread at times—of manipulating the dates of stock options grants to coincide with low points in their value. Chances are you know what backdating is because lots of companies have done it—Monster Worldwide Inc., Apple Computer, Comverse Technology, Affiliated Computer Systems, Brocade Communications Systems. And those are just a few that come to mind. Leave it to executives to come up with yet another innovative way to max out their pay. Is backdating illegal? Nope. But it's not very nice either. Shareholders don't take it well when they find out their highly paid executives are spending their time finding accounting loopholes that allow them to take lots and lots of money from the company cash flow—while shareholders pay the price.

There's another term we've heard associated with options: spring loading—when options are granted just before good news is announced that sends stock prices higher. A little digging around reveals that spring loading is completely legal as long as the board knows what's going on when the options are granted. In other words, if both board and executives are both in on this dubious practice it's a-okay. Of course, it's perfectly legal to leave shareholders, who think that the options are granted at market value, in the dark.

Examples of spring loading abound. Let's take Apple Computer, who granted several large stock option grants two days after ousting CEO Gilbert Amelio, but before the company announced its acquisition of the software maker Next and the return of Steve Jobs. The date was July 11, 1997, a day that marked a ten-year low in Apple stock.[5] But in the span of 19 months Apple went from being in some serious trouble to being on top of the world. Were the executives who were granted stock options on the bad days just plain lucky? Hmmmm. Apple also awarded a bunch of grants on August 5. On the 6th Jobs announced that Microsoft had invested $150 million in Apple. Double hmmmmm.[6]

So what do you think? Are backdating and spring loading legitimate forms of compensation, or are they thinly veiled forms of insider trading? We think the answer is simple. Companies that don't tell their investors that they are awarding options prior to good news that will potentially send stocks higher are misleading them. Period. And that's not good for any company's long-term outlook.

How Much Are These Things Worth, Anyway?

Since the SEC has required expensing of options, a flurry of suggestions regarding how to value them has cropped up. While some see this as just another way companies are playing the "numbers game," in all fairness the question of how to value options has had accounting and securities regulators pulling their hair out for more than a decade.

The most commonly used method is the Black-Scholes method. But critics of this method say that it overstates the value of options and reduces a company's net income.

INVESTOR ALERT #23

REPRICING STOCK OPTIONS

Option repricing is a very common design feature that continues to upset and concern most investors. And the practice should be very upsetting. In fact, we think it is so upsetting that the investor should take their money someplace else. We see very little reason to provide executives with "Mulligans" or "do overs" at the expense of investors. It is a little bit like saying, "I didn't get it right the first time, but if you let me try a second time I'll get right." The only thing that should be right about this situation is to show the executives the right way to the door.

Yes, we think there's some value in learning from mistakes. But those should happen before they get to the executive suite. What is even more frustrating is that some plans provide for option repricing without even getting shareholder approval.

You know the old saying, "A deal is a deal."

But there's something else you should know about Black-Scholes as well as another common method, the lattice method. Both include assumptions and estimates that can be tweaked, allowing many companies to manipulate the numbers as they see fit. Here's an interesting stat. According to a report by Credit Suisse Analyst David Zion, the value of options granted by companies in Standard & Poor's 500 index dropped from $104 billion in 2000 to $30 billion in 2004.[7] Sure, companies granted fewer options. But does this account for the entire drop, or can stock option valuation be seen as another form of the numbers game? Quite possibly. With the introduction of the new disclosure rules, many companies changed the way they value their options. Intel's valuation method, for example, allowed them to reduce last year's stock options costs by $570 million, while Cisco reduced its expenses $640 million.[8] Could options valuation turn out to be the next scandal *du jour*? We shall see.

Investors Say, "Show Me the Money"

How often do executives pony up their *own* money to buy stock in the companies they run? Not very often. When an executive is said to be heavily invested in a company he runs, let there be no doubt about it—most of his equity ownership is in the form of stock options and restricted stock.

But some investors are wondering why they should continue to invest in companies when those who are running it aren't. Kornitzer Capital Management, Inc., for example, sold its last shares of Sara Lee because it felt that top-tier executives were showing a lack of faith in the company by not buying shares with their own money.[9] Not exactly a ringing endorsement, is it?

Of course, some executives put up their own money, most notably in turnaround situations. Jamie Dimon at Bank One (i.e., before the acquisition of JP Morgan Chase) and Edward J. Zander of Motorola Inc. have both bought company shares in the open market. Does this send a strong message to investors? You bet it does.

Payment for Pulse

The fierce criticism that has recently surrounded stock options is certainly one of the reasons why today's trend is moving away from options and more toward restricted stock. There's no doubt that giant option grants at Enron, for example, encouraged executives to fudge accounting practices, hoping to cash in the options and then dump them before anyone noticed how creative they had been. Nobody wants to be another Enron. And so some companies are dropping option plans altogether in favor of restricted stock plans.

But we have to wonder if moving solely into restricted stock isn't going a bit overboard. Two issues basically drive the value of restricted stock: the number of shares awarded and the stock price at exercise. If the stock price goes up between the time of grant and exercise, the executive is a two-time winner—he gets the value of the grant and the value of the appreciation. But, if the stock price goes down from the grant to vesting, the executive still enjoys some value, but it is less than the grant value. Unlike stock options, the value proposition is relative, not absolute, which gets us to our main point. Warts and all, because of their valuation linkage to stock price appreciation, stock options are a much more leveraged long-term incentive vehicle than restricted stock with time-based vesting. We would actually go so far as to say that over the past few years, the increased use of restricted stock with time-based vesting is counterintuitive to the clamor for more pay for performance.

Let's take Exxon Mobil as an example. Exxon Mobil has canned their stock option plan and now only hands out real stock. How is that hurting them?

Well, Exxon Mobil reported that in 2005, it spent more money buying back its own stock than it did on integral things like R & D, capital spending, and exploration.[10] Sure, this may be part of a plan not to invest until oil prices come down, but it sure did not hurt the retired CEO Lee R. Raymond's compensation plan. With his long-term incentives made up of restricted stock, Raymond didn't stand to gain anything by taking a significant risk. If oil prices stay high, the company would have missed out on some good investments but would still be profitable. But what if prices fell? You got it. The value of the stock would suffer.

All this goes to show that while long-term incentives shouldn't be structured in a way that allow them to steal money from shareholders, they should be structured so that executives care about whether or not stock rises. When long-term incentives are made up entirely of restricted stock, an organization gives executives the message that they will get rich even if the company's stock stays put. Can you expect such a plan to drive executives? The answer is no.

Close, but Not Perfect

Unlike stock options and restricted stock, performance shares tie the award to the achievement of pre-established performance goals, which may or may not be based on stock price. Lots of companies are hopping on the performance share bandwagon. The media company Viacom, for example, long criticized for its excessive executive pay packages, approved a long-term incentive for CEO Philippe P. Dauman with a target value of $12 million, half in stock options and half in performance shares. The payouts of both go hand-in-hand with Viacom's stock performance, effectively tying most of Dauman's compensation to the value of the organization's stock.

That being said, performance shares aren't perfect. Especially for companies in volatile markets, it's difficult to figure out what the right metrics are to drive performance over a longer period of time. And while performance shares usually work well for mature companies that can develop sufficiently grounded "look back" and "look around" baselines to develop financial and/or stock performance goals for the next two or three years, they don't work well for an immature company that can't develop this baseline. Finally, some companies design their performance share plans with ridiculously low bars. And that defeats the whole purpose—the award isn't really performance-based after all.

A Trip Down Memory Lane

What about the types of plans that specify an amount of cash that will be awarded based on the achievement of defined, long-term objectives?

In most cases, these plans represent a throwback to the olden days when executives received portions of the net earnings of the organization. The most critical difference in non–market based plans is that they rely on internal financial measures to determine the value of the award. Since the plan is denominated in cash, and therefore insulated from market factors, the amount of value believed appropriate at the target level of performance is highly predictable. In addition, while the expected amount of the award must be amortized over the performance period, there is no additional adjustment for the movement in company stock, since the company stock value has no impact on the dollar value of the award.

Giving It Back

In these days of corporate malfeasance yet another new trend has emerged—claw back policies. These policies are now a part of many organizations' long-term incentive programs, stating that companies—and their shareholders—can basically get their money back if executives take money they haven't earned. While in some cases this means money executives were paid despite not meeting a goal or because of an accounting error, claw back policies are also used to recoup money paid because of executive misconduct. In either case, if someone has paid you too much it's only right to return the money, right? Right?

While Barney Frank has proposed legislation designed to help shareholders achieve claw backs, other companies are adding rules and amendments to their long-term incentive programs in order to make claw backs easier. International Paper, for example, has regulations that state that they can recoup money if results are significantly revised, and also pays bonuses in restricted stock that can't be sold for a number of years, giving them some time to catch both mistakes and executive misconduct.[11]

How important are claw back policies? Consider this tale of woe. In December 2000 Florida Power and Light's shareholders approved an $8 billion merger with Entergy Corp., setting off about $92 million in cash bonuses for 700 managers.[12] Did the deal have to be completed before executives took home their windfall? Nope, just approved by shareholders.

Here's where things blew up. In April of 2001, the deal was called off. Shareholders demanded a repayment, but it seems the board was loath to insult CEO James Broadhead. Apparently he had some hunting buddies in the crowd and a few other friends who didn't want to damage a friendship over, oh, millions of dollars. Shareholders were furious, and in January of 2002 two groups sued. To add insult to injury, while FPL's executives were enjoying fat—and undeserved—bonuses, things were so bad at the company that employee pay was cut and—this is good—discount coupons for Thanksgiving turkeys were no longer offered.[13] Not only did the company eventually decide to let the bonuses slide, they also found out during the investigative period that, due to an accounting error, an extra $9 million in bonuses was overpaid. We know, this story just keeps getting uglier and uglier. Eventually the company recouped $22.25 million, $9.75 of which was paid by Broadhead and other executives, the rest of which was picked up by insurers.[14] If the moral of this story isn't evident we'll spell it out to you. Don't pay your long-term incentives until the goals attached to them are complete, and make sure your plan includes a claw back policy.

Things to Consider

With all of these long-term incentive instruments, how do you know which ones will work for your executive total reward program? While there is no one-size-fits-all answer (yes, we know, there's *never* an easy answer) there are some key general considerations that must be taken into account when designing your plan.

- **Efficiency.** Efficiency favors restricted stock/RSUs and cash if an organization is thinking about financial statement expense. Why? Well, it's pretty likely that the cost of restricted stock/RSUs will equal or exceed the value delivered to the executive, and cash payments match the related expense.

If your organization is a private organization that intends to stay so, this is less of a concern.

- **Shareholder Alignment.** Both stock options and restricted stock align executives with shareholders. Does one do a better job than the other? There are actually arguments for both sides. Those in favor of stock options say they better align executives with shareholders because executives must increase the value of the company in order to receive any benefit. On the other hand, others say that restricted stock has better alignment power, because executives almost always have an interest in company value.
- **Retentive Power.** Restricted stock and cash come out the winners. Restricted stock because executives almost always have value, and cash because it doesn't erode, except with inflation.
- **Tax Effectiveness.** Both stock options and SARs are better than restricted stock when it comes to tax effectiveness. Some private companies introduce a deferred compensation element to control liquid liability and keep the LTI payouts more predictable. In addition, the deferred compensation element can also make an LTI plan more attractive to participants.
- **Private Company Considerations.** These include voting rights, dividends, and financial reporting and valuation. If restricted stock or stock options are used, real shares will be transferred to executives. But issues like voting rights of outside shareholders, state law, shareholder rights, higher scrutiny of the financial statements, and worries regarding selection status, mean that outside shareholders aren't always wanted by closely owned or family-owned businesses.

*C*ase Study #22

One of our private clients came to us and asked us for assistance on their long-term incentive plan design. The first effort was to understand how they had evaluated and compared their long-term incentive plan awards with the mar-

ketplace awards. We assigned one of our top economists to work with the organization to help determine the likely value of their long-term incentive awards.

It became clear that the comparison was, in fact, invalid. Ultimately we had to translate the award from a private company with all its appendages into an award that was an "apples to apples" comparison with the marketplace on an ordinary income basis.

When the final comparison was made it was clear that the value that had been ascribed to the awards by the human resources and finance departments was approximately one-third of the award's comparable value. While our conclusion did not sit well with the human resources and finance departments, they agreed we were correct.

The outcome of this discrepancy was to grant four times as many shares to the client's executives than was necessary to attain the market attachment the company was targeting. And information did indicate that the historic grants had been extremely valuable to the executives. Until we developed our evaluation, it was not clear how much more valuable they were in the marketplace.

Sometimes when you want an evaluation it may be necessary to go to a third-party if the results of the evaluation may affect the income of the evaluators.

The Portfolio Approach

If you've read this chapter carefully, you understand that while there are plenty of long-term incentive vehicles to choose from, none of them are perfect. And this is why most of the companies we work with are taking a double-pronged approach when it comes to long-term incentive strategy. In most cases, a thoughtful mix of equity compensation as well as performance-based vehicles gets the right message across and accomplishes what long-term incentive plans are supposed to do: attract and retain top executives while also holding them accountable to the organization's long-term success.

Using a portfolio approach—an approach that uses several different vehicles—is often the best way for a company to meet its program objectives. For example, stock options are great if you are looking to align executive success to shareholder success, but they may not speak at all to other important goals, like meeting specific objectives.

A long-term incentive can be one of the most complicated components of a total executive reward strategy. In addition to ensuring that the plan is effective and gels with environmental factors, shareholder issues, and business and people strategies, it also has to meet complex government and tax regulations. For this reason it's a good idea to use a design team who can not only create an effective program, but can also sell it to executives. If you want the results you are after here's a no-brainer—your executives need to understand the plan. Finally, a good balance of vehicles ensures that your long-term incentive plan doesn't speak to just one area of your organization, but allows your organization to accomplish a wide variety of goals.

*C*ase Study #23

A technology company asked us to help develop an executive total reward strategy. After reviewing the major components of the plan, we were surprised to find out that all employees at the organization were awarded stock options. We developed an analysis that determined what the average gain on exercise was for the entire population, and several cuts of executives.

Everyone at the organization was surprised to find out that the average gain on exercise for the entire participating population was approximately $1,000. This meant that *the average employee received a $1,000 benefit, which oc-curred almost annually as a function of both the growth of the stock in the number of shares that had been awarded. Most of the shares were exercised relatively soon after they vested.*

The actual analysis for the executives was not much differ-ent. The average holding period after vesting was less than two years, and the average amount gained upon exercise was less than $10,000. Few executives hung around for more than five years.

Our recommendation was to eliminate all employee partic-ipation in a stock option program except for the very senior executives, and to lengthen out the vesting period to five years from three. In addition, we installed a minimum stock holding amount, and provided the executives with a cash award roughly equivalent to the taxes that they would owe on exercise shares.

Sometimes, just because your competitors are giving stock options to all employees, it doesn't make it right for your company. When stock options are used like a short-term savings account it's a waste of shareholder resources. The objective of stock or equity based compensation ought to be to make senior management owners of the company and align their interest to shareholders. Rank-and-file employ-ees' interests cannot be aligned with shareholders through the use of an equity program which provides them with $1,000 gains annually.

Long-term incentives that work best are those that are used with mix in mind. Nicely balanced with other components, long-term incentives can send the right message—and can be highly motivating. The goal should be to thoughtfully de-sign your long-term incentives so that you are rewarding ex-ecutives for making decisions that will serve your organiza-tion well and up the ante for long-term success.

References

1. National Center for Employee Ownership Study.
2. Ibid.
3. "Value of Employee Stock Option Grants Declines Sharply." *Watson Wyatt*, 7 December 2006. Available online at http://www.watsonwyatt.com/news/press.asp?ID=16796, accessed 1 October 2007.
4. Greenberg, Herb. "Seeking Out Firms That Don't Bother With Stock Options." *Wall Street Journal*, 26 August 2006.
5. Hesseldahl, Arik. "Apple's Options Overdose." *Businessweek*, 7 August 2006. Available online at http://www.businessweek.com/technology/content/aug2006/tc20060817_404045.htm?chan=search, accessed 1 October 2007.
6. Ibid.
7. Sasseen, Jane. "Cheaper Stock Options." *Businessweek*, 13 July 2006. Available online at http://www.businessweek.com/bwdaily/dnflash/content/jul2006/db20060713_765011.htm?chan=top+news_top+news, accessed 1 October 2007.
8. Waters, Richard. "New Accounting Rules Help Corporate USA Slice Expenses." *FT.com*, 24 April 2006. Available online at http://search.ft.com/iab?queryText=New%20Accounting%20Rules%20Help%20Corporate%20USA%20Slice%20Expenses&aje=true&id=060424000626&ct=0&location=http%3A%2F%2Fsearch.ft.com%2FftArticle%3FqueryText%3DNew+Accounting+Rules+Help+Corporate+USA+Slice+Expenses%26aje%3Dtrue%26id%3D060424000626%26ct%3D0&referer=http%3A%2F%2Fsearch.ft.com%2Fsearch%3FqueryText%3DNew+Accounting+Rules+Help+Corporate+USA+Slice+Expenses, accessed 1 October 2007.
9. Jargon, Julie. "Sara Lee Investors Note Execs Not Buying Stock." *Crain's*, 1 October 2006. Available online at http://www.chicagobusiness.com/cgi-bin/news.pl?id=22276, accessed 1 October 2007.
10. Norris, Floyd. "Perhaps Exxon Really Needs Stock Options." *New York Times*, 10 February 2006. Available online at http://topics.nytimes.com/top/news/business/companies/exxon_mobil_corporation/index.html?query=STOCKS%20AND%20BONDS&field=des&match=exact, accessed 1 October 2007.

11. Thurm, Scott. "Extra Pay: Many CEOs Receive Dividends on 'Phantom' Stock." *Wall Street Journal*, 4 May 2006. Available online at http://online.wsj.com/article/SB114671224745343502. html, accessed 1 October 2007.

12. Ibid.

13. Ibid.

14. Ibid.

CHAPTER 13

Wealth Accumulation Incentives

The executive compensation reward component that we are calling "wealth accumulation" is a new category for most executives, as well as for most designers. How new is it? Well, check out any index in our competitors' books, and chances are you won't find it listed.

Lots of people make the mistake of lumping wealth accumulation into the category of executive compensation associated with long-term incentives (since much wealth has been accumulated as a result of equity incentives) or equity-based incentives or, even more off base, they liken it to supplemental executive retirement programs (SERPs). We believe it's important for the category of wealth accumulation to stand on its own. Used correctly, wealth accumulation incentives have immense power. Any organization that chooses not to evaluate this new species of executive compensation is, in our opinion, missing out. And in a big way.

Viva la Difference

Let's talk first about the difference between this new category—wealth accumulation—and the more traditional ways that executives create wealth, including SERPs, deferred compensation, and long-term incentives like stock options and restricted stock.

The biggest difference between wealth accumulation incentives and the categories listed above is that wealth accumulation incentives are—well—*incentives*. Because the first criterion for determining whether a program falls into this new category is whether or not it is performance based. The second criterion is whether it is truly "super long term" or career based.

Let's talk about traditional retirement plans. Traditional retirement plans are not tied to stock or company performance, yet executives accumulate lots of wealth through them anyway.

When we hear of a mediocre-or-worse CEO receiving substantial retirement money, the news gives us pause and makes us think about the design of the compensation plan. While no two plans are designed exactly the same, traditional retirement plans are not tied to stock or company performance. In other words, an executive will receive the same retirement benefits regardless of whether the company prospered or failed during his tenure. Hardly motivating, right?

INVESTOR ALERT #24

THE CEO GETS DISPROPORTIONAL AMOUNTS OF THE TOP TEAM'S COMPENSATION

If you look at the top five officers on a company's proxy statement and find the CEO receives a disproportional amount of the total compensation, you have strong evidence of an imperial CEO.

If an imperial CEO is appropriate for the organization at this point in time, then there's no need to be concerned. But if there's nothing in the organization's current situation that explains the need for an imperial CEO, you might want to consider that the disproportionate pay is going toward a disproportionate need to feed a disproportionate ego.

When a CEO's compensation indicates that they believe "they are the team" rather than an individual contributing to the team, there's probably not a good portfolio of management talent at the top.

So how does retirement work into all of this? Traditionally, retirement has been a static figure based solely on the executive's retirement age and how many years of service he has put in with the company, multiplied by his last years of compensation. However, today's headlines have everyone thinking:

Should an executive's retirement benefits fluctuate depending upon his performance?

Okay, if you had doubts before, here's where you are really getting your money's worth for this book. We've identified and developed a new wealth accumulation plan approach that links long-term wealth accumulation directly to performance. This plan, unlike traditional retirement or stock option plans, is designed so that a portion of the executive's total reward program and ultimately their wealth accumulation rewards are based on company performance, stock performance, or a combination of both. If you are thinking that this sounds familiar, it is. These plans harken back to the days when owners ran their own companies. These plans go beyond the "alignment of shareholders" and effectively combine career incentives and defined contribution retirement plans with deferred compensation awarded only when the corporation beats the competition.

Before we get in the details regarding these types of plans (which we called gPB-WARP, grahall Performance-Based Wealth Accumulation and Retention Plans), let's talk about the traditional plans.

Traditional Plans

The first plan, a defined benefit retirement plan, is a plan we've already mentioned that is dependent only on the executive's last few years of compensation and his qualified retirement age, with sufficient years of service. The benefit *does not* vary with financial and stock price performance. While other parts of an executive's compensation plan may be performance-based, traditional retirement plans are not. Usually the plans vest after five years of service.

The second type of traditional plan, the "long-term" incentive program, is typically a plan that has either stock option awards or restricted stock awards that vest after three or four years.

This "long-term" plan's benefit (or the gain in the stock price) is available for the executive to cash in on whenever he or she feels is an opportune time, which can be simply an overall stock market or sector rally.

INVESTOR ALERT #25

SHORT TIME VESTED MEGA GRANTS OF OPTIONS OR RESTRICTED SHARES

Sometimes you'll read about a mega grant of options being awarded to some lucky executive. The rationale usually given is that the grant is necessary to either hire a new executive or align the present executive with the shareholders and the business. When these options are vested over a short (three–five years) prorated time frame, the only thing getting "lined" is the executive's pocket.

Even worse is when the executive is given a mega grant of restricted stock.

Regardless of how well the shareholders do, unless the stock price collapses, the executive will quickly become wealthy. In the worst-case scenario he may also become risk-adverse and complacent.

In both cases, investors should give themselves a mega tip and sell the shares.

However, if the options or restricted shares come with a real performance requirement (something in the 75th percentile, for instance), hold onto the shares during the restructuring period if you have the stomach for it.

The third type of traditional plan is the deferred compensation plan, where the executive is required to (or can voluntarily) defer their current compensation into either a fixed rate of return account or a broad set of stock mutual funds. These plans allow the executives to choose when they will receive the normally 100 percent vested money at some date in the future.

Each of these traditional plans may have a place in any company's executive total reward strategy, however, none of them really puts the executive in the actual shoes of the owner based upon their company's absolute and relative performance, and none of them require the executive to invest and hold the stock through "thick and thin." Two of the three—SERPs and deferred compensation—don't even require that the wealth be held in company stock.

The grahall Performance-Based Wealth Accumulation and Retirement Plan (gPB-WARP)

So how does the gPB-WARP differ from the other traditional plans? Well, the plan has been designed in response to the needs of the market today, as well as for the sometimes competing interests of the various stakeholders and other interested parties in the current business environment. A gPB-WARP is an alternative for boards and organizations who feel excessive retirement plans, despite performance, are inappropriate, stock plans have too short a horizon, and deferred compensation isn't invested in company stock and all of the plans vest based on too short a period of time. In other words, the gPB-WARP provides an alternative way of looking at wealth accumulation for those organizations that believe some portion of retirement, equity incentives, and deferred compensation should be tied to the value an executive brings to an organization and how that value compares to other possible investments the shareholders could have made.

How So?

Well, these new reward components uniquely integrate retirement, deferred compensation, and incentive compensation programs and then lengthens the time frame. Shareholders, and the public, are tired of seeing executives walk away with something for nothing. A gPB-WARP addresses that issue by giving the executive an incentive to grow the stock on both an absolute and a relative basis.

In addition, a gPB-WARP operates within a performance-based, defined contribution framework. There is a clear, and highly leveraged, link between the creation of long-term career company value and the compensation from the plan when the executive leaves at retirement. In other words, if an executive adds value to an organization, his wealth accumulation and retention account will go up, but if the company performs poorly prior to his retirement, the plan's account is indexed to the company's stock and will go down.

What does this mean? It means that there is an opportunity for key employees to "buy in" and share in the growth and appreciation of the business, much like owners did in previous generations. In addition, there is a relatively modest impact on the budget, as plan contributions are largely funded out of earnings in excess of target. While the executives have all of their current, short, and mid-term incentive plans to live on, these plans treat or require that they not just think like owners but really become owners.

Why is this plan exciting? Well, it should certainly be exciting to organizations and their shareholders, who can design plans that ensure that generous retirement plans are reserved for only those executives who perform excessively well. Organizations implementing a gPB-WARP know that their executives have more of an incentive to perform. And even executives should be excited about grahall Performance-Based Wealth Accumulation and Retention Plans. Why? Because these plans reward good executives for jobs well done, and give them a certain level of control over their wealth accumulation. Maybe not such great news if you are a mediocre executive, but great news if you are above average!

As an example, let's talk about different gPB-WARP designs— the first is nearly funded from above target long-term incentive payouts, the second is tied only to company performance, while the third is tied to company performance and share price appreciation.

Figure 13.1 shows the projected Supplemental Retirement Benefit for an example Firm's CEO, assuming a target of 30 percent.

In the second example, in a gPB-WARP driven by company performance, the percentile of company performance would determine what percentage of total rewards that would be deposited into the wealth accumulation account. For the sake

FIGURE 13.1 Typical Defined Benefit SERP

Supplemental Retirement Plan - After Offsets

Year	End of Year Age	Salary @ 5.0%	100% Target Bonus	Total Comp	% Target Benefit	$ Target Benefit
1	45	500,000	500,000	1,000,000	0%	—
2	46	525,000	525,000	1,050,000	0%	—
3	47	551,250	551,250	1,102,500	0%	—
4	48	578,813	578,813	1,157,625	0%	—
5	49	607,753	607,753	1,215,506	0%	—
6	50	638,141	638,141	1,276,282	0%	—
7	51	670,048	670,048	1,340,096	0%	—
8	52	703,550	703,550	1,407,100	0%	—
9	53	738,728	738,728	1,477,455	0%	—
10	54	775,664	775,664	1,551,328	0%	—
11	55	814,447	814,447	1,628,895	30%	488,668
12	56	855,170	855,170	1,710,339	30%	513,102
13	57	897,928	897,928	1,795,856	30%	538,757
14	58	942,825	942,825	1,885,649	30%	565,695
15	59	989,966	989,966	1,979,932	30%	593,979
16	60	1,039,464	1,039,464	2,078,928	30%	623,678
17	61	1,091,437	1,091,437	2,182,875	30%	654,862
18	62	1,146,009	1,146,009	2,292,018	30%	687,605
19	63	1,203,310	1,203,310	2,406,619	30%	721,986
20	64	1,263,475	1,263,475	2,526,950	30%	758,085

Annual Benefit @ Retirement: 758,085

Lump-Sum Equivalent @ Retirement (18 payments @ 6%): 8,700,739 of argument, let's say that a company performance percentile of 15 percent would yield a retirement contribution of 3 percent of total compensation, while a company performance percentile of 95 percent would yield a retirement contribution of 25 percent of total compensation. As company performance improves, the contribution is increased because of both an increasing contribution rate and an increasing bonus to which the rate is applied. The leverage can be surgically applied, with significant increases in contribution rates at specified company performance levels, thereby creating a situation where plan contributions are funded out of earnings in excess of a target.

Figure 13.2 illustrates the two parts of the long-term incentive plan. "On Target" performance against three year performance period goals results in a payout competitive with the market 50th percentile (approximates 100 percent of base salary). Performance above target over this period earns an additional "WARP" (Wealth Accumulation and Retention Plan) payment. In conjunction with the LTIP payout, the WARP allows executives to earn a total long-term incentive—where merited by performance—that is competitive with the market 50th to 90th percentile. WARP payments also have a retention feature, as they are subject to an additional five to ten years of ratable vesting. WARP payments would be capped at the market 90th percentile (approximates 250 percent of base salary). We believe that this LTIP payout structure is a unique design for focusing executive attention on above-target performance and retaining executive talent while allowing for wealth accumulation.

INVESTOR ALERT #26

VESTED WEALTH ACCUMULATION

Whenever an investor sees large amounts of vested wealth as result of either: (a) long-term incentive plans in the money equity, (b) vested retirement benefits, (c) vested deferred compensation accounts, or (d) even large 401(k) plan balances, then the investor should be concerned about the amount that the CEO, or executives in general, can take when things turn bad.

Don't misunderstand—if executives have accumulated a great deal of wealth as a result of shareholder wealth created, large account balances in the various

Figure 13.2 Performance-based warp on top of long-term incentive.

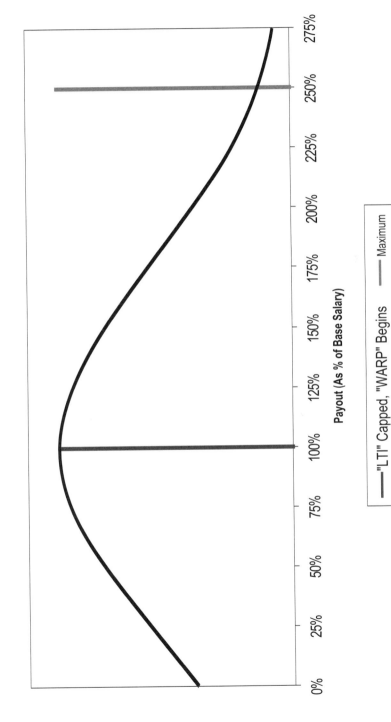

Long-Term Incentive Payout as % of Base Salary

Payout (As % of Base Salary)

— "LTI" Capped, "WARP" Begins   — Maximum

wealth accumulation plans are well and good. But what happens when all that wealth is vested and things start to look less rosy for the executive and the company? You can bet the executive will opt to take the money and run instead of hanging in and toughing it out through the rough period. We don't blame the executives. We blame the compensation committee and the board of directors.

What if an organization wanted to base a gPB-WARP on both company performance and share price appreciation? In that case, wealth accumulation balances would be linked to both company performance and share price appreciation. The contributions of the plan each year would vary depending on company performance, as illustrated in the previous example. Once contributed to the plan, a percentage of the account would be "pegged" to company stock performance, with the remaining percentage pegged to other investment indices. Converted into a table, the gPB-WARP would show the potential lump-sum equivalent at retirement, at various combinations of company performance and stock performance.

Figure 13.3 illustrates a Performance-Based Wealth Accumulation and Retention Plan which varies based on company performance. Uniquely there are two different aspects: (a) as company performance improves, the contribution is increased because of both an increasing contribution rate and an increasing bonus to which the rate is applied and (b) the leverage can be surgically applied, with significant increases in contribution rates at specified company performance levels (see 50th and 75th percentile), thereby creating a situation where plan contributions are funded out of earnings in excess of target.

Figure 13.4 illustrates a link of the plans benefits to both company performance and share price appreciation. The weighting of these two factors can vary to appropriately reflect the relative importance of each. The contributions to the plan each year would vary depending on company performance, as illustrated in the previous example. Once contributed to the plan, a percentage of the account would be "pegged" to company stock performance (in this example, 50 percent), with

FIGURE 13.3   Performance-based WARP—driven by company performance.

Percentile Company Performance	Plan Parameters		Year 1 Sample				SERP Benefit	
	Potential Bonus	PB-WARP Contrib as % Total Comp	Year 1 Salary	Yr 1 Bonus	Total Comp	PB-WARP Contrib	% of Total Comp	Lump Sum Equivalent
5%	0%	0.0%	500,000	0	500,000	0	0.0%	0
10%	0%	0.0%	500,000	18	500,018	0	0.0%	0
15%	19%	3.0%	500,000	95,610	595,610	17,868	5.7%	989,613
20%	34%	4.0%	500,000	171,621	671,621	26,865	7.6%	1,487,875
25%	47%	5.0%	500,000	236,831	736,831	36,842	9.5%	2,040,424
30%	59%	5.5%	500,000	295,392	795,392	43,747	10.5%	2,422,850
35%	70%	6.0%	500,000	349,658	849,658	50,979	11.5%	2,823,435
40%	80%	6.5%	500,000	401,150	901,150	58,575	12.4%	3,244,092
45%	90%	7.0%	500,000	450,970	950,970	66,568	13.4%	3,686,782
50%	100%	15.0%	500,000	500,000	1,000,000	150,000	28.6%	8,307,567
55%	110%	15.5%	500,000	550,000	1,050,000	162,750	29.6%	9,013,710
60%	120%	16.0%	500,000	600,000	1,100,000	176,000	30.6%	9,747,545
65%	130%	16.5%	500,000	650,000	1,150,000	189,750	31.5%	10,509,072
70%	140%	17.0%	500,000	700,000	1,200,000	204,000	32.5%	11,298,290
75%	150%	25.0%	500,000	750,000	1,250,000	312,500	47.7%	17,307,430
80%	163%	25.0%	500,000	812,500	1,312,500	328,125	47.7%	18,172,802
85%	175%	25.0%	500,000	875,000	1,375,000	343,750	47.7%	19,038,173
90%	188%	25.0%	500,000	937,500	1,437,500	359,375	47.7%	19,903,545
95%	200%	25.0%	500,000	1,000,000	1,500,000	375,000	47.7%	20,768,916

Note: Lump Sum Equivalent is calculated based on 18 payments (age 65 retirement to death at age 82), and a 6% discount rate.

FIGURE 13.4   Wealth Accumulation & Retention Plan based on company financial and stock performance

% Company Performance	6% Fixed	Stock Performance								
		10%	20%	30%	40%	50%	60%	70%	80%	90%
10%	0	0	0	0	0	0	0	0	0	0
20%	1,487,875	1,202,277	1,458,240	1,642,808	1,800,513	1,947,917	2,095,321	2,253,027	2,437,595	2,693,558
30%	2,422,850	1,957,783	2,374,592	2,675,141	2,931,949	3,171,981	3,412,013	3,668,821	3,969,369	4,386,178
40%	3,244,092	2,621,388	3,179,477	3,581,899	3,925,754	4,247,146	4,568,539	4,912,393	5,314,815	5,872,904
50%	8,307,567	6,712,928	8,142,099	9,172,633	10,053,185	10,876,217	11,699,248	12,579,801	13,610,335	15,039,506
60%	9,747,545	7,876,502	9,553,397	10,762,556	11,795,738	12,761,428	13,727,118	14,760,300	15,969,459	17,646,354
70%	11,298,290	9,129,581	11,073,255	12,474,780	13,672,332	14,791,655	15,910,978	17,108,530	18,510,055	20,453,729
80%	18,172,802	14,684,529	17,810,842	20,065,134	21,991,343	23,791,725	25,592,106	27,518,315	29,772,607	32,898,920
90%	19,903,545	16,083,056	19,507,113	21,976,099	24,085,757	26,057,603	28,029,449	30,139,107	32,608,093	36,032,151

the remaining percentage pegged to other investment indices (in this example, a fixed rate of 6 percent is assumed). Figure 13.4 shows the potential lump-sum equivalent at retirement, at various combinations of company performance and stock performance.

The Result

Due to new proxy disclosure requirements, coupled with shareholder sensitivity to executive compensation, boards may find the gPB-WARP a good alternative to the traditional three types of retirement plans. The gPB-WARP will ensure that CEOs who are not performing up to snuff will not receive excessive retirement money at company and shareholder expense. The gPB-WARPs will also give executives a good incentive to perform at their best, allow them to share in the growth of the business, and, to a certain degree, place their wealth accumulation in their own hands, just like the owner did in "the good old days."

Buying into It

Also unique to what we call wealth accumulation is that we feel it should not be strictly in the form of company stock. There is an optimal amount of ownership that should be required by an executive within an organization. No doubt, some of this wealth should be subject to lengthy vesting, and therefore lost if the executive leaves the organization to pursue other interests.

INVESTOR ALERT #27

STOCK OWNERSHIP GUIDELINES

Most of you will think we're crazy, but stock ownership guidelines often send messages to us that send us straight for the door. Here's why. Most organizations that set the guidelines set them too low. More importantly, once the goals are published, that level of share ownership becomes the acceptable level, or "norm," within the company. This creates the constant exercising and selling cycle, which in turn creates the regranting cycle and results in more shareholder dilution. There is something inherently wrong with an organization that needs to dictate the necessary share ownership to the individuals entrusted with the future of the organization.

If we really want executives to operate like long-term owners of the company and be aligned with the shareholders, then significant ownership ought to be a condition of the position, period.

Executives ought to be able to sell a small percentage of the shares they are granted and exercise, but their wealth should be on the same line as the shareholders.

And here's an interesting fact for you. Study after study has shown that organizations perform better if their executive team, as well as the middle management teams that report to executives, hold sufficient shares of the organization's stock. In addition, studies have shown that the value creation is sub optimized if the executives own *too much* of the organization's stock. It's pretty reasonable to expect that an executive, when considering future wealth, would want to pursue a diverse portfolio. To that end, we believe that wealth creation should be a balance between a threshold level of ownership in the company's stock, as well as a portfolio of stocks that allow the executive to benefit from a diversity of investments consistent with their personal needs.

Hitting the Target

Although controversial, we believe executive wealth creation, once the organization performs above the 50th percentile over a five-year or more period, should be directly proportional to the wealth that is created for the investors. What do we mean by this? Well, if the executive team is able to generate sustained wealth that is at the 75th percentile for a particular risk category, then it follows logically that the wealth accumulation of the executive should also be paid, in terms of wealth creation, at the 75th percentile of organizations of similar size and complexity. Simple math!

What we have to say next might be obvious, but we are going to say it anyway. If the organization's performance is below the 50th percentile for its risk category, then the executive, of course, should receive little or no wealth creation at all.

Short-Term Miracle Makers Need Not Apply

Now that you know a bit about the gPB-WARP, how do you maximize it? In other words, in what situations do you use it to motivate your executives?

Certainly, critical strategic initiatives would fit the category of our concept of performance-based, even if they did not, in the short term, generate significant price appreciation for the shareholders. Because they are extremely motivational and directional in nature, they would be appropriate to install in a gPB-WARP program.

We can easily imagine a group of secondary performance factors that could be used in conjunction with, or in place of, our definition of performance (which is, we hope you recall, performance above the 50th percentile over an extended period of time versus organizations in similar risk categories). Strategic acquisitions, geographic expansion, repositioning of an organization's value stream, and integrating new acquisitions or products are all factors that could be tied to a gPB-WARP.

To that end, no short-term miracle makers need apply. Our general feeling is that a gPB-WARP should be used for periods of time greater than five years, and we certainly wouldn't argue if someone suggested that a gPB-WARP plan should be used for a ten-year period or more. Sure, organizations may have occasional spurts of success or short-term setbacks. That's just part of the game and should be expected. On the other hand, it's the executive's job to position the organization for success. We think of the time period, then, as being somewhat generational in nature.

Pay Really Reflects Performance

If an executive isn't performing well, then by all means he should be given a little encouragement to leave. And gPB-WARPs work quite well in the encouragement department. An executive who isn't adding value above the 50th percentile in terms of wealth creation for shareholders will be, under the gPB-WARP, underpaid compared to their peers. So what? Let another organization benefit from his sub par management, while you go out and attract an executive with the goods to make your organization a premium performer.

No Hit-and-Runs

You've probably noticed that we have strong opinions about just about everything, and vesting is no different. There should be no—we repeat no—hit-and-run opportunities with a PB-WARP plan. As a matter of fact, we've suggested to many clients that the earliest vesting be 50 percent vesting after five years, with prorated vesting of the additional 50 percent over a second five-year period. We actually prefer 10- and 15-year cliff vesting. Is this extended vesting appropriate? Absolutely. Especially when the other components of the executive reward program are carrying their appropriate levels of compensation for the executive.

Compare and Contrast

We would like to end this chapter by leaving you with two important thoughts. First of all, it's not okay to take your eye off the ball when it comes to how much wealth an executive stands to accumulate. It's not good for the organization, it's not good for the shareholders—hey, it's not even good for the executive who gets all the negative attention. And now that we've given you a fairly simple solution, you can say good-bye to those "Holy Cow" moments.

Second of all, we would like to see more companies replace what we feel are the most misused total executive reward strategy components—executive retirement plans, deferred compensation, and stock options—with some real long-term performance based, wealth accumulation for executives

We hope that a great deal of the major organizations in the future will give serious thought to the benefits of developing versions of wealth accumulation and retention plans based on performance for their executive team. We know shareholders will find this new category of reward strategy pretty exciting; we're not so sure that the executives whose companies perform above average will also find these new wealth accumulation plans very exciting. Those executives whose organizations underperform in absolute or relative terms won't see the "glitter," and that's fine. They should continue to try and convince their boards they deserve both time-based restricted stock and defined benefit supplemental retirement plans. So be it!

CHAPTER 14
Executive Benefits

Here's a short (and playfully exagerated) quiz to test your total executive reward strategy savvy.

Do You Know the Difference Between Executive Benefits and Executive Perks?

1. Your wife went nuts decorating your Italian villa, the company picked up the tab, and now the media has made you the poster child for executive excess. What went wrong here?
   (a) You abused your executive perks.
   (b) You abused your executive benefits.
   (c) Someone forgot to hide this better. And when you find out who that someone is . . .

2. Your kid needs braces, but why should you pick up the tab? After all, anyone who makes a gazillion dollars should also have their medical bills taken care of, right? This type of thinking represents a misunderstanding of:
   (a) Executive benefits.
   (b) Executive perks.
   (c) Real life in general.

3. On a trip to Bora Bora, you were injured in a mishap with an angry headhunter. (No, *not* the same headhunter that tried to poach you from your company. Different guy. Definitely different wardrobe. But that's a story for another time.) Now it looks like you are going to need some time off to recover. Whether or not your long-term disability provides enough for you and your family to maintain your current standard of living is a function of:
   (a) Your executive benefits program.
   (b) Your executive perquisites program.

(c) How sorry your company feels for you once they get a load of you looking small and bewildered in your hospital bed.

4. In light of the new SEC disclosure rules, the organization has decided not to allow your dog, otherwise known as G. Shepherd, to book flights on the company plane. This represents a decrease in your:

(a) Executive perquisites.

(b) Executive benefits.

(c) Time and money. Not only are you going to have to pick up the phone and arrange to have someone drive your dog to his weekly psychiatry sessions, you are going to have to pay for it to.

Okay, put your pencil down. How do you think you did? If you answered *a* for every question, then you know the difference between executive benefits and executive perquisites. If you didn't answer every question correctly, don't feel so bad. Lots of people confuse executive benefits with executive perks.

In fact, executive benefits and executive perquisites are two very distinct components of an executive reward strategy. How are they different? In a nutshell, executive perquisites are extra benefits that executives receive that rank-and-file employees do not receive. Club memberships, use of the company airplane, paid tax and investment advice, and automobile usage are all good examples of common executive perquisites.

By contrast, executive benefits are employee benefits—those supplied to rank-and-file employees—that are supplemented in order to be appropriate for executives. In many cases statutory rules and regulations place limits on employee benefits. Executive benefits are excess benefits designed to fill in those gaps created by the various limitations. Income replacement, income protection, future financial security, pay for time not worked, and deferred compensation all fall under the category of executive benefits.

Our philosophy on executive benefits is relatively straightforward and simple. If the benefit is provided to all employees, but has a maximum limitation for no good reason other than "because Congress says so," then the executive should be provided supplemental benefits that extend, on a proportional basis, those benefits that are limited by statutory regulation. The mantra here, folks, should be "All things in moderation." In no case should the benefits provided to executives be substantially greater than those provided on a proportional basis to all employees. Unless, of course, there is a business reason to do so.

When More Than Pride Is Injured: Income Replacement

Let's go back a few pages to our executive who was injured in the ugly headhunter mishap. It's never pretty when a top-ranking executive sustains an injury or illness that takes him away from the organization for an extended period of time, even when natives are not involved. An extended illness or injury can have drastic consequences not only on the executive, but on the organization as well.

The fact is, about 20 percent of all working Americans will suffer an illness or an injury that takes them away from work for 90 days or more before they are 65. Some of the best executives have had long and seasoned careers and are a little on the older side. They know there's a chance they will face a short-term or long-term disability or illness—at least those who realize they are mortal do! So here's the problem. The short-term and long-term disability packages offered to rank-and-file employees just aren't going to cut it for a highly paid executive.

Let's do the math, and you'll see what we mean. Most disability programs allow income replacement of 60 percent, with a total maximum of $5,000 per month. For highly paid executives, that amount might just barely cover the wife's clothing allowance, you know what we mean? If you look at studies that show how much the average American worker makes, you'll realize that many people would be thrilled to bring home $5,000 per month. It's just that executives aren't part of this group.

We know. It's hard to be sympathetic when you know that executives making millions in compensation should probably be able to put aside, oh, a quarter million, just for this reason. But the fact is we all get used to certain standards of living, and executives are no different.

This concept is really pretty simple, which is why we are always amazed to find clients who are clueless when it comes to the gaps between employee limitations and what is appropriate for executives. As a matter of fact, time and time again income replacement is one of the most poorly executed categories of executive benefits.

The goal of any income replacement plan should be to ensure that executives can maintain their standard of living when faced with a short- or long-term disability or illness. When you think about it it's a pretty good incentive for an executive to come on board, as well as a good incentive for him to stick around.

Keeping Executives in Good Form: Income Protection

The corporate world got a wake-up call in 2005 when two of McDonald Corp.'s chief executives, James Cantalupo and Charlie Bell, died within nine months of each other.

In addition to being sad, the deaths caused an incredible corporate disruption, causing many companies to think about the benefits of offering top officers company-paid physical exams.

We know what you're thinking. A guy who brings in a salary of a couple million a year should be able to foot his own medical exam. And it all starts to smack a bit of Marie Antoinette.

Until you stop looking at medical exams as executive benefits, and put them in the category of "business necessity" instead.

So here's the question: should executives receive extra medical and dental insurance? That's an interesting question.

Most companies don't distinguish between top executives and the rank-and-file work force when it comes to health benefits. As health care costs skyrocket and employees pay higher premiums, co-pays, and deductibles, employers have a tough time asking employees to shoulder more of the burden while high-paid executives pay no penalties. It can also be a tough sell: average workers don't like it when the top-level executives get better health care than they do. And they really get mad when they learn that the company has grossed out the benefit paid so the executive receives the reimbursement on an after-tax basis. And we don't blame them. There is absolutely no ethical or business-based reason for a gross-up of an income protection benefit. It's just a misuse of corporate resources. Period.

Despite all of this, certain extra medical benefits are reasonable. For example, paid medical exams. Any time a benefit can have a positive impact on the health and security of an employee, it should be considered necessary. And executive health is an asset to the company.

If you think an executive should be in charge of his own health, then think again. It's always amazing to us that a large number of executives we've worked with don't provide the kind of self-service that they would provide if health were considered an asset to the company. Annual physical exams are low-cost, high value, and all in all a great benefit for a company to offer.

Aside from this one exception, medical benefits for executives should mirror those of rank-and-file employees. In other words, the organization shouldn't foot the bill for the executive's premiums. The same goes for dental insurance. There is no reason we can think of that companies should pick up the tab for the child's braces and the wife's teeth whitening. What's next? Breast implants? If an organization isn't paying its executives enough to afford their own medical and dental insurance premiums, there are bigger issues at stake.

When it comes to life insurance policies, supplemental benefits are also often needed for executives. Many employers pay two times base salary up to a maximum of $100,000, and allow employees to buy supplemental life insurance which comes in additional multiples of the salary. Executives should be provided the same deal that all employees are provided *without* the artificial cap.

The Golden Years Are Green, too: Future Financial Security

When word got out that former New York City Stock Exchange chairman Dick Grasso's retirement package was a sweet $139.5 million, you could practically hear the stunned silence. This created one of the first of many "holy cow" moments when directors, shareholders, and the general public realize the startling results of retirement packages.

Okay, we know what you are thinking. How can directors— as those on the NYSE claimed—*not* know what their top executive stands to take home in retirement. Especially if that figure is high enough to freeze the expressions on their faces? When all is said and done you just can't put $140 million into the "oversight" category. To do so is a clear violation of shareholder's interest. It's just not okay.

But it's not impossible. To understand how easy it is for boards and directors to take their eyes of the ball, you have to understand how Supplemental Executive Retirement Plans— otherwise known as SERPs—work.

INVESTOR ALERT #28
_____
                                    A SUPERLATIVE SERP

If the company decides it's time to have a supplemental executive retirement plan (SERP) that far exceeds the norm, then it is probably a good time to place your retirement income in another organization.

SERPs are good, up to a point. A SERP should replace some portion of the executive's base salary and occasionally total cash compensation. A reasonable replacement ratio is between 40 percent and 60 percent. If the replacement ratio of all the various retirement plans exceeds 60 percent, that exceeds the executive's ongoing needs as a retiree, and is actually a wealth accumulation plan in sheep's (SERP's) clothing.

Simply put, retirement plans focus an executive's interests on retirement, not employment. And executives should be confident that their retirement needs are going to be met in proportion to the amount of time they contributed to the organization.

At the same time, if the executive incentive or supplemental retirement plan is replacing all of the executive's pre-retirement income, then the focus of the reward program is in the wrong place, or least on the wrong time frame.

There needs to be a balance between where you are and where you're going to be. If an executive looks too far forward to the "times of comfort," he is bound to trip over a stone on the way down the path.

First of all, let's talk about the intention of the SERP. The SERP has become an increasingly important tool for recruiting new executives in mid career. This is because in most cases, retirement vehicles like Social Security, regular retirement plans, and 401(k) plans cap out and would cover only a small portion of their pay. The SERP is designed to ensure that executives maintain their standard of living during retirement. And this is perfectly reasonable—as long as it's reasonable, that is.

But the fact is that the retirement windfalls that some executives are taking with them are so ridiculous that they are moving executive pay out of the spotlight—and retirement plans are taking their place.

Executives guaranteed some pretty sweet golden years (though green years actually describes them better) include Pfizer's Hank McKinnell, who will be paid $6.5 million per year in retirement, and Exxon Mobil's Lee R. Raymond, who will rake in $5.9 million per year.[1] Lockheed Martin's Vance Coffman will receive a $31.5 million lump sum.[2] So all this begs the question: Is a retirement plan intended to replace income, or is it intended to replace wealth creation?

The answer is, of course, the former. But the way SERPs are set up these days, they are doing the latter. How did things get so out of control?

The typical SERP is based on average salary and bonus, as well as years of service. So far so good. Where things get out of hand is when the plan adds long-term incentive awards and grants of restricted stock into the mix, too. When these elements get treated as annual pay, the value of the retirement plan stands to increase dramatically. This is what happened in the case of Dick Grasso and the NYSE. The board knows what the executive stands to make at target, but doesn't spend too much time figuring out what the executive stands to make in alternate scenarios. The problem occurs, as we've seen in the case of Mr. Grasso, when the executive performs way above target. No one is disputing that our friend Dick did a great job. But enough is enough already. This is just one of the reasons why we think the gPB-Warp, which we talked about in the last chapter on wealth creation, is such a great alternative to the SERP.

How much do long-term incentives and restricted stock impact retirement plans? Well, let's go back to Pfizer's Hank McKinnell again. With McKinnell's $6.5 million annual retirement bonanza, he stands to pull in more than $70 million. But if restricted stock and long-term incentives hadn't been factored in? McKinnell would be entitled to only about $37 million.[3]

This is exactly why some critics call SERPs "camouflage compensation," saying that if you want to award compensation without anyone finding out about it, the SERP makes a great hidey hole. This is because traditionally, the cost of SERPs was rarely shared with shareholders. If you wanted to know how much a SERP cost, you not only had to know where to look and be willing to spend the time and effort to dig for the information—you had to be really, really smart in order to calculate it.

How did the SERP get to this point? Well, let's add one more installation to Congress's museum of good intentions gone horribly wrong. In 1974 Congress passed legislation that required companies to fund the pensions they promised to their employees, and to keep pensions of executives proportional to those of regular employees.[4] Sounds pretty good, right?

But instead of dissuading companies from giving executives excessive retirement pay as intended, it encouraged them to set up separate retirement plans for executives. And before you knew it, stock options, bonuses, and other long-term incentives snuck into the retirement calculations. By themselves each of these components might not add up to much. But when you add them all together—*kaboom!*—there's the potential for some crazy money.

No more. The happenings at the NYSE did more than raise a few eyebrows. It raised the public's ire. After all, we're talking about a non-profit organization here (we know, it's hardly the Red Cross)! Amid public hand-wringing, a media circus, and a court order that stipulated that Grasso must return a good portion of the money, the SEC stepped in with new rules and regulations designed to make SERPs more transparent. Now even a shareholder of average intelligence can see what's up.

All this has organizations running scared. The NYSE debacle has boards and organizations, as well as compensation committees, taking a good, hard look at their SERPs. After all, no one wants to have the next celebrity CEO taking up their corner office. It looks like boards and organizations are going to have to get creative and find another way to hide the wealth.

Of course, not all companies have SERPs. United Airlines and Bank of America recently got rid of its supplemental retirement plans, while companies like Cisco, eBay, and Microsoft never used SERPs to begin with. Companies who claim to have a more egalitarian culture eschew SERPs in general, because they feel they send the wrong message to employees.

Whether or not that's true, organizations should be wary of how their SERPs are perceived. Many organizations have cut or frozen pension plans for regular employees so that they can pay their executives' retirement benefits. GM, for example, cut pensions for 42,000 workers, claiming that these "legacy costs" were the reason they were in the hole.[5] In fact, GM's pension plan contained an excess of about $9 million. The real drain? Unfunded executive pension plans, which weighed the company down with a $1.4 billion liability.[6] So while the rank-and-file reluctantly bid adieu to their pensions, executive pensions exploded.

Not only does this create issues with the company's finances, it also sends a bad message, don't you think? GM is not alone. General Electric, AT & T, Exxon Mobil, International Business Machines, Bank of American, and Pfizer all have executive pension obligations that have ballooned to more than $1 billion.[7] And more and more companies are cutting or freezing the pension plans of regular employees while executive pension plans grow unchecked. According to Bureau of Labor stats, only 21 percent of private sector workers are covered by pension plans, while 69 percent of Fortune 1,000 executives are.[8] Exxon Mobil's Lee Raymond will be compensated more than $6.5 million a year, based on his highest average salary and bonus over a three-year period.[9] So basically, Raymond's pension is tied to the energy prices that have allowed the organization to record high profits.

While we certainly believe that executives are entitled to the same retirement benefits as rank-and-file employees on a proportional level, we believe excessive retirement payouts are costly to the company and to shareholders. Most pension plans replace 20 to 35 percent of a regular employee's income. By contrast, executives often get 60 percent or higher. And if you are Hank McKinnell, you get 100 percent! We believe pension plans should replace wealth, but they shouldn't create it.

Recharging the Batteries: Pay for Time Not Worked

Okay, by this time you know us pretty well. So it probably won't surprise you when we tell you that we don't think executives should get any more vacation, holiday, and sick time than the average rank-and-file employee.

That being said, should an organization who is trying to woo a top-notch executive really quibble over a week or two when they are already doling out millions in compensation? Doesn't really make sense, does it?

Here's the deal. Most regular employees start with two weeks of vacation time and, depending upon years of service, earn additional weeks up to four weeks. It's going to be tough— and may even come across as niggling—if you offer an executive the same amount of vacation time as that offered to short-term employees. Most executives we work with effectively negotiate a minimum of four weeks of vacation. We're always a little suspicious of executives who really go to bat trying to negotiate substantially more vacation time than regular employees. In addition to making you wonder about their work ethic, it also makes you wonder whether or not they care about the type of message they are sending to other employees. Part of an executive's job is to set a good example, and complaining about not getting enough time off—or worse, taking an excessive amount of time off—makes regular employees who work really hard kind of, well, angry. Most major organizations provide ten days of holidays and upward of four weeks of vacation for top-level executives. If you are recruiting an executive from Europe this won't cut it, but it should be perfectly sufficient for most U.S. executives.

All that being said, it's a rare executive who can operate at full efficiency 12 months per year, year after year. Executives work more than 40 hours per week—way more. They sacrifice time with family that other workers don't. As stewards of their organization—as those designated with the task of making shareholders money by making critical decisions—you can bet that most executives are working even when it looks like they are lying in bed sleeping. In addition to normal vacations and holidays, we often recommend that executives should be able to recharge their batteries—and competitive juices—by taking a sabbatical every three to five years. The sabbatical should be less than six months, but longer than two.

Go Ahead, Pile on the Debt: Deferred Compensation

In addition to pensions, how do executives add to their green—oops, we mean golden—years? Deferred compensation.

Simply explained, a deferred compensation plan allows executives to defer portions of their salary and bonuses until retirement. Some plans even let executives defer gains from exercising stock options. The sums grow tax-free, and sometimes even increase at an above-market interest rate guaranteed by the company. Some companies even make contributions to deferred compensation plans under certain circumstances.

Deferred comp plans are a pretty sweet deal for the executive, and are a great way for companies to attract and retain top talent. But shareholders often look on them less kindly. Why? Well, if you consider the fact that deferred compensation plans represent money the company has to pay tomorrow for work done today, they fall under one category: debt. And this debt must be deducted from a company's earnings each quarter.

Similar to many executive retirement plans, deferred compensation isn't funded. Which basically means that an organization doesn't sock away assets in the plans so that they can pay the money when the time comes. What are we getting at here? When all is said and done, deferred compensation plans reduce company profits.

If someone tries to tell you that deferred comp plans are just like 401(k) plans, stop them right away and take them to school. Employees fund 401(k) plans with their own pay, so they don't create corporate debt or liability.

So when we talk about deferred compensation, how much liability are we talking about here? Umm, a lot. General Electric's liability for deferred compensation is a whopping $2.4 billion, while Countrywide Financial Corp.'s executive retirement debt—deferred compensation plus pensions—was $340 million at the end of 2005.[5] About $305 million of that was for deferred compensation alone. Compare this to $373 million, which is Countrywide's pension obligation for 25,915 retirees and ordinary workers.[5] See what we mean here?

Because of the cost, most companies do fund their deferred compensation plans—it's just that they do it informally. In a study done by Clark Consulting in 2005, it was found that the majority of companies—70 percent in fact—funded their deferred compensation plans through Corporate Owned Life Insurance (COLI).[10]

Like anything associated with high-paid executives, deferred compensation plans have enjoyed their share of controversy. In 2005, MassMutual Financial Group fired chairman and CEO Robert O'Connell for inflating the value of his retirement account by tens of millions of dollars.[11] As a matter of fact, deferred compensation plans have increasingly been seen as an innovative way to secretly ratchet up executive pay. O'Connell, who was incredibly creative, was accused of buying fake stakes in hot IPOs at the original offering price, as well as crediting his account with securities trades after markets had closed.[12] The end result? His account exploded 37 percent a year. That certainly beat the pants off the Dow Jones Industrial Average over the same time period, which was 2.2 percent.[13] Enron, which racked up about $220 million in deferred comp liabilities for just 285 executives, really brought deferred compensation into the spotlight. About three dozen of those executives withdrew a total of $32 million the year before Enron declared bankruptcy, most under a haircut provision.[14]

Since deferred compensation has joined the newsworthy ranks of swollen retirement packages and backdated options, Congress has decided to step in and keep this liability under control by tax code 409A, which regulates various types of deferred compensation arrangements allowed under the tax laws. In a nutshell, 409A is designed to cut down on abuses related to election timing, distribution timing, and the ability to accelerate payouts. Thanks to Enron, it's now a lot harder to get a haircut. The downside? The laws are costly, confusing at best, and some critics even say they are incomplete. Are you curious to know under what situations deferred compensation becomes taxable income? So are we. Hire an attorney and tell us what you find out.

We all know that history repeats itself, so let's take a quick trip down Memory Lane to "things that Congress has tried to do to make things better that have really made things much worse." We're talking Section 208G, the golden parachute rules, as well as Section 162(m), the million dollar cap on employer deductions. Both of these regulations were designed to reign in excessive executive pay. Congress gets a gold star for a really good effort, but in both cases the regulations encouraged organizations to find loopholes. The result? After every well-intentioned attempt to keep executive compensation at reasonable levels, it just got higher. Will 409A be more of the same? We can't wait to find out.

References

1. Dash, Eric. "New Executive Bonanza: Retirement." *New York Times*, 3 April 2005. Available online at http://www.nytimes.com/2005/04/03/business/yourmoney/03pensions.html, accessed 1 October 2007.
2. Ibid.
3. Ibid.
4. Ibid.
5. "Hidden Burden." *Wall Street Journal*, 23 May 2006.
6. Ibid.

7. Ibid.
8. "Updated AFL-CIO Executive Paywatch Site Includes Top 25 Pension Packages for CEOs." *Pension & Benefits Daily*, 7 April 2006.
9. Ibid.
10. "Clark Consulting Survey Reveals Growing Trends in Executive Benefits." *Business Wire*, 7 November 2005.
11. Francis, Theo. "Phantom Accounts for CEOs Draw Scrutiny." *Wall Street Journal*, 13 June 2008.
12. Ibid.
13. Ibid.
14. Ibid.

CHAPTER 15

Executive Perquisites

The Skinny on the Fat

To help define executive perquisites, and to give you a little history lesson on where they all began, let's go back to the time of George Washington. That's right, the father of our country is also the father of executive perks.

In the summer of 1775, Congress offered George Washington the position of commander-in-chief at an annual salary of $25,000. A captain was paid $20 per month! And what was Mr. Washington's response? "As to pay, sire, I beg leave to assure the Congress that . . . no pecuniary consideration could have tempted me to have accepted this arduous employment. Those I doubt not they will discharge, and that is all I deserve."[1]

Done deal! Congress accepted Washington's proposal and enthusiastically praised him for his patriotism. But you can imagine that they were slightly less enthused eight years later, at the end of the war, when faced with Mr. Washington's expense account. It was to the tune of $449,261.51, almost 25 percent of which was listed as miscellaneous. Mr. Washington was apologetic that his expense report lacked receipts but hey, there was a war on, what did folks expect?

Today's executives, especially those with hefty perquisites, perhaps owe some serious gratitude to General Washington, the father or perquisites and executive benefits, and to Marvin Kitman, whose research brought General Washington's ledgers to light.

It cost Congress a fair amount to ensure that Washington and his wife got together a few times during the conflict, but it was no doubt worth it to keep the General's morale in top shape. It's also interesting to note that George Washington listed 25 percent of his expenses as "miscellaneous." All we can say is, anyone who has the guts for this move certainly has the guts to win a war.

Today we define executive perquisites as any benefit provided to the executive that is above and beyond the benefits provided within the executive benefits framework. While General Washington's perks may have fallen into the "four w's" categories of wagons, women, wig care, and wine, modern perquisites are often defined by the "four c's"—cars, clubs, counseling, and contracts. That being said, executive perquisites are often custom-tailored to the company and its individuals and can be numerous and extremely unique in design. They range from the practical, like cell phones and computers, to the truly outrageous, like $1 million parties and horses.

Why Executives Wax Nostalgic About the 1950s

The 1950s gave us poodle skirts, rock and roll, . . . and executive perquisites. That's right. While perks fell out of favor after General Washington, they came back into style in the 1950s.

To understand how executive perks were viewed in the 1950s, go out and rent the 1957 comedy, "Will Success Spoil Rock Hunter?" In this film the protagonist, played by the late Tony Randall, is focused on climbing the corporate ladder. And while more money and authority are all part of the plan, what Rock really wants is something he can lay his hands on—the key to the company washroom. It's the tangible item—that will show that Rock has really arrived—that drives him.

In the 1950s, high income taxes meant that high paychecks weren't practical. Compared to today, companies made up for the relatively low salaries they paid their executives with things like cars, country club memberships, and big offices. Back then, it wasn't unheard of for an executive to get any one of these things instead of a big raise.

How are things different today? Today the executive gets the raise *and* the car, country club membership, and big office.

Transparent Is the New Black

So what's the problem? Nothing, if you are the executive. Oh, and if you are the media you love executive perquisites too. After all, nothing sells papers hot off the press like a big, juicy article on Dennis Kozlowski's flagrant perk abuse. And who has the willpower to change channels when Larry King is interviewing Buca's former chief executive Joseph Micatrotto, who has been charged with using company funds to buy— and redecorate—an Italian villa. Don't look at us!

But here's the problem. Nothing gets a shareholder upset as much as outrageous executive perks. Especially if that shareholder is wearing Hanes.

As a matter of fact, in light of recent scandals regarding company planes, lavish parties, vacation homes, and art collections, executive perquisites are coming under greater review by various governmental, regulatory, and general employee groups.

We may even be saying farewell to perks as we know them. The Security and Exchange Commission's (SEC) new compensation disclosures, which call for detailed disclosure of any perquisite in excess of $10,000, may put a speedy end to the wine cellars, golf memberships, and stipends that were easily buried yesterday. Previously, regulators required companies to disclose benefits whose value exceeded $50,000, or 10 percent of total pay and bonus. The SEC's new regulations call for a transparency that will bring to light company expenditures, which is great news for company shareholders who feel executives are overcompensated. The new regulations are part of the SEC's plan to get companies to name one compensation figure for each top executive, allowing investors to learn more about the fringe benefits of top corporate officers.

Are There Perks in the Afterlife?

As far as we know no executive has negotiated for perquisites that will follow him to the big office in the sky. However, some pretty sweet deals have been negotiated that put executives into a very comfortable retirement. We are talking specifically about employment contracts that call for big payments when a CEO's employer changes hands. Often referred to as "golden parachutes," these were initially designed to align the interests of the shareholders with that of the executive.

Change of control plans were designed to protect the executive in the case of a hostile takeover. In the case of a merger or acquisition that put the executive out of a job, they were guaranteed a certain amount of money. This gave the executive financial security, but also gave shareholders peace of mind as well, as they could rest assured that those in the driver's seat would not make decisions for the company based on whether or not they would have a job in the morning.

INVESTOR ALERT #29

TERMINATION PROVISIONS ON CIC

An investor should be concerned about the quality of an organization's earnings when termination provisions upon a change of control are too liberal. It is reasonable to have the top management team protected in the event of a change in control. But if this protection is too widespread—if there is a single trigger termination clause, if the size of the awards seem to be disproportionate to the risk of not being reemployed, or if there are too many executives in the change of control provision—then investors should consider whether or not the management team is chasing a rainbow like a leprechaun looking for a pot of gold.

So if you see a rainbow and a pot of gold you had better start looking for leprechauns, because they are sure to be in the neighborhood. And leprechauns do not make good executives.

In theory this policy works in favor of both the company and the individual executive. But has it been abused? You bet.

What's interesting now is that "single trigger" events, such as a change of control, are enough to put the payout in action. Take Gillette's CEO, James Kilts, as an example. The Gillette takeover was friendly, but the change in ownership alone was enough to kick Kilt's parachute agreement into action. The end result? Kilt received everything stipulated in the provision— and he got up and went to work the next day. Same office, same job. Big check in the bank. Sweet!

Yes, it's becoming more and more common for executives to sign contracts that ensure when they leave the company, they are set for life. Just take Charles K. Gifford, past chairman of Bank of America Corp.

When Gifford left Bank of America in 2005, it was with an annual pension of $3.1 million—for life. Gifford also receives up to 120 hours of flight time on the company's private jet per year, as well as tickets to the Boston Red Sox.[2]

How did the Bank of America justify this perk with the Securities and Exchange Commission? Like many other companies put in the same position, it said this perk was part of Gifford's compensation for continued advice and consultation. General Electric Co., Citigroup, Honeywell International, and a whole host of other companies have also awarded these types of pensions and perks to retiring executives.[3]

INVESTOR ALERT #30
SINGLE TRIGGER CHANGE OF CONTROL RIGHTS

Let's talk about the "sell and move on" phenomenon.

There's a pretty good chance that if executives have single trigger opportunities to cash in and move on during a change in control, they may be in a better position to understand the company's future opportunities than investors. It's quite possible they could be "dressing down" the company for sale. Yes, there are two ways to sell a company. One is to dress it up for sale in hopes to get the very best price for the shareholders and themselves. The other way is to dress it down in hopes that someone will see great value in purchasing the organization and incorporating it into their own future. In either case, it's a pretty clear indication that the executives do not want to be around after the sale.

When someone says it's time to leave the party make sure you're not the last person out the door, unless, of course, you don't mind cleaning up the mess.

Oh, the Beauty of It All!

Okay, let's go back to that 1957 film called "Will Success Spoil Rock Hunter?" Does he finally get the key to the executive washroom? He does, and with all the pomp and circumstance it deserves. When he unlocks the door and gets his first look at the hallowed halls, he cries, "Oh, the beauty of it all!"

Despite the uproar created by naysaying activist shareholders, executive perquisites play an important role in any company, especially when it comes to attracting talented executives. More popular in traditional, blue chip companies, perks in technology companies have always seemed downright Spartan in comparison. But now, even companies like Microsoft and Google are unleashing a perk war in an effort to attract and retain employees.

During the courtship period, perquisites tell the executive he or she is really special and is joining an elite cadre of other special executives. In addition to the role perks play during the hiring process, they can give an executive a sense of security, status, and overall well-being.

INVESTOR ALERT #31

CEO-ONLY PERQUISITES

When the CEO has a significant number of perquisites which only he has, that's pretty good evidence of the imperial president. If they are the only ones who need the specific perquisite to get their job done, then there must be many aspects of their job that are unique to them. But that's hardly ever the case.

You can bet that the reason other executives don't have the perquisites is not because of the cost of such programs, but more because the CEO doesn't want other individuals to have what he has.

One of Michael's favorite saying goes something like this, "If you need a symbol you should use one."

While the media has sunk its teeth into some juicy perquisite exposes during the past few years, we do need to remember that the media is prone to hyperbole. While their abuse has been in the spotlight, perquisites should not be synonymous with pure excess. In fact, many companies use perks exactly as they were designed to be used: to mutually benefit both company and executive without negatively affecting the shareholder.

Executives should expect certain perquisites since they have additional expectations and obligations compared to the rank-and-file workforce. Perquisites can be offered for many different reasons and structured to accomplish various goals. Executive perks are a symptomatic indicator of the organization's vision, mission, and values. If the vision or mission has become cloudy or lost, then it's a good bet that the perquisites program shows great diversity but very little business logic. If, on the other hand, executive perks are specific and targeted to key business needs that reflect the organization's mission or vision, then the perquisite program will be seen as complementary, not contradictory.

What's in, What's Out

There are several studies that show that executive perquisites boost production and have a good effect on the company overall. A 2004 study done by Raghuram Rajan of the International Monetary Fund and Julie Wulf of the University of Pennsylvania's Wharton School measured productive boosts resulting from access to the corporate jet—and yielded positive results.[4] And there's no doubt that perks like footing the bill for yearly medical exams, providing sabbaticals, and offering financial counseling are good for executives and therefore ultimately the companies they work for. These perks fall into quite a different category than, say, yachts, villas, and horses.

INVESTOR ALERT #32
BOATLOADS—OR YACHTS—OF PERQUISITES

Whenever we go into a company and discover a large amount of perquisites, it's a sure bet we've found a company that has lost its way and mission. And there's probably an imperial CEO walking down the hallways.

EFFECTIVE EXECUTIVE COMPENSATION

The imperial CEO is a lot like Marie Antoinette. When asked what the peasants should eat for lunch since they had run out of bread, she merely responded that they should eat cake. An executive with perquisites that encourage him to lose sight of other stakeholders who do not share the same perquisites is eventually going to lose sight of both the customers who buy the products and the employees who make the products.

Perquisites make executives feel like they can walk on water without "keeping to the stones." Before they know it, they are wet. And so are the shareholders who were cheering from the boat.

What about perks like dining clubs, golf memberships, and health club access? While these perks fall into more of a gray area, here's our rule of thumb: if they benefit the company in the long term, there's no reason not to include them on your roster of company perquisites. In other words, can you explain how this perk is necessary for your company to the SEC? Then go for it.

Some perks are ego driven, and these are hard to justify. Like Rock's key to the restroom, a lavishly stocked wine cellar or top-of-the-line hot tub might be more gratifying to the executive than a check.

But executives might nevertheless find themselves bidding adieu to excessive perks, particularly with the advent of the SEC's new compensation disclosure rules, which will make certain perks more difficult to explain.

Case Study #24

One of our clients was recruiting an executive who would be responsible for developing investor interest, and came across an individual who seemed eminently qualified. We agreed to negotiate the employment contract for the organization's CEO, as he was an incredibly generous man and we felt it would be best if we provided a certain level of discipline to the discussion.

We negotiated the contract for the next several weeks, but it soon became clear that the individual was pushing the

> *envelope on what seemed reasonable. In particular, we reached a big impasse when the individual listed the numerous perquisites that he thought were important for him to do his job. The list is too long to go into, but included the usual cars, golf and country clubs, financial and legal counseling, first-class plane travel, etc.*
>
> *When we showed the list of perquisites to the CEO, in one significant bolt of insight he realized that if the individual needed all of these things in order to do his job, maybe he wasn't such a great candidate after all. Of course, when we conveyed this thought back to the candidate, he suddenly became very quiet on the subject of perks. Sometimes you just have to say no.*

Critics of executive perks are not always annoyed by the dollar amount of the excesses. In fact, when you compare the dollar value of perks they are a mere pittance compared to executives' salaries. What bugs the critics is what excessive perks stand for. First of all, they tend to go hand-in-hand with rigid hierarchies. And they separate executives from the rest of the work force, which affects good decision making. Executives with excessive perks get used to living on the company's dime, and spend freely. Do they spend as freely with the shareholders' money? Absolutely! The culture of waste spills over into corporate decisions. A study done by David Yermack, an economist at N.Y.U. who specializes in executive compensation, showed that the long-term stock market performance of companies with excessive perks was much worse than that of their more frugal peers.[5]

When an organization provides a tremendous number of status-based perquisites that do not have the requisite business benefits, then executives learn to focus on appearance rather than results. But these days we see the pendulum swinging back. We're no longer focused on the wants and needs of the individual, but are considering the overall requirements of all parties—the executive, the company, and its shareholders. Compensation and executive perquisites are heading in a direction where they are directly tied to a set of criteria that reflect the company's performance. So what's this mean? It means that today's CEOs should expect remuneration after they succeed, not before. What a concept!

INVESTOR ALERT #33

THE CEO'S CONTRACT IS A "ONE-OFF"

When a CEO's contract has significant protections or benefits not afforded to other executives, then bells go off. These are the same bells, incidentally, that go off in the heads of the subordinates. It changes the entire relationship at the top. Unless the organization is in trouble, the executive team needs to work together to be successful. What this phenomenon exhibits is that the imperial CEO walks the halls of his own mind saying, "It's ok for me, but not for you."

It's not that we are against imperial CEOs in specific instances for specific periods of time, but if the CEO's contract is substantially different, then the contract won't be the only distance between the CEO and other executives.

So, what kind of perks are right for your company? As we've said before, setting up a perk program is a great time to get creative and tailor it to the mission and vision of your company. In other words, there's no one-size-fits-all. That being said, let's go through, in detail, the types of perquisites and how they might affect your company's business and people strategies.

Real Money Going in: Signing Bonuses

In today's world of acquiring executive talent, it's almost a given that an individual executive will receive a signing, or "hire-on," bonus. But a signing bonus doesn't always take the shape of a check in full. As a matter of fact, a signing bonus can take many shapes, and is not always given at the time the individual accepts or starts the job.

Why would a company offer an executive a signing bonus? Well, while today's signing bonuses are designed for a number of instances, most instances are for the losses associated with the executive's unvested benefits from the former employer. To the extent that the executive is going to lose some incentive amounts, retirement accounts, or other unvested incentive payments such as long-term restricted stock, it is typical, and probably required, that the executive receives a signing bonus that makes them whole.

The best sign-on bonuses are ones that are earned based upon performance, and have vesting requirements that are consistent with the dollar amount of lost benefits. We're always a little surprised when we hear about signing bonuses that are given for the purpose of making up the unvested losses from their prior employer that are given, in cash, at the date of hire. Why are we surprised? Because it makes no sense for the new employer to do this. If the executive was likely to earn the benefit for five years, it is quite appropriate to make vesting period for the signing bonus, roughly equivalent to the benefits he was losing at his prior employer.

Here's a Big Check, Now Go Away: Severance Packages

Severance pay packages have grown more generous in recent years, especially for the executive ranks, according to a study done Lee Hecht Harrison, a consulting and career-services company in Woodcliff Lake, New Jersey.[6] But you don't need a fancy study to know that executives are being paid big bucks just to go away. All you need to do is be up on current events. Consider some of the big payouts that have been in the news lately:

- Coca Cola awarded a $17.7 million severance package to former chief executive M. Douglas Ivester, who stepped aside in early 2000 after about two years on the job.[7]
- Mattel Inc. paid its former president, Matthew Bousquette, a lump sum of $5.4 million. According to regulatory filing with the SEC, the amount included an annual bonus plus three times Bousquette's salary, as required by his employment agreement.[8]

- Morgan Stanley paid former CEO Philip Purcell $44 million just to go away.[9]
- Burger King Corp. gave former chief executive Gregory Brenneman a severance package that paid him his annual base salary of $1.03 million for three years, plus his annual bonus of $2.06 million.[10]
- Bristol-Myers Squibb awarded its former chief executive, Peter R. Dolan, a $1.2 million severance payment plus enhanced pension benefits worth about $9.5 million.[11]
- And the mother of all severance programs, $210,000,000 for Home Depot's Nardelli.
- Some severance packages even include the lifetime use of company planes, donations to charitable organization, payment of taxes, and use of vacation homes.

These, and other examples, have caused a raised eyebrow or two. But once an individual crosses the middle management line into the executive ranks, you have to realize that in addition to this very much esteemed position, the half-life of the executive director is proportional to the height within the hierarchy that he has risen.

Executives are the gladiators of the corporate world. The competition within the upper deck of major corporations is brutal and ruthless. We love reading the Booz Allen Hamilton study that comes out annually on the number of CEOs that have left their positions as a result of termination for cause. The last few years the number of organizations that have terminated their CEOs for lack of performance has doubled, and the new percentage on an annual basis is about 14 percent.

That being said, in addition to nonperformance there is always the constant and real circumstance in which an organization is acquired, and the acquiring organization no longer needs the services of the CEO or, for that matter, large numbers of the executive team. When you add that to the number of companies acquired or that go out of business, 50 percent of the S & P 500 have changed each decade.

So what does all of this mean? It means that in today's world, it's just not possible to acquire the services of a talented chief executive officer without providing a severance benefit.

Nevertheless, large payments have sparked criticism and shine a light on the fact that there is a difference between reasonable and excessive. Media attention and public outcry from shareholders has caused many companies to look at their compensation practices, including Coke, who recently adopted a policy of obtaining shareholder approval for its severance arrangements with senior executives if the payout exceeds 2.99 times the sum of the executive's annual base salary and bonus. Other big names like Hewlett-Packard, Electronic Data Systems, American Electric Power, Union Pacific, and AutoNation already have such rules.

Even some executives are jumping on the backlash bandwagon and rejecting lavish exit packages. Take Edward J. "Ned" Kelly III, chief of Mercantile Bankshares Corp. Stating that the public was "frankly irritated" by excessive payouts, Kelly surprised the board by suggesting they drop stipulations in his contract that would have brought him a $9 million settlement when and if the Baltimore bank were sold.[12]

No doubt the mergerpalooza that occurred in the 1980s brought about the golden parachute syndrome that we see today. While in the 80s such arrangements ensured that executives wouldn't turn down acquirers to save their own skins, some critics today say the arrangements have ballooned to such a degree that they could actually encourage executives to sell out.

So what's the answer? Severance packages are necessary for any company who hopes to attract talent, but first make them reasonable, and second, follow in the footsteps of Coke. Keep them in check by requiring board approval. If an executive candidate wants an excessive amount of severance, you should "walk away."

Keeping Clean: Counseling

At Washington Mutual's annual meeting, a shareholder, after reading the fine print in the financial statement, asked this question:

"What amount of compensation would top managers require before they could afford their own accountants?"

The question, which was greeted not by an answer but by a round of applause from those attending the meeting, brought to light that despite $1 million salaries, bonuses, stock awards, and other compensation, executives are often treated to legal, personal, and financial counseling services that add up to a few thousand dollars at most.

But the question here is not really whether executives can afford their own counseling services. Of course they can. Still, we've always believed that the key members of an executive team should have a certain amount of paid financial counseling. It's to the benefit of the organization that executives understand their financial planning program, and also for them to understand how the program can best be used.

It's also important for the executive to have tax and estate preparation on an annual basis. If you can't see how this benefits the company, then consider this: the last thing an organization needs is to have an executive's tax discrepancy all over the media. Remember, the media loves that kind of thing! The executive is tried and guilty right off the bat. A few years down the road when the executive is cleared of all charges the silence on the part of the media will be deafening.

What about legal counseling? Most executives we know are in need of significant legal counsel. This not only keeps their noses clean in the first place, but in the case where they do find themselves in a bit of a snag, good legal counsel provides two important benefits. Legal counsel hopefully clears the executive's name and keeps the company out of the media, and also allows the executive to concentrate on his job while the legal team manages an out-of-work distraction.

Is Your Name Tiger Woods? Clubs for Eating, Meeting, Greeting

At a time when executive perks are under scrutiny by regulators, not to mention the public, *USA Today* did an interesting study of 115 chairman and CEOs of Fortune 1,000 companies who also scored good to excellent according to the Golf Handicap and Information Network (GHIN) database. The findings? Fifty-one of them belong to at least two clubs, while 25 belong to three or more.[13] So who is footing the bill?

It might surprise you to find out that some of these executives are paying for their own memberships. But of course, others are not. Since 1994, when the U.S. Tax Code was updated to clarify that memberships to sporting and entertainment clubs were not a deductible expense (unless, of course, you are Tiger Woods), companies have had to prove that such memberships were business related in order to get a tax break.

However, CEOs do use club memberships for a variety of reasons, including entertaining customers and recruits, and giving job evaluations to top executives. And while the public is quick to get up in arms about executive club membership, we all need to realize that a lot of CEOs don't have personal lives. In fact, their business lives are inextricably woven into their personal lives.

Proponents of club memberships argue that leisure boosts workplace productivity, and we're not going to argue that 18 holes of golf or two sets of tennis sure clears the head and shines a new perspective on things. But as with all perks, the goal of the company should be to determine how a particular perk benefits the business as a whole, and not just the individual.

We like to break the issue surrounding clubs into two categories. The first category is for business need only. Eating clubs, for example, can be a very effective perquisite if they are used for eating with an associate, customer, or supplier.

The second category of clubs are those used for recreation. In our opinion, clubs used for recreation are like perquisites gone wild.

Most top-level executives make important decisions all day long. So it wouldn't stretch their gray matter any to keep track of when a golf club is used for personal use, and when it is used for business use. Our take on this is quite simple: if you are using the club for business purposes, the company pays; if you are using it for personal purposes, you pay.

It should be interesting to see whether the SEC's new disclosure regulations curtail company-paid memberships, as well as whether the IRS weighs in to determine whether memberships are taxable perks. As far as golf clubs are concerned, the GHIN makes it possible to see where the executives who post their scores are hanging out. In the meantime, CEOs can always fly under the radar by electing not to post their scores with GHIN.

Red Sox, the Opera: Entertainment

The stories abound of executives who have season's tickets to the Red Sox, a box at the opera, or any other number of entertainment venues—all on the company's dime. But is entertainment a legitimate executive perquisite?

If the entertainment is business-related, experienced with a potential customer, and helps you deliver your service, then the perk is of value to the company.

Whenever anyone asks us about entertainment and its role as an executive perquisite, we tell them a story that dates back to Michael's early years in the compensation business.

When Michael was younger he flew around the world, sat down with CEOs, and went through a process called job grading. Well, he had just met with the CEO of the French division of a major organization and was preparing to leave when he realized he had forgotten to grade the sales people. And what does the CEO tell Michael? He tells him that he doesn't have any sales people on his staff. He doesn't need them.

For a company with such large sales figures, Michael found this perplexing. The CEO of the French division went on to explain that he had a home in the South of France. Each July and August, he invited his customers and their families to enjoy that home while also discussing business with them. He negotiated his entire year's worth of sales during this two-month period. He charged the company for his villa for this period, but you can bet the expenses were significantly less than those that would support a sales force called upon to do the same job. Was the CEO of France's South of France villa a business-based perquisite? We think so.

That being said, entertainment is one of the most difficult perks to regulate. The problem with entertainment is that it is black and white on one end, but gray in the middle. Taking a client to dinner? Sounds fair. Taking a client on a boat cruise in the Mediterranean? Probably excessive.

Entertainment can be hard to regulate because senior executives feel insulted and that their integrity is on the line when you start asking them questions. So it becomes difficult to set guidelines. Consider the CEO of a major corporation, who submitted, on her expense account, 87 dinner evenings in one year. So out of 365 days of the year, she suggested that 87 of them were spent buying food and wine for someone related to business. To us, that would be difficult to explain. Which makes us glad that we're just compensation guys, and not auditors.

Preventative Medicine: Executive Contracts

Executive contracts serve two main purposes: they benefit the executive, and they benefit the organization. We say thumbs up to executive contracts.

A correctly done contract not only makes expectations clear to both parties, it spells out the remedy should either of the parties veer from the stipulations in the contract. Not only does this reduce litigation, it makes debates between executives and companies less public. As we've said many times, celebrity CEOs aren't like regular celebrities. While negative press might sell more movies for celebrities, shareholders tend to not support companies whose executives find themselves smack in the middle of a negative spotlight. Best to avoid that altogether.

That being said, a word of caution regarding contracts. A contract should protect the interests of both the executive and the organization. And that means a contract shouldn't give an executive permission to do his job poorly without having to worry about his financial security. A contract that gives an executive extreme protection takes the pressure off the executive to perform. Remember, all things in moderation.

INVESTOR ALERT #34

THE EXECUTIVE'S DEFINITION OF TERMINATION "FOR CAUSE" IS TOO LONG OR TOO COMPLICATED

While it's not very easy to read the long and complicated contracts that are developed for executives of today's modern corporations, it is absolutely mandatory to read and understand them if you are an investor. One absolutely critical area to read is the organization's definition of "termination for cause." If this definition becomes extraordinarily complicated and convoluted, we're probably dealing with a CEO with a persecution complex, or one that is terribly insecure.

Unless the executives deserve to be persecuted or are by necessity insecure, then you as an investor should probably seek out a more confident group of executives.

Safe and Sound: Security

With excessive executive compensation a media favorite, sometimes it's easy to jump on the bandwagon. It's really easy for the average person to criticize an executive for private plane travel or because he has a car and driver. But before you really lambaste executives who put these things on the company tab, stop and consider.

In many situations, the tab for private planes and cars and drivers isn't picked up because organizations want their executives to be as comfortable as possible. It's picked up because companies want their executives to be safe. For executives who are in the public eye, this can be perfectly legit. This is also a perfectly good way to spend company money for an executive who travels overseas to countries with security issues.

So while a chauffeured trip from the American Embassy to the airport is fine, that same executive shouldn't expect to be driven from his house to the opera. Unless the opera is in Central America. Here's a good rule of thumb when it comes to security: If there is a real security threat, then security should be paid for by the company. But if the perk is given just to make the executive feel like a rock star, it is the misuse of corporate resources.

Gross Out: Gross-Ups

Gross-ups are perfectly legal. They are also perfectly gross, and we tell our clients not to do them. Gross-ups are the most aptly named executive perk, because they make us gag.

What is a gross-up? Basically, it's a tax buy-off that allows executives to receive gross pre-tax sums rather than net post-tax sums. The IRS regards benefits that have a dollar value—benefits like severance payments, supplemental health benefits, and relocation expenses, to name just a few—as taxable income. So that executives won't have to suck up a hefty tax bill on these generous benefits, companies reimburse them with gross-up payments. And shareholders get to foot the bill.

And the bill can be pretty big. Here's an example that will make your head spin. North Fork CEO John Kanas will have $66 million in restricted stock, $15 million in severance, $6 million in stock options, and $4 million in stock-based units to play with in retirement. And just when you think this deal can't get any sweeter, here's the kicker: he'll owe a big, fat $0 in taxes. That's because the shareholders at North Fork—as well as those at Capital One, which bought the company—will foot the $44 million bill.[14]

In 2005 Equilar Inc. did a study, paid for by the *Wall Street Journal*, of the 100 largest companies. It found that in 2004 a little more than half of the companies—52 percent—paid gross-ups to one or more of their top executives. Home Depot's Bob Nardelli received gross-up payments that well exceeded his $2 million base salary.[15] Shareholders had to love the idea of paying Nardelli's taxes while their stock headed south.

There is no earthly reason why executives shouldn't pay taxes when the rest of us have to. Next thing you know, they'll figure out how to cheat death, too.

INVESTOR ALERT #35
GROSS-UPS ON EXECUTIVE BENEFITS

Whenever you see a "gross-up" on a medical or dental benefit, you have good evidence of a CEO who is out of touch with the workforce and quite probably other issues.

There is no reason for executives to be awarded substantial benefits above and beyond those benefits provided to the rank-and-file. If they need to have their medical insurance paid on a pre-tax basis and then grossed up for taxes, then they probably can't afford to be sick. If they can't afford to be sick, you probably shouldn't have them managing your company's assets.

Sweetheart of a Deal: Post Retirement Consulting

When chairman Charles Gifford left Bank of America Corp. in January of 2005, one of his many parting gifts was 120 hours of access per year to the company plane. How did the company explain this expensive—and excessive—perk? They claimed in filings with the SEC that the use of the company plane was part compensation for Mr. Gifford's continued consulting services.

In most cases, post-retirement consulting adds up to lots of money for very little work, and is a poor use of company and shareholder funds. Aren't those pension plans hefty enough?

Sometimes companies draw up these consulting agreements for what they think are the right reasons. They may want to ease the transition between the departing executive and the new leader, or they may want to dissuade the leaving executive from working with a competitor. In fact, the executive ought to feel obligated to assist the company he is leaving, when you consider that a lot of his benefits are still tied up with the company. Drawing up a contract that gives an executive large amounts of money just for being accessible doesn't make sense, and is a misuse of corporate funds.

The Biggest Myth: The Company Is Paying for It

The next time your buddy stops you from reaching for your wallet after a round of golf or a nice dinner and says, "This one's on me, the company will pay for it," know that he's perpetuating one of the greatest myths about executive pay. The company isn't "paying for it" at all. The shareholders are. Our opinion on the use of perquisites is fairly straightforward. If they provide value to the business that outweighs their cost, then it's reasonable to use them. But if they are used as a status symbol or a way to ensure that executives don't have to pay for things the rest of humankind has to, then they are a big waste of corporate dollars.

References

1. Kittman, Martin. *George Washington's Expense Account.* New York: Simon and Schuster, 1970.

2. Berk, Christina. "A Perk Takes Off." *Wall Street Journal,* 11 April 2005. Available online at http://online.wsj.com/article/ SB111265106931397636.html?mod=2_1147_2, accessed 1 October 2007.

3. Ibid.

4. Durfee, Don. "A Farewell to Perks? The SEC's new compensation disclosure rules could mean the end of luxurious wine cellars and questionable stipends." *CFO Magazine,* 7 November 2006. Available online at http://www.cfo.com/article.cfm/8100464/ c_7932402, accessed 1 October 2007.

5. Surowiecki, James. "Perk Hogs." *The New Yorker,* 7 June 2004. Available online at http://www.newyorker.com/archive/ 2004/06/14/040614ta_talk_surowiecki, accessed 1 October 2007.

6. "Severance Packages Grow More Generous." *Dow Jones News Wire,* 7 December 2005. Available online at http://www.careerjournal. com/salaryhiring/hotissues/20051209-djn.html, accessed 1 October 2007.

7. Romanek, Broc. "Coke Adopts `Shareholder Approval of Severance Arrangements' Policy." *The Corporate Counsel.net,* 27 December 2005. Available online at http://www.thecorporatecounsel. net/blog/archive/000852.html, accessed 1 October 2007.

8. "Mattel Former Pres to Receive 5.4 million Separation Payment." *Dow Jones Corporate Filing Alert,* 28 December 2005.

9. "Morgan Stanley Shareholders Vote for Severance Oversight." *Wall Street Journal,* 5 April 2006.

10. "Exiting Burger King Chief Gets Big Severance Package." *Wall Street Journal,* 25 April 2006.

11. Saul, Stephanie. "Former Bristol-Myers Chief to Get 9.5 million Package." *New York Times,* 4 November 2006. Available online at http://www.nytimes.com/2006/11/04/business/04dolan.html? adxnnl=1&adxnnlx=1191262757-2EQ6GjkLKZTm3yuSccc75w, accessed 1 October 2007.

12. "Golden Parachutes Tarnished." *Baltimore Sun,* 15 April 2006.

13. "CEOs Belong to Fore—or 5 or even 6 golf clubs." *USA Today,* 2 November 2001.

14. "Gross Up Gross Out—The latest abomination in CEO pay." *slate.com,* 15 March 2006.

15. Ibid.

Development Rewards

It's not all about the money. Despite the stories you've read that focus on executive excess and greed, executives can be motivated by stuff other than, well, *stuff*. And that's where development rewards come into play.

Let's start by defining development rewards. Development rewards allow an executive to develop and grow in a way that will positively impact his ability to perform. Performance management, career pathing, succession planning, special training, and mentoring—all are examples of development rewards.

If you've ever read the book *Human Capital* by Gary Becker (if you haven't, you should—Becker won the 1992 Nobel Prize for Economics and obviously knows what he is talking about), you know that when all is said and done, total compensation isn't just a big, fat paycheck or mountains of stock options. Additional education, mentoring an executive so that he truly understands the company's values and vision, and programs that allow executives to pursue a certain career path are equally as important capital investments. Why? Because they've been proven to raise earnings and add to a person's good work habits. When all is said and done, you can separate a person from their financial or tangible assets. But you can't separate them from their knowledge, skill, and values.

And that's why any good total executive reward program realizes the importance of development rewards. It's a win-win situation for both the company and the executive. Why? Well, development rewards ensure that executives are competent to do their jobs. Executives who are trained to do their jobs retain their jobs, perform better, and earn more money. How does this help the company? Well, it's pretty simple, really. When executives perform better, company and stock performance rises as well. In addition, executives who are given access to education, training, and mentoring programs often better understand a company's vision, mission, and values, which is critical to the company's success. Making an investment in your executives through developmental rewards means that you can often hire your executives from within, instead of hiring them from outside. Would Carly Fiorina have fared better at Hewlett-Packard if she had had the benefit of mentoring before she had taken over the helm? While we don't want to suggest that Fiorina's lack of understanding of HP's culture was the *entire* reason for her downfall, we do believe that had she bought into and supported the company's culture, things would have been different.

How do development rewards motivate the executive? Simple. The company providing the development rewards is investing in the executive. He is receiving education, training, knowledge, or mentoring that will only serve to further his career.

*C*ase Study #25

One of our clients created one of the first development reward programs that we are aware of. It created a skills inventory of each of its candidates for management positions. It also created a list of positions within the organization with known skill requirements. Throughout the year it continued to match job openings with the skills inventory of individual people, allowing them to determine who might be the most appropriate person to fill a particular position.

Careers were managed like gardens—they were watered, tended, and inspected for insects. It was common knowledge that the organization encouraged and preferred an "up from within" promotion approach. It also dramatically

> *encouraged people to transfer horizontally within the division, in order to broaden their knowledge of the requirements for each of the major functions within the company.*
>
> *Turnover at this organization was probably the lowest of all the major competitors, and was extraordinarily low for the industry in general. Making development rewards part of the overall total reward strategy for executives seems to us like a no-brainer. Inevitably, the individuals who are promoted from within are fully aware of the benefit provided to them in the form of career enhancement.*

The New Normal

Let's take a trip down Memory Lane for a second. Do you remember the organization guy of the 1960s? You know, the one who started with a company right out of college, moved his way up the executive ranks, and retired with a nice, fat pension?

No? Well, that's because today's executive is hardly the organization man of the 1960s. As a matter of fact, we're just going to come right out and say it. Let's deal with the facts. A lot of CEOs are losing their jobs.

A recent study done by Booz Allen Hamilton says it all. In 2005, more than one in seven top companies worldwide replaced their CEOs. The study looked at 2,500 of the world's largest public companies, and found that 15.3 percent of chief executives left their jobs. To put this into perspective the study's authors, Chuck Lucier, Paul Kocourek, and Rolf Habel, said that this is a 70 percent jump from the first year they did the study, in 1995.[1]

Welcome to the new normal. As more and more shareholders refuse to put up with poor returns, executives are getting the message. They will be allowed to keep their jobs only if investors find their performance acceptable.

Booz Allen Hamilton's study went on to show that the turnover rate in North America was 16.2 percent. And here's

FIGURE 16.1   CEO turnover. (From the top 200 U.S. industrial and service companies.)

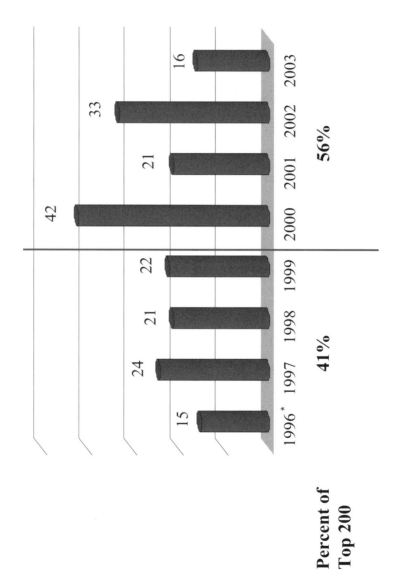

Percent of Top 200

41%   56%

* Estimated

the clincher. A record-breaking 35 percent of CEOs who left their posts were ousted because of performance reasons. That's about one-third.[2]

So, what do we think studies like this mean? Well, it means that performance management is certainly a viable non–cash way of motivating executives to get the job done. Forget about stock options and access to the company plane, today's executives are motivated to perform *just so they can hold on to their jobs.*

What else does the study tell us? It tells us that governance reforms are doing exactly what they were intended to do. Boards are keeping their finger on the pulse of regulatory pressure, and are being more responsive to shareholders who are looking for results. Instead of the CEO managing the board, the board is now managing the CEO. Which is exactly the way it should be, don't you think?

The Myth of the "Repeat Chief"

We're not yet done with the above study done by Booz Allen Hamilton. Because it also gives us some great insight on how companies recruit executives, and whether or not traditional methods should be looked at and possibly revamped.

Let's talk first about how most organizations find their CEOs. The most often used strategy among the world's biggest companies is to hire CEOs with prior chief executive experience. Which sounds great in theory, but let's think about that a little bit.

A company that decides to recruit an executive with experience, a so-called "repeat chief," often has to pay big bucks to get top talent. At the highest levels, the deal has to be pretty sweet—not only when it comes to salary, bonuses, and stock options, but executives are usually compensated for any unvested options they leave behind. Let's face it. Hiring executives from outside costs a lot of money.

Does it work? Let's check out the study, which says that former CEOs perform no better than new, untested CEOs. And even more interesting, more than one in eight of the CEOs who left their position had been the leader of another company before.[3]

Which means that while repeat CEOs are expensive, they might not give an organization the most bang for their buck. Why? Well, outside CEOs face difficult challenges like leading an unfamiliar company. The best kind of CEOs, in fact, are those that have experience in their own company, or at least within the industry.

The study showed that while outside CEOs tend to start off with a bang, they lag well behind inside CEOs as their tenure grows longer. In addition, companies in trouble who hire outside CEOs tend to get themselves into even deeper trouble—their performance records are much worse, on average, than those of executives hired from within.[4]

What are some of the reasons why inside executives do better than outside executives? In most cases, they better understand the company's vision, mission, and values, as well as the specific challenges it faces. They have a better understanding of outside environmental issues affecting the company, including specifically the needs of key stakeholders. They have often watched others succeed—and sometimes fail—before them. In many cases, inside executives are put on a specific career path, or are mentored by other executives. They may have received specific industry training that gives them a better shot at success. Allowing executives access to such development rewards throughout their careers gives an organization an excellent return on their investment, while also allowing the executive to feel as if he is being invested in as well.

Who's Next?

Why are some of the best executives gray? Because with age comes wisdom. But unfortunately for the organizations these aging executives head up, with age also comes inevitable retirement.

The challenge, of course, comes when it's time to name a successor to an executive who has had a long and successful career with an organization. Sometimes these executives are so responsible for the culture of a company, it's very difficult for anyone to imagine anyone filling their shoes.

We are always amazed when we have clients who haven't spent the time to make succession plans. They spend decades building a successful company but don't ensure its continued prosperity by naming a successor should their CEOs health fail or should they suddenly pass away. While no one wants to think about their own demise, it is inevitable. While it's more convenient when it happens after someone has taken over your post, some CEOs who are used to controlling just about every aspect of their corporations start to think they can control their own demise as well. Well, they can't. And someone needs to tell them.

It is up to boards to ensure that a good, solid succession plan is in place. To wing it when the time comes isn't good for the company, isn't good for the shareholders, and can cause a certain amount of divisiveness among remaining top-level executives.

Let's take the case of Frank Lanza, the now deceased chairman and chief executive of defense contractor L-3 Communications Holdings. Lanza, a spirited entrepreneur who built the company so that it had a market value of $10 billion, was 74 years old and had just gone undergone esophagus surgery when he admitted in May of 2006 that he didn't have a designated successor. His plan? Well, he'd get to that once he was within a year of retirement.[5] But in early June, Lanza went into the office one morning and died later that afternoon. Chief Financial Officer Michael Strianese was named interim CEO, but amid shareholder uncertainty about the growing company's strategy.[6] Shareholders weren't comfortable about the lack of a succession plan, and who could blame them?

Or how about Mr. Lanza's friend, Bernard Schwartz, aerospace industry icon and former chairman of Loral Space & Telecommunications. After three successful decades leading the company, Schwartz made a fatal error that drove the company into bankruptcy.[5] Schwartz stepped down—reluctantly, we may add—at the age of 80. Many bitter shareholders were left with nothing, wondering why a succession plan wasn't put into place well before Schwartz's final faux pas.

Other organizations are taking note and putting succession plans into place that ensure that knowledgeable, trained executives can take over and keep things operating smoothly in the case of CEO demise or decline. Hiring younger executives, and then grooming them for the top position, ensures a smooth transition for the organization.

For example, Procter & Gamble Co. recently made it known that they were concentrating on succession planning for CEO A.G. Lafley—despite the fact that Lafley has seven years to go before retirement age.[5] United Technologies Corp.'s long-time CEO, George David, designated his successor in 2006 at the age of 64, despite the fact he had no intentions of stepping down any time soon.[5]

Even Warren Buffett, septuagenarian CEO of Berkshire Hathaway, Inc., told shareholders in February 2006 that a succession plan was in place and would be put into play by the board should Buffett need to be replaced.[5] Buffett stated he was confident the board would act in the best interest of the shareholders. And plans like that just make shareholders sleep better at night.

We would even go so far as to say that boards have an obligation to their shareholders to put a succession plan in place. Why the board? Well, it can be tough for the CEO to see the forest through the trees, if you know what I mean. Often long-time CEOs are so entrenched in their organizations—it's their life, really—that they have a hard time letting go while they are still able to make the decision. But when the time comes and it really is time for them to step down, they often no longer possess the same sharpness that they once had and may not be capable of making the right decision.

Succession plans are not only good for the company and the shareholder, they are good for executives as well. Any executive that is being groomed for the top position is going to be motivated to perform, and is also going to have good knowledge of the inner workings of the company and its challenges long before he's standing at the helm.

Keeping All Your Horses in the Race

We've already talked about how succession planning, as well as putting certain executives on a career path, can have positive results for both the organization and the individual. But can they have negative results as well?

Of course they can. Internal succession battles can be compared to horse races, where the victor gets to wear a wreath of roses and the losers are taken out back and shot.

But a company with a thoughtful reward system can minimize the damage. How? Well, take a lesson from Jeffrey Kindler, the CEO who, after 18 months, won Pfizer Inc.'s succession battle. A mere two hours after his victory was announced, he reached out to his competitors to ask them for their help and support in keeping the company afloat.[7] When all is said and done, it's up to new chiefs to retain their top talent. Positioning rivals in new and challenging roles, providing education and training that allows them to succeed and grow, and setting them on a career path all send the message that the executive is important to the organization, and has a potentially bright future. When Jeffrey Immelt was chosen to succeed General Electric's John Welch, three executives were named as backups for the front-runners and were given bigger jobs.[8] Remember, executives have big egos, and this type of public praise and support goes a long way!

Secret Rites and Other Custom Designed Programs

Sometimes, just the thought of being one of the "it" guys is enough.

While there are all kinds of custom-designed development reward programs out there, one particularly effective one that comes to mind is Goldman Sachs Group's "partner" club.

The 300 or so people who make "partner" at Goldman Sachs not only bring home a good portion of the company's profits, they also have the satisfaction of belonging to one of Wall Street's most elite clubs.

As a matter of fact, we'll go so far as to say that Goldman Sachs' exclusive club may be one of the best motivational tools in the corporate world today. How does it work? Every year, candidates are divided by letter grade—A, B, and C—then are nominated and vetted by senior management. Not only is the group of partners guaranteed big money—last year the group shared more than $2 billion—but they also get sweet perks like opportunities to invest with the firm when it buys stakes in other companies and the ability to buy Goldman shares at a 25 percent discount.

So who has the best chance at making partner? Goldman's top money makers, of course.

But while the money and perks may be enough to make anyone perform their best to win a spot in Wall Street's hottest club, there's something even bigger at stake. While candidates who don't make partner sometimes get another shot two years later, in most cases those who are turned down can effectively say good-bye to their career at Goldman. Because if you're not a winner in this race, chances are you aren't performing up to expectations.

Things have changed since Goldman was founded in 1869. Back then, if you did your job and showed a little promise you had a good chance of making partner. Today, the stakes are a little higher. And with everyone trying to outperform each other and win a the coveted title of partner, it's no surprise that Goldman's stock was up about 40 percent in 2006, significantly beating the 17 percent gain for the Dow Jones Wilshire U.S. Financial Services Index.[9]

Okay, we know what you are thinking. Couldn't Goldman Sachs motivate its top performers by paying them large wads of cash, without going through this whole, long process? Well, if you truly believe that then you are not getting the point of this chapter. Money-making isn't the only thing that drives executives. Honestly. Despite what you've read in the newspaper and, okay, even in this book.

What makes Goldman's program so motivating is that the "clubby" aspect of it appeals to those who yearn to be part of the company's culture. This type of development reward is, in effect, killing several birds with one stone. In addition to putting executives into high gear, it promotes a certain culture and values that executives want to buy into. Are executives who make partner at Goldman rich? Of course they are. And equally as important to them, they belong to a very cool club.

And then there's the fact that once an executive makes partner, he'll most likely stick around to enjoy it. While other firms compete with hedge funds that pay top dollar for star traders, Goldman uses the partnership process to help retain its top talent. Are there firms out there clamoring for Goldman's best performers? Of course. But they have a pretty powerful incentive to stay, don't you think?

Good Stuff Rolls Downhill, Too

When all is said and done, an organization is only as good as its leadership. And good leadership trickles down. By that we mean that the example that the CEO sets will be the one that other executives follow.

So how do you develop good leadership? How do you factor that into your reward structure? Well, there are lots of factors that come together to make the process of developing or mentoring executives at the corporate level a big challenge. We believe a large portion of this challenge lies in the environment and culture of the organization itself.

You can't pay executives a lot of money and say "Here, be a good leader." Instead, the CEO typically sets the cultural and values norms. We believe that there are three important steps to structuring a reward system for good leadership.

First of all, executives must be aware of their own behavior, specifically how investors, auditors, the general public, and other stakeholder groups perceive their various leadership skills. Second, you must give them a reason to change.

That's right, a little extra push never hurt anyone. Even if individuals understand that their leadership skills are ineffective, they probably won't change unless you give them a good reason to. There needs to be a "downside" when executives don't make positive changes to their behavior. Pay and promotion are two great motivators, and should be tied to how an executive develops as a leader.

Finally, there needs to be a supportive environment that reinforces the qualities associated with the more successful leadership models. In other words, executives should be given all the tools to succeed, whether this is in the form of training, mentoring, or something else. Executives that do succeed should be rewarded.

When the environmental conditions are set—when the developmental leadership rewards are in place—there is a substantial opportunity for the executive to develop increased capabilities with respect to those aspects of their job that require the confidence associated with leadership.

References

1. "Global CEO Turnover Sets New Record in 2005." 5th Annual Survey of CEO Turnover, *Booz Allen Hamilton.*

2. Ibid.

3. Ibid.

4. Ibid.

5. "Tough Question for L-3's CEO: Who's Next?" *Wall Street Journal,* 8 May 2006.

6. "L-3 Taps Interim CEO." *Wall Street Journal,* 10 June 2006.

7. "CEO Can Mend Division Caused by Race to the Top." *Wall Street Journal,* 11 August 2006.

8. Ibid.

9. "Inside Goldman's Secret Rite." Wall Street Journal, 13 October 2006.

CHAPTER 17

Director's Pay

Check this out:

HELP WANTED: High-level executives needed to spend several days per year hanging out in boardrooms. Primary duties include enforcing regulations and keeping a close eye on your friends. The individuals must be comfortable with the significant personal liability that goes with the territory. Average pay: $200,000 per year.

If you guessed that the above advertisement is for a director, then you are right on the money. And it's no wonder that a good director is hard to find. Over the past few years, the role of director has become more demanding and fraught with risk. Not surprisingly, director compensation has increased over this time. And while the increase in director compensation is noteworthy, far more meaningful and fascinating is the shift in focus from how much directors are paid to what they do and how that pay is delivered.

Is It Really Worth It?

Why are so many executives hesitant to sit on today's corporate boards? The WorldCom story tells it all. If you aren't familiar with the WorldCom story, here it is in a nutshell. Twelve former WorldCom directors had to cough up $25 million of their own money—that's right, their own money—to settle shareholder claims. Ouch. So what's going on here? Well, we can credit Sarbanes-Oxley and other antifraud laws and regulations for upping the ante. The lesson here? If you are serving on a board and want to keep your stuff, you had better be doing your job. Let things slip under the radar—intentionally or not—and you're screwed.

Is it any wonder that boardroom turnover has reached a record high, with 25 percent of directors quitting at FORTUNE 1,000 companies? When all is said and done, being on the board is no longer the cushy appointment it once was. Now it's time-consuming and risky. And when all is said and done, what happened at WorldCom has had a fairly widespread effect: a general unwillingness of experienced executives to place themselves in the hot seat.

Director's Get Their 15 Minutes, Too

Being on the board used to be a pretty low-profile gig, but now directors, much like executives, are getting their 15 minutes of fame too. For a while there being on the board was a pretty sweet deal. Pay was ratcheting up. But then shareholders and litigators started paying attention. And they didn't like what they were seeing. So directors and their pay (and for that matter their personal assets), much like executive pay, hit the headlines. This means that being on the board doesn't necessarily net you a sweet deal anymore. It does mean that directors' personal wealth may be more exposed to plaintiffs. People are paying attention, and companies are responding. It's fair to say that directors' pay is getting more attention than it ever has before, forcing companies to shift their focus from how much directors are paid to what they do and how that pay is delivered. Our opinion? It's about time. For example, way too many boards' members are paid based strictly on the size of the organization on whose board they serve, regardless of the state of the organization, the relationship between the board and the organization, the performance of the organization, and the number of board members. The other confounding effect is the "regression to the norm" of the board's compensation pay mix. Most companies we know start the review of board of director pay by determining not only how much other companies are paying but also how they are paying; consulting reports we have read often report in the "recommendations" section of the report (and we are paraphrasing here), "the average of the comparator group pays its board compensation in the following ratio: 40 percent retainer, 50 percent stock, and 10 percent fees and since you pay less retainer than the average you should increase your retainer to become 40 percent of the total compensation for your directors! NALNA (No Additional Logic Need Apply!)."

Departing from the Norm

We've said this many times when it comes to executive compensation and the same holds true for director's compensation: no two organizations are the same. Similarly, no two organizations have the same relationship with—or expectations of—their board of directors. So what does this mean? It means, of course, that a board's role will vary accordingly. A clear and comprehensive understanding regarding the relationship of the board of directors with the organization, as well as the role each director will play, is a fundamental first step in determining how to develop a board of directors total reward strategy.

So where's the starting point? Good question. The relationship, responsibilities, and roles should be the starting point for boards as they set the amount and form of compensation they receive for the total reward strategy. This is a departure from past practice, when companies tended to align director compensation with the principles that governed executive compensation (in other words, defined competitive posture as compared to organizations of like size, in like industries).

New notions of corporate governance demand that director compensation be separate from operating management, and be treated differently. Executives responsible for executing the business strategy have incentives linked to corporate performance, whereas directors who are elected by shareholders to serve as stewards of their investments would have broader reward components focusing on longer-term success factors consistent with the various shareholders interests, be it "risk adjusted returns," or organization sustainability, for example. They should also consider other stakeholders beside just their specific shareholder interests. In this context, director total reward strategy should visibly reflect this distinct role, and should also have a different underlying philosophy.

The Issues

Similar to the way one would design a total executive reward strategy, the review and evaluation of any particular organization's board of directors' reward strategy should begin by addressing a series of issues designed to determine the responsibilities and roles of the directors.

- **The business environment** in which the organization operates. For example, a business environment that is fairly controlled, regulated, and heavily unionized will have significantly different implications for board leadership than a business environment that is fast-paced, unregulated, and marked by many competitors.
- **The key stakeholders** are a secondary factor. If key stakeholders (executives, employees, customers, suppliers, or partners) have unusual influence over the organization by way of controlling the development or execution of the organization's business strategy, then the board may operate in a more informational "contractual" or advisory "conditional" manner than in a shared "conventional" or primary "consensual" manner, for instance.
- **The vision, mission, and values** of an organization will affect the relationship between the organization and the board. If the organization has a strong vision, mission, and values, the board will be less likely to be involved in a day-to-day strategy or tactics, and may be more involved in major organizational processes that ensure the continuation of

the business, such as organizational culture and management succession.

• Last and most important, the board's relationship will be reflective of the **general, value chain, and specific business strategies**. If the strategies are effective and are in the extension phase, then the board's role will be more likely to be advisory or even informational. To the extent that the business strategy is under stress, then the board's relationship with the organization will more likely be consensual or conventional in nature.

The Categories

As a result of the review of the above business issues, we have defined the types of board relationships or roles in four general categories.

• Contractual (informational)—Here boards meet to review and approve, typically at quarterly meetings, whatever management puts in front of them. Out of 100 board votes, 99 will be determined consistent with management recommendations. They are really just providing or exchanging information, much like the role of a business consultant with "no oar in the water."

• Conditional (advisory)—In the conditional approach, the board's role is to fulfill whatever role is dictated by the management and or the situation. These types of boards tend to have neither lead directors, nor non–executive chairmen, and besides working solely on management's agenda, they predominantly provide advice and counsel.

• Conventional (shared)—In this case, the role of the board members is to contribute based upon some specific knowledge, skills, or contacts that they have. These boards tend to have lead directors, and the board, with management's input, sets the agenda and reviews and approves strategy.

• Consensual (primary)—In this relationship, the board is critical and has substantial influence over management and the organization. These boards tend to have non–executive chairmen, and tend to create and be responsible for strategy, development, and execution.

The overall role of the board should be reflected in the total reward strategy chosen for the board of directors. Generally, the above factors and the defined roles will have an impact on at least one or more of the three reward architectural strategic axes—money, mix, or messages.

For example, if the board's role is "consensual" or primary, then we would expect to see the level or money expended in total to be somewhere between the 75th percentile and the 90th percentile for boards of similar size organizations. If, on the other hand, the board's role was "contractual" or informational, then we would expect the level of the reward to be more between the 10th and 25th percentile. If the role were to be defined as either advisory or shared, then we would expect the board to be paid somewhere near the median, or 50th percentile, in total rewards.

Quantity Versus Quality

Here's another interesting theory when it comes to board of directors pay. It is important to note that when we are talking about board compensation, we should first consider the total cost of the board to the organization. In other words, it's like shopping for anything else. How much do you want to spend? Once you have a budget, you can decide how you want to spend it. Do you want to spend it on fewer, more highly qualified individuals, or does it suit your needs to have a greater number of less qualified individuals?

INVESTOR ALERT #36

LARGE BOARDS OF DIRECTORS

Investors should be concerned whenever the board of directors becomes unusually large for the task of governance. The only thing that is worse than having too small a board of directors is having one that is too large.

The board of directors shouldn't be a bureaucracy. If the board of directors is a bureaucracy then it is quite likely that the company is too. Bureaucracies can't last in today's competitive environment.

So, once an overall budget or target level of rewards for the entire cost of the board has been set based upon the relationship and the role of the board with the organization, the next key step is to determine the balance between the quality and the quantity of the board members.

Let's go with an example. Let's say an organization has $2 million to spend on a board. If your needs call for 10 non–employee directors, then each director will be paid $200,000. But what if you want fewer, more qualified board members, say, a total of five? Then the annual pay for the individuals should be expected to be $400,000 per year.

Now let's say the board was placed in a situation that required it to be either primary or informational. Then we would expect the board pay levels to reflect those different requirements. For example, if the board were primary and therefore correctly targeted at the 75th percentile—let's say $3 million total—the organization would have the choice of paying 10 average qualified directors an amount equal to $300,000 each, or five highly qualified individuals $600,000 each.

If, on the other hand, the organization's business strategy or model was well developed and operated in a steady state run mode, then we would expect to see the board of directors, in aggregate, receive an amount that would approach $1 million instead of the average of $2 million. Obviously, if the same 10 directors were retained, then the compensation of each should be $100,000.

So when all is said and done, here's the deal: the compensation level of reward for any individual on the board should first reflect the organization's environment, key stakeholders, and business strategy. Secondarily, it should reflect the role those board members play and the responsibilities they have. And finally, it should reflect the total number of directors carrying the load.

The Two Other M's—Mix and Messages

When thinking about the mix and messages portions of the reward architecture for directors' pay, it is best to capture the five different categories of rewards. Each has its own very distinct message. Those five categories are membership, performance, contribution, benefits, and status, gratuitous, and prestige rewards.

Membership Rewards or Retainers send a message that, regardless of the company's performance or the director's contribution in terms of hours or expertise, all directors will be paid a straight dollar or share amount. Essentially, like the American Express advertising campaign once stated, "Join the club and receive the benefits of membership." This is all good if the requirements and time commitments of the board are relatively similar between board members. The message is, regardless of your own rewards, the membership requires operating ethically and without regard to any spurious interest in the rewards. The individual board member needs to be obligated to only his or her shareholders and maybe other important stakeholders such as the general public, customers, etc. While this form of reward has traditions going back to the knights of King Arthur's roundtable, very few directors would accept the premise that all directors contribute the same amount. Or for that matter, that the exposure of the head of the audit committee has the same exposure as the other members of the board. On most of the boards with which we consult the majority of members would agree that "they don't do it for the money!" However, I don't think many of them would continue to do it without the pay!

Performance-based rewards, most often seen in the form of company equity but also occasionally in the form of cash, are an attempt to tie the directors' rewards to both the shareholders' interests and the performance of the company.

Historically, awards of stock were made in the form of stock options but are (like lemmings) being made in the form of restricted stock or units today.

Contribution rewards for directors take the form of fees. Fees for board or committee meetings, fees for chairmanships of the board or various committees, and fees for committee membership in general. Regardless of how this reward approach feels like a mercenary or even like other professionals we know (we were thinking consultants, not the "oldest profession"), when we objectively analyze the actual hours contributed on most of today's boards there is a significant difference in the number of hours each board member commits. This may not have been the case in the most recent past, but with today's compliance issues, there is going to be very different time requirements from individuals chosen for these glorious additional responsibilities and obligations. Most individuals believe that the board's reward program will need to reflect these gross differences in contributions.

Benefits such as retirement programs, deferred compensation, medical, dental, and life insurance programs are becoming less common but are still provided in some organizations.

Prestige-, gratuitous-, or status-based rewards have to do with special rewards that range from airplane travel for free or reduced amounts (typical of boards of directors of the airline industry), or contributions made to a board member's favorite charity, all the way to discounts on the company's products. Not to mention the benefit of traveling to board meetings in warm climates during the winter month and cool locations during the summers.

It's not hard to conclude that each of the above categories of director's rewards carry very different messages by themselves, but that different mixes or combinations of rewards from the above categories would send different messages to not only the directors, but also the entire list of other organizational stakeholders (executives, employees, customers, partners, suppliers, and yes, ultimately the owner investors!).

So how does one go about determining the appropriate mix and messages for the board of directors? Well, one could certainly find out what the averages of all of the competitors are paying. Hopefully by now you realize that's not how we would recommend you approach the issue. Of course, one could call a consultant and ask for "best practices," another no from our perspective!

We would recommend reviewing the business environment, key stakeholders, company's business strategy, and the people strategies to determine the most appropriate compensation levels and messages—and resulting components (membership, performance, contribution, benefits, or prestige)—that make good business sense. Believe us when we say that many of you will not end at the bus stop the organization is presently parked outside of.

INVESTOR ALERT #37

PROFESSIONAL BOARDS OF DIRECTORS

Whenever the board of directors is made up of a lot of individuals who are not very senior executives but who are serving as professional directors, we would be concerned as a new investor that the executives are receiving advice from those who can teach versus those who can do. Professional directors have their place on today's boards. But if the board is stacked with too many professional directors who are relying on the board compensation to be a form of their retirement plan supplementation, it is unlikely they would go against the grain when it comes to opposing an inappropriate—or not well thought-out—direction for the company.

It is true that today's boards of directors are required to do more work than they have in the past. We don't, however, think that having too many professional directors who only sit on other boards is a good solution. It does not provide for the balance of those people who know how to do, versus those people who know how to advise.

They Work Hard for the Money

Most boards are singing this Donna Summer tune loud and clear. The basic message? Boards are working harder. And when they work harder, you are going to have to pay them more. It's that simple.

Additionally the increased risk, prestige, and experience are no longer enticing reasons to sit on a board. In a nutshell, companies have to make board service more appealing by sweetening the pot. In addition to major increases in board pay, pay structure is being transformed as restricted stock grants replace stock options. Why? Well, in large part because of the regulatory changes that are afoot, not to mention pressure from investors.

Boards Go Better with Coke

In addition to the total cost of the board relative to the overall market value of the organization, we do believe that in many cases it is appropriate—in spite of the editorials of many pundits to the contrary—to pay the board for performance. As a matter of fact, we are big fans of the trend that Coca Cola has put into motion. What have they done? Well, they've introduced an innovative new plan for compensating directors. Basically, the board doesn't get paid unless the company hits its financial targets.

Coke's plan used to be more standard—each director got $50,000 in cash, $75,000 in share units, and other fees, regardless of the soft drink giant's performance. This new system puts the board on the same level as shareholders.

The Future

So what does the future hold when it comes to director responsibility, roles, and rewards?

Director responsibilities, roles, and rewards will become more dramatically defined in the future. We expect boards to develop fairly specific charters and define what their responsibilities are. Some of this will be a result of high-profile cases where role confusion put the board in a position of enhanced liability and shareholder suits. An "advisory" board will have a clearly different set of responsibilities from a "primary" board.

The total cost of the board will be a discussion subject, and should lead to choices with respect to the quality of directors required. In our many years of attending meetings and advising boards, we have never heard much discussion regarding the cost and number of members, and for that matter, how their rewards should be related to organizational performance. With the Coca-Cola board leading the way, this will be a relatively well-debated subject in the near future.

Director roles will be better defined. All specific director roles will become better defined in the form of official position or role descriptions. These descriptions will specifically outline the range of responsibilities and duties and, very importantly, will also determine the limits of accountabilities. This will be critically important in all of the major leadership roles.

Director total reward strategy will be dramatically restructured. Director pay can be structured in many ways, but we believe that simplicity and transparency should be the guiding principles in all cases. Each company will have to determine the optimal level (money), mix, and messages of components, as a reflection of the organization's size, situation, and the role and importance of directors to a company's long-term success.

Retainers for board service will continue to increase and annual full-service retainers will become more common as board meeting fees lose popularity.

Committee chair retainers, particularly premiums for audit and compensation committee chairs, will increase to reflect the additional time these roles now require. This increase may be dramatic, because these retainers, where they have been used, have historically been relatively modest.

Committee meeting fees will increase modestly, because they are the simplest way to recognize additional time demands. Nonetheless, we believe more boards will adopt a retainer strategy for committee service in lieu of meeting fees. This may be particularly true once companies become more familiar with the requirements imposed by Sarbanes-Oxley and compliance becomes more routine. We believe that meeting fees should become a thing of the past. Either the organization pays for experience and the role of the board member or it is paying for their time commitment. We don't think, with the exception of the boards that are advisory or informational, that director compensation should be on a time basis exchange rate.

Lead director compensation will continue to grow, reflecting continued expansion of the role, as more companies realize its value.

Equity compensation will continue to shift from options to full value shares. We expect directors' programs to maintain a roughly equal balance between cash and equity.

Stock ownership guidelines for directors will continue to spread. Attaining ownership goals will be supported by increased use of full value shares.

Finally, *holding requirements for directors will and should become increasingly prevalent.* Directors will be expected to hold company-derived shares for extended periods, perhaps even until retirement from the board.

So what's the "takeaway" from this topic, and why was it added to a book on executive total reward strategy? Simply put, if the directors are not rewarded appropriately, then it's very doubtful that the executive reward program will be effective either. And the fact is, as poor, unstrategic, and just plain pedestrian as the executive reward strategy generally is, the same or worse is true for those individuals' reward programs that are supposed to be setting executive pay.

CHAPTER 18
Final Thoughts

A few hundred pages later, we think you'll agree that there's a lot to be thought about on the subject of executive total rewards. Our goal in writing this book was to take the fairly complex but extremely timely subject of executive total rewards and break it down in a way that gives you, the reader, all the information you need to design and implement an effective total executive reward strategy. One that works in *today's* world. And of course in tomorrow's as well.

Why is this important? Because a total executive reward strategy can make or break a company. If you have a well thought-out and implemented plan, chances are your stock and company performance are high and executives and shareholders alike are happy. But if there are kinks in your plan you are going to feel the consequences. At the very least your company won't meet its potential, and at the very worst you'll end up in the headlines. As conscientious consultants (yes, there is such a thing) we wanted to share what we had learned throughout our careers with the goal of giving the entertainment spotlight back to the people who want to be there—comedians and movie stars, for example. Enough of this nonsense already.

That being said, we realize we've given you a lot of information to absorb, so we wanted to end this book with a few solid thoughts that will get you off on the right foot when it comes to designing your total reward strategy. Here are our predictions regarding total executive rewards, organized by topic of each chapter.

Business Environment

Survival of the fittest is going to become the name of the game as the business environment becomes more competitive. The economy will be robust, legislators will continue to talk, regulatory bodies are going to be pretty busy interpreting the latest round of regulations, shareholders will be sharing more than their two cents worth, and companies will strive to produce more for less. Put all this together and what do you have? Organizations that aren't in top shape competitively can expect to be swallowed whole by the market. As a result, competition for the very best people—those who have track records of success—will be ruthless.

We also predict that politics will continue to be a "side show" in this area, as Congress debates a proposal that will require proxy votes on executive compensation plans. The "Protection Against Executive Compensation Abuse Act" focuses on increasing exposure, not limiting pay.

But between now and then, expect to see lots—really, lots—of debate regarding the SEC's first overhaul of executive pay disclosure rules. We expect what we've called the "out of bounds" organizations will have some second thoughts, while the rest will continue with the current formula of following the market trend, plus or minus 5 percent to ensure that their executive rewards programs drive their executive pay programs—and their organizations—towards the mean. What's this boil down to? Simply the law of regression, discovered hundreds of years ago and still alive and well. In other words, everything will need to be disclosed, but when all is said and done nothing will change. Tally sheets may serve as a model for presenting compensation data more clearly than in the past, but few companies will use the true economic impact analysis approach. So no need to say goodbye forever to those "holy cow" moments. As a matter of fact, pull up a chair and bring some popcorn, because these are going to be fun to watch. Expect a little more public hand-wringing too, as the structure of executive pay becomes more transparent to the general population.

How about on the tax front? As companies continue to struggle with the implications of new Tax Code section 409a, expect some confusion and bewilderment. As we write, there are lots of issues on the table that need to be resolved before final documents are put into place. Issues like whether companies should try to retain option gain deferral programs by allowing participants to make irrevocable elections in advance as to when options should be exercised. Or the impact of the new rules on deferred compensation plans. What constitutes performance-based pay, how executive fringe benefits are reported, and how to decide when an executive retires if the option term should be extended are just a few more issues that have organizations scratching their heads.

Other new landmark accounting and regulatory changes include FAS123R. Besides strict new limits on deferred compensation programs, accounting experts are going to be working overtime while companies try to figure out how to present stock-based compensation costs in the income statement, as well as 2007 and beyond earnings to investors. Early reports show that many companies will continue to use the Black-Scholes model to estimate the fair value of employee stock options, though alternative models will be explored. As a matter of fact, you can expect to see some pretty creative option valuation techniques.

Stakeholders

Key stakeholders will continue to complain, push, pull, and remain more concerned about the golden goose than about executive compensation largesse. And that's exactly how it should be. In fact, the "self cleaning oven" aspect of the American economy will continue to work as it has in the past. Not perfect—in fact, messy—but in the end it will reward the best organizations and penalize the worst. And while it might take a little longer than you think it should, poor performing executives with high rewards levels will ultimately be replaced.

You can expect shareholder proposals on compensation and governance issues to surge in the upcoming years, with a focus on more specific compensation practices—the use of performance requirements in equity grants, for example—rather than generic efforts to restrict total pay. Extensive activity is expected on majority votes. While a relative few companies will adopt a form of majority vote, requiring that Directors who receive a majority of "withhold" votes resign, this approach won't find widespread acceptance. And it shouldn't. Shareholders, rather than just pursuing costly reforms along the lines of Sarbanes-Oxley or seeking outright limits on pay, have shifted their attention off of getting access to the information needed to judge pay programs for themselves. Ultimately, what they need to judge is whether the company is performing well enough to retain the stock. If not, they should sell the stock right into the cellar!

How about boards? Ironically, many boards themselves are in need of better information on pay. As a result, much of the interest in transparency is centered around boards' growing use of tally sheets, which have allowed many companies to capture, for the first time, the accrued costs of complex pay components approved incrementally over the years. The often surprising results, combined with pressure from governance critics, have prompted an ongoing reexamination of common compensation practices—from the use of hiring bonuses and peer group comparisons to compensation and benefits provisions for retiring and terminated executives.

Vision, Mission, Values/Business Strategy/ Organizational Capabilities, and People Strategy

Organizations will continue to gain an understanding of the power of the "line-up." Vision, Mission, and Values is the threshold that supports Business Strategy, which in turn requires Organizational Capabilities and People Strategy for implementation. Many organizations have been good at developing winning business strategies. And yes, business strategy is certainly the meat, but when all is said and done are you going to enjoy your hamburger as much without the bun? All meat analogies aside, most organizations will understand that the execution of business strategy requires the acceptance of the Vision, Mission, and Values of the organization, and can only be implemented through the Organizational Capabilities and People Strategy.

So what about predictions when it comes to business strategy? All we have to say is this. Beware of executive compensation consultants that give you predictions on business strategy. It can't really be done with any success, so we won't do it.

Base Salaries

Base salaries will continue to be taken for granted. And you know what? Companies will get what they pay for. In other words, executives will continue to discount base salaries. And because of the continuing pressure from the layers within the organizations, salaries will continue to be pushed up against the $1 million barrier.

Short-Term Incentives

Short-term incentives will continue to serve as a compensation workhorse, with many organizations increasing award opportunities to make up for reduced option values. But performance targets are likely to be set higher in light of improved results in 2006 and 2007, as well as greater awareness of the competitor marketplace. Crossing a long-time threshold, some companies will set target bonuses for chief executives that will exceed 200 percent of salary. Maximum bonus opportunities are also rising, with stretch awards of 300 percent of target bonus becoming more commonplace.

Mid-Term Incentives

FASB-mandatory expensing of stock options has already caused many major companies to make deep cuts in options use—and significantly boost awards of full-value shares. The extent of change is highly dependent on the particular industry and financial circumstances of each company, and will be more fully revealed in 2007 proxy reports. For now, time-based vesting remains the standard for both option and share grants, but growing opposition to "pay for a pulse" is likely to prompt more companies to incorporate specific financial goals into grant terms.

Mid-term incentives will become the new workhorse for motivating the vast number of middle management in many large corporations. Some organizations will go so far as to remove top executives from their annual incentive pools. This, under the right circumstances, should be applauded.

Long-Term Incentives

Prepare for substantial change in equity compensation structure. There are a few things we expect from organizations. First of all, we expect them to abandon traditional methods for determining equity compensation grant amounts. We also expect them to be persistent on executive ownership. We also expect that restricted stock will not be paid for performance. We'll probably see an increase in the use of stock SAR's, attached dividend rights, discount prices, indexed prices, performance vesting, and third-party transferability. On the other hand, we expect to see a decrease in cash SAR's, ISO's, premium price options, and reloads. We also predict that run rates will decrease, and executive grant values will continue to come down.

The implementation of mandatory option expensing will continue to drive major reductions in option utilization, particularly broad-based programs, and more use of full value awards. The one-third of top 200 companies that were early adopters of FAS123R used fewer than half the options of non–expensers, while the adopters' utilization of full-value shares increased fourfold. Among all major companies, option awards in excess of $10 million—so-called mega-grants—

have fallen sharply in the past two years. There will be increased pressure from investors to tie both option and share awards to executives' meeting specific targets related to financial performance.

Wealth Accumulation

Intended to revert those oh-so-amusing "take the money and run" scenarios, executive equity retention and ownership requirements are becoming more common features of equity programs. In another bid to better align executive interest with shareholders, more companies are writing restrictive covenants into the terms of equity grants and employment contracts and are also turning to the courts—with mixed results, mind you—to recapture performance-based compensation based on discredited financial results.

Regulatory changes and governance concerns are spurring revisions—and some cuts—in executive benefit and perquisite programs. Highly leveraged stock options are being replaced with other wealth accumulation vehicles, while SERPs and other deferred comp programs—while they are certainly attractive long term—face some serious hurdles under IRS Section 409A. In addition to discouraging executives from deferring to company stock, the new rules might also delay delivery of SERP benefits and change-in-control payments to executives.

That being said, providing new executive wealth accumulation opportunities will be controversial, especially considering widespread cutbacks in employee defined benefit plans. Another problem? Older pension plans were structured at a time when compensation was a fraction of current levels. And guess what? They've grown exponentially. So how to deal with this criticism? Our guess is that new SERPs may include performance hurdles.

Executive Benefits

Executive benefits should continue to be evaluated and reduced to "make whole" types of programs. The golden rule, "Do unto others as you would have others do unto you," will give good guidance for executives and designers.

Executive Perquisites

In lieu of executive excesses that have made it onto the front pages, you can bet that both employers and investors are going to be keeping better tabs on who uses the company jet and why. When things do go awry, boards are going to get pressure to recapture excess money and revoke privileges. The problem? Possession, as they say, is nine-tenths of the law, and proving fraud and culpability can be close to impossible. In the end perquisites will be business-based for most organizations, not status-based.

Executive Development Rewards

What's going to change here? Well, there will certainly be less tolerance when it comes to retaining executives who are surrounded by controversy. Organizations are beginning to realize—finally, we might add—that there's no such thing as an irreplaceable executive. And boards are becoming more comfortable rejecting outlandish compensation demands from swollen-headed leaders, instead opting to hire less egotistical managers who are team players. Succession planning, as a result, is becoming a hot topic on the boardroom agenda.

Directors' Compensation

Expect less catch-up in director compensation. While director pay has seen a 15 to 20 percent growth over the past several years, it's more likely that you'll see a 5 to 10 percent growth in the near future. And just like they are with executive pay, the public, as well as activists, are demanding better disclosure of board pay. You can just about bet you'll see more information, as well as formal statements regarding the board's pay philosophy.

And Finally—Some General Trends for Executive Reward Strategies

As much as we wish it could be different, we think the development of integrated, holistic executive reward strategies will remain elusive. Most organizations will continue to see the executive reward strategy as a single dimensional effort in determining an amount, while defaulting to the market averages for the mix of rewards. Even worse, companies will continue to adopt the crowd consensus, otherwise known by the oxymoronic name "best practices," to determine the messages component of the executive reward architecture.

Still, the process itself of developing an appropriate executive reward strategy will become more thoughtful and better documented in most companies. And there will be a more intense concentration on pay strategy. A typical board of directors might debate issues like how programs should be designed for competitive advantage. As a result, pay for performance will continue to make progress as a general concept.

Yes, we know, we've thrown a lot at you and there's a lot to keep track of and understand in today's new business environment. But when all is said and done we would encourage you to keep at the forefront the whole reason for executive total reward strategies to begin with. So while regulatory concerns are certainly important, be sure that they don't distract you from the whole point of your compensation plan to begin with—to attract, retain, and motivate key talent.

Ten Simple Rules

You may have finished this book and said to yourself, "Wow! I didn't realize executive compensation was so complicated. I just don't have the time to follow all those steps." Well, *make* the time. Look at the chart on page 4 and follow it. While the goal might be simple, accept the fact that there's no simple way of reaching that goal. Like life, when it comes to total executive rewards, most shortcuts end in unhappiness for someone—either the company, the executive, or the shareholders. If you skip a step, you do so at your own peril. And don't say we didn't warn you!

1. Ignore What the Other Guys Are Doing

We admit that "They are doing it so I'm going to do it too" is a somewhat valid argument. When you are much younger. It's not valid when the same argument is used by grown-ups discussing total executive rewards. If you take one concept away from this book let it be this: there is no such thing as "best practices." The *only* best practices are those that work best for your company. If someone tells you that you need to pay at the median or 75th percentile because everyone else is, ignore them! Statements like "This is the way we did it in the past," "This is the way they do it at Otherguy Industries," and "This is the way they did it at my prior company" are also pretty silly and won't get you anywhere close to where you need to be. Unless, of course, you want to be average. Then, by all means, do what everyone else is doing.

2. Identify the Real Driving Factors

And after reading this book you should know what they are. The issues that should play into your total executive reward strategy include (a) the business environment; (b) key stakeholders; (c) vision, mission, and values; (c) business strategy; (d) people strategy; (e) organizational capabilities; and (f) organizational structure, processes, and culture. Get to know and understand them intimately before you design your program.

3. Make It About More Than Just Money

If you think total rewards is just about the money, you are wrong. A complete reward architecture takes mix and messages into the equation. Your organization's specific goals will determine the best mix of short-term, mid-term, and long-term incentives. Used correctly, top executives will receive the messages necessary for the organization to operate at its best. If you think that by taking care of the money part of the executive reward strategy you are finished, then you are probably right. You are "finished," if you know what we mean.

4. Watch Your Boundaries

When it comes to the business environment, think of our analogy of the playing field. You want to play the whole field and not just between the hash marks. That being said, you don't want to play outside the lines, either. Figure out how big your field is and where the boundaries are, and work within them.

5. Listen to Your Stakeholders

Your key stakeholders are integral to the success of your business in the long term, so don't make them mad. Measure their influence and proactively incorporate their input. Involve the right stakeholders in the process and you have a much better chance of success. At the same time, just because a key stakeholder doesn't like an aspect of the program doesn't necessarily mean you should change it. It's all about driving the success of the organization. Stay focused.

6. Keep Your Vision Clear

Do all companies have great vision, mission, and values statements? Nope. And is it possible to design an effective total reward strategy without them? It's been done before. That being said, if your vision, mission, and values statements are visible, clear, and meaningful, your total executive reward program should be designed to complement them. Things just work better when everyone is on the same page and conflicting messages aren't being sent!

7. Nail Down Your Strategy

Your organization's business strategy is the most important influence—that's right, *the most important influence*—on your reward strategy's overall design. So clarify and decode all of your organization's business strategies (general, value chain, or specific). If you don't like Michael Porter's concepts, then use someone else's, or your own, for that matter. That being said, determining the impact of business strategy on your organization, as well as how it should be incorporated into the total executive reward strategy, is absolutely imperative. So don't skimp here. Have a good understanding of your business strategy and work with it.

8. Dig In

Both organizational capabilities and people strategy are threshold conditions when it comes to designing a total reward strategy. A compensation strategy with good traction always hits upon an organization's structure, process, and culture paradigms. Keep your eye on culture in particular, which can take on a life of its own. Designing a total executive reward strategy without taking into consideration the nuances of an organization's culture is sure to result in you getting bitten you-know-where. If it can happen at Hewlett-Packard, it can happen at your organization too. We mean it when we say that culture has a mind of its own.

9. Know What You Are Doing, and Use the Right Analytical Tools

It sounds obvious, but you must understand all aspects of your executive compensation plan if you want to keep your nose clean. And by that we mean you need to be in the know when it comes to minimum and maximum payouts and consequences under all scenarios. Knowing what an executive stands to make at target just isn't good enough. Because how many executives just make target? In addition to knowing what they might make in one year, know what they will make over their executive careers, and what they are walking away from if they choose to leave.

10. Respect the Power of Total Executive Rewards

Designed correctly, a good plan can be an organization's greatest ally—aligned not only with an organization's goals and strategies, but also with the interest of the shareholders. If there is a silver lining to the recent failures when it comes to executive compensation maybe it's this: with compensation in the spotlight investors and shareholders are demanding that executives no longer be excessively rewarded for poor performance. For the first time in years, this heightened focus has led many organizations to take a more detailed look at their pay practices, and the increasingly important role compensation plays in attracting, retaining, and motivating executives. It's about time, don't you think?

CHAPTER 19
Case Study 1

What happens when you take the concepts in this book and apply them to your total reward strategy? The results are nothing short of inspiring (and believe us, that's not a word we use every day).

We wanted to share the following case study, in order to show the reader what a profound effect a good total reward strategy has on an organization's environment, business, and culture. We'll tell you what we recommended, what changes were made as a result of those recommendations, and the resulting implications. The end result? Well, you'll see . . .

First, a Bit of Background

So who is the client in this case study? We'll never tell. Suffice it to say that they are a highly successful U.S.-based S&P 500 industrial conglomerate with extensive international operations. The company comprises several different businesses and a variety of different models, all under the leadership of about 200 executives and 500 management employees.

Where We Came In

The company wanted to take its future in its hands, but felt it was impeded by a total reward strategy that was a bit, well, moldy. So they asked us to review the design of the total reward strategy and come up with some recommendations that would be more aligned with the company's external environment, key stakeholders, business strategy, organizational structure, people strategy, and vision, mission, and values.

Getting Started

Our first step was to determine what the company expected from its total reward program.

The organization's mission was to balance the company's overall success formula with the need for each business to be successful competing for people, without developing a disadvantage in the overall cost of the client service. The business models throughout the company were different, and because of this, significant portions of the total reward architecture needed to be responsive to the businesses and industries where the organization competed for people resources. What does this mean in the end? Well, when all was said and done, the critical mission of the reward program was to provide competitive advantage to the company by facilitating both the competitive realities of the market for people talent, while encouraging internal cooperation at the critical points of organizational interface—between the different business segments, as well as within the company and its clients.

When it came to the General Business Strategy (GBS), the goal was, as far as each business segment was concerned, that each boat floated on its own. In other words, each business needed its own economically sustainable and appropriate cost structure when it came to people costs.

When it came to the Value Chain Strategy (VCS), the goal of the reward program was to put the money where it was needed. Strategically appropriate rewards would be allocated to increase the overall competitiveness of the organization.

Finally, when it came to the Specific Business Strategy (SBS), rewards needed to be based on total results and success, thereby providing reinforcement to the overall human capital message of meritocracy, not bureaucracy.

Our Recommendations

Once we had looked at these three strategies, we had some general recommendations when it came to motivating, retaining, and recruiting.

- Motivation would be accomplished by shifting the executive reward program to a more meritocracy-based program, and significantly increasing the differential for performance.
- In addition to providing more attractive performance-driven incentive opportunities, retention characteristics of the rewards architecture would be enhanced by creating a wealth accumulation program that had the potential for significantly above market accumulation, with longer than market practice vesting rates, and a performance-driven component directly linked to the delivery of shareholder value.
- The rewards architecture should be an enhanced recruiting tool, as high performers are attracted to performance-leveraged and performance-specific opportunities.

The Overall Impact

The impact of all of this? Let's talk about organizational impact first. We expected that the revised executive reward strategy design would provide substantial thrust to the cultural transformation, building on the cultural change process begun several years ago. Included in the prospective cultural transformation would be an enhanced ability for the organization to build out its professional services capabilities, which was viewed as a critical component of its growth and revenue diversification strategies. To the extent that overall recruitment, motivation, and retention were enhanced, we believed the company's performance would be further improved, which was critical because of the highly competitive nature of its business.

And what about the impact of this strategy on executives? As far as individual employees were concerned, the goal of the program was to attract, motivate, and retain high-performing executives, while encouraging low-performing executives to hit the road. The fact that poorly performing executives would find the program discouraging and would leave in greater numbers gave the company another opportunity to further raise the management talent bar.

Now that you have an overall idea of the total reward program's mission, as well as our reaction to it as far as recommendations and potential impact were concerned, let's talk about what we found when it came to the company's external environment, key stakeholders, business strategy, organizational structure, people strategy, and vision, mission, and values. Then we'll let you in on how all of that factored into the specific recommendations we made, as well as the impact we expect those recommendations to have on the organization.

External Business Environment Findings and Implications

When it came to the company's external environment, we found that the company faced intense competition. It also had extensive international operations and, accordingly, needed to be highly sensitive to country-specific governance and regulation matters, particularly regarding employment, safety, and technology deployment. Finally, a significant portion of the company's revenue was derived from a handful of its U.S. legacy clients.

When it comes to a situation like this, the reward design needs to triangulate between:

1. Shareholder expectations for continuation of recent excellent performance, reflected in stock price and total shareholder return.
2. Cost and margin-based sensitivities, related to competitor and local market practices.
3. Investments in people, processes, and technologies required to continue to grow and diversify its client base.

Stakeholders Findings and Implications

Because of the company's business services and mix—and in addition to typical shareholder, employee, and supplier stakeholder concerns—we found that there were two stakeholders that required special attention. These two groups were customers, especially those in its key legacy industries, and governmental agencies in the United States that wanted to attract the company's plant operations.

We found that while retaining its core strength with its legacy clients, the company needed to develop more diversified clients, as well as product offerings and services that effectively counteract the strengths of its competition.

Vision, Mission, and Values Findings and Implications

The company wanted to be the world leader in its businesses, and cited core values such as unparalleled client satisfaction, teamwork, shareowner's trust, respect for the individual, diversity, and corporate citizenship.

We decided that rewards design needed to balance changes required for the company's prospective continued success, without fracturing the core values that had driven its legacy of success. We also found it interesting that the company's core values didn't reference the depth and breadth of its considerable human and intellectual capital.

Business Strategy Findings and Implications

The company triangulated three general business strategy components (GBS) around its mission critical value chain strategy (VCS). The general business strategy focused on a differentiation advantage, which was characterized by harnessing the company's unique production capabilities with an absolute commitment to client satisfaction. The general business strategy was also characterized by production and design efficiencies, and it was a recognized leader with high brand recognition for quality and cost. When it came to the value chain strategy, this called for exceptional client knowledge with unique capabilities for design and operational excellence, and global production capabilities driven by developing expertise in consultative engineering services as a "feeder" to its core businesses.

When it came to specific business strategies (SBS), the company wanted to focus on large, multi-national potential clients, where its breadth and depth of experience and core capabilities could be fully leveraged into highly profitable long-term client relationships. The company wanted to expand its industry vertical penetration, while preserving its dominance in its legacy industries.

We found that the company's GBS was a robust combination of differentiating factors that, with the right front-end engineering/consulting, could provide unique cost and production advantages to a wide variety of clients.

From a human capital point of view, the company's VCS placed a balanced emphasis on solution generation and operational execution.

Finally, a key component of the company's prospective SBS was to enhance and expand the developing engineering services it provided to current and potential clients. This enhancement, and the accompanying increased industry vertical penetration, was a critical element to its client "pull through" strategy, that begins with engineering consulting and leads to profitable ongoing relationships.

Organizational Capabilities Findings and Implications

We found that the company took a diffused approach:

- Customer capabilities were a mix of industry specific and matrixed services.

- Product-and-service capabilities were primarily industry vertical business units with direct P & L responsibility; engineering services were primarily functional, without P & L responsibility.
- Management capabilities were a mix of industry verticals, matrixed services, and centralized decision making.
- People capabilities were centralized, for the most part.
- Technology capabilities were also primarily centralized.

Stemming from its "one organization" cultural change process begun several years earlier, the company implemented a uniform balanced scorecard approach for management that was:

- 75 percent based on corporate EPS performance vs. its internal targets set by the board, and;
- 50 percent based on achievement of personal goals, specifically including client satisfaction and talent development.

In our view, developing the required organizational capabilities to drive the GBS and SBS represented a key challenge in rewards design, particularly regarding the level of rewards opportunity. On the one hand, the emphasis on developing a "one organization" approach to organizational capability had been a critical part of the company's success over the past years, reflected by its stock price performance. On the other hand, with its reliance on EPS as the key financial metric for rewards, many management members lacked significant "line of sight" to GBS and SBS objectives related to growth and diversification.

People Strategy (Organization, Structure, Processes, and Culture): Findings and Implications

The organizational structure was stratified and hierarchical.

Decision making was a mix of team-based and top down. In contrast to its complex hierarchical structure, the company's legacy approach to process featured an open door policy. Resource planning, allocation, and monitoring were also centralized, as was communications, which emphasized corporate identity over divisional identity.

In line with its history and core business lines, the company had a primarily internally focused, process-based culture emphasizing global execution and customer satisfaction.

In our executive interviews, it was positively noted that this culture required a very hands-on approach by senior management, but it was also negatively noted that the legacy culture at times lacked accountability, particularly for management below the top rungs of the organization. Also, in our executive interviews some concern was also expressed about a cultural tendency to be more short-term and top-line focused than long-term and bottom-line focused.

Structure Implications

Although simplified, the structure design was still stratified vis-à-vis the goal of being able to move people between roles, functions, and BUs with relative ease. We though that reward design needed to consider placing more emphasis on differentiated pay for performance through variable compensation, and less emphasis on fixed compensation.

Rewards design and program implementation had historically been centralized at the company and, in light of its competitive pressures and sensitivity to its price structure, needed to stay that way for the foreseeable future. However, as the company grew and further diversified, divisional leaders would need to take on more accountability for differentiated pay for the performance aspects of rewards program design.

The company's emphasis on diversification of its revenue streams, and the concurrent increased reliance on a more consultative approach to current and prospective clients through consultative engineering services, would lead to important culture changes that would better accommodate certain aspects of a network-based culture, within its bedrock of process-based culture. We believed that the company's process-based culture would gradually transform to include some aspects of a network-based culture, which is typical of a professional services approach.

In addition, in our experience, individual and team accountability are particularly important issues to address clearly in rewards design within matrixed organizations.

Our Next Step

Now that we had a good background on the external environment, key stakeholders, business strategy, people strategy, and vision, mission, and values, it was time to use our understanding to ensure that each aspect of the reward structure aligned with the above.

The Way It Was

When it came to salaries at the company, we found that annual increases typically brought average salaries and grade midpoints to or just below market median. In terms of differentiation, we found that the company's salary increase practices were very consistent across positions and divisions. The same could be said for the company's short-term incentive program.

When it came to long-term incentives, we found that award valuations were below market median for almost all positions. However, increases in the company's stock price and sustained improved financial performance could close the gap over time.

The relatively rich and varied menu of wealth accumulation programs offset incentive program market gaps, particularly for higher-paid, longer-tenured employees. The same could be said of the company's perquisites program.

The overall rewards mix was relatively more attractive to highly tenured, higher salaried employees, and relatively less attractive to new hires and less tenured and lower-paid employees. The company's overall fixed people costs were relatively inflexible.

When it came to the message that the rewards program sent, for those employees who made a long-term commitment, the company's approach could have been perceived as attractive, retentive, and supportive of a "grow your own" approach to talent cultivation. However, the approach was not as supportive for the attraction of outside talent, and for the retention and motivation of more junior internal talent required to drive the company's business strategies of increasing consultative engineering services and the accompanying increase industry vertical penetration.

So that's the way it was. And here's how we suggested it should be. In addition to our recommendations, we've also included the potential impact of our suggestions.

Recommendations for the Reward Architecture (Money, Mix, and Messages)

Except for those with Corporate Asset Designation (which we determined were roughly the top 100 executives), we recommended a more surgical overall market attachment for the other various positions, based on the General, Value Chain, and Specific Business Strategies. When it came to the Organizational Capabilities Strategy (OCS), we found that there were certain positions within the company that had a disproportionately large ability to make or break specific business strategies, and even value chain strategies. We felt those positions should be rewarded in relation to their ability to leverage desired results.

We felt the mix of rewards needed to shift more toward performance-based variable rewards—short-term incentives, long-term incentives, and performance-based wealth accumulation—and away from fixed entitlement-based rewards.

Finally, the message needed to continue to be pay for both individual and organization performance. In order to get this across, we believed the performance component of the pay should be medium-term, long-term, and "positional" for the executive team and/or individuals with the Corporate Asset Designation; and short-term and medium-term for the other individuals. We also recommended that the company eliminate the hierarchy bureaucracy-based rewards like perquisites, their current SERP design, etc., in order to facilitate a progression from a process culture to a limited network-based culture for the senior leadership and Corporate Asset groups.

Our Recommendations for Corporate Asset Designation

We recommended that the company carve out a small and select group of individuals for proactive corporate career management, as well as those who needed to be extremely transferable across organizational boundaries as needed. We suggested that eligibility be limited to employees designated as high-performing/high-potential individuals. These individuals would have a separate reward architecture, corporately managed, that consisted of salary, mid-term incentives, long-term incentives, and a grahall Performance-Based Wealth Accumulation Plan (gPB-WARP). When it came to program design, we saw two possible—but not necessarily mutually exclusive—program designs. One approach focused on the need to facilitate the movement of key individuals between business units with relative ease, while the other focused on the need to further develop the pool of candidates with high potential for upward mobility in the company, inclusive of the need for developmental moves across business units.

We envisioned two approaches to rewards architecture. In the first approach, a separate reward architecture—in other words, one that was not business unit specific—would be developed for these individuals, regardless of where they were assigned in the organization, targeted at either the 50th or 75th percentile. The second alternative started with the same reward design as the assigned business unit, but included several different alternatives when it came to what programs were targeted for the individuals.

Impact Analysis

The program could be designed to be cost-neutral—in other words, it would take the cost from other programs. It's important to note that any positive cost impact should be accompanied by improved performance and reduced retention concerns and costs for key performers. We mentioned before that one of the goals of the company was to ensure that all its business units were supported by one another, and this design builds on that. How? Well, it provides a manageable platform for the development of managerial talent, while also facilitating key individuals to move across business units. We believe the program design will have a direct and positive effect on the attraction, motivation, and retention of top talent.

Our Recommendations for Salary

We suggested the company abandon targeting all jobs to market median, and instead develop a surgical approach differentiated by business strategies, initially within several job families. We also felt a greater differentiation in salary increases—three or four times greater than what was in place—was needed, particularly when targeted "at market" or "above market."

Another recommendation was to tie salary increase policies to business and people strategies. For Operations and Staff functions, for example, salary increases should be driven primarily by a combination of responsibilities and hierarchy. For Technology and Professional Services/Project Management functions, salary increases should be driven by competencies, with little or no regard to time in position and/or hierarchical considerations.

We also thought that if individual performance and retention concerns warranted one-time salary adjustments could be implemented—of significant size if necessary—to bring selected high-performing individuals to market levels, particularly for individuals in professional services and project management positions, and for other key performers who are off their differentiated market targets and considered to be vulnerable. A similar surgical approach to more senior management individuals who are significantly off market and perceived as vulnerable could also be implemented

For average performers who were over their designated market target, we suggested implementing policies to more significantly slow the rate of salary increases. Examples include calculating salary increases on range midpoint rather than actual salary; stretching salary increase consideration beyond 12 months, or providing lump sum salary increases.

Impact Analysis

Salary increase matrixes were designed to be cost neutral, neither positive or negative versus the current distribution of dollars. In order to implement a more differentiated program, we also recommended that the organization consider increasing total spending by 1 to 2 percent. Salary is re-established as part of the pay-for-performance program. An annual salary increase is no longer an entitlement.

Our Recommendations for Short-Term Incentives

In the same manner as salaries, we thought it was a good idea to abandon targeting *all* jobs to market median and develop a surgical approach, differentiated by business strategies, initially within several job families:

- Operations: market attachment
- Staff: off market attachment
- Technology: market attachment
- Engineering Services: above market attachment

We also recommended using short-term incentives to drive home the meritocracy message. How? By carefully analyzing the degree of differentiation achieved in 2006 awards vs. 2005, by prospectively achieving significantly greater differentiation in short-term incentive awards, and by training management to do this, while holding senior management accountable by making it a compensable factor in their incentive awards.

We also thought it was important that individual performance goals consistently reflected Division performance metrics across the company. For engineering positions, we also asked the company to consider weighing individual performance (inclusive of BU and team performance metrics) more than 50 percent, and corporate EPS performance less than 50 percent, as well as providing the opportunity for bonus awards connected to project completion dates rather than annual reviews. Finally, because of competitiveness concerns, we suggested they increase short-term incentive opportunities for most or all of the most senior positions.

Impact Analysis

There were some minor adjustments to differentiated incentive targets, and the volatility of the performance/pay out slope was increased. By customizing the mix of EPS and individual scorecard/role-based scorecards, better alignment between the business units and organizational goals was achieved. High-performing executives were motivated by a plan that has higher targets and greater leverage. Lower-performing executives were motivated to make constructive changes in their level of their contribution, or to leave the organization.

Recommendations for Long-Term Incentives

We believed the company's approach to long-term incentives design was sound.

But we did not recommend either continuation of the current approach of common award opportunities by grade, or the same sharpness or degree of differentiation in market attachments as recommended for salary and short-term incentive. Instead, we recommended that the company achieve greater differentiation in long-term incentives awards based on:

- Contributions to present and future revenue and net income streams;
- Concerns related to the motivation and retention of talented individuals identified as having potential to take on greater responsibility in the company;
- The need to reward individuals for taking on developmental moves (i.e., to smooth out any loss in total cash compensation opportunities related to the developmental move); and,
- Total equity holdings for individuals—for example, if certain highly tenured individuals had built significant equity awards over many years and were not perceived to be at risk for retention, it is appropriate to cut-back on their award levels and/or frequency (i.e. consider for awards every other year).

In addition, we felt that long-term incentives awards for the Corporate Asset Group should be managed at the corporate level, as well as coordinated with performance-based Wealth Accumulation awards.

Impact Analysis

The financial impact was assumed to be neutral, but could be cost positive if the company chose to close gaps in competitiveness. Because short-term incentive is directly linked to performance, execution of multi-year business plans should improve significantly. Because of the performance leverage, executives who executed against a multi-year business plan were attracted to the design and, conversely, executives who could not plan and execute dropped out of the organization.

Our Recommendations for Wealth Accumulation Programs

To the extent that the company was able to achieve significantly more performance and retention-based differentiation in its STI and LTI awards, we recommended that the current WA design be kept in place.

However, we also recommended that the cost of the WA benefits be ratcheted back, through selective reductions in matches and/or caps on total benefit levels, with cost savings shifted to performance-based incentive programs. How? Well, the nonqualified deferred compensation (NQDC) match on deferred cash could be reduced over time and/or tied to corporate performance, rather than exclusively based on the level of individual deferral, regardless of corporate performance; and the NQDC match on RSUs could be capped at established career levels.

We also suggested the company implement a grahall Performance Based Wealth Accumulation and Retention Plan (gPB-WARP) for the Corporate Asset Group.

Impact Analysis

There was an increased cost by adding a handful of executives to the gPB-WARP component of the plan, and a slight increase in target Total Wealth Accumulation. The potential increase in the variable award would be offset by extraordinary company performance. The cost savings in poor performing years would be a result of shifting the fixed/entitled award from 66 percent to 20 percent. We witnessed a shift in the culture from short-term management to long-term management. Executives had incentive to focus on long-term strategic positioning rather than short-term, non-sustaining gains. Finally, you saw a higher retention of key executives. Longer vesting periods drove executives' focus on long-term positioning, while there was a greater potential for significant growth in total wealth accumulation. Finally, executive compensation was more closely tied to the organization's long-term performance.

Our Recommendations on Perquisites

We recommended that the company eliminate many of the hierarchical perquisites like car allowance, luncheon and club memberships, etc., and put the cost savings into greater performance-based short-term incentive opportunities for the most senior individuals.

Impact Analysis

Eliminating perquisites resulted in significant annual savings. The recommendations demonstrated and supported the message of the organization, which is to operate as one business, while providing a strong message that the entitlements of the current culture are rapidly fading away. The change may be viewed negatively by current executives receiving these benefits, but those same executives may also benefit from increased salary. Executives with fewer perquisites will also be delivering the company message of unity.

When All Is Said and Done . . .

We can't tell you exactly how this organization responded to the total executive reward strategy we recommended, but we can tell you that they are substantially higher performing today than when we did the assignment three years ago. As we've said in the text, while stock price appreciation isn't everything, the price has risen considerably since the new reward program—in marked contrast to direct competitors. If there's one thing this case study accomplished, we hope it turned you on to the potential of change—specifically, how removing an old, outdated, and inappropriate executive reward strategy and putting in its place a fresh strategy aligned with the organization's business and people strategies—can completely and profoundly change the future of an organization. If you have forward-thinking ideas it's time to get rid of your backward total reward strategy, and replace it with a more effective strategy that gives careful consideration to where you compete, and how.

CHAPTER 20

Case Study 2

In the last chapter we talked about how a total executive rewards strategy would impact an organization. In this chapter, we'll talk about how it would affect the individual executive.

In the Beginning

It all started when one of our clients called us in for a meeting. The problem? After 20-plus years as CEO, he felt it was time to recruit and hire his replacement. The organization was predominantly in the financial services market, but was truly a conglomerate of a number of different types of organizations. Its environment was very competitive with major worldwide and niche players.

The key stakeholders were the investment managers who tended to hold the stock for long-term appreciation.

The organization's vision and mission were to provide superior risk-adjusted returns for shareholders, and the values espoused and followed the highest degree of integrity, as well as conservative assumptions and business practices.

How about the CEO himself? Well, he was one of the most successful CEOs we had ever met. During the 20 years he was there, the organization's compounded annual increase was close to 20 percent. This put the organization's performance above the 90th percentile in total return to shareholders for most large organizations. Since this individual was a fairly open-minded person, we suggested starting with a white paper on the various marketplaces, which could be sources for the candidate to replace the long-standing CEO of this cor-

EFFECTIVE EXECUTIVE COMPENSATION

poration. This white paper is something we like to call the gra-hall Marketplace Map—or gMM.

Checking Out the Other Guys

Since this organization was unique and represented a combination of an industrial company, an investment company, an insurance company, etc., we looked at several different marketplaces and the relevant compensation structures for each of the various marketplaces in order to create the gMM. In fact, we looked to the compensation program for investment banking, asset management (mutual funds, hedge funds, and private equity), insurance organizations, and ultimately corporate industrials.

The CEO wanted to understand the entire range of market compensation programs from which his potential successor would arrive. Obviously, the packages were quite different. So, based on conversations with the current CEO, other executives at the organization, and external executives, we identified four organizational categories from which the new CEO could be recruited.

• Comparable Companies. CEOs from competitors of smaller or similar revenue size.
• Larger Companies. COO, CFO, and CIO level executives from competitors of larger revenue size.
• Investment Companies. Top executives from investment banking organizations.
• Consulting Companies. First-year partners from management consulting firms.

Given the diversity of the target organizations being considered, the actual offer and transition process would have to be customized based upon the candidate's current situation.

After some lengthy discussions, an executive search firm was retained and we were instructed to assist the firm in developing an appropriate package at the point of time we wanted to

(text continues on page 472)

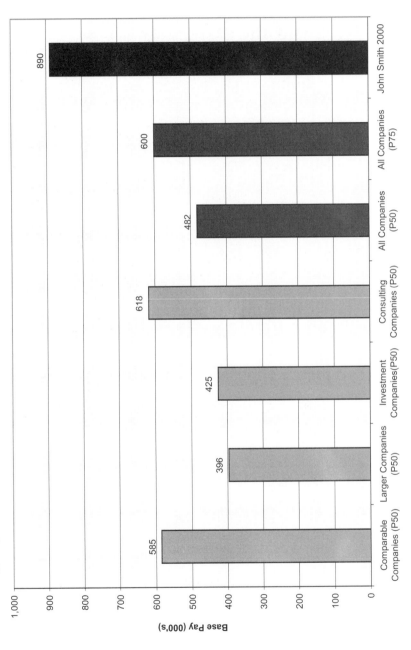

FIGURE 20.1   grahall Marketplace Map (gMPM) for base salary. The base pay amounts for each group are the median, for the whole group at the median and 75th percentile, and for John Smith are shown here.

FIGURE 20.2 grahall Marketplace Map (gMPM) for total cash compensation. The total cash compensation for each group at the median and 75th percentile, and for John Smith are shown here.

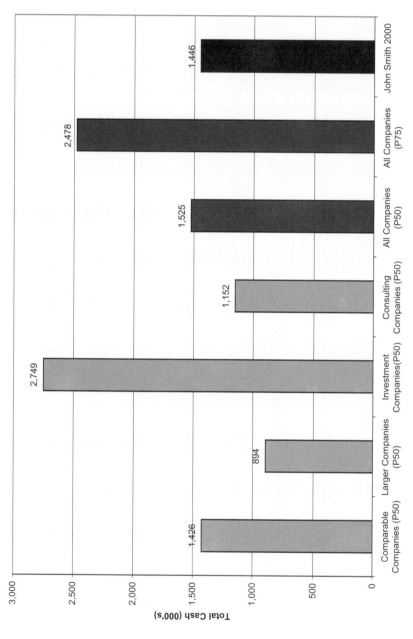

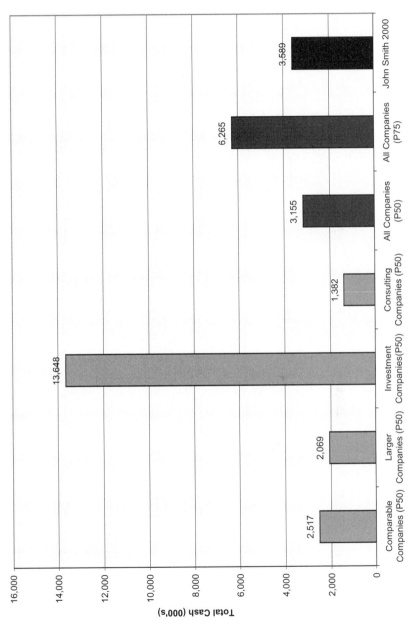

F𝗂𝗀𝘂𝗋𝖤 20.3   grahall Marketplace Map (gMPM) for total direct compensation. The total direct compensation for each group at the median, for the whole group at the median and 75th percentile, and for John Smith are shown here.

offer the job to an individual. The gMMs below—one for base pay, one for total cash compensation, and one for total direct compensation—helped us map things out, and illustrate amounts for each group at the median, for the whole group at the median and 75th percentile, and for the candidate.

Getting to Know You

As soon as the candidate was identified, we interviewed him to see what kind of compensation program seemed appropriate. We explained to the candidate that we wanted to completely understand his present reward program at his current employer, so we could better configure a program specific to him. During the interview we developed a rapport that allowed us to talk about his family, his history, and what he liked to do during his free time. In addition, we were able to determine his own moderately developed philosophy on CEO compensation. Armed with this information, we were able to develop the details of his present compensation program for his present employer. We were able to determine what he had earned and was vested in, as well as what he had earned but was not vested in. While we are sure that from his perspective the interview flowed like a nice conversation between gentlemen, we had, in fact, pre-scripted our questions and were categorizing all of the information that came from the candidate into a conceptual schematic that would help us determine what the most appropriate compensation program would be to attract, and ultimately retain, this individual.

Our Observations

- The philosophy at the candidate's current employer was that when you join the team everyone rises or falls with the performance of the organization.
- The candidate was more comfortable with focusing on specific results and being rewarded when those results were accomplished.

- The candidate believed that it was most demotivating when an executive had specific objectives and they were accomplished, but because the organization or certain key divisions missed goals, there is no incentive payout for all the executives.
- The individual had a very long-term view of performance.
- The right way to run a long-term program is to have the awards be driven by individual performance with the reward medium being a company-wide stock or stock-like compensation.
- In general, the candidate didn't like stock options. He believed that they compensated people at the expense of shareholders. Instead he preferred a structure that paid them on how they do each year in the form of equity and enough cash to pay the taxes.
- We also felt that it was important that the reward package indicated that the candidate was in line to take over the top position. The candidate wanted to see a certain level of cash compensation, but beyond that believed the best result for both parties would be for him to become aligned with shareholders by receiving stock-based rewards.
- If the executive was successful in ten years, he would expect a meaningful level of ownership in the company.
- If the candidate could create a deferral of compensation that would assist in the tax avoidance area, that would be preferred.

When all was said and done, we learned that the candidate was very interested in the challenge, and thought that it was an opportunity for him to become a CEO where he could put many of his theories on managing a corporation into play. His past history indicated that he only had experience in one corporate position, which was the CFO of a major insurance organization. Prior to that, he was a renowned stock picker in that particular industry. It appeared to us that he wanted the top job of CEO, even though his experience would not normally have made him a good candidate for the job. We—as well as he—recognized that while he was extremely intelligent and thoroughly knew the industry, it was, in fact, quite a stretch for him to be considered for the top job.

Getting to Know the Candidate's Current Program

Now that we had a handle on the candidate, we needed to get the essential details of the candidate's present reward program. Why? Because we wanted to make a side-by-side comparison of the reward plan components of each company.

Through this comparison we were able to come up with an understanding for the strengths and weaknesses of the candidate's current program, and how it stacked up to our client's current program. We immediately went to work to discover elements such as the significant reliance on the overall stock of the company the candidate currently worked for, versus compensation that would be more related to this individual's own contribution to the organization. It was clear from the beginning that the candidate felt his contributions to the organization, while significant, paled beside the sheer size and number of the other senior executives within his current organization. We reasoned that he wanted more compensation to be specific to his own contributions.

The Comparison

Next it was time to make a side-by-side comparison in a quantitative and projected manner. When projected over the next 10 years, what would the candidate receive if he stayed with his current employer? And what would he receive if he were to take the job of CEO with our client? In calculating the proposed package for the candidate, versus his current package and the potential wealth generated at our client's firm, we made a few assumptions.

Current Employer

- Estimated stock price increase = 10 percent per year
- Estimated increase in base salary = 5 percent per year
- Target short-term incentive payment = 100 percent of base salary
- Stock option value = Black-Scholes value for 2002 grants, increased by 10 percent each year
- Restricted stock value increase = 10 percent per year
- Performance share increase = 10 percent per year

Client Firm

- Estimated stock price increase = 10 percent per year
- Estimated increase in base salary = 5 percent per year until 2004, where $1 million is assumed the base to reflect his potential promotion to CEO, and 5 percent per year thereafter.
- Target short-term incentive payment = 50 percent of base salary
- LTIP grant targets increase at 5 percent per year, payout increases based on the stock price increase
- Challenge grants = payout based on 25 percent of the value, times the stock price each year
- Matching grant = payout based on 10 percent of the value, times the stock price each year

As you can see from the following tables, the two programs did not result in similar amounts of money being earned over the ten-year period. In fact, his present employer would pay him $10 million more than we were expecting our client's firm to pay him.

The Challenge

Now came the real challenge. To come up with a program that, while less in total dollars, closed the deal. We somehow managed to convince both the compensation committee and the present CEO that we would be able to do this.

(text continues on page 481)

FIGURE 20.4

	Current Employer's Program	Potential Employer's Program
Change of Control	Upon termination within 2 years of a CIC, candidate is entitled to (a) 2× the sum of current annual salary and the average of annual awards over the prior 3 years; (b) individual maintains insurance and disability benefits for 2 years or upon acceptance or employment with another company; (c) accelerated vesting of LTI awards. Potential Severance Payout 2002: $70,000	TBD
Base Pay	$400,000	$500,000
Incentive Pay	Incentive Target—100 percent of base salary	Incentive Target—75 percent of base salary
LTI Plan	(a) LTIP awards granted as performance shares, which are paid out based on 3-year performance cycle; (b) the number of target shares earned is dependent on achievement of specified EPS targets for the 3-year period; (c) settlement of awards may be in shares/cash or a combination of both; (d) target awards granted for the candidate in 1999 = 6,000	(a) LTIP awards granted as performance shares, which are paid out based on 4-year performance cycles; (b) the number of target shares earned is dependent upon achievement of specified EPS growth for the 4-year period; (c) settlement of awards have been half in cash, and half in common stock; (d) CEO LTIP payout under 1993 LTIP: $3,000,000 ($1.5 million in cash and 30,000 performance shares)

	Current Employer's Program	Potential Employer's Program
Stock Option Grants	80,000 in 1999, granted as follows: 40,000 reload options granted at FMV, with a 10-year term and 40,000 options granted at a 25 percent premium over FMV, with a 5-year term. All options vest over 2 years ratably.	None.
Restricted Stock	10,000 shares in 1999. Dividends are paid in restricted stock.	None.
Deferred Compensation	None disclosed	$100,000 of savings benefits credited pursuant to the company's deferred compensation plan in 2001 for the current CEO.
Health and Welfare	None disclosed.	In 2001, the current CEO received insurance benefits valued at $12,000 of life insurance, and other insurance coverage valuing $7,000.
Pension Plan	The candidate will only be eligible for the cash balance portion of the pension plan beginning January 2000. (a) Total number of years participating in pension plan multiplied by the difference between 1.75 percent of average compensation for the "final average earnings" and the amount related to the employee's primary Social Security benefits.	(a) All executive officers participate; (b) payout— choice of either a life annuity or a lump sum; (c) amount for an executive with 15 years or more of service and paid as a life annuity equals 50 percent of the "average compensation."

FIGURE 20.5 Current employer corporation estimated ten-year payout.

	2002	2003	2004	2005	2006	2007	2008	2009	2010	2011	Total Value After 10-Years
Base	$450,000	$472,500	$496,125	$520,931	$546,978	$574,327	$603,043	$633,195	$664,855	$698,098	$5,660,052
Target Short-Term Incentive	$450,000	$472,500	$496,125	$520,931	$546,978	$574,327	$603,043	$633,195	$664,855	$698,098	$5,660,052
Stock Option Grants	$2,500,000	$2,750,000	$3,025,000	$3,327,500	$3,660,250	$4,026,275	$4,428,903	$4,871,793	$5,358,972	$5,894,869	$39,843,562
Restricted Stock Grant	$221,000	$243,100	$267,410	$294,151	$323,566	$355,923	$391,515	$430,666	$473,733	$521,106	$3,522,171
Performance Shares		$847,000	$931,700	$1,024,870	$1,127,357	$1,240,093	$1,364,102	$1,500,512	$1,650,563	$1,815,620	$11,501,817
Executive Car Program	$10,000										$10,000
Value Earned Per Year	$3,631,000	$4,785,100	$5,216,360	$5,688,384	$6,205,129	$6,770,944	$7,390,606	$8,069,362	$8,812,978	$9,627,791	$66,197,653

Total Value For 10-Years is equal to the total earnings, as determined in the year the rewards are granted, in accordance with our assumptions listed on the first page.

Because of the difficulty in projecting future grants and actual stock option payouts, the value earned per year equals the total value awarded each year (Performance shares are determined at the payout date) based on general assumptions and the stock price for that year.

FIGURE 20.6 Client firm corporation estimated ten-year payout.

	2002	2003	2004	2005	2006	2007	2008	2009	2010	2011	Total Value After 10-Years
Base	$600,000	$630,000	$1,000,000	$1,050,000	$1,102,500	$1,157,625	$1,215,506	$1,276,282	$1,340,096	$1,407,100	$10,779,109
Target Short-Term Incentive	$300,000	$315,000	$500,000	$525,000	$551,250	$578,813	$607,753	$638,141	$670,048	$703,550	$5,389,554
LTIP Grants				$1,197,900	$1,317,690	$1,383,575	$2,196,150	$2,305,958	$2,421,255	$2,542,318	$13,364,846
Challenge Grant 1	$1,187,500	$1,425,000	$1,698,125	$2,011,625							$6,322,250
Challenge Grant 2			$1,436,875	$1,724,250	$2,054,731	$2,434,066					$7,649,922
Match Grant	$570,000	$684,000	$815,100	$965,580	$1,138,005	$1,335,259	$1,560,584	$1,817,622	$2,110,461	$2,443,691	$13,440,302
Value Earned Per Year	$2,657,500	$3,054,000	$5,450,100	$7,474,355	$6,164,176	$6,889,337	$5,579,993	$6,038,002	$6,541,860	$7,096,660	$56,945,983

Total Value For 10-Years is equal to the total earnings, as determined by the share price at the time of vesting. While the Challenge Grants or Matching Grants are not vested until the final year, we spread the total value earned upon vesting over the total period, to more accurately reflect the amount earned per year (based on stock price at the beginning of the period).

Value earned per year equals the total amount earned each year, based on general assumptions and the stock price for that year.

FIGURE 20.7   Shareholder wealth created versus executive wealth accumulation.

Wealth Generated

Amounts generated over time

Shareholde Created	Value upon entry	10% after 10 years	Increase in Value	Aggregate Candidate Value
Market growth	$1,406,000,000	$3,646,801,899	$2,240,801,899	$56,945,983
	Shares Outstanding=7.4 Million			
	Market=190$ times number of outstanding shares			

In addition, it was also decided that the client would not make the candidate a direct transfer to CEO, but would bring the candidate in as executive vice president for a period of time in order to evaluate him to determine if, in fact, he was going to be effective as CEO.

The solution? We developed a program that stepped up in two tiers. The first tier was to have the candidate come in as an executive vice president initially, and then be promoted to CEO within two years. We presented an employment contract sheet to the candidate and walked him through the various reward components to get his feedback, including:

- Base salary increase by 5 percent each year.
- Bonus is equal to 100 percent of base salary.
- There is a 10 percent growth in the stock price each year.
- Performance shares are granted to the candidate over his entire tenure as the CEO. Performance shares are paid out at 200 percent to the candidate's base salary after 2007.
- The first challenge grant of 31,836 (shares adjusted for stock dividends) restricted share units vest in 2004, and the second challenge grant of 26,530 (shares adjusted for stock dividends) restricted stock units vest in 2006.
- Matching shares vest in 2010.

As amazed as we were, the candidate liked the program! Ultimately, we needed to calculate the candidate's annual projected compensation (Figure 20.8).

We went through a significant amount of effort to understand the type of program that would be more effective for this candidate. In addition to that, we created an economic impact analysis (Figures 20.9 and 20.10), which showed how the individual would fare depending upon how the various performance factors within his composition program worked, and how the company stock reacted. In addition, we performed a walk-away analysis (Figure 20.11) which indicated how much the individual would leave on the table of "earned but not vested" compensation over his entire career at our client's firm. We also developed a wealth accumulation analysis which

(text continues on page 486)

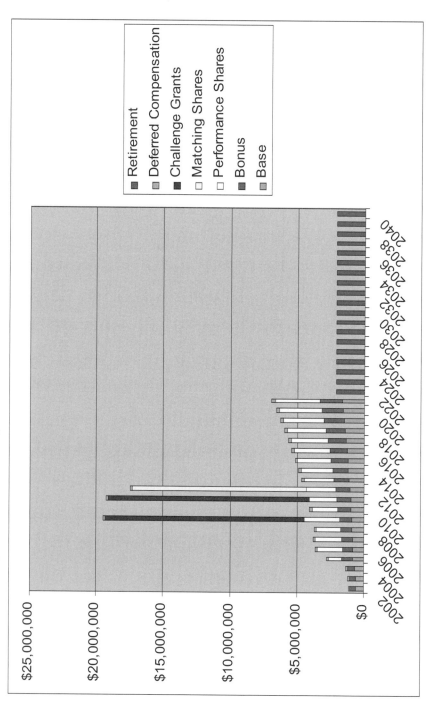

FIGURE 20.8 Current analysis: forecasted compensation.

FIGURE 20.9   grahall Economic Impact Analysis (gEIA); total over five years.

Company Performance

Stock Performance	10	20	30	40	50	60	70	80	90
10	$6,339,996	$6,339,996	$6,339,996	$6,339,996	$8,389,167	$14,423,844	$16,141,437	$16,578,937	$17,016,437
20	$6,774,905	$6,774,905	$6,774,905	$6,774,905	$9,029,234	$15,829,789	$17,662,729	$18,100,229	$18,537,729
30	$7,736,599	$7,736,599	$7,736,599	$7,736,599	$10,426,497	$18,905,208	$20,981,246	$21,418,746	$21,856,246
40	$8,596,976	$8,596,976	$8,596,976	$8,596,976	$11,659,872	$21,625,878	$23,908,495	$24,345,995	$24,783,495
50	$9,572,809	$9,572,809	$9,572,809	$9,572,809	$13,043,817	$24,684,232	$27,191,500	$27,629,000	$28,066,500
60	$10,927,405	$10,927,405	$10,927,405	$10,927,405	$14,943,915	$28,891,256	$31,696,941	$32,134,441	$32,571,941
70	$13,938,492	$13,938,492	$13,938,492	$13,938,492	$19,102,350	$38,124,265	$41,552,161	$41,989,661	$42,427,161
80	$15,252,577	$15,252,577	$15,252,577	$15,252,577	$20,895,427	$42,114,339	$45,800,236	$46,237,736	$46,675,236
90	$19,500,468	$19,500,468	$19,500,468	$19,500,468	$26,625,156	$54,892,635	$59,371,621	$59,809,121	$60,246,621

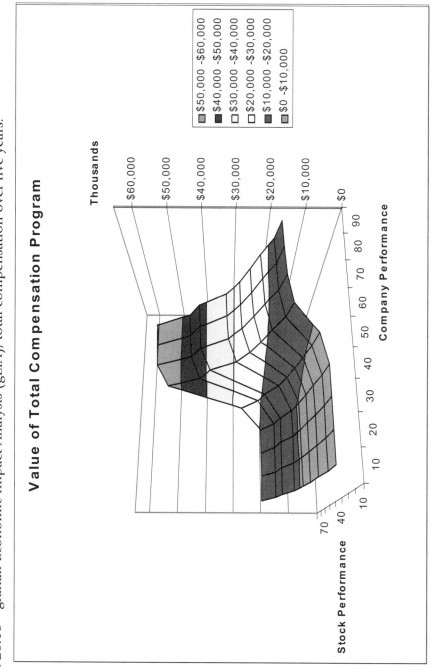

Value of Total Compensation Program

Thousands

$60,000

$50,000

$40,000

$30,000

$20,000

$10,000

$0

Company Performance

Stock Performance

- $50,000 -$60,000
- $40,000 -$50,000
- $30,000 -$40,000
- $20,000 -$30,000
- $10,000 -$20,000
- $0 -$10,000

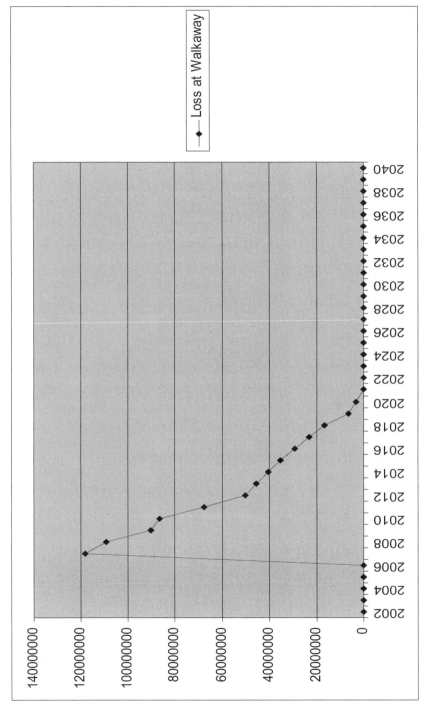

FIGURE 20.11 grahall Walk Away Analysis (gWAA): loss at departure.

showed how much wealth this individual would develop over his working career with the organization.

The cummulative compensation value varies with incremental wealth creation for shareholders. The 90th percentile stock and company performance needed to deliver $60 million in compensation would result in $5 billion of incremental market value for the company as illustrated in Figure 20.13.

The Counter Offer to the Counter Offer

We like to be prepared when we know we are recruiting a key executive from a major corporation. They almost always counter offer. We took the time to understand and predict where the present employer would counter within the constraints of their overall executive reward program. With a large employer like this one, it's fairly easy to determine how many degrees of freedom they have in creating a counter offer that is interesting enough to the candidate to retain his services, but doesn't break the bureaucratic policies of the company.

First of all, there were the intangible benefits that the candidate would receive upon accepting our client's offer. These included the reputation and status that the candidate would enjoy as a result of his future CEO position, along with an offer of a position on the client's board of directors. The idea behind this? If the candidate has a larger, reputable position, he will have general control of the company-wide investment choices, and the ability to impact not only the company's future, but his own future.

In addition, strategic responses to potential counter offers were developed by reward element, with a general "strategic order" of responses in mind.

- Where performance factors are involved, prove the greater value of the client's offer by introducing the increased probability of achieving performance measures at the client's company versus the current employer.

FIGURE 20.12 Total career-to-date wealth accumulation.

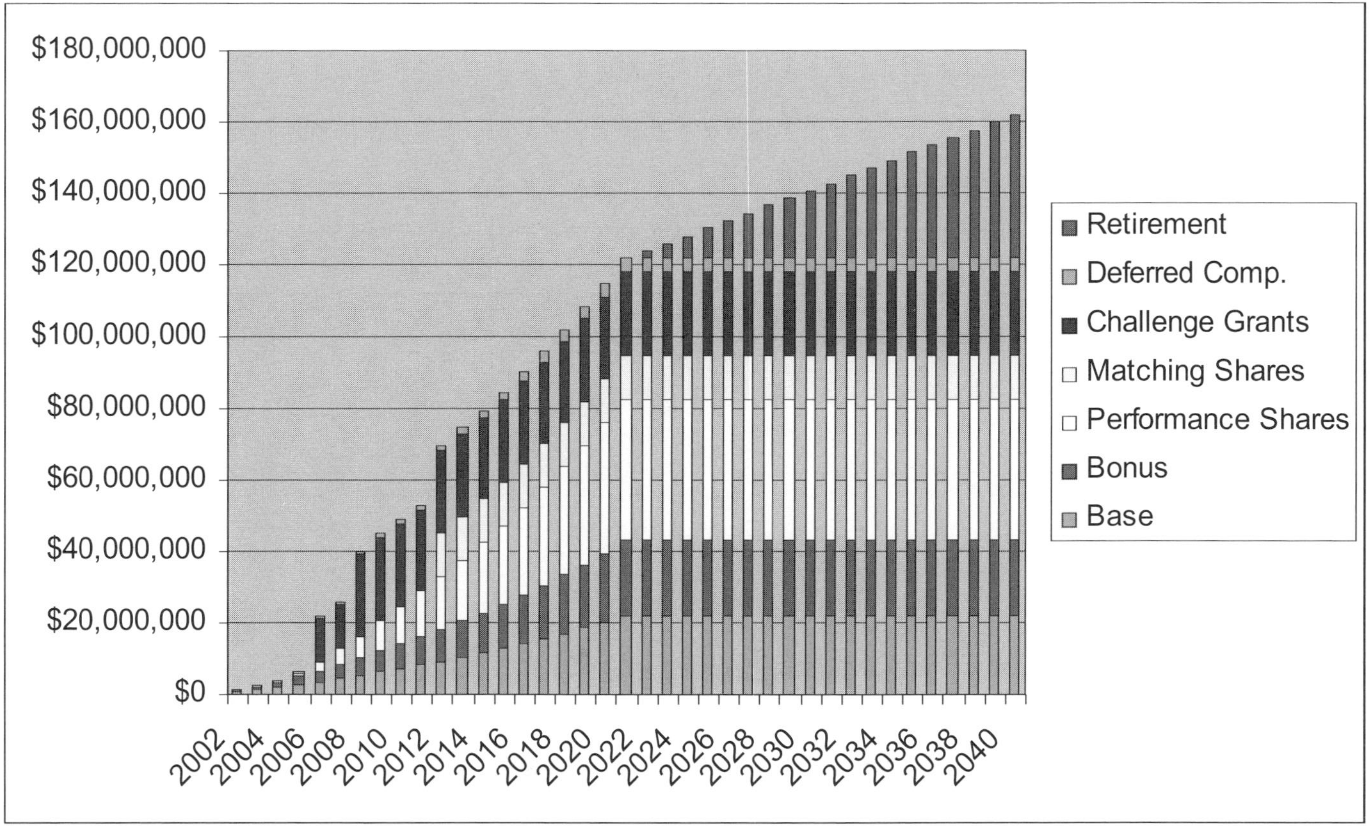

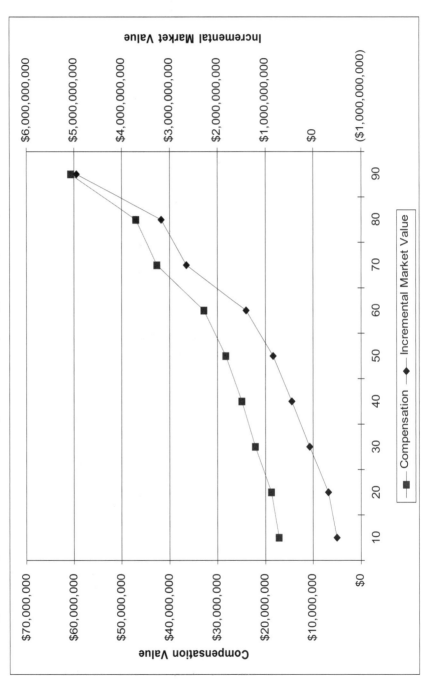

FIGURE 20.13   grahall Pay for Performance Alignment Analysis (gP4PAA): five years.

- Attempt to match the current employer's offer value in accordance with the candidate's desired form. For example, if the current employer offers increased short-term incentives, the client offers more matching grants.
- Attempt to match the current employer's offer in spirit. For example, if the current employer offers equity as options, the client offers some value in restricted shares, or some other equity form.
- Attempt to match the current employer's offer in kind, or "reward for reward." For example, if the current employer increases base, the client increases base.

We got specific with certain scenarios. Let's say the current employer offered to increase the base salary above $600,000. What could some responses to that counter offer be? The client could guarantee an increase in base salary to $750,000 in 2003, increase the base salary to $800,000 and reduce the challenge grant, reduce severance to $500,000 in exchange for an increase to $800,000, or the client could increase base salary with no offset to other reward elements.

What if the candidate thought the client's short-term incentive goals were too discretionary, and the current employer's short-term incentive goals were more attainable? A good response would be to quantify goals to reflect the candidate's specific performance and eliminate discretion. We would suggest that for the first year, they evaluate only on returns from "investment capital" and not operating assets; in the second year, evaluate upon 50 percent investment returns and 50 percent operating assets; in the third year, begin to evaluate all of the organization's performance requirements.

If the current employer's STI program allows for more "upside," some responses might be to guarantee a maximum bonus for 2002, by taking the additional from the LTI transitional grant (for example, $450,000 guaranteed bonus, $450,000 transitional bonus), or to increase the challenge grant to 30,000 shares.

What if the performance share incentive is not adequate, and the current employer has a shorter vesting period and is offering more target value per grant? Well, that "inadequacy" could be supplemented by the challenge grant and the matching grant. In addition, the transition grant could be increased to 900,000, and the date of vesting for the challenge grant could be altered to accelerate vesting if 15 percent annual growth of the organization's stock is reached in the first two years.

What if the current employer is offering more stock options or restricted stock with no performance-based vesting? Quite simply, our package offers a higher potential ownership position than will ever be attainable at the current employer. In addition, the client could grade the vesting of challenge grants so that the candidate receives 1/4 if the company book value grows by 10 percent compounded annually, they could lower the threshold of challenge grants that the candidate must achieve to vest in the grant, they could increase the challenge grant award amounts to 30,000 shares per grant, and they could offer stock options or restricted stock with comparable value and vesting.

If the candidate notes that his current employer promises a more substantial retirement package, a good response would be to offer to work with the candidate to match their offer in terms of value, or to increase the matching grant limit to 20,000.

We also included some responses to indirect benefits to the candidate, like the fact that he has a shorter commute at his current employer. A good response to this issue is to offer to arrange a flexible schedule, and pay for the candidate's stay in the city when necessary.

A Happy Ending

The end of this story is a tale of success. The executive accepted the offer in 2000, and in 2002 was promoted to CEO. By the year 2006, the stock of the company had doubled. The executive understudied the current CEO for two years, was promoted on time, and has developed an even more successful organization than already existed. Most of the credit for the success goes to both the new CEO for executing a business strategy, and to the prior CEO and board of directors for choosing a strong individual. We do believe most of the success is about choosing great executives. However, it helps to have the right program design (in this case, a very custom design) to attract, motivate, and retain.

CHAPTER 21

Books We Love and That Should Be on Your Bookshelf

CHAPTER 1

Environmental Business Issues
Listed by Order of Authors' Preference

Mintzberg, Henry. *Power In And Around Organizations.* Englewood Cliffs, NJ: Prentice-Hall, Inc., 1983.

Lawrence, Paul R. and Jay W. Lorsch. *Organization and Environment, Managing Differentiation and Integration.* Boston: Graduate School of Business Administration, 1967.

Pfeffer, Jeffrey and Gerald R. Salancik. *The External Control of Organizations, A Resource Dependence Perspective.* New York: Harper & Row, 1978.

Bernstein, Peter L. *Against The Gods, The Remarkable Story of Risk.* New York: John Wiley & Sons, 1996.

Taleb, Nassim Nicholas. *Fooled by Randomness, The Hidden Role of Chance in the Markets and in Life.* New York: Texere LLC, 2001.

Fuld, Leonard M. *Competitor Intelligence. How to Get It; How to Use It.* New York: John Wiley & Sons, 1985.

Weidenbaum, Murry L. *The Future of Business Regulation, Private Action and Public Demand.* New York: AMACOM, 1979.

Green, Scott. *Sarbanes-Oxley and the Board of Directors, Techniques and Best Practices for Corporate Governace.* Hoboken, NJ: John Wiley & Sons, Inc., 2005.

Thurow, Lester C. *Head to Head, The Coming Economic Battle Among Japan, Europe, and America.* New York: William Morrow and Company, Inc.,1992.

Porter, Michael E., ed. *Competition in Global Industries.* Boston: Harvard Business School Press, 1986.

Galbraith, James K. *Created Unequal, The Crisis in American Pay.* New York: The Free Press, 1998.

National Association of Corporate Directors Series. Washington, DC: National Association of Corporate Directors, 1994–present.

Corporate Governance in Employee Ownership Companies. Oakland, CA: National Center for Employee Ownership, 1996.

Carpenter, Jennifer N. and David L. Yermack, eds. *Executive Compensation and Shareholder Value.* Norwell, MA: Kluwer Academic Publishers, 1998.

Nystrom, Paul C. and William H. Starbuck, eds. *Handbook of Organizational Design,* Vol. 1, *Remodeling Organizations and their Environments.* London: Oxford University Press, 1981.

Varallo, Gregory V. and Daniel A. Dreishbach. *Fundamentals of Corporate Governance: A Guide for Directors and Corporate Counsel.* Chicago: American Bar Association, 1996.

DiNardo, John, Kevin Hallock, and Jorn-Steffen Pischke. *Unions and Managerial Pay.* Cambridge, MA: National Bureau of Economic Research, 1997.

CHAPTER 2

Key Stakeholders Issues

Mitroff, Ian I. *Stakeholders of the Organizational Mind, Toward a New View of Organizational Policy Making.* San Francisco: Jossey-Pass Inc., 1983.

Drucker, Peter F. *The Unseen Revolution, How Pension Fund Socialism Came to America.* New York: Harper & Row, 1976.

Blasi, Joseph, Douglas Kruse, and Aaron Bernstein. *In The Company of Owners, The Truth About Stock Options (and Why Every Employee Should Have Them).* New York: Basic Books, 2003.

Bowen, William G. *Inside the Boardroom, Governance by Directors and Trustees.* New York: John Wiley & Sons, Inc., 1994.

National Association of Corporate Directors Series. Washington, DC: National Association of Corporate Directors, 1994–present.

Corporate Governance in Employee Ownership Companies. Oakland, CA: National Center for Employee Ownership, 1996.

CHAPTER 3

Vision, Mission, and Values Issues

Listed by Order of Authors' Preference

Gates, Bill, Nathan Myhrvold, and Peter Rinearson. *The Road Ahead.* New York: Viking Penguin, 1995.

Wang, An and Eugene Linden. *Lessons, An Autobiography.* Boston: Addison-Wesley Publishing Company, Inc., 1986.

Armstrong, Karen. *A History of God: The 4,000-Year Quest of Judaism, Christianity, and Islam.* Westminster, MD: Alfred A. Knopf, Inc., 1993.

CHAPTER 4

Business Strategy

Listed by Order of Authors' Preference

Poter, Michael E. *Competitive Strategy, Techniques for Analyzing Industries and Competitors.* New York: The Free Press, 1980.

Poter, Michael E. *Competitive Advantage, Creating and Sustaining Superior Performance.* New York: The Free Press, 1985.

Buzzell, Robert D. and Bradley T. Gale. *The PIMS Principles, Linking Strategy to Performance.* New York: The Free Press, 1987.

Rappaport, Alfred. *Creating Shareholder Value, The New Business Performance.* New York: The Free Press, 1986.

Stewart, G. Bennett III. *The Quest For Value, A Guide For Senior Managers.* New York: Harper Business, 1991.

Young, S. David and Stephen F. O'Byrne. *EVA and Value-Based Management, A Practical Guide To Implementation.* New York: McGraw-Hill, 2001.

Goold, Michael, Andrew Campbell, and Marcus Alexander. *Corporate-Level Strategy, Creating Value in the Multibusiness Company.* New York: John Wiley & Sons, Inc., 1994.

Bogue, Marcus C. III and Elwood S. Buffa. *Corporate Strategic Analysis.* New York: The Free Press, 1986.

Stringer, Robert A. Jr. and Joel L. Uchenick. *Strategy Traps, and How to Avoid Them.* Lexington, MA: Lexington Books, DC. Heath and Company, 1986.

Bruner, Robert F. *Applied Mergers and Acquisitions.* Hoboken, NJ: John Wiley & Sons, Inc., 2004.

Rock, Milton L., Robert H. Rock, and Martin Sikora, eds. *The Mergers & Acquisitions Handbook*. Lexington, MA: McGraw-Hill, Inc., 1987.

Boulton, Richard E.S., Barry D. Libert, and Steve M. Samek. *Cracking The Value Code, How Successful Businesses are Creating Wealth in the New Economy*. New York: Arthur Andersen, 2000.

Black, Andrew, Philip Wright, and John E. Bachman. *In Search of Shareholder Value, Managing the Drivers of Performance*. London, England: Financial Times Management, 1998.

Carpenter, Jennifer N. and David L. Yermack, eds. *Executive Compensation and Shareholder Value*. Norwell, MA: Kluwer Academic Publishers, 1998.

Michaelson, John. *Restructuring for Growth*. New York: McGraw-Hill, 2003.

Kaplan, Robert S. and David P. Norton. *The Strategy-Focused Organization, How Balanced Scorecard Companies Thrive in the New Business Environment*. Boston: Harvard Business School Press, 2001.

Ansoff, H. Igor and Edward McDonnell. *Implanting Strategic Management*. Englewood Cliffs, NJ: Prentice Hall, 1984.

Bogue, Marcus C. III and Elwood S. Buffa. *Corporate Strategic Analysis*. New York: The Free Press, 1986.

CHAPTER 5

Organizational Capabilities and People Strategy
Listed by Order of Authors' Preference
Organizational Capabilities

Ulrich, David and Dale Lake. *Organizational Capability, Competing From the Inside Out*. New York: John Wiley & Sons, Inc., 1990.

Hamel, Gary and C. K. Prahalad. *Competing for the Future, Breakthrough Strategies for Seizing Control of Your Industry and Creating the Markets of Tomorrow*. Boston: Harvard Business School Press, 1994.

Hammer, Michael and James Champy. *Reengineering the Corporation, A Manifesto For Business Revolution*. New York: HarperCollins Publishers, Inc., 1993.

People Strategy

Branham, Leigh. *Keeping the People Who Keep You in Business*. New York: AMACOM, 2001.

Michaels, Ed, Helen Handfield-Jones, and Beth Axelrod. *The War For Talent*. Boston: Harvard Business School Publishing, 2001.

Herman, Roger E. and Joyce L. Gioia. *How to Become an Employer of Choice*. Winchester, Virginia: Oakhill Press, 2000.

Kimberly, John R. and Robert H. Miles. *The Organizational Life Cycle, Issues in the Creation, Transformation, and Decline of Organizations*. San Francisco: Jossey-Bass Publishers, 1980.

Likert, Rensis. *The Human Organization, Its Management and Value*. New York: McGraw-Hill Book Company, 1967.

Peters, Thomas J. and Robert H. Waterman, Jr. *In Search of Excellence, Lessons from America's Best-Run Companies*. New York: Harper & Row, Publishers, 1982.

Organization Structure

Mintzberg, Henry. *The Structuring of Organizations, A Synthesis of Research*. Upper Saddle River, New Jersey: Prentice-Hall, Inc., 1979.

Galbraith, Jay R. *Designing Organizations, An Executive Briefing on Strategy, Structure, and Process*. San Francisco: Jossey-Bass Publishers, 1995.

Galbraith, Jay R. *Organization Design*. Boston: Addison-Wesley Publishing Company, Inc., 1977.

Wheatley, Margaret J. *Leadership and the New Science, Learning about Organization from an Orderly Universe*. San Francisco: Berrett-Koehler Publishers, Inc., 1992.

Nystrom, Paul C. and William H. Starbuck, eds. *Handbook of Organizational Design*, Vol. 2, *Remodeling Organizations and their Environments*. London: Oxford University Press, 1981.

Organization Processes

Hall, Richard H. *Organizations, Structure, Processes, and Outcomes*. 4th ed. Englewood Cliffs, NJ: Pub. Prentice-Hall Inc., 1972.

Perrow, Charles. *Complex Organizations, A Critical Essay*. 3rd ed. New York: Random House, 1972.

Dalton, Gene W., Paul R. Lawrence, and Larry E. Greiner, eds. *Organizational Change and Development*. Homewood, IL: Richard D. Irwin, Inc., 1970.

Mintzberg, Henry. *Structure in Fives, Designing Effective Organizations*. Englewood Cliffs, NJ: Prentice-Hall, 1983.

Senge, Peter M. *The Fifth Discipline, The Art & Practice of the Learning Organization*. New York: Doubleday, 1990.

The Price Waterhouse Change Integration Team. *Better Change, Best Practices For Transforming Your Organization.* Burr Ridge, IL: IRWIN, 1995.

Tomasko, Robert M. *Rethinking The Corporation, The Architecture of Change.* New York: AMACO, 1993.

Seashore, Stanley E., Edward E. Lawler III, Philip H. Mirvis and Cortlandt Cammann, eds. *Assessing Organizational Change, A Guide To Methods, Measures, and Practices.* New York: John Wiley & Sons, 1983.

Organization Culture

Kotter, John P. and James L. Heskett. *Corporate Culture and Performance.* New York: The Free Press, 1992.

Denison, Daniel R. *Corporate Culture and Organization Effectiveness.* New York: John Wiley & Sons, 1990.

Flannery, Thomas P., David A. Hofrichter, and Paul E. Platten. *People, Performance, & Pay, Dynamic Compensation for Changing Organizations.* New York: The Free Press, 1996.

Cameron, Kim S. and Robert E. Quinn. *Diagnosing And Changing Organizational Culture, Based On The Competing Values Framework.* San Francisco: Jossey-Bass, 2006.

Kilmann, Ralph H., Mary J. Saxton, and Roy Serpa. *Gaining Control Of The Corporate Culture and Associates.* San Francisco: Jossey-Bass Inc., 1985.

Schein, Edgar H. *Organizational Culture and Leadership.* San Francisco: Jossey-Bass Inc.,1992.

Graves, Desmond. *Corporate Culture-Diagnosis and Change, Auditing and Changing the Culture of Organizations.* New York: St. Martin's Press, 1986.

Frost, Peter J., Larry F. Moore, Meryl Reis Louis, Craig C. Lundberg, and Joanne Martin. *Organizational Culture.* Beverly Hills, CA: Sage Publications, Inc., 1985.

Sherriton, Jacalyn and James L. Stern. *Corporate Culture Team Culture, Removing the Hidden Barriers to Team Success.* New York: AMACOM, 1997.

Church, Allan H. and Janine Waclawski. *Designing and Using Organizational Surveys, A Seven-step Process.* San Francisco: Jossey-Bass Inc., 1998.

Neuhauser, Peg, Ray Bender, and Kirk Stromberg. *Culture.com, Building Corporate Culture in The Connected Workplace.* Etobicoke, Ontario: John Wiley & Sons, 2000.

CHAPTER 6

Executive Total Reward Strategy
Listed by Order of Authors' Preference

Davis, Michael L. and Jerry T. Edge, Series Eds. *Executive Compensation, The Professional's Guide to Current Issues & Practices.* San Diego, CA: Windsor Professional Information, 2004.

Peter T. Chingos, ed. *Responsible Executive Compensation for a New Era of Accountability.* New York: John Wiley & Sons, Inc., 2004.

Foulkes, Fred K., ed. *Executive Compensation, A Strategic Guide for the 1990s.* Boston, MA: Harvard Business School Press, 1985.

Kay, Ira T. *Value At The Top, Solutions to The Executive Compensation Crisis.* New York: Harper Business, A Division of Harper Collins Publishers, 1992.

Crystal, Graef S. *In Search of Excess, the Overcompensation of American Executives.* New York: W. W. Norton & Company, Inc., 1991.

Sirkin, Michael S. and Lawrence K. Cagney. *Executive Compensation.* New York: Law Journal Press, 2005.

Melbinger, Michael S. *Executive Compensation.* Chicago: CCH Incorporated, 2004.

Fay, Charles H., Michael A. Thompson, and Damien Knight, eds. *The Executive Handbook on Compensation, Linking Strategic Rewards to Business Performance.* New York: The Free Press, 2001.

CHAPTER 7

Executive Total Reward Architecture
Listed by Order of Authors' Preference

Bok, Derek. *The Cost of Talent, How Executives and Professionals Are Paid and How It Affects America.* New York: The Free Press, 1993.

Bebchuk, Lucian and Jesse Fried. *Pay without Performance, The Unfulfilled Promise of Executive Compensation.* Boston: Harvard University Press, 2004.

Manas, Todd M. and Michael Dennis Graham. *Creating a Total Rewards Strategy, A Toolkit for Designing Business-Based Plans.* New York: AMACOM, 2003.

CHAPTER 8

Total Reward Strategy Components

Listed by Order of Authors' Preference

Melbinger, Michael S. *Executive Compensation.* Chicago: CCH Incorporated, 2004.

Ellig, Bruce R. *The Complete Guide to Executive Compensation.* New York: McGraw-Hill, 2002.

Overton, Bruce and Susan E. Stoffer. *Executive Compensation Answer Book.* 5th ed. New York: Panel Publishers, 2002.

Crystal, Graef S. *Questions And Answers On Executive Compensation, How to Get What You're Worth.* Englewood Cliffs, NJ: Prentice-Hall, Inc., 1984.

CHAPTER 9

Base Salary

Listed by Order of Authors' Preference

Berger, Lance A. and Dorothy R. Berger, eds. *The Compensation Handbook, A State-of-the-Art Guide to compensation Strategy and Design.* 4th ed. New York: McGraw-Hill, 2000.

CHAPTER 10

Short-Term Incentives

Listed by Order of Authors' Preference

Berger, Lance A. and Dorothy R. Berger, eds. *The Compensation Handbook, A State-of-the-Art Guide to compensation Strategy and Design.* 4th ed. New York: McGraw-Hill, 2000.

Bruns, William J, ed. *Performance Measurement, Evaluation, and Incentives.* Boston: Harvard Business School Press, 1992.

Chingos, Peter T, ed. *Paying For Performance, A Guide to Compensation Management.* New York: John Wiley & Sons, Inc., 1997.

CHAPTER 11

Mid-Term Incentives
Listed by Order of Authors' Preference

Berger, Lance A. and Dorothy R. Berger, eds. *The Compensation Handbook, A State-of-the-Art Guide to Compensation Strategy and Design.* 4th ed. New York: McGraw-Hill, 2000.

Ericson, Richard N. *Pay to Prosper, Using Value Rules to Reinvent Executive Incentives.* Scottsdale, AZ: WorldatWork, 2004.

CHAPTER 12

Long-Term Incentives
Listed by Order of Authors' Preference

Longnecker, Brent M. *Stock Option Alternatives, A Strategic and Technical Guide to Long-Term Incentives.* Scottsdale, AZ: WorldatWork, 2006.

Longnecker, Brent M. *The Power of Restricted Stock, The Definitive Guide to a Resurging Long-Term Incentive.* Scottsdale, AZ: WorldatWork, 2006.

Berger, Lance A. and Dorothy R. Berger, eds. *The Compensation Handbook, A State-of-the-Art Guide to Compensation Strategy and Design.* 4th ed. New York: McGraw-Hill, 2000.

Weeden, Ryan, Corey Rosen, Ed Carberry, and Scott Rodrick. *Current Practices In Stock Option Plan Design.* 2nd ed. Oakland, CA: The National Center for Employee Ownership, 2001.

Chriss, Neil A. *Black-Scholes and Beyond, Option Pricing Models.* New York: McGraw-Hill, 1997.

Nadel, Alan A., Thomas M. Haines, and Gregory M. Kopp. *Accounting for Equity Compensation.* Oakland, CA: The National Center for Employee Ownership, 2003.

CHAPTER 13

Wealth Accumulation Incentives
Listed by Order of Authors' Preference

Berger, Lance A. and Dorothy R. Berger, eds. *The Compensation Handbook, A State-of-the-Art Guide to compensation Strategy and Design.* 4th ed. New York: McGraw-Hill, 2000.

Thurow, Lester C. *Building Wealth, The New Rules for Individuals, Companies, and Nations in a Knowledge-Based Economy.* New York: HaperCollins Publishers, Inc., 1999.

Chasman, Herbert, ed. *Deferred Compensation, A Guide to Design, Funding, and Administration.* Homewood, IL: Dow Jones-Irwin, 1978.

CHAPTER 14

Executive Benefits

Listed by Order of Authors' Preference

Raffaeli, John and Campbell Gerrish. "Executive Long-Term Disability." *Managing Employee Health Benefits* 6 (Spring 1998).

Liebeskind, Michael B. "Executive Long-Term Disability Insurance Update." *Journal of Compensation and Benefits* 13 (July-August 1997).

Hewitt Associates. *Approaches to Funding Supplemental Executive Death and Survivor Income Benefit Plans.* Lincolnshire, IL: Hewitt Associates, 1997.

Jenei, Jeffrey J. and Anthony M. Sardis. "New Vistas for Survivorship Split Dollar." *National Underwriter Life & Health-Financial Services Edition* 102 (February 2, 1998).

Greve, Michael. "Executive Benefits: Carving up Group Term Life Insurance." *Newsbriefs* 16 (July-August 1997): 9.

Glass, Richard D. and Stan Marshall. "Is Variable Universal Life an Appropriate Funding Vehicle for Deferred Compensation Plans?" *Journal of the American Society of CLU & ChFC* 50 (May 1996).

"Executive Participation Plans—An Executive Benefit." *CRG Executive Trends* 1 (First Quarter 1998).

CHAPTER 15

Executive Perquisites

Listed by Order of Authors' Preference

Baehler, James R. *Book of Perks.* New York: St. Martin's Press, 1983.

Tarrant, John and Paul Fargis. *Perks and Parachutes, Negotiating Your Best Possible Employment Deal, from Salary and Bonus to Benefits and Protection.* New York: Times Books, 1997.

Salwen, Robert and Gail McGowan. *2001 Guide to Executive Employment Contracts.* 3rd ed. Orlando, FL: Harcourt, 2001.

CHAPTER 16

Executive Development Rewards
Listed by Order of Authors' Preference

Rehfeld, John E. *Alchemy of a Leader, Combining Western and Japanese Management Skills to Transform Your Company.* New York: John Wiley & Sons, Inc., 1994.

Goleman, Caniel. *Emotional Intelligence, The Groundbreaking Book that Redefines What It Means to be Smart.* New York: Bantam Books, 1995.

Spencer, Lyle M. Jr. and Signe M. Spencer. *Competence at Work, Models for Superior Performance.* New York: John Wiley & Sons, Inc., 1993.

Tichy, Noel M. and Eli Cohen. *The Leadership Engine, How Winning Companies Build Leaders at Every Level.* New York: HarperCollins Publishers, Inc., 1997.

Giber, David, Louis Carter, and Marshall Goldsmith. *Linkage Inc.'s Best Practices In Leadership Development Handbook, Case Studies, Instruments, and Training.* San Francisco: Jossey-Bass/Pfeiffer, 2000.

Goldsmith, Marshall, Laurence Lyons, and Alyssa Freas. *Coaching For Leadership, How the World's Greatest Coaches Help Leaders Learn.* San Francisco: Jossey-Bass Pfeiffer, 2000.

Barner, Robert. *Executive Resource Management, Building and Retaining an Exceptional Leadership Team.* Palo Alto, CA: Davies-Black Publishing, 2000.

CHAPTER 17

Director's Pay
Listed by Order of Authors' Preference

Rehfeld, John E. *Alchemy of a Leader, Combining Western and Japanese Management Skills to Transform Your Company.* New York: John Wiley & Sons, Inc., 1994.

Kaback, Hoffer. "The Case for Cash for Directors." *Directors & Boards* 20 (Winter 1996).

Johnson, Alan M. and Francine C. McKenzie. "Director Compensation . . . Here's How to Keep Your Stockholders Happy." *Directorship* XXII (June 1996).

Zaleznik, Abraham, Robert Stobaugh, Charles M. Elson, et al. "A Spirited Debate over Director Compensation." *Directors & Boards* 20 (Spring 1996).

EFFECTIVE EXECUTIVE COMPENSATION

National Association of Corporate Directors. *Director Compensation: Purposes, Principles and Best Practices*. Washington, D.C.: National Association of Corporate Directors, 1995. Davis, Michael L. and Robert Stobaugh. "Best Practices in Director Pay." *Directors & Boards* 20 (Fall 1995).

Frederic W. Cook & Co., Inc. "How Should Corporate Directors Be Paid? NACD Presents Its Views." *Alert Letters* (July 12, 1995). Carey, Dennis C. "Performance-Based Director Pay." *Directors & Boards* 19 (Spring 1995).

Fischer, Judith M. "The Effective Use of Director Talent." *Directors & Boards* 20 (Summer 1996).

Index